| Sikh Kirtan and Its Journeys

| CHICAGO STUDIES IN ETHNOMUSICOLOGY

A series edited by Philip V. Bohlman and Timothy Rommen

Editorial Board

Richard C. Jankowsky
Margaret J. Kartomi
Anna Schultz
Anthony Seeger
Kay Kaufman Shelemay
Martin H. Stokes
Bonnie C. Wade

Gurminder Kaur Bhogal

Sikh Kirtan & Its Journeys

Instruments, Theories, Technologies

The University of Chicago Press   CHICAGO AND LONDON

An open-access digital edition of this book is available thanks to funding provided by the Uberoi Foundation for Religious Studies, Wellesley College, and the General Fund of the American Musicological Society (AMS).

The terms of the license for the open-access digital edition are Creative Commons Attribution-Non-Commercial-No-Derivatives 4.0 International License (CC BY-NC-ND 4.0). To view a copy of this license, visit https://creativecommons.org/licenses/by-nc-nd/4.0/. Note to users: A Creative Commons license is only valid when applied by the person or entity that holds rights to the licensed work. This work may contain components to which the rightsholder in the work cannot apply the license. It is ultimately your responsibility to independently evaluate the copyright status of any work or component part of a work you use in light of your intended use.

The University of Chicago Press, Chicago 60637
The University of Chicago Press, Ltd., London
© 2025 by The University of Chicago
Subject to the exception mentioned above, no part of this book may be used or reproduced in any manner whatsoever without written permission, except in the case of brief quotations in critical articles and reviews. For more information, contact the University of Chicago Press, 1427 E. 60th St., Chicago, IL 60637.
Published 2025

34 33 32 31 30 29 28 27 26 25   1 2 3 4 5

ISBN-13: 978-0-226-84593-7 (cloth)
ISBN-13: 978-0-226-84595-1 (paper)
ISBN-13: 978-0-226-84594-4 (ebook)
DOI: https://doi.org/10.7208/chicago/9780226845944.001.0001

Library of Congress Cataloging-in-Publication Data

Names: Bhogal, Gurminder Kaur, author.
Title: Sikh kirtan and its journeys : instruments, theories, technologies / Gurminder Kaur Bhogal.
Other titles: Chicago studies in ethnomusicology.
Description: Chicago : The University of Chicago Press, 2025. | Series: Chicago studies in ethnomusicology | Includes bibliographical references and index.
Identifiers: LCCN 2025025131 | ISBN 9780226845937 (cloth) | ISBN 9780226845951 (paperback) | ISBN 9780226845944 (ebook)
Subjects: LCSH: Kirtana (Sikhism) | Sikh music—History and criticism.
Classification: LCC ML3197 .B49 2025 | DDC 782.346—dc23/eng/20250617
LC record available at https://lccn.loc.gov/2025025131

Authorized Representative for EU General Product Safety Regulation (GPSR) queries: Easy Access System Europe—Mustamäe tee 50, 10621 Tallinn, Estonia, gpsr.requests@easproject.com
Any other queries: https://press.uchicago.edu/press/contact.html

For KIRTANIYE, celestial and earthly, divine and mortal, animate and inanimate. For the first DHAADHI and the first RABABI — bound by bliss and steeped in song.

Contents

Notes on Transliteration, Accompanying Website, and
    Classroom Teaching xi
Preface: The Vast Ocean of Sikh Kirtan xv
Acknowledgments xxi

| INTRODUCTION 1

Historicizing *Kirtan* in Punjab and the Diaspora:
    Case Study—Kenya 3
Navigating Gender Inequality 6
Crosscurrents: The Many Tides of Sikh *Kirtan* 12
The Journeys of Sikh *Kirtan* 17
Why Sikh Musicology? 20

1 | THE MUSICAL AND SONIC DIMENSIONS
   OF *SRI GURU GRANTH SAHIB* 26

From *Bhakti* to *Kirtan*: *Rāg* Compilation and Implications for
    Musical Performance 31
Other Musical Details in Verse Titles: *Partāl* and *Aasa ki Vār* 39

A Mystery Term: *Ghar* 45
How Should *Kirtan* Be Listened to and What Does *Kirtan* Do? 51
Listening Expansively to the *Kirtan* of the Cosmos 59
Avian Yearnings for the Divine in Birdsong 63
Chapter Summary 67

2 | TRACKING THE HARMONIUM FROM CHRISTIAN MISSIONARY HYMNS TO SIKH *KIRTAN* 69

Destination Punjab: The Harmonium Arrives in India 73
"Civilizing the Heathen": How Female Missionaries Used the Harmonium to Signal Modernity and Spiritual Progress 77
A Missing Link? Missionary Dependence on *Mirasi* as an Entryway to Sikh *Kirtan* 83
The Issues at Stake 93
Showcasing the Harmonium in Sikh *Kirtan* 98
Pedagogical Reform and the Rise of Female *Kirtaniye* 104
Chapter Summary 108

3 | *ANAHAD NĀD* AND THE SONIC EMBODIMENT OF DIVINITY 110

Toward a Theory of *Anahad Nād*: The Case of Bhai Hira Singh (1879–1926) 114
The Critical Commentaries of Bhai Vir Singh and Bhai Randhir Singh 118
From Hath Yoga to Raj Yoga: Arrival at the Tenth Door (*Dasam Dwar*) and Beyond 127
The Fourth State and Timbral Resonance of *Panch Shabad* 136
Chapter Summary 141

4 | HEARING (*ANAHAD*) INSTRUMENTS AND THE *RABAB* IN SIKH ART 144

Anahad Instruments 146
The *Rabab* in Sikh Art 152
The Rise and Flows of the *Rabab* 157
(*Anahad*) *Rabab* as Seen Through Sikh Iconography 160
The Extant Sikh *Rabab* and Its Stories 174
The *Rabab* in the B-40 *Janamsakhi* Manuscript 177
Anahad Nād and Pictorial Resonance: The Halo and Sonic Vibration in Sikh Art 180
Chapter Summary 183

5 | ENGINEERING *ANAHAD NĀD* AS DIGITAL BLISS: THE CASE OF AMRITVELA TRUST   184

Kirtan and Acoustics   187
Current Mediations of Technology in Sikh *Gurudware*   190
Establishing Amritvela Trust in Ulhasnagar (Maharashtra)   196
Amritvela Trust's *Kirtan*: Mediating *Darshan* Between
  the Metaphysical and the Digital   200
Headphones and Absorption   209
Experiencing Digital *Anahad Nād*   212
A Vibratory Feedback Loop Between *Kirtan* and *Seva*   215
Vibrating Bodies of the Twenty-First Century   217
Chapter Summary   218

6 | THE DIGITAL JOURNEYS OF *KIRTAN*: PURSUING INNOVATION AND GENDER EQUALITY   220

Davwinder (Dindae) Sheena: Crafting a "Sikh Sound"   223
Taren Kaur: "Integrate Women into *Kirtan Darbar*"   228
Jasleen Kaur: "You Can't Stop the Revolution"   234
Veer Manpreet Singh: The Innovation of *Slow
  Kirtan* and Healing with *"Tuhi Tuhi"*   239
Bhai Nirmal Singh Khalsa (Pipli Wale) and Kirtan Studio:
  "*Kirtan* Is Life"   244
Shivpreet Singh: "Listening to Guru Nanak"   248

| EPILOGUE   253

Appendix   257
Glossary   265
Notes   269
Index   329

Notes on Transliteration, Accompanying Website, and Classroom Teaching

References to *Sri Guru Granth Sahib* (*SGGS*) are based on srigranth.org. All translations are my own unless stated otherwise. I also refer readers to khojgurbani.org. The work of translating *SGGS* is ongoing among scholars and members of the Sikh community.

It is customary among some scholars to remove the prefix "Sri" for reasons that have to do with its Brahmanical gesturing. My decision to retain this honorific takes into account how Sikhs refer to sacred verse in their practice. The format "2-8" indicates that I am referencing page 2, line 8, as shown on srigranth.org. The format "173-4/5" indicates that I am referencing page 173, lines 4 and 5.

This book has been written with (broadly speaking) three types of readers in mind: those who are familiar with the Punjabi language and will be able to recognize terms without relying heavily on diacritical marks (which might prove distracting and confusing); those readers who are not familiar with Punjabi but who have experience with interpreting diacritical marks and thus rely on these notations to help with pronunciation; and those who are familiar with neither the Punjabi language nor the convention of reading diacritical marks.

I have tried to accommodate these three groups of readers by offering a separate glossary and a brief translation of terms when they are first mentioned. Throughout, I have opted for minimal use of diacritical marks, hoping that the second type of reader might be willing to accept my attempts at simple transliteration and translation in accommodating reader types 1 and 3. I apologize to those readers who value the precision afforded by diacritical marks.

I do not pluralize Punjabi words by adding an *s* to the end (except for terms that are now common in English, such as "Sikh," "guru," and "yogi"). For example, historical stories that recount Guru Nanak's life are called *Janamsakhi* whether in the singular or plural, as I would say in Punjabi. I do not pluralize frequently used words like *shabad* or *rāg*, but I do use the plurals *Gurudware* and *kirtaniye*, as I would in spoken Punjabi. I opt for the common pronunciation of *shabad* (divine word) with *sh* rather than *s* (*sabad*), as written in *SGGS*.

Speaking of *shabad*—this frequently used term has two meanings, which the reader will be able to determine from the context. Sometimes it refers to a musical rendering of a verse. For example, "I sang the *shabad* 'Rasna Japti Tuhi Tuhi' at *Gurudwara* yesterday." At other moments, *shabad* retains its literal meaning of divine word/primal utterance.

I use Punjabi terms (for example, *rāg*, *ras*, and *dhurpad*) instead of their Hindi equivalents (*raga*, *rasa*, and *dhrupad*). All musical instruments are italicized.

Interviews have been conducted in English, Punjabi, or Hindi. All translations are mine.

Finally, names. Since Sikh last names usually use Singh for men and Kaur for women in an effort to eliminate casteism, professional practitioners of *kirtan* (called *kirtaniye* or *ragi*) sometimes include their affiliation with a particular town or city as an identifying marker. Thus, Bhai Harjinder Singh (Srinagar Wale) means I'm talking about the Bhai Harjinder Singh who is associated with Srinagar.

ACCOMPANYING WEBSITE AND USING THIS BOOK IN THE CLASSROOM

The accompanying website, https://sikhkirtananditsjourneys.wordpress.com, provides a variety of materials that are referenced in the book and in the endnotes: audio recordings, video recordings, artwork, tables, figures, and a bibliography.

I realize that the topic of Sikh *kirtan* will be unfamiliar to many in the Euro–North American academy. For instructors, here are some tips on how you might teach this book.

The preface, introduction, and chapter 6 can be used for high school seniors, undergraduate students, and graduate students.

Chapter 1 is divided into two sections: The entire chapter is suitable for graduate students. Undergraduates might find the second section, "How Should *Kirtan* Be Listened to and What Does *Kirtan* Do?" a sufficient reading assignment.

Chapter 2 can be assigned to undergraduates and graduates. Those looking for a shorter read that skips a study of missionary sources can start with the introduction and then pick up at "The Issues at Stake."

Chapter 3 explores the topics of sound and timbre through the lens of *SGGS*. The section "From Hath Yoga to Raj Yoga: Arrival at the Tenth Door (*Dasam Dwar*) and Beyond" might be omitted for readers less interested in exploring connections between yoga and timbre. This chapter can be assigned to all students.

Chapter 4 studies instruments of *SGGS* in the first half and the depiction of the *rabab* in Sikh painting in the second half. This chapter can be assigned to all students.

Chapter 5 focuses on how digital technology facilitates worship through a case study. This chapter can be assigned to all students.

Chapter 6 is the easiest reading assignment in that it is a series of interviews with *kirtaniye* who discuss how they innovate using technology.

Preface

The Vast Ocean of Sikh Kirtan

A book devoted to the topic of Sikh devotional music is inherently vibrating with the sung poetry of Guru Nanak, the first of ten Sikh gurus. His verses took flight in the musical imagination of Bhai Mardana, Guru Nanak's cherished companion and player of the plucked chordophone, the *rabab*. Echoing through the centuries, Guru Nanak's voice and Bhai Mardana's *rabab* are lodged deep within Sikh consciousness. Together, the two men traveled by foot through parts of India, Pakistan, Afghanistan, Iran, Iraq, Tibet, Bangladesh, Ceylon (Sri Lanka), Saudi Arabia, and other regions. Their collaborative offering of divine praise (*kirat*) is the original *kirtan* that suffuses the Sikh cultural imagination. Devotees imagine and reimagine the moments when Guru Nanak calls out to Bhai Mardana to touch the strings of his *rabab* because "bani has arrived" (the utterance of the divine one has become manifest/revealed).[1] Sikh *kirtan*, in the Sikh imaginary, has its origins in revelation—in a moment of clarity, insight, focus, devotional love (*bhaav*), and, above all, a connection with the divine. The simultaneity of this feeling is what the living tradition of Sikh *kirtan* seeks to invoke and sustain.

    Sikh Kirtan and Its Journeys is written against the backdrop of these journeys and traces myriad more paths as it considers where Sikhs have traveled to and established their homes in the centuries following

Guru Nanak and Bhai Mardana's travels (known as *udasi*). Whether they moved to New Zealand, Australia, Kenya, Uganda, Zambia, Tanzania, South Africa, Burma (now Myanmar), China, Singapore, Hong Kong, Thailand, Malaysia, Japan, Afghanistan, Iraq, Canada, America, the United Kingdom, or many parts of continental Europe, Sikhs have taken *kirtan* with them.[2] This devotional music was cherished as a key component of their spiritual nourishment, but it was also bound up with their "movement capital" and how they "negotiate[d] disequilibrium... and dissonance" in foreign lands, as observed by sociologist Parminder Bhachu.[3] Regular emphasis is placed on the importance of listening to and singing the divine word of Sikh sacred verse formally known as *Sri Guru Granth Sahib* (*SGGS*) or informally known as *Gurbani* or *Bani* (the utterance of the Guru). Sikhs are instructed to hear *Gurbani* whether it is offered by another devotee — through being spoken, intoned, or sung — or as an individual (including silent reading in one's mind). Devotional music is an intrinsic feature of Sikh worship, and everyone is encouraged to offer and participate in *kirtan*: children and adults, experts and amateurs.

The living tradition of *kirtan* is practiced across many places, in different ways and — as understood within the Sikh context — by a variety of matter taking human, animal, plant, elemental, and celestial forms. As a devotional practice *kirtan* is multifaceted since it is a reflection of the spiritual needs and shifting musical tastes of devotees and practitioners in India and across the Sikh diaspora. This book draws on musical and spiritual theories that underpin the practice of *kirtan*, while exploring the instruments that carry its sounds and the technologies that facilitate a communal experience of bliss. The introduction and six chapters work together in arguing that there is no singular expression of *kirtan*. A central goal is to show the diversity of Sikh *kirtan* in an inclusive way that embraces its agents, as well as the theories, instruments, and technologies that sustain its practice.

How can an expression of devotion that began with two people who were skilled musicians, Guru Nanak and Bhai Mardana, become open to all regardless of educational background or social status? A well-known *sakhi* (a story relating to the historical period of the gurus) drawn from the wellspring of Sikh oral history offers an answer to this question.[4]

The male descendants of Bhai Mardana were known as *rababi*, players of the *rabab*, and this instrument was cherished in the *darbar* (courts) of the ten Sikh gurus, whose lives spanned the fifteenth to the eighteenth centuries. During the late sixteenth and early seventeenth centuries, Guru Arjan, the fifth guru, had employed the brothers Bhai Satta and

Bhai Balwand (descendants of Bhai Mardana) in his court. They were among the first *rababi* to offer *kirtan* at the revered Harmandir Sahib in Amritsar (popularly known as the Golden Temple today), and a large *sangat* (gathering of devotees) flocked to hear them, making generous offerings of gold and money during their visits. As the wedding of Bhai Satta's daughter drew near, the brothers decided they would ask Guru Arjan for financial help—to which the guru readily agreed. When he asked what they required, their greed got the better of them: Instead of asking for a specific amount, they envied the offerings made by the *sangat* and responded that they would like to collect whatever was offered during the period of a single day, from morning to night. The guru agreed to give them the next day's offerings of gold and money, but, as it turned out, the *sangat* in attendance was sparse and the offerings were similarly small. The brothers were upset by this situation and were even more perturbed when Guru Arjan's jealous brother, Bhai Prithi Chand, added fuel to the fire. He insinuated that the guru had tricked Bhai Satta and Bhai Balwand by asking the *sangat* not to attend. The brothers made a decision: "When we do *kirtan*, the *sangat* attends. When we don't do *kirtan*, the *sangat* does not attend. Let us not rise in the morning to sing *Aasa ki vār* [a ballad in *rāg Aasa*]."

When the *sangat* arrived early the next morning, Bhai Satta and Bhai Balwand were missing. Guru Arjan inquired after them and was told they refused to come because they felt deceived. The guru then sent his revered companion, Bhai Budda, to collect them from their home, but again they refused, stating with great arrogance that Guru Arjan had to learn a lesson: If the brothers don't come and perform *kirtan*, then the *sangat* will not attend either. At this point the guru himself went to their home, but they continued to refuse his requests even when he told them they could take as much as they wanted to cover their wedding expenses. As the brothers continued to reject the guru, they made remarks that were insulting to him and to all the gurus before him. Having crossed the line, the brothers received a curse from the guru: They were never to offer *kirtan* again, and if anyone should dare negotiate with the guru on their behalf, they would be paraded around town on a donkey.

At this juncture Guru Arjan returned to Harmandir Sahib and declared that the tradition of *rababi kirtan* was to end and that the Sikhs themselves must take up the practice of *kirtan*. He ordered his *sangat* to pick up *tanti sāz* (traditional string instruments of the time), but members of the *sangat* pleaded that they knew nothing about *rāg* (melodic modes) or how to play these instruments. The guru repeated his instruction and asked them to trust his words—as the instruments were lifted, *rāg* began to bloom forth from the depths of their beings, and the *sangat* was soon united in the offering of *kirtan*. From that moment on, the tradition of Sikh *ragi* was born, and to this day Sikhs are encouraged to offer *kirtan* regardless of their level of skill.

Meanwhile, Bhai Satta and Bhai Balwand became emotionally distraught, financially ruined, and physically unwell. In a moment of clarity they had a realization: Guru Arjan and the *sangat* do not exist because of the brothers — it is the brothers who exist because of the guru and the *sangat*. Finally, they traveled from Amritsar to Lahore to plead with Bhai Ladha, who was known for his willingness to always help those in need. He asked the brothers to return to Amritsar and await his arrival. When Bhai Ladha appeared, he was seated on a donkey and began to traverse the town. Upon hearing of this incident, Guru Arjan immediately summoned Bhai Ladha and the brothers to his court. Bhai Ladha's plea was accepted by the guru, and the brothers were forgiven on the condition that after bathing they would sing *kirtan* that praised the very gurus they had previously decried. The *vār* (ballad) that they sang in *rāg* Ramkali is recorded in *SGGS*.[5] Of the twenty-two *vār*, it is the only one that has not been composed by one of the gurus.

I retell this story at length for several reasons. First, for its importance in Sikh consciousness — this *sakhi* is often narrated to children within the unit of the family and community, but it also features in gatherings of devotees at Sikh places of worship (*Gurudware*) as a warning against greed and slander and as a lesson in humility. Second, in parallel with the *kirtan* of Guru Nanak and Bhai Mardana, this episode deepens Guru Arjan's commitment to creating equality and equity by prompting him to democratize the practice of devotional music. Following the efforts of the preceding gurus to establish social justice, Guru Arjan continued to dismantle divisions of caste by instructing all Sikhs to undertake *kirtan*, just as they were invited to participate in *guru ka langar* by making and eating food together as a group (*pangat*) — an ambition that some in the community regarded as radical at the time, given the trenchant observance of caste separation in early modern India. Guru Arjan's momentous decision created a new space for *kirtan* that evaded the highly simplified dichotomy of Indian music as either *desi* (folk/"Little Traditions") or *marg* (classical/"Great Traditions") — a characterization that continues to this day in scholarly and nonscholarly discussions of Hindustani music.[6] *Kirtan*, throughout the period of the Sikh courts, transcended — stood at a distance from — these boundaries. Relatedly, the question of how *kirtan* should be offered is latent in this observation: *Kirtan* must be undertaken in a state of humility — it is not (primarily) a musical act of virtuosity that seeks validation and admiration from others, but a sonic means of facilitating a spiritual experience for all.[7]

Third, this *sakhi* is a lesson in forgiveness. Guru Arjan did not have to include Bhai Satta and Bhai Balwand's *vār* when he compiled *SGGS*, but he chose to—not only to indicate their realization of grave misdeeds but also to remind devotees of the central place that *rababi* have played in Sikh *kirtan*. After Guru Arjan, the gurus continued to keep *rababi* in their courts, alongside Sikh *ragi* and *dhaadhi* (singers of folk or historical ballads called *vār*). Sikhs continued to learn *kirtan* from the descendants of *rababi* up until the time of the partition of India and Pakistan in 1947.[8] *Rababi* are essential knowledge bearers who have played a key role in the development of Sikh *kirtan*.[9] Today most *Gurudware* allow *kirtan* to be offered by professional *kirtaniye* as well as the *sangat*.

Finally, this *sakhi* forces us to consider the issue of why Guru Arjan was insistent on Bhai Satta and Bhai Balwand offering *kirtan*. Why were they repeatedly asked to attend to this activity? Could morning worship not have continued without it? Gobind Singh Mansukhani explains that *kirtan* offers a direct link to divinity, "after which there are no more journeys to undertake, no more births to redeem. One reason why this happened only in Sikhism, was because its founder was a musician."[10] In recalling Guru Nanak's sung verses, this answer reveals why devotees consider *kirtan* an essential expression of Sikh devotion.

After opening my book with a story familiar to many Sikhs, and one that is foundational to my own upbringing, I consider it essential to clarify my position and methodology. The scholarly research and fieldwork for this book have taken place over the last two decades, although my devotional immersion in Sikh *kirtan* has been lifelong. I write not only from the perspective of an academic; indeed, I navigate the multiple identities of researcher, practitioner, and devotee. Thus, there are occasional moments when my method calls for a deliberate shift from a scholarly third-person voice to a more intimate first-person voice to lend nuance and detail to the argument. To be clear, my book is not, strictly speaking, a form of autoethnography. Rather, this style of writing has been informed by similar approaches that navigate insider/outsider status in ethnomusicology. My training in music and the humanities equips me with the necessary tools and methodologies from musicology, music theory, ethnography, sound studies, media studies, religious studies, and art history, as I explore and understand devotional expression. I draw on distinct ways of thinking and doing in assembling an idiosyncratic method whose plurality works toward highlighting the many expressions, agents, and identities of Sikh *kirtan*.

In writing this book I wish to honor as far as I can the full spectrum of *kirtan* as it is practiced today, knowing that as Sikhs negotiate their lives in different corners of the globe, they are finding their own ways to make a connection with *Gurbani* that is unique and meaningful. To my mind, I am not writing the definitive book on Sikh *kirtan*. This is hopefully the first of many that will engage with the challenges of negotiating Sikh identities in a globalized environment.

Acknowledgments

It is a joy to extend my gratitude to all those who made this book possible. I am thrilled to receive financial support for open access publication from the Uberoi Foundation for Religious Studies, the Wellesley College Library and Technology Services Open Access Fund, the Wellesley College Luce Moore Grant, and the American Musicological Society's General Fund.. The Uberoi Foundation and Wellesley College have provided financial support for this project in many ways, and I remain deeply grateful for their generosity.

There are many individuals whose voices are interwoven into this book. I wish to thank my parents, and my mother in particular, who introduced me to *kirtan* while I was in utero. I remain convinced that this was the first music I ever heard, and Bhai Harjinder Singh's (Srinagar Wale) *kirtan* seeped into my consciousness during the earliest years of my life. For this connection to *Gurbani*, I am deeply grateful to my mum—this is the greatest gift of all. My parents-in-law have always supported me, and their help in making vital connections with the *sangat* in Ulhasnagar has been indispensable. Rajee Hazari and family warmly welcomed us into their home, and Rajee Ji helped with my research in Ulhasnagar every step of the way. I also wish to thank Gurmukh Ji for answering many queries about Amritvela Trust and Mukesh Ji for his guidance when I first started my work in this city. The *sangat* in Ulhasnagar, indeed the global *sangat*, has inspired me at every moment: Complete strangers filled out a survey, graciously shared their innermost thoughts with me, and inspired me to reflect on the variety and power of *kirtan*. Many more individuals deepened my understanding through conversation, sharing materials, and teaching. I wish to thank Ustad Surjit Singh, Ustad Gurtej Singh, and Dr. Ashwini Purohit for accepting me as their student. I have also learned a great deal from Bhai Kultar Singh and Ustad Baljit Singh (Delhi Wale). My guru-bhai, Gurvinder Singh, has been supportive and resourceful, along with many others in the Boston *sangat*, including Sarbpreet Singh, Jitinder Singh, Amritpal Singh, Mandeep Khanna, and the *dilruba* group of the Khalsa school. Amardev Singh in Malaysia remains a constant resource, always at the ready to answer any query about *kirtaniye* and recordings. Many archivists have come to my help: Shubha Chaudhuri, Suresh Chandvankar, Jonathan Ward, Taranjiet Singh Namdhari, Dr. Mohinder Singh, and Maninder Kaur of the Bhai Vir Singh Sahitya Sadan in Delhi. Several in-depth conversations with leading practitioners led me to think about *kirtan* and issues of production deeply. My heartfelt gratitude is extended to Jasleen Kaur, Taren Kaur, Navpreet Kaur, Bhai Nirmal Singh Khalsa (Pipli Wale), Veer Manpreet Singh, and Dindae Sheena. I am fortunate I was able to speak with the late Bhai Raghbir Singh Diwana and his son, Rajinder Singh, who helped me with my research on Kenya. I wish to thank Priyanka Mac for the honor of using her evocative painting for the front cover of my book.

I remain deeply indebted to my academic communities. At Wellesley College, I wish to thank the Newhouse Center for a summer fellowship, the Mellon Foundation for a grant to develop and co-teach a new course about sacred sound in South Asia, the Music Department for their willingness to incorporate South Asian music into the concert series and curriculum, Carol Lubkowski at the music library, and Angie Bates and her team at Interlibrary Loan, who worked hard to obtain obscure sources. A wonderful student, Vivian Stewart, helped build the accompanying website, and I am hugely grateful for her diligence and commitment. Another former student, Aislinn Bohot, did an excellent job of organizing audio and video examples for the website. Grace Pechianu created a bibliography from an enormous list of sources. I was invited to give keynote lectures and colloquia at several institutions, including the University of Oxford, Case Western Reserve University, the University of Notre Dame, the Center for Diaspora Studies (Punjabi University), Amherst College, and the Eastman School of Music. I wish to thank my colleagues and their excellent students for sharing insightful comments, which helped me refine my work. Lively banter with colleagues and friends has also helped me clarify ideas: I wish to thank David Collins, Claire Fontijn, Kaleb Goldschmitt, Reinaldo Moya, David Russell, Jonathan Dunsby, Peter Smith, Berthold Hoeckner, Dr. Gurnam Singh, Parminder Bhachu, Nikky-Guninder Kaur Singh, Dr. Gurdeep Kour, Dr. Usha Khurana, Gibb Schreffler, Virinder Kalra, Harjinder Lallie, Pritam Singh, Bhai Baldeep Singh, Dr. Dupinder Rattan, Pashaura Singh, Jeffers Engelhardt, Francesca Brittan, Daniel Goldmark, Cory Hunter, Anaar Desai-Stephens, Matthew Rahaim, Ramneek Kaur, Neelima Shukla Bhatt, Inderjit Kaur, Inni Kaur, Jasjit Singh, Manjeet Singh, Suhail Yusuf, Jonathan Cross, Esther Cavett, John Baily, Amy Catlin-Jairazbhoy, Linda Hess, Winand Callewaert, and Anna Yu Wang.

I have been working on this book for at least two decades. It began as a graduate student paper in 1998 at the University of Chicago, where I sat around a large seminar table in Professor Philip Bohlman's proseminar on mode, sandwiched between two peers who would go on to become shining lights in the field of ethnomusicology (Rich Jankowsky and Timothy Rommen). I remain indebted to this experience and to these brilliant thinkers, whose critical mindsets and kind support stayed with me as I slowly worked on this project, never quite believing it would come to fruition. My dear friend Charles Hiroshi Garrett was the one who told me to "just finish it." I'm sad I can't share it with him, for he left us too soon. Over many years, our chitter-chatter about this project helped me keep going, and I'm glad he told me to stop procrastinating. I am ecstatic this book finally found its home at the University of Chicago Press under the wise counsel of the editorial board of the Chicago Studies in Ethnomusicology series and the close supervision of my wonderful editor, Mollie McFee.

My large, loving family helped me get to the finish line. My gratitude extends to the Bhogal, Channa, Mehta, and Panesar families. I'm grateful to my sons, Vir and Armaan, for being part of this journey, and I hope that *kirtan* will always be a part of theirs. My deepest love and gratitude go to Mridul, who does what it takes to make things happen.

Introduction

The power of *kirtan* is frequently highlighted in Sikh sacred verse. Hearing and offering *kirtan* is a means to feeling physically healthy (*kirtan* removes disease), mentally healthy (*kirtan* removes anxiety), spiritually uplifted (*kirtan* raises one's consciousness by amplifying inner vibration), environmentally attuned (devotees are encouraged to perceive the *kirtan* offered by nature, organic and nonorganic matter, the elements, and the cosmos), and communally connected (*kirtan* orients the corporeal vibration of a community toward building social bonds and promoting service, which improves the well-being of all).

This unique conception of devotional music points to a tradition where social bonds are forged through the force of amplified corporeal vibration catalyzed by *kirtan*. This experience of *kirtan* stands at a distance from the realm of aesthetics and an experience of *ras* (intensified emotion) as facilitating individual bliss. A *sangat* attunes to "the divine Word as an aid to ethical and spiritual development" while cultivating an inner "shant rasa (emotion of peace) and nam rasa (devotional mood)," as noted by Pashaura Singh and Mansukhani.[1] The foundational role of *kirtan* in communal Sikh worship ensures its centrality as it accompanies Sikhs wherever life takes them. Over time, as *kirtan* undertook multiple journeys to distant places with different Sikh communities, it also changed in its musical character, an observation that highlights the contentious topic of musical taste.

SGGS has a distinctive formal structure characterized by its indexical organization into thirty-one major *rāg*. The association of a verse with specific *rāg* has been understood by some devotees as nothing short of a divine command—*hukam*—that must be obeyed, which has led to the musical practice of *nirdharit rāg kirtan* (offering sacred verse in designated *rāg*), where verse titles themselves are sung in *rāg* to preface the main composition. This style of *kirtan* is often called "classical" by practitioners and devotees; it has become synonymous with a growing practice called *Gurmat Sangeet*, which prioritizes *nirdharit rāg* played on traditional instruments.

The theoretical framework outlined here seems straightforward. In reality historical forces have tampered with the transmission of musical knowledge within the Sikh community (*panth*). Broadly speaking, the formation of the *panth* coincided with a period that saw the tyrannical rule of Mughal emperors during the time of the gurus and the collapse of the Sikh empire by the middle of the nineteenth century, only to be followed by brutal imperialism and the first waves of immigration among Sikhs to British colonies during the nineteenth and twentieth centuries. As a response to rapid colonization, some Sikh scholars advocated for the importance of preserving knowledge about *rāg* as it was practiced in a style of *kirtan* defined as *Gurmat Sangeet* in publications of the early twentieth century.[2] By 1931, as Virinder Kalra observes, specific rules and regulations had been codified in the form of the Sikh *Rehat Maryada* (1950).[3] Bob van der Linden views the resulting canonization of *kirtan* as a response to the imperial encounter by Singh Sabha reformists who sought to restore a sense of Sikh spiritual identity.[4] Later in the twentieth century *kirtan* reform was spearheaded by the Shiromani Gurudwara Prabandhak Committee (SGPC), which oversees the management of *Gurudware* across India. Since 1991 the Ludhiana-based institution Jawaddi Taksal, dedicated to teaching *Gurbani* and *Gurmat Sangeet*, has endeavored to institutionalize the practice of *nirdharit rāg*.

As one might expect, political interventions have been interpreted differently by others. Against these sociopolitical initiatives, Bhai Baldeep Singh asserts his position as a "representative of the oldest pre-*darbāri* [pre-courtly] and pre-colonial Gurbānī Sangīta tradition's emic knowledge stream," a thirteenth-century tradition that he sees as having resisted colonization. In parallel, Francesca Cassio views these reforms as propagating a "'neo' kirtan repertory" as opposed to a "Sikh Renaissance," led by Bhai Baldeep Singh and which "foster[s] the recovery of the existing body of *rāga*-based heritage compositions (the actual *purātan śabad rīts*) and their pedagogy which have survived in oral and written forms."[5] Since the founding of the Chief Khalsa Diwan in 1902, political debates surrounding *kirtan* reform and decolonization have seen the rise of multiple narratives—some speak of lineage and continuity between knowledge bearers, while others acknowledge a need to rebuild a music-theoretical foundation even if this requires incorporating more recent ideas about *rāg* and musical instruments (chap. 2 shows these debates are ongoing).[6] The historical figures of the colonized and uncolonized Sikh loom large in these debates.

HISTORICIZING *KIRTAN* IN PUNJAB AND THE DIASPORA: CASE STUDY—KENYA

While these theories allow us to productively examine the impact of colonization on Sikh history, closer attention to the lived reality of a growing diaspora sheds new light on the transformation and evolution of *kirtan*. For many, the volatile geopolitical landscape of the late nineteenth and early twentieth centuries disrupted lineages for transmitting oral and written knowledge pertaining to the practice of *kirtan*, particularly within the diaspora. Living in precarious socioeconomic circumstances in locations remote from Punjab made it harder for some Sikhs to follow the *hukam* of *nirdharit rāg* over time, especially among communities that did not have access to knowledge bearers of *rāg*. Sikhs who began their migration to distant lands such as East Africa during the nineteenth century—the "pioneering generations" as Bhachu calls them—included laborers, craftsmen, artisans, tailors, and mechanics.[7] In the case of those who traveled to Kenya, for instance, these pioneers carried inherited cultural and religious knowledge, which they drew on in the absence of *granthi* (custodians of *Gurudware*) and professional *ragi/kirtaniye*, who were not always participants in the first journeys. Many first-generation diasporic Sikhs did not have access to a *Gurudwara* as a place of worship—Bhachu shows how the first immigrant Sikhs were often involved in building *Gurudware* from the ground up using *mabati* (Swahili for "corrugated iron").[8]

Some of these migrants were versed in *rāg*, and others likely relied on their own memories of tunes (based on *kirtan* or folk/popular melodies) (see fig. I.1). This photo from the early twentieth century, possibly of the earliest pioneers, shows they had taken a percussion instrument (a *tabla* or *dholki*) with them. Later migrants took instruments, too. Gopal Singh

FIGURE I.1 Pioneer Sikhs offering *kirtan* and prayer in East Africa. Photograph courtesy of Lakhvir Singh Khalsa.

Chandan reminisced about his preparation for his long journey to Kenya in 1929 on a "huge ship called [SS] *Rawalpindi*." He recalled the events of the night before his travel: "In the evening Rattan Singh, a lifelong friend from Nakodar, and I sang a *shabad* [devotional composition] in Basant raag: *Sadho mann ka maan tiyago*—get rid of false pride, oh the pious ones. I played the harmonium which I had manufactured with my own hands while Rattan Singh . . . accompanied me on the tabla." Having traveled to Bombay from Nakodar (Punjab) to board his ship, Gopal Singh Chandan made sure he "bought a trunk to keep the harmonium" to protect his instrument. Describing Gopal Singh Chandan's journey to Kenya, his son Amarjit Chandan gives an insight into how *kirtan* literally traveled with him: "On his first voyage to Kenya in 1929, he . . . sang *shabads* which fellow-travelers joined in with while sailing through the Arabian sea."[9]

In addition to harmoniums and *tabla/dholki*, which were prized possessions that passengers took with them as essential companions, other instruments also crossed the ocean: In **figure I.2**, we see two *dilruba* and a *tanpura*. A violin and clarinet are also shown as part of the *kirtan jatha* (ensemble)—while a violin was occasionally played in *kirtan*, the clarinet likely crossed over from the military band, which had been established in Punjab by the British; it would never have been played in *kirtan*, since the only wind instrument that is (rarely) incorporated is the *bansuri*

FIGURE I.2 Sikh *Rāgis Kirtan Jatha*, Nairobi, 1942 (Amarjit Chandan Archive). The instruments shown here include two bowed *dilruba*, a plucked *tanpura*, two harmoniums, two sets of *tabla*, a clarinet, and a violin.

(bamboo flute). My guess is that its use here is more as a prop. This photo is a valuable document for another reason: It was taken in Nairobi at a photography studio started by Gopal Singh Chandan in 1939, showing the entrepreneurial spirit of the early migrants, much noted by Bhachu.

In the coming decades, diasporic communities would turn to records and commercial radio, with its broadcasting of Indian cinema tunes, as musical fodder for *kirtan*. In India the first *kirtan* had been recorded by the Gramophone Company at the turn of the twentieth century, and in the following decades the commercialization of *kirtan* continued to grow in tandem with the ascent of Indian cinema.[10] Existing Gramophone Company records show that by the 1930s *kirtan* was also being recorded in studios in a *filmi* style, hence the emergence of another category, *filmi shabad*.[11] The pace picked up by the 1970s when Kesar Singh Narula, who had established his career within the film industry as a composer, arranger, and producer, turned his attention toward producing commercial Punjabi folk music and commercial *kirtan*.[12] Kimani Gecau explains that the wind-up gramophone was in use in Kenya during the early decades of the twentieth century and that Indian immigrants "started playing music in their shops to attract customers in the 1920s." They were selling the new gramophone as well as "imported Indian, European and American (including black American) music." By the 1950s Indian immigrants were contributing to Nairobi's "vibrant popular music industry" by establishing local record companies; Gecau observes how the "setting up of a pressing plant in Nairobi in 1952 made Nairobi the centre of East Africa's music industry."[13]

NAVIGATING GENDER INEQUALITY

Just as diasporic Sikhs offered *kirtan* in keeping with the resources they had at hand, women have participated in *kirtan* in ways that have been shaped by the gender expectations and opportunities at sites of practice and worship. The *filmi* musical style and aesthetic became a template for diasporic communities, particularly for women who were homemakers and who did not have access to skilled training in *kirtan*. When All India Radio banned the playing of Hindi film songs on its airwaves in 1952, Radio Ceylon began broadcasting hit cinema songs across South Asia and the diaspora during its popular segment *Binaca Geetmala*. During a car journey on the way back from a *Gurudwara* in Nakuru one afternoon, I heard a film tune played on the radio that was exactly the same as one I had been taught on the harmonium for a *shabad* (a devotional composition). I was around ten years old at the time, and I still recall my surprise that a film tune should resemble a *shabad*. I had it the wrong way around, of course: Although I had arrived at the film tune after learning the *shabad*, the women who taught me had encountered the film tune first.

Over time, as communities were able to accumulate enough wealth to bring male *ragi* from India to various diasporic hubs, they began to forge strong connections with *rāg*-based *kirtan*. In Malaysia Bhai Tara Singh and Bhai Santokh Singh Nirpukh (a student of the *rababi* Bhai Lal Mohammad Amritsari) arrived in the mid-1930s.[14] In Kenya students of Bhai Darshan Singh Komal (a disciple of the renowned *rababi* Bhai Sain Ditta) staked a long presence from the 1950s up until a decade or two ago: Among them were Bhai Beant Singh Bijli, Bhai Ajit Singh Mutlashi, Giani Gurcharan Singh, and Bhai Raghbir Singh Diwana. By the 1960s, however, with the advent of cassettes and the growing interest from Indian recording companies in marketing a popular style of *kirtan* influenced by Indian cinema, the Sikh diasporic community had become active and powerful consumers whose tastes for *kirtan* had shifted considerably.

When *ragi* traveled outside of India (this is also true to some extent for their service within India), they were often asked to deliver *kirtan* in a "light or popular style" because most of the local *sangat* no longer understood or appreciated *rāg*, as Bhai Raghbir Singh Diwana informed me.[15]

In his study of the impact of recording industries on religious music in India, Scott Marcus argues that the "commercial recording industry is dominated . . . by males" even when it comes to consumption. This is not the case with Sikh *kirtan*, since many women, particularly diasporic, consumed *kirtan* on cassettes within the domestic sphere, thereby playing a critical (and understudied) role in how this industry flourished and evolved.[16] Pioneer Sikhs performed *kirtan* themselves and, when they began to access recordings, these materials kept them connected to their faith and their homeland. To be clear, recordings are not played in *Gurudware* to replace live *kirtan* (to my knowledge); following the *hukam* (command) of Guru Arjan, Sikhs are compelled to offer *kirtan* in the absence of—and in addition to that offered by—professional *kirtaniye*. For those *ragi* who made commercial recordings, it's difficult to determine whether they amassed much wealth. What many popular *ragi* did accumulate, without a doubt, is celebrity status and renown in the recording industry, which led to a demand for their live presence in *Gurudware* (which remains the case today for certain *kirtaniye*).

This shift in listening behaviors was accompanied by a change in attitude toward musical instruments. The harmonium, which had entered Harmandir Sahib in Amritsar by around 1903, had become a defining instrument of Sikh *kirtan* by the 1930s: It was robust and relatively cheap, didn't require constant tuning, and was easy to play, unlike the traditional string instruments (*tanti sāz*) of the Sikh courts. The consumption of *kirtan* had increased considerably due to cassette technology by the 1980s, but the growth of this industry (coupled with the impact of colonization) came at a cost: The vibrant *rāg* and instruments that had enlivened the courts of the gurus for nearly three centuries had begun to fade away from practice and, even worse, from memory. As early as 1906 Sikh intellectual Bhai Vir Singh observed a decline in the practice of offering *Gurbani* in stipulated *rāg*, as well as decreasing interest in hearing *rāg* among the *sangat*. In parallel he saw a growing curiosity to hear *sakhi* (spiritually inflected narratives) rather than *kirtan* because, as he explained it, the *sangat* had lost an understanding of *rāg*.[17]

Practitioners had been lamenting tendencies toward a *filmi* style in *kirtan* since its crossover in the middle of the twentieth century in tandem with the commercialization of *kirtan* on LP record, cassette, and later, CD.[18] Several factors contributed to the turn of the tide toward a *rāg*-based *kirtan* beginning in the early 1990s using *tanti sāz*. Chief among these is the attack on the Golden Temple by the Indian government in 1984, a catastrophic event whose aftermath of violence and mass killings prompted deep introspection among Sikhs over the revival and preservation of their cultural values, traditions, identity, and heritage. Given my multi-migrant background (having lived in Kenya, the United Kingdom, and now the United States), I also see first- and second-generation Sikhs (who are now entering middle age) as active participants in this cultural introspection: Although we were teens during the time of these massacres, the atrocities of these events have left an indelible imprint on our diasporic Sikh identities and senses of the colonized/decolonized/neocolonized self.[19]

As I see it, these generations are now actively involved in inviting practitioners of *nirdharit rāg kirtan* (mostly called *Gurbani Sangeet* or *Gurmat Sangeet*) to local *Gurudware* and community centers and in promoting festivals (called *kirtan darbar*, *samagam*, or *samelan*), camps, and workshops focused on learning compositions in the thirty-one principal *rāg* of *Gurbani* (see **fig. I.3**). Opportunities to learn traditional string instruments like the *taus*, *dilruba*, *sarangi*, and *rabab*, along with percussion instruments like the *pakhawaj* and *jori*, are sought out. An even greater push for historical awareness is coming from millennials and postmillennials who want to learn more about their Sikh heritage. As will be discussed in chapter 2, the standard *kirtan jatha* (ensemble) is now

FIGURE I.3 Poster advertising a three-day performance of thirty-one *rāg* from *SGGS* at the Sikh Gurdwara of San Jose, California, September 2023.

FIGURE I.4 Photograph of a summer *kirtan* camp at Gurdwara Sahib, Westborough, Massachusetts, led by celebrated *sarangi* player Ustad Surjit Singh. Students are learning to master techniques of *rāg* on bowed instruments, *dilruba* and *sarangi*, August 2023. Author's photograph.

changing its profile from that of two harmoniums and *tabla* to a small orchestra of string instruments (see **fig. I.4**). This chapter highlights the changing optics of Sikh *kirtan* during an era of historical awakening, which includes a much-needed discussion about female-led *kirtan*.[20] The juxtaposition of **figures I.3** and **I.4** reveals the gender imbalance at play: **Figure I.3** features ten *kirtaniye*, one of whom is a woman. **Figure I.4** shows a workshop led by celebrated *sarangi* player Ustad Surjit Singh, with fourteen women and three men.[21] This difference raises an important question: Why is the representation of women at the professional level so small?

While *kirtaniye* tend to be predominantly male, this is not the case in a majority of cases where string instruments are now being taught. As highlighted in chapters 2 and 6, more and more female *kirtaniye* are excelling in Sikh *kirtan*, and in some cases, accomplished women have been welcomed into diverse spaces, including elite music festivals in Punjab (such as Jawaddi Taksal's Adutti Gurmat Sangeet Samelan and Harivallabh Sangeet Sammelan), the Punjabi reality TV show *Gavo Sachi Baani*, and high-profile *kirtan* competitions (such as the Hemkunt Kirtan Darbar). I note, in this chapter, that women are not permitted to offer *kirtan* at the holiest site, Harmandir Sahib.

A barrage of *Gurudwara* politics, coupled with an overall lack of opportunity for female *kirtaniye*, led Navpreet Kaur (California) to establish a

FIGURE I.5 Poster from Gaavani: Celebrating the Female Voice in Gurbani Kirtan featuring lead *kirtaniye*. Guneet Kaur, Dallas, 2024.

new organization that provides a space for professional women and girls aspiring to be professionals: Gaavani, whose motto is "Celebrating the female voice in *Gurbani kirtan*." This initiative began when she envisioned female representation in the multiday *kirtan darbar* that she organized in 2018 at the San Jose *Gurudwara*, whose inauguration included a celebrated female *kirtaniya*, Guneet Kaur. Over the next few years female participation increased at this *kirtan darbar*, which led Navpreet Kaur to create Gaavani in 2021, with the support of the scholar and practitioner Dr. Gurnam Singh (chapter 6 explores how having a male counterpart helps female *kirtaniye* enter and navigate the patriarchal world of *kirtan*). Gaavani's first event took place in May 2022 at Fremont Gurudwara and gave female *kirtaniye* from North America an opportunity to gather and offer *kirtan* in *nirdharit rāg* (see **fig. 1.5**).²² As seen in a recent *darbar* organized in Dallas (January 2024), Navpreet Kaur's multimedia melding of sacred poetry with *rāg* and original painting by female Sikh artists presents a holistic vision of *Gurbani*, where the female voice and expression is front and center—literally in the form of vocal timbre but also figuratively, given *Gurbani*'s use of the female poetic register to explore themes of yearning, separation, love, and joy.

Gaavani's bold efforts work in tandem with a gradual rise of women over the last few decades in a folk tradition that runs parallel to *kirtan* and that is sometimes featured at *Gurudwara*: *dhaadhi vār*.²³ **Video example 1.1** shows a female *dhaadhi jatha* led by Rajwant Kaur (Fatehgarh Sahib Wale).²⁴ *Dhaadhi* are musicians who perform folk music using the *dhadh*, a small, double-headed, handheld drum, and the folk *sarangi* (constructed and played differently from the classical *sarangi* sometimes used in *kirtan*) in small (mostly single-sex) groups of three or four men or women. Since *dhaadhi jatha* do not only sing verses from *Gurbani*, they are permitted to play standing up in *Gurudwara*; in comparison, all other offerings of *kirtan* are made in a seated position on the floor in a show of humility and to maximize the transduction of vibration. Nowadays, *dhaadhi* interweave historical episodes (*sakhi*), current political events, and phrases from *Gurbani* into their ballads (*vār*). In his valuable discussion of female *dhaadhi*, Michael Nijhawan explores the political role played by the *nabhewale bibian* in bolstering Sikh resistance prior to the Indian government's attack on Harmandir Sahib in 1984.[25] Bhai Vir Singh views the tradition of *dhaadhi jatha* as an important counterpart to the practice of *kirtan*. In an essay from 1906 he lamented that oral interpolation, a *dhaadhi* trademark, had been taken over by *ragi* and *rababi* who, by incorporating exegesis, prevent an unbroken (*akhand*) offering of *kirtan* from occurring, which is essential to keeping the mind connected to *Gurbani*.[26] Folk and classical styles are both respected in the practice of *kirtan*, and Guru Nanak, in a gesture of humility, often described himself as a *dhaadhi* (summoning up the cultural figure of the low-caste folk musician or ballad singer).

Amateur women have other options for creating their own distinctive devotional music. *Gurudware* around the world have a separate schedule for women to meet and offer *kirtan* at events called *satsang*. These gatherings are also held at community centers and at people's homes, where the harmonium and the percussion instruments *chimta/chhainay* (steel tongs with added steel disks) and *dholki* (double-headed drum played sitting down) feature prominently (see **fig. 1.6** and **video ex. 1.2**). Many of the women who participate in *satsang* are untrained, but they often teach one another how to play simple melodies on the harmonium in a *dharna* (call-and-response) style—the strongest (loudest) singer will sing the main line of text, and the remainder of the *sangat* will repeat it. While playing rhythm and meter on the *dholki* is a learned skill that is usually taken up by someone who has had some training, playing the *chimta/chhainay* is fairly self-explanatory—one just has to keep track of the beat and know when to stop and start.[27] "Ladies Satsang" (*bibian da satsang/istri satsang*), as these gatherings are often called, are important social and spiritual events: Since the patriarchal structures of many *Gurudware* make it difficult for women to be involved in governance, the *satsang* provides a communal space for devotional practice where women have full control. This practice is worthy of further research, especially given the unique corpus of compositions that has evolved within the context of the "Ladies Satsang" over time.

As these overlapping cases have showed, the long history of Sikh

FIGURE I.6 Photograph of "Ladies Satsang" featuring one harmonium, one *dholki*, and two sets of *chimta/chhainay* at Ramgarhia Sikh Gurdwara East London, June 2023. Author's photograph.

devotional practice has offered many opportunities to reconnect with tradition and explore new expressions. One tide (addressed in chap. 2) continues to pull toward the Sikh courts of days past under the guise of purity and authenticity. However, the ocean is vast, and there are other waves whose currents flow in multiple directions.

CROSSCURRENTS: THE MANY TIDES OF SIKH *KIRTAN*

In writing this book, I found myself constantly negotiating multiple vantage points, given my role as both participant and observer. Relatedly, I was unsure how other Sikhs felt about the modern development of *kirtan* following the partition, since devotees are not socially and culturally encouraged to critique sacred expression. Several years ago, as I scanned a blog post on the Langar Hall website (thelangarhall.com), where Sikhs were reflecting on the style of *kirtan* that they enjoy—with an emphasis on *rāg*-based *Gurmat Sangeet*—I was intrigued by how comfortable people felt giving their opinions in the "safe" anonymous space of the internet. I yearned to know more. Even though I had grown up learning the *vaja* (harmonium) from women in my community, I shifted in my adult years toward learning the *dilruba*, a fretted and bowed string instrument, from a master player of the *sarangi* in the Namdhari tradition, Ustad Surjit Singh (see **fig. 1.4** above). I enjoy playing and hearing *kirtan* in *rāg* and there are many instances when I agree with practitioners who argue that the true essence of a verse can only be grasped when it is communicated through the designated *rāg*. At these moments I am utterly moved and deeply touched by the resonance of *shabad* (the divine word) through *rāg*. This experience honors the command—*hukam*—of the gurus, and the experience of hearing *nirdharit rāg* by such experts as Ustad Baljit Singh (Delhi Wale) is like no other (**video ex. 1.3**).

At the same time, I am empathetic toward the women who taught me my first *kirtan* on the harmonium, and I remain greatly appreciative of their dedication and efforts. Being part of first- and second-generation East African diasporic communities and, beyond that, being women, they were mostly self-taught and took opportunities to teach one another and the children of the community without having had the chance to receive formal training themselves. It is these kinds of interaction with amateur *kirtaniye* that compel me to view *kirtan* as a multifaceted tradition and one that is inclusive of different ideas and practices as they coalesce among evolving communities settled around the world. As I undertook close listening to the harmonium during my research for chapter 2, there were many moments when I stumbled upon a *shabad* or two that jolted me back to my childhood memories. My mother was particularly partial to playing Bhai Harjinder Singh (Srinagar Wale) during the 1970s on cassettes (many of which I now own). When I listen to his *"Amrit Bani Har Har Teri,"* Bhai Satvinder Singh and Bhai Harvinder Singh's (Delhi Wale) *"Sunn Yaar Humare Sajan"* (1980s), or Bhai Anantvir Singh's *"Madho Hum Aise Tu Aisa"* (2000), I am drawn in (**audio exs. 1.1, 1.2, and 1.3**). These recordings of mainstream *kirtan*, with their pairing of voice, harmonium, and *tabla*, are the stuff of nostalgia. Even though these examples fall under the larger category of "Sikh *kirtan*," there are subtle and notable differences between these *kirtaniye*. Bhai Harjinder Singh's focus on simple, repeating melodies and a calm delivery of *Gurbani* epitomizes what he calls *nirol kirtan*, which places primary emphasis on *shabad*, the divine word. Bhai Satvinder Singh and Bhai Harvinder Singh reach for a commercially oriented audience, and thus their choice of melody is more elaborate, sometimes opting for a wistful vocal delivery reminiscent of *ghazal*. Meanwhile, Bhai Anantvir Singh is renowned for the rousing voice and vibrant energy of his *kirtan*, which characterizes the fully participatory *AKJ* (*Akhand Kirtani Jatha*) style.

| Classical/*Rāg*-based (*Gurmat Sangeet, Gurbani Sangeet, Gurmat Kirtan, Namdhari Kirtan*) |
| Mainstream |
| Semi-Classical |
| *Akhand Kīrtanī Jatha* (AKJ) |
| New Age/Contemporary |
| Digital |
| *Partāl, Puratan Reet, Dhurpad Shailly, Dodra Samagam,* Bollywood, *Ghazal, Thumri* |

FIGURE I.7 Styles of *kirtan* in order of popularity, as identified by respondents.

Figure I.7 shows that there are many styles of *kirtan* being played and heard today, and some of these use assigned *rāg*, traditional instruments, or both. The categories shown here have been suggested to me by a virtual *sangat* through an anonymous survey (discussed in the appendix). In this book I refer to styles that adhere to designated *rāg* as *nirdharit kirtan* and those that do not follow this practice as *rāg*-flexible *kirtan*. While some practitioners and listeners use a variety of terms to describe *kirtan*, others are more particular about which formulations capture their efforts.[28] The categories shown here reflect the most common labels, but I acknowledge that these are not sufficient since they embrace a diversity of styles within a single category.

For example, Namdhari *kirtan* might come under the umbrella of classical *kirtan*, which is based strictly on the use of designated *rāg* as heard in *Gurmat Sangeet/Gurbani Sangeet/Gurmat Kirtan*. Even then, there are differences among these styles because Namdhari *kirtan* is sometimes offered in *rāg* that are not used in *Gurbani* (such as *Shivranjani, Bhimpalasi, Pahadi, Jaunpuri, Shankara,* and *Pilu*), even as Namdhari practitioners remain committed to the use of traditional instruments. They prefer to use *taus, dilruba, tār-shehnai, sarangi,* and *tanpura*, rather than a harmonium, which is reserved mainly for *diwan* (religious assembly) along with *kainsi* (hand cymbals, also called *jhanjh* or *manjira*).[29] Styles of singing are also different between Namdhari *kirtaniye* and *Gurbani Sangeet* as practiced by someone like Bhai Baldeep Singh, for instance: Both offer *kirtan* in a variety of genres and styles, although we hear slightly more emphasis on *khyal* (a more ornamented lyrical style) with Namdhari *kirtaniye*. Their style of *dhurpad* is also different in comparison to that of Bhai Baldeep Singh (see **video exs. 1.3** and **1.4**).[30]

Figure 1.7 shows a category for mainstream *kirtan* (commercially described as *shabad kirtan* or *Gurbani kirtan*), which refers to a style that one would typically hear in a *Gurudwara* by a visiting *ragi jatha* (ensemble) comprised of two harmoniums and a *tabla* (often *rāg* flexible). Also captured in this figure is the distinctive, *rāg*-flexible style of the *AKJ*: Using the harmonium and percussion (usually *tabla* and *chimta/chhainay*), the *shabad* is presented through a simple melody in a call-and-response style. *AKJ kirtan* gradually builds in intensity through a paced, temporal progression that incorporates a rhythmic form of cyclic breathing (*saas giraas*), which contributes to an ecstatic delivery. The new age/contemporary category includes *kirtaniye* who are *rāg* flexible and experimental in their choice of musical instruments. Again, this category is vast and incorporates styles as diverse as Dya Singh's "new Australian 'world' music" and Snatam Kaur's meditative and healing *kirtan*.[31] The final category I outline here is digital, another broad umbrella term, which includes musicians who offer *kirtan* in a way that makes creative and innovative use of digital technology (including Bhai Gurpreet Singh, Veer Manpreet Singh, and Jasleen Kaur; see chaps. 5 and 6). There is overlap with the new age/contemporary category, since Dya Singh, Snatam Kaur, and Taren Kaur all use technology in skillful ways to communicate their unique sacred aesthetics. The final list—including *partāl, puratan reet, dhurpad shailly, dodra samagam,* Bollywood, *khayal, ghazal, thumri*—is discussed below.

Figure I.7 encapsulates an argument I will revisit throughout the book: There is no singular expression of Sikh *kirtan*. In certain instances the act of journeying across the globe has led some communities to expand their practice of *kirtan* to include cultural and technological currents that pervade their lives. In other instances practitioners hold fast to past traditions to preserve hereditary knowledge. Against these contexts, I still contend with the question of whether it is necessary to demote devotional expressions that do not adhere to *nirdharit kirtan*. Personal reflection on this issue creates considerable inner turmoil: If one hears or plays *kirtan* through melodies that are not in the stipulated *rāg*, does that mean divine *hukam* (command) is being interpreted as mere suggestion as opposed to a spiritual imperative? This question is explored in the appendix, and it guides my observations about diverse *kirtan* practices in this book.

In whatever way it is expressed musically, *kirtan* plays a key role in the Sikh spiritual economy. Oral knowledge suggests that it has always been this way, given that Guru Nanak's delivery of *kirtan* during his travels often catered to the tastes of his local community, which he accommodated through (a) linguistic adaptations in his verses to catch the nuances of local dialects; (b) musical styles, from a folk aesthetic for rural audiences to, as it is believed, a more austere expression in the form of *dhurpad* for more informed listeners; and (c) inflections in his choice of *rāg* to reflect regional practices or spiritual leanings. *Rāg Tilang* is said to have appealed to the Sufis, while in his travels to the South, Guru Nanak altered *Gauri, Wadhans, Maru, Bilawal, Ramkali,* and *Prabhati* into *Dakhni* (Deccani) forms, which is why these *rāg* exist in pure (*shudh*) and hybrid (*mishrat*) versions (e.g., *Gauri Dakhni, Wadhans Dakhni*). A hundred years later, one might argue that Bhai Satta and Bhai Balwand's acute awareness of their critical role in the *kirtan* economy was behind their attempt to exploit it—until, that is, Guru Arjan realized the importance of expanding a single market by encouraging broad participation. By the turn of the twentieth century, Bob van der Linden suggests, *kirtan* had again become "a commodity, whereby the chief *ragi* at the Golden Temple between 1910 and 1930, Bhai Moti, charged the highest fee for a public *kirtan*."[32] The vast proliferation of *kirtan* across the spaces of live, recorded, and digital practices points once more to the continued tendencies of *kirtan* toward the marketplace.

Based on manuscript study, Pashaura Singh shows that Guru Arjan was

> fully aware of the needs of various sections of the Panth [community] coming from different backgrounds. That is why he stressed the use of classical, semi-classical and folk tunes in devotional singing, keeping in mind the sociological significance of the folk tradition. At the end of his response, Guru Arjan made the most significant point—that the appropriation of the meaning of the Divine Word depends to a large extent upon the capacity, preparation, and interest of the listeners. That is why he stressed the power of listening with focused attention at *kirtan* sessions.[33]

Guru Arjan is often thought of as having democratized *kirtan*. By placing the execution of *kirtan* within the purview of every Sikh, he also wrested it from the hereditary dominance of lineage and gave Sikhs the opportunity to bring their own backgrounds and beings into musical conversation with the divine utterance of the guru. In one respect coexistence has been inscribed into the Sikh imagination of *kirtan*: The voice and *rabab* of Guru Nanak and Bhai Mardana constituted one of several devotional expressions in a sonic landscape marked by *bhakti bhajan* and *Sufi qawwali*, among other sacred vocal genres of the fifteenth century. Furthermore, when I think of how the gurus were scattered throughout Punjab during their lifetimes, and how the instruments associated with their courts changed over time, it is clear that the practice of *kirtan* was always evolving and never static. To my mind, this logic might also extend to the interpretation of *rāg*: Was the delivery of *Aasa* in the court of Guru Gobind Singh identical to that of Guru Nanak three centuries earlier? Was it identical to forms of *Aasa* that were played at Harmandir Sahib during the time of Guru Ramdas? I wonder whether the practice of *kirtan* was conceived by the gurus as singular or whether, as Pashaura Singh's manuscript source suggests, it was broad enough to embrace the various musical offerings of the *sangat*.

It is clear in *Gurbani* that *rāg* is a musical device whose inherent *bhaav* (a feeling of heightened or ecstatic devotion) should be oriented toward conveying the sentiment of the *shabad*, as the third guru, Guru Amardas, makes clear: "*Rāg*, sound (*nād*), and sacred word (*shabad*) appear beautiful to us when they offer an easeful meditation." The third and fourth gurus made the point repeatedly that *rāg* is an aid to contemplation and its use should not overshadow the verse. Guru Amardas explained, "Only sing in *rāg* Bilawal when the divine name has become manifest in one's mouth."[34] He also composed a verse in *rāg* Sri where he explains, "Among all the *rāg*, Sri *rāg* is exemplary if it stirs up love for the divine" and "*Rāg* Gauri is auspicious if it allows one to remember the divine beloved."[35] Similarly, *rāg* Malar, associated with rain, cools the mind through contemplation of divinity. Guru Ramdas observed, "Among all the *rāg*, the one that is the most pleasing is that which allows the divine one to pervade the consciousness."[36] In *kirtan* a devotionally attuned delivery of *shabad* oriented toward a synesthetic experience of *amrit ras* (the embodied perception of sweet nectar) is paramount and should never be overshadowed by musical prowess.

THE JOURNEYS OF SIKH *KIRTAN*

An anonymous survey discussed in the appendix helped me navigate questions about *nirdharit rāg* vs. *rāg*-flexible *kirtan* as I was writing the first two chapters of this book. Chapter 1 turns to the topic of theories (flagged in the book's subtitle) to show the importance of *rāg* as an organizing device and as a spiritual tool through a detailed study of verse titles (*sirlek*). I explore how a theory of *rāg* resides at the core of the devotional experience while also examining the broad conception of music signaled by the vibrant soundscapes of *Gurbani*, which encompass nature, animals, the elements, and the cosmos. The historical-cultural significance of *nirdharit rāg* remains a concern in chapter 2, which is oriented around another topic flagged in the subtitle, musical instruments. While showing how the harmonium became embroiled in recent debates around *rāg*, heritage, preservation, and lineage, I draw on missionary accounts to trace a history of this instrument in Punjab, arguing that how it is played and constructed by practitioners of Sikh *kirtan* has been carefully honed.

Another question that had been vexing me for some time anchored my continued investigation of theory and instruments in chapters 3 and 4, which were conceived as a pair. This concerns the topic of *nād*, divine sound, and what it means within Sikh epistemology. Guy Beck, Lewis Rowell, and others have explored ideas about *nād* within the Vedic context, and while their attention to the dualistic notion of *nād* as *ahata* and *anahata* (struck and unstruck) is a helpful starting point, these discussions do not fully capture the immense importance given to the latter, and described as *anahad nād*, in *Gurbani*. Chapter 3 turns again to theory, exploring the different formulations of *anahad* in *SGGS*, the emergence of *anahad* as an embodied experience that is marked by timbral heterogeneity, and the intertwined relationship between the struck origins of *kirtan* in the physical effort of playing musical instruments and the unstruck origins of divine sound in its existence as a permanent, effortless vibration. The gurus were not only knowledgeable about the theory of music, but they were accomplished musicians in their own right. The principal collection of instruments in the Sikh courts included the *rabab, saranda, sarangi, taus, tanpura, pakhawaj, dholak, dhadh,* and *jori,* as well as, later, the *sitar, dilruba,* and *tabla*. It is no surprise then that the specific timbres of inner corporeal vibration are not described in *SGGS* as divine sound, *nād*, but in terms of the specific instruments that vibrate *anahad* timbres through the body. Few scholars have drawn attention to how the internally vibrating timbres of the *bheri, rabab, kinguri, tura, sinyi,* and other instruments articulate each juncture of the spiritual journey. At the pinnacle of the meditative experience, these instruments contribute to the vibration of an inner timbral intensity described in *Gurbani* as *panch shabad* (literally "five primal sounds" but experienced as timbral plenitude).

Devotees hear, recite, and sing about *anahad* instruments in their daily worship in such compositions as *Japji Sahib, Anand Sahib, Rehras Sahib,* and *Kirtan Sohila*. Yet few would claim to know what *anahad nād* means and fewer still might confess to hearing these timbres as an embodied experience. This chapter fulfills a need to understand the concept of *anahad nād* as articulated in *Gurbani* and to grasp its essential role in *kirtan*. It is not enough to conceive of *ahat* and *anahad* as opposites, as Vedic epistemology suggests. *Kirtan*, rather, is a catalyst that allows devotees to be forever attuned to *anahad nād* in the form of corporeal vibration. Devotees live in the flow of *kirtan*.

Chapter 4 merges the topics of theories and instruments: Extending the discussion of *anahad nād* from chapter 3, I study "*anahad* instruments" to create an inventory of instruments that contribute to the experience of inner bliss. This work is vital because certain musical instruments continue to be mistranslated and misidentified in scholarship. These errors reduce the impact of the writings of the gurus and bhagats, which often drew on the distinctive structure and unique timbres of musical instruments in bringing metaphysical and physical domains into close alignment. This chapter makes an iconographical turn to focus on the most important instrument in the Sikh cultural imagination, the *rabab*. Because of the central role played by this instrument in the "first" *kirtan* of Guru Nanak and Bhai Mardana, the *rabab* is the most frequently depicted musical instrument in Sikh art. This chapter examines illustrations of the *rabab* to explore its role in *kirtan*. In the absence of written documentation I turn to iconographical sources in attempting to unearth the idiosyncrasies of this plucked chordophone and other instruments that it was in dialogue with during the time of the gurus.

Informed by this deep study of *anahad nād* in relation to the theories and instruments of *SGGS*, the final chapters were also conceived as a pair that shifts the focus toward how technology mediates experiences of *anahad nād*. Taking Amritvela Trust as a case study in chapter 5, I explore how digital technology creates an immersive experience of *kirtan* that increases corporeal vibration and, in turn, orients this vibration toward social responsibility and undertaking service in the community (*seva*). The practice of *kirtan* using a combination of acoustic and electronic instruments expands the Sikh orchestra even further, while a lack of adherence to playing in designated *rāg* brings into focus Guru Arjan's emphasis on conveying the *shabad* in a way that seems most suitable to the *sangat*. In this instance Bhai Gurpreet Singh's digital *kirtan* uses simple melodies in a clearly structured musical format and call-and-response style to appeal to the tastes of the large Sindhi Sikh community that settled in Ulhasnagar (Maharashtra) after the partition. Meanwhile, his use of Bluetooth headphones to avoid noise pollution during the early hours of the morning (a sacred time known as *amritvela* in *SGGS*) in a multimedia setting that incorporates multicolored lighting, opulent fabrics, extravagant flower arrangements and interior design, LED screens, drones, and more facilitates a synesthetic experience of bliss that amounts to a digital encounter with *anahad nād* for up to forty thousand devotees in person and many more thousands online (indeed, it was my own digital consumption of Amritvela Trust's *kirtan* on YouTube that first drew me to learning more about this community). During their conversations with me, many devotees expressed their feeling of having reached *jannat* (celestial paradise) or *swarag* (divine abode) when participating in this digitized *kirtan*. Whereas chapter 3 explores a conception of *anahad nād* that is experienced by a chosen few (*virlai*), Amritvela Trust's use of technology reimagines this experience for all.

Chapter 6 examines how digital *kirtan* contributes to an experience of digital *darshan* (a sensing of divine presence) and feelings of bliss among a virtual *sangat*. While the thoughts of the *sangat* steer how my book unfolds in this introduction, the closing chapter continues the conversation around similar topics but from the perspective of the practitioner. The chapter presents interviews with a leading audio engineer and five *kirtaniye* who have been at the forefront of *kirtan* innovation in recent years: Davwinder (Dindae) Sheena, Taren Kaur, Jasleen Kaur (Monga), Veer Manpreet Singh, Bhai Nirmal Singh Khalsa (Pipli Wale), and Shivpreet Singh. In their distinctive ways, each of these individuals is reimagining *kirtan* in the twenty-first century using digital technology. During my conversations, I ask them to explain their relationship to *Gurbani* while inviting them to share the creative process behind their unique musical compositions. The responses are honest and revealing: Jasleen Kaur and Taren Kaur pick up again on issues of gender inequality and the difficulties of pursuing *kirtan* for a female professional musician. Other interviewees point to problems surrounding the institutionalization of *kirtan* and the precarity of hereditary knowledge. For all, digital media offers a refuge of sorts for forms of innovative expression that are unfettered and bold.

No matter how one might choose to label these expressions—digital, world, pop, cinematic, new age, healing—the music of these *kirtaniye* is broadly consumed by listeners (and not only by Sikh devotees) through social media platforms and apps. These styles of *kirtan* have received little interest from scholars, likely because they are the furthest away from realms of *rāg* and traditional instruments. Many listeners report being drawn into *Gurbani* through these offerings. It is my goal to honor these experiences and to better understand the motivations of musicians in their efforts to reimagine *Gurbani* through contemporary sonic expressions of *kirtan*.

WHY SIKH MUSICOLOGY?

Despite the steady stream of scholarship on North Indian musical traditions in the Euro-North American academy, one would be hard-pressed to find a sustained study of Sikh *kirtan*. Mentions of this devotional tradition in scholarly literature are typically superficial or marginal, although there is an increase in PhD dissertations about this topic at universities outside of India.[37] To be sure, language is a barrier, since few institutions teach Gurmukhi script, whereas Devanagari and Urdu have much longer curricular histories in universities and colleges. Still, it's hard to believe that research on early modern North India, whether focused on the musical culture of the Mughal courts or the practice of *bhakti*, has managed to sidestep Sikh *kirtan* for so long: The richness of parallel activity that was taking place within Sikh circles with regard to musical forms such as *dhurpad*, *dhammar*, and *khyal*; innovations in *rāg*; and the development of musical instruments is a crucial part of this body of research. Without a consideration of Sikh *kirtan*, an understanding of musical culture in North India between the fifteenth and eighteenth centuries is incomplete and skewed.

Scholarship on *kirtan* by Indian scholars was likely first undertaken by Bhai Charan Singh during the middle of the nineteenth century in the context of a detailed analytical study of *SGGS* (*Sri Guru Granth Bani Biaura*, 1902) and continued by his son, the aforementioned Bhai Vir Singh, through numerous publications.[38] There was considerable focus in their writings on explaining what is distinctive about the practice of Sikh *kirtan* in comparison with other devotional musical traditions, and both father and son were committed to an approach that conveys the *shabad* clearly, with a devotional intention and in the designated *rāg*. The synthesis of these three elements was paramount in their theories of what truly constituted Sikh *kirtan*. In addition to being a poet, novelist, exegete, translator, entrepreneur, and advocate for social justice, Bhai Vir Singh established a weekly newspaper in 1899, *Khalsa Samachar*, where articles about *kirtan* were also published. He was passionate about holding on to orally transmitted melodies (*purania dhaarna*), and it is striking that he was already lamenting the loss of musical knowledge over a century ago.[39] Against the encroaching violence of British colonialism and with the increased opportunity for publication, Sikh practitioners and scholars slowly began to record their musical heritage in sound and print.[40]

An essay by Bhai Vir Singh heads an important volume on *Gurmat Sangeet* that was published in 1958, although his essay, and likely those of the other four contributors, including his father, was written many years prior.[41] These five essays were first published separately before being brought together in this volume, and Rishpal Singh argues that it was the impact of this book that inspired others to publish on the topic of *Gurmat Sangeet*.[42] We see valuable examples of such publications in the form of Gian Singh Abbotabad's *Gurbani Sangeet* (1961), Bhai Avtar Singh and Bhai Gurcharan Singh's *Gurbani Sangeet Prachin Reet Ratnavali* (1979), and Dyal Singh's *Gurmat Sangeet Sagar* (1984). These volumes provide critical information about how to play the *rāg* of *SGGS*, rhythmic and metric patterns (*tāl*), and notation for compositions. In the case of Abbotabad, who worked closely with Bhai Taba, a renowned *rababi*, these notations capture a musical vestige of the *rababi*'s practice during a period when many had migrated to Pakistan following the partition. These invaluable texts are now among those used to train young *ragi* at major *taksal* (centers of learning). As Rishpal Singh documents, many books have been written in recent decades along these lines to preserve and revive existing precarious knowledge about specific *rāg* and *puratan reet* (orally transmitted traditional melodies).[43] Important within this body of work is the research of Ajit Singh Paintal and Gobind Singh Mansukhani, which is also available in English.[44]

Perhaps it is in relation to this historical-political context that the term "Sikh musicology" began to be introduced by scholars by the late twentieth and early twenty-first centuries in efforts to create a defined space within the English-speaking academy for the serious study of Sikh music as an academic discipline. Dr. Gurnam Singh (who holds a chair in *Gurmat Sangeet* at Punjabi University, Patiala) was among the first to use this term in the title of his book from 2001, *Sikh Musicology: Sri Guru Granth Sahib and the Hymns of the Human Spirit*. Many others soon followed suit in adjoining the term "Sikh" to "musicology." This association was cemented in 2008 with the establishment of a chair in Sikh musicology at Hofstra University (currently held by Francesca Cassio). There has been little reflection on the history of the term "musicology," given its origins in nineteenth-century Germany, where a scientific approach to the study of music—as demonstrated through a preoccupation with issues of acoustics, the physical properties of sound, theories of hearing and attention, and the psychology of perception—was prioritized. Moreover, given efforts to decolonize Sikh studies, it is surprising that scholarship on *kirtan* continues to be produced under the banner of "musicology" with little attempt to explain why a field that was initially organized around Western European notions of music theory and compositional grammar should be allied with Sikh musical practices. Certainly, the label "musicology" lends some heft to the newly emerging field of Sikh studies. I also believe there are some useful connections to be drawn between German scientific theories and Sikh approaches to sound articulated in *Gurbani* and in the writings of scholars such as Bhai Vir Singh and Bhai Randhir Singh (see chap. 3). As the field of Sikh musicology grows, it will become necessary to address the question of how Western musicology—which is itself a sprawling, evolving, and diversifying field—speaks to the specific concerns of Sikh studies (which are similarly evolving and diversifying, as seen in the vast scope of topics in and contributors to the latest volume edited by Pashaura Singh and Arvind-Pal Singh Mandair, *The Sikh World*).

In terms of my own contribution, this project has been a long time in the making. It began during my graduate studies at the University of Chicago in a seminar about mode in 1998 with Philip Bohlman. The boundaries between the subdisciplines of music theory, musicology, and ethnomusicology were open in my department, and I recall writing a final paper that directed my learning in these other areas toward the study of Sikh *kirtan*. Given my interest in *rāg*, a topic that was explored in the seminar alongside Arabic *maqam* and Persian *radif*, I soon found myself fascinated by the *kirtan* of Bhai Avtar Singh and Bhai Gurcharan Singh. Today, there is a good amount of scholarship on their important contributions to *kirtan*—notably by their successor, Bhai Baldeep Singh—but there was very little in print at the time.[45] I worked closely with their recordings, which I listened to repeatedly on cassettes I had bought in Toronto. At that moment I found myself at a crossroads: The tide was being pulled toward the powerful currents of a revival of *Gurmat Sangeet/Gurbani Sangeet*. At the same time, the discipline of Sikh studies in the Euro-North American academy was still in its early days. Those scholars whom I now see as having played a vital role in defining the field had recently completed their doctoral dissertations and, in the cases of Nikky-Guninder Kaur Singh, Pashaura Singh, and Gurinder Singh Mann, their first books in English. The academic study of *kirtan* was not yet established in Sikh studies, and I wasn't quite sure how to create a conversation around a diasporic experience of *kirtan* at a time when the conservation and production of instruments, and preservation and transmission of knowledge about *rāg*, were top priorities.

It was imperative for the first English-language scholarship in Sikh studies to introduce readers to *Sri Guru Granth Sahib* (*SGGS*) and other textual traditions, such as the *Janamsakhi* corpus, through attention to translation, exegesis, and source study against the historical backdrop of colonial and postcolonial encounters. Given the centrality of sound and music in *SGGS*, it wasn't long before scholars had to contend directly with the topic of *kirtan*, although few were professionally trained to do so. My attempts to redress this imbalance result in a methodology oriented around music, even as I rely on the earlier body of work to inform my translations and understanding of how sacred text intertwines with musical gesture. The act of translating and interpreting sacred verse is not one that I take lightly: My efforts are informed in particular by Mandair's critique of the "repetition of the colonial event" and cautioning around the "ideologies of sacred sound." My deliberate use of oral narrative to introduce this book participates in a longing for "return to some kind of origin," even as I repurpose the imagined *kirtan* of the past to help readers understand how a concern with origins steers present-day discourse around *nirdharit rāg* and historical musical instruments and to galvanize innovative forms of devotional expression.[46]

Gurinder Singh Mann has somewhat downplayed the importance of *kirtan/rāg*, but Pashaura Singh has remained attuned to its central role in Sikh worship.[47] In tandem with the scholarship of Paintal and Dr. Gurnam Singh, Pashaura Singh and Balbinder Singh Bhogal have undertaken significant research on Sikh music, and many others have made valuable contributions, including Nikky-Guninder Kaur Singh, Virinder Singh Kalra, Francesca Cassio, Inderjit Kaur, Bob van der Linden, Bhai Baldeep Singh, Harjinder Singh Lallie, Radha Kapuria, Nirinjan Kaur Khalsa-Baker, Gurdeep John Singh Khabra, Navtej Kaur Purewal, and Kristina Myrvold. Research on music in and around Punjab by Gibb Schreffler, Michael Nijhawan, and Suhail Khan has contributed in vital ways to learning about specific musical instruments, such as the *dhadh*, *dhol*, and *sarangi*, while offering opportunities to imagine their contributions to the variegated soundscapes of the Sikh courts, as musical ideas were developed by *rababi*, *ragi*, and *dhaadhi*. In view of the importance given to folk, literary, and musical genres in *SGGS*, I see scholarship on Punjabi popular traditions as being an important source for scholars of *kirtan* as we mull over missing melodies (*vār* and *dhuni*) and puzzling title designations for verses (*ghar* and *rahoe*).[48] As I watched from the sidelines over the years, and slowly gathered my sources, I became deeply indebted to all these scholars and many more in adjacent fields of sound studies, sensory studies, digital and media studies, and South Asian cultures and religions, for the ways in which they have enriched and broadened my thinking.

As the field of Sikh studies grows and expands, one of the biggest hurdles facing researchers is the slow digitization of primary sources and, in the cases of rare manuscripts, a reluctance to give full access to materials held in private collections. The challenging task of translating the many languages and dialects of *SGGS* in a way that feels up to date is ongoing thanks to the initiatives of SikhRI (Sikh Research Institute), a collaboration between scholars and volunteers. In this vein, I would also like to mention two collectors of recorded sound, Amardev Singh (https://

kirtansewa.net) in Malaysia and Sarbpreet Singh (gurmatsangeetproject.com) in Boston, who provide a tremendous service to scholars and the community through their commitment to preserving musical knowledge. Similarly, Bhai Baldeep Singh's Yaar Anad Virtual Baithak series offers a treasure trove of conversations with leading practitioners of *kirtan*—and other celebrity musicians working across different genres of South Asian music—many of whom I would never have the chance to meet in person and from whom I have learned a great deal due to this tremendous and original effort.

All this is to say that this book has taken many journeys—literal, virtual, metaphorical, and emotional—before arriving at its current form. My companions—whether they were encountered in print, in the digital realm, or in person—have been unfailingly generous. In grappling with many different forms of knowledge from a multi-migrant perspective, *Sikh Kirtan and Its Journeys* situates Sikh *kirtan* within a whole world of theories and practices.

The Musical and Sonic Dimensions of *Sri Guru Granth Sahib*

> The aim of my life is to be absorbed in religious discourse [*katha*], devotional singing [*kirtan*], *rāg* [melodic modes], and divine melody [*nād, dhun*].
>
> GURU ARJAN, *rāg Bilawal* (*SGGS* 818-8)

One thousand four hundred thirty pages constitute the standardized volume of sacred verse known today as *Sri Guru Granth Sahib* (*SGGS*). Sikhs refer to these verses as *Gurbani* (the sacred utterance of the gurus) or *bani*. They revere *Gurbani* as the living embodiment of a divine, sovereign guru. Each folio is sometimes referred to by page number (*ank*) or, in keeping with Sanskrit literary conventions, as a limb (*ang*). These poetic compositions carry sound in a variety of ways. Devotees might read and hear the text internally, in their minds, while outwardly projecting an aura of silence.[1] Verses can also be intoned softly in private prayer or delivered in a declamatory vocal style during a larger gathering (both methods are called *paath*). Finally, the organization of verses into groups identified by *rāg* (melodic mode), as shown in **figure 1.1**, points to the ordered, musical characterization of Sikh sacred verse in keeping with the ancient tradition of *rāg* poetry (*rāgakāvya*).[2] This index, which

FIGURE 1.1 Manuscript of an index featuring *Rāg Ramkali*, *Natnarayan*, and *Maru* from Panjab Digital Library. *Sri Guru Granth Sahib Ji*, accession no. MN-000234-0033.

is from an early (possibly eighteenth-century) manuscript, lists a group of verses in *rāg Ramkali*, followed by a set in *rāg Natnarayan* and another in *rāg Maru*. SGGS intertwines spiritual contemplation with the practice of music, while keeping in focus the manifestation of primordial word (*shabad*) as divine sound (*nād*).

When verse is sung, whether in *rāg* and whether solo or accompanied by musical instruments, poetry becomes a spiritual offering broadly described as *kirtan* (derived from *kirat*, the musical act of praising divinity). The term *shabad* (divine word) also refers to this sung rendition at times. Hearing and singing *kirtan*, and playing *kirtan* on musical instruments, intensifies the internal resonance of the body and elevates the consciousness while inviting devotees to contemplate divinity. Script and scripture embody a latent vibration that becomes palpable when sonic expression is manifested in the forms of intoned speech and song. Nikky-Guninder Kaur Singh reminds us, "There is no hierarchy between the reciter and the listener, the musician and the hearer, the interpreter and the reader."[3] Bound together through vibration, Sikh bodies attuned to divinity are always resonating with divine *nād* (primordial sound/timbre).

At the same time that *SGGS* is a spiritual guide for millions of Indian and diasporic Sikhs, it is also a relatively untapped musicological treasure trove with an immense potential to enrich our understanding of musical life in early modern North India. A study of verse titles calls attention to the variety of melodies (*dhuni*), musical genres, musical styles, *rāg*, and *partāl* (relationships of metric proportion) that establishes the musical parameters of Sikh sacred verse. The musical and sonic dimensions of *SGGS* draw connections with other literary and musical conventions, particularly the devotional practice of *bhakti*.

The unique structure of *SGGS* is seen in its organization according to thirty-one principal *rāg*, said to be *shudh* (pure). Some scholars and practitioners prefer to catalog *rāg* in another way, where the thirty-one *shudh rāg* are distinguished from thirty-one *mishrat* (hybrid/compound) *rāg* — that is, melodic modes comprised of two different *rāg*, such as *Aasa-Kafi* (a combination of *Aasa* and *Kafi*) — thereby giving a total of sixty-two *rāg* (see **fig. 1.2**). Other scholars eliminate *Bilawal Mangal* and *Asawari Sudhang* to offer a complete count of sixty *rāg*.[4] The accompanying website invites readers to explore these *rāg* through a range of recordings. Each section offers a few compositions in the designated *rāg* to help readers become acquainted with the unique affect of each *rāg* when aligned with sacred verse.

Given this book's emphasis on the topic of the journey, the first half of this chapter traces the psychological and spiritual trajectory suggested by the progression of *rāg*, beginning with the somber and introspective *rāg Sri* and ending with the cautiously jubilant *rāg Jaijawanti*. My interpretation of data gleaned through digital analysis offers a direct way to understand the "musicological coherence" ascribed to *SGGS* by Pashaura Singh, which is difficult to grasp at first glance.[5]

Driven by preservationist and decolonizing impulses, scholarship on *kirtan* over the last century has been oriented toward performance. Since the earliest scholarly contributions of Charan Singh's *Sri Guru Granth Bani Biaura* (1902), researchers and practitioners have been preoccupied with determining the correct structures of *rāg* and issues of performance practice. To be clear, this chapter does not function in this way: Readers

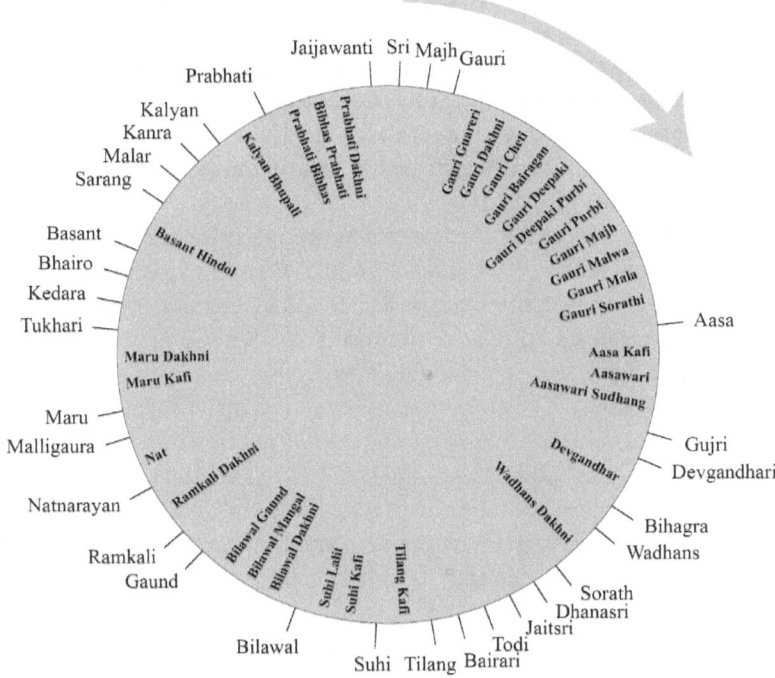

FIGURE 1.2 The progression of the thirty-one *shudh* (pure) and thirty-one *mishrat* (hybrid or compound) *rāg* of SGGS.

will not come away knowing how to play *nirdharit rāg kirtan*. Unlike many Punjabi-language texts focused on teaching *kirtan* to professional and lay musicians, my book's pedagogical focus is geared toward the academic classroom, where live and recorded devotional examples of *kirtan* showcase the core traditions and concepts that provide the foundation for the multiple expressions of *kirtan* we hear today.

The second half of this chapter sketches a model for listening that follows the journey outlined in the first half, allowing audio recordings to guide our understanding of *kirtan* while urging reflection on the important (and mostly unasked) question of how to listen to *kirtan* and on the unique dynamics that are established between *kirtaniye* (practitioners) and the *sangat* (gathering of devotees), performers, and listeners. Throughout *Gurbani* devotees are not instructed to play (*bajao*) *kirtan* but to do (*kar*) *kirtan* and sometimes to sing (*gaavho*) *kirtan*. Listening to *kirtan* is also highly valued. It must be remembered then that *kirtan* is not (only) performance oriented toward entertainment; it is (also) a spiritual offering where the acts of singing and listening are intertwined in a circular relationship, allowing outwardly made music to be manifested as an inwardly attuned experience of bliss (*anand*). Corporeal bliss satisfies a personal need, but experiencing and amplifying vibration when listening to *kirtan* as a *sangat* is especially coveted in Sikh spiritual practice because this collective energy facilitates *seva* (social responsibility and service) through *simran* (a constant remembrance of divinity).⁶

Notably, in the Sikh tradition, a heightened state of spiritual bliss activates social action. Poet and scribe Bhai Gurdas explains in his *vār* (ballads) how singing *Gurbani* facilitates a deep transformation of the self that is manifested through community service.⁷ Gobind Singh Mansukhani also hears in *kirtan* "a higher element [of] . . . 'super-aesthetics,'" linked to a "quality of transformation" that lies "apart from the *rasas*."⁸ These end goals ultimately distinguish Sikh *kirtan* from other devotional traditions such as Bengali *padāvalī-kīrtan*, Nepali *dāphā*, and Marathi *kirtan*, even as there are other overlaps, as seen in how these practices of devotional music relate to commerce and the marketplace, efforts at cultural preservation, and the construction of nationhood and regional identity.⁹

While Sikh *kirtan* functions within the same spiritual orbit as early modern practices of *bhakti*, its impact is felt beyond the realm of *ras* as a form of savoring that facilitates the experience of individual, internal corporeal bliss.¹⁰ Abhinavagupta's theory of *rasa* from the eleventh century focuses on "spiritual liberation" for an individual, where *rasa* is created for and relished by an audience. In contrast, in Sikh *kirtan* there is no audience, so to speak: The *sangat* is as important a participant in musical practice as the *kirtaniye* themselves, and it must be remembered that *kirtan* is ultimately a collective offering. While Abhinavagupta's theory of *rasa* focuses on the individual, the Sikh tradition emphasizes experiencing *kirtan* as a *sangat* so that everyone can contribute to and benefit from amplified corporeal vibration. The effects of *rasa*, as Kathleen Higgins explains, are transient and last only as long as the performance itself, whereas those of *kirtan* are considered by the gurus to be long-lasting and ripe for replenishment through constant *kirtan* and *nām simran* (recitation/remembrance).¹¹

The penultimate section of this chapter will broaden our understanding of hearing *kirtan* further yet, showing how the authors of sacred verse admire another category of music: the sonic gestures of nature, animals, the elements, and the cosmos. This discussion places emphasis on how hearing, singing, and playing *kirtan* are central to a state of being that is attuned to the divine both inwardly and outwardly, as an individual, and as part of a larger matrix of vibration.

FROM *BHAKTI* TO *KIRTAN*: RĀG COMPILATION AND IMPLICATIONS FOR MUSICAL PERFORMANCE

The fifth guru, Guru Arjan, took the first steps toward compiling the definitive version of *SGGS* as we know it today through the creation of the *Adi Granth* in 1604. In addition to writing his own verses, Guru Arjan arranged the compositions of the first four gurus (Guru Nanak, Guru Angad, Guru Amardas, and Guru Ramdas), fifteen bhagats (holy figures), *bhatts* (bards), and notable musicians Bhai Mardana, Bhai Satta, and Bhai Balwand to form this sacred volume. Several scholars have studied the complicated process of compilation, examining early manuscripts where possible and noticing differences and variations between them, all the while keeping in view Guru Arjan's efforts to create an authoritative *granth* (sacred book) that would be used by devotees for the purposes of worship through recitation and singing and marking life-cycle events such as births, naming, marriages, and funerals.[12] *SGGS* is no mere anthology of poetry. The tenth guru, Guru Gobind Singh, proclaimed — after adding the compositions of the ninth guru, his father, Guru Tegh Bahadur, during the last decades of the seventeenth century — that he is to be the last living guru. Since Guru Gobind Singh's death in 1708, Sikhs revere *SGGS* as their eternal, sovereign guru.[13]

How is *SGGS* different from and similar to other sacred texts of this time and place? Typically, when scholars reflect on the idiosyncratic features of *SGGS*, one of the first observations they tend to make concerns the arrangement of its verses according to *rāg*. Certainly, it is unique for a volume of this length and scope to be organized in this manner, as Pashaura Singh makes clear: "No other contemporary or near-contemporary religious compilation can be compared with the doctrinal consistency and complexity of the Adi Granth structure."[14] There are some notable precursors that reveal points of structural overlap and difference between *SGGS* and other sources of a devotional nature. The practice of linking poetry to melodic forms and rhythmic patterns is ancient, as Raman Sinha explores. Guru Arjan and his chief scribe and amanuensis, Bhai Gurdas, may have been aware of older devotional practices where *rāg* and *tala* were used, such as in Vajrayana and Sahajayana Buddhism and in *Gorakh-bani* of the eleventh century.[15] Composed in the twelfth century, Jaidev's *Gita Govinda*, which explores Krishna's love for Radha, offers a useful perspective from which to appreciate the unique musical/poetic format of *Gurbani*.[16]

The musician-dancer Jaidev organized his volume into verses that give simple performance indications in their titles. Especially significant is Jaidev's division of the text into twenty-four *prabandha* (a multipart, structured composition) whose vocal form mirrors the *astapade* (eight stanzas) that are common in *SGGS*.[17] Another overlap between *Gita Govinda* and *SGGS* is that their titles indicate the *rāg* to which verses are linked. Arvind Mangrulker observes the use of several *rāg* in *Gita Govinda*, some of which suggest overlap with certain *rāg* of *SGGS*, including *Gurjari* (Gujri), *Vasanta* (Basant), *Ramakari* (Ramkali), *Kedara* (Kedar), and *Bhairava* (Bhairo). *Gita Govinda* mentions *tāl* in later manuscripts, including *Prathimat, Rupak, Ektāl, Yatitāl, Astatāl,* and *Adavatāl*.[18] Although *tāl* are not specified in *SGGS*, a relationship of metric proportion is sometimes indicated by the term *partāl*. In terms of expressive delivery, Mangrulker's claim that *Gita Govinda* would have been performed in a way where "singing (*gāna*) is thus charmingly punctuated by recitation (*pathana*)" captures the multivocal registers of *SGGS*: The entire volume can be recited/intoned, but given that many verses are prefaced by information about their musical dimension, it is clear they were conceived to be sung and accompanied by instruments.[19] Finally, similarities can be seen in the metric construction of the verses, which can be syllabic (*aksara-vrattas*) or patterned/moric (*matra-vrattas*). *Gita Govinda* offers just one point of comparison, but as Sinha suggests, there are likely several other medieval Sanskrit texts that are worth investigating to gain a broader sense of the literary conventions Guru Arjan inherited and modified to suit the purposes of Sikh devotion.

In addition to Sanskrit texts such as *Gita Govinda*, it is likely that contemporaneous collections of *pada* in notebooks and anthologies kept by singers and scribes, devoted to the *bhakti* verses of Kabir, Sur Das, Mirabai, and others, were also familiar to Guru Arjan and Bhai Gurdas. Sinha notes that *rāg Dhanasri, Aasawari, Sarang, Sorath, Ramkali, Bilawal, Malar, Maru,* and *Todi* were commonly used in *bhakti* poetry.[20] It is no coincidence, then, that all these *rāg* feature in *SGGS*. Another scholar of *bhakti* poetry, Winand Callewaert, notes how nomadic musicians sang the *pada* of bhagats such as Namdev, Ravidas, and Kabir as they traveled through Northwest India in exchange for local hospitality.[21] As their oral repertoire grew, Callewaert argues, musicians began to keep notebooks as an aid to memory and to capture their evolving inventory of songs. Although many of these notebooks are now lost, copies of them can be seen in the form of seventeenth- and eighteenth-century anthologies made by professional scribes who were involved in the process of recording poetry in writing. Both singers and scribes associated verses with a particular *rāga* and *tāla*.[22] On their part, scribes were likely following the musical conventions established by singers and communicated through

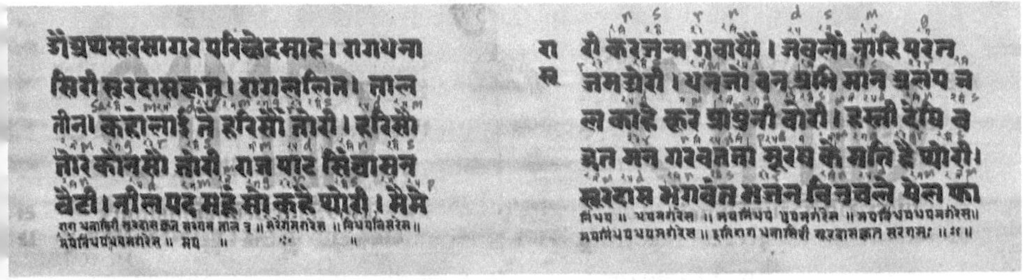

FIGURE 1.3 Sur Das, *Sur Sagar*, with music notation (and my annotations). Approximately eighteenth century.

their notebooks and in practice. **Figure 1.3** shows an eighteenth-century source for Sur Das's *Sur Sagar*, where *rāg Dhanasari*, *rāg Lalit*, and *teentāl* are mentioned alongside *sargam* notation for this *rāg* in smaller letters at the bottom.[23] *Sargam* notation is also written above the words in the main text, which suggests that this copy may have served as a notebook from which singers learned and possibly sang these verses (my own annotations are visible in this scan).

Scribes occupied a professional class of their own in early modern India. It is unlikely that they were also singers of this poetry, although this point is challenged in the Sikh courts: An important scribe of Guru Nanak, Bhai Lehna, who later became the second guru, Guru Angad, was undoubtedly singing *kirtan*.[24] We also learn from the *vār* of Bhai Gurdas that scribes and singers were part of the close-knit community at Dalla (Punjab).[25] Bhai Gurdas himself was likely a *kirtan*-singing scribe, given the importance of *kirtan* to daily worship. During these moments of literary activity, written verse probably existed alongside its sung counterparts in oral practice, although it is unclear how one medium might have impacted the other in Punjab. It is intriguing that in Maharashtra around this time, as Christian Novetzke observes, literacy was conceived as "subservient to performance" in the context of *Marathi Varkari kirtan*, a tradition whose founder is revered as Bhagat Namdev. His verses are also contained in *SGGS*.[26]

Guru Arjan's efforts to compile verses into groups organized by *rāg* had a parallel in the efforts of traveling musicians who clustered together poems according to *rāg*. However, their intentions were radically different. Oral practices of music-making allowed for flexibility. As Callewaert explains, "The same song could be sung to different *rāgas* and as a result we find songs classified under different *rāgas* in different manuscripts."[27] Performers might change their choice of *rāg* for a poem according to their location, their audience, or the occasion, season, or time of day. Therefore, the same verse might be recorded in one *rāg* in a particular manuscript and in a different *rāg* in another document. In addition, it is highly plausible that different communities of performers were singing the same verses in different *rāg*. And performers might not strictly follow a written format just because one exists. In the absence of concrete answers, one can merely wonder whether the presentation of a poem in *rāg Ramkali* in an anthology meant that singers would only want to sing it this way. The question of whether the written form of a poem served to freeze its musical interpretation, ensuring that it was only rendered in the *rāg* stipulated in the verse title, is of extreme importance to current debates surrounding the practice of Sikh *kirtan* and *nirdharit rāg*.

My preoccupation with the issue of obedience to the text highlights a major difference between contemporaneous anthologies and *SGGS*. The flexibility afforded to singers and scribes with regard to interpreting the same verse in multiple *rāg* is (generally) not at play in the interpretation of *rāg* in *SGGS*. While Guru Arjan likely heard traveling musicians sing the compositions of the bhagats in a variety of *rāg*, his efforts in compiling *SGGS* were oriented toward carefully organizing the verses of the gurus and bhagats under specific *rāg*.[28] Thus, when he placed Kabir's verse "Tann raeni munn punn rupp" in *rāg Aasa* in *SGGS* (482-2), the implication is that the guru is instructing devotees to sing this verse in this particular *rāg* even if singers or scribes might have ascribed it to a different *rāg*, as we see in the *Dadupanthi Niranjan Sampradaya MS*, where it appears in *rāg Gauri*. We can see this also with Kabir's "Gaj nav gaj dass gaj ikees pooriya ek tanayi," which appears in *rāg Ramkali* in the *Dadupanthi* sources but in *rāg Gauri* in *SGGS* (335-3).[29]

The early Sikh manuscripts inherited by Guru Arjan, and upon which he based the *Adi Granth*, did not always include mention of *rāg* or author attributions (*mahala*) in titles. Thus, Guru Arjan picked his thirty-one *rāg* very carefully. Although some *rāg* were already indicated in the manuscripts, others were chosen with a devotional purpose in mind. *Rāg Deepaki*, for example, was believed to generate intense heat, even fire, as told in the legend of Emperor Akbar's famous court musician, Tansen, so it is not included except in combination with the contemplative *rāg Gauri*, the most popular *rāg* of *SGGS*, which serves to temper the heat. Thus, we have *rāg Gauri Deepaki* and *rāg Gauri Purbi Deepaki* in compositions by Guru Nanak.

Guru Arjan's editorial interventions with regard to the choice and trajectory of *rāg* throughout *SGGS* are essential to the devotee's spiritual journey, as *SGGS* commences in a space of somber reflection, initiated by *rāg Sri*, and progresses to a state of restrained jubilation, indicated by the final *rāg Jaijawanti*.[30] To be clear, even before the tenth guru, Guru Gobind Singh, added his father Guru Tegh Bahadur's verses in *rāg Jaijawanti* to *SGGS*, Guru Arjan's last verses in *rāg Prabhati* already indicated the final ascent of the spiritual journey: Their optimistic association with sunrise (early dawn, *prabhaat*) indicates a new beginning in contrast to *rāg Sri*, which denotes sunset and evening. Gurnam Singh reminds us that Guru Arjan's "selection of particular ragas was particularly suited to the nature and expression of the sacred text."[31] Thus, these thirty-one *rāg* were those Guru Arjan considered the most conducive to spiritual attainment.

As implied in **figure 1.2**, journeying is undertaken across two levels in *SGGS*. From a musical perspective, the first level is suggestive and based on the quality of *ras*, informed by a theory of *rāg*, as devotees traverse the realms between *Sri* and *Jaijawanti*. This progression is not linear since there are a few moments when the choice of *rāg* indicates morning followed by a retreat to evening. For example, a morning *rāg*, *Ramkali*, is followed by an evening *rāg*, *Natnarayan*, and similarly, *Prabhati* is followed by *Jaijawanti*. Relevant to this observation is the topic of *rāg* time theory and whether the association between time of day and *rāg* as established by the twelfth century was of concern to Guru Arjan.[32]

The association between *rāg* and season is well established in theoretical texts by the eleventh century, according to Mukund Lath, particularly in the writings of Abhinavagupta (who cites an ancient authority, Kashyapa) and in Narada's *Sangita Makaranda*. At various moments in *SGGS*, *rāg* are also associated with seasons, as seen in the use of *Basant* to herald the spring or *Malar* to signal rain. However, it remains unclear as to whether time theory—the belief that specific *rāg* are performed at circumscribed hours to experience their full, affective potential—is behind the organization of *rāg* in *SGGS*. On the one hand, the establishment of *kirtan chaunki* (sittings/services) by Guru Arjan at Harmandir Sahib (Golden Temple) suggests a correlation between *rāg* and time of day (*pehar*) in Sikh musical practices by the early seventeenth century (see **fig. 1.4**).[33] On the other hand, an emphasis on continuous recitation and *kirtan* in *SGGS* would remove this practice from the domain of *rāg* time theory, and many practitioners today see the musical rendition of *Gurbani* as "timeless" in that it can be offered at any time, even as certain performance conventions continue to hold, such as the association of *rāg Aasa* with morning. Also worth noting is the special role of Guru Amardas, the third guru's, composition, "Anand Sahib," in *rāg Ramkali*, a favorite *rāg* of *bhakti* poets and singers, which is used to conclude various *chaunki* at different times of the day and night. These observations keep

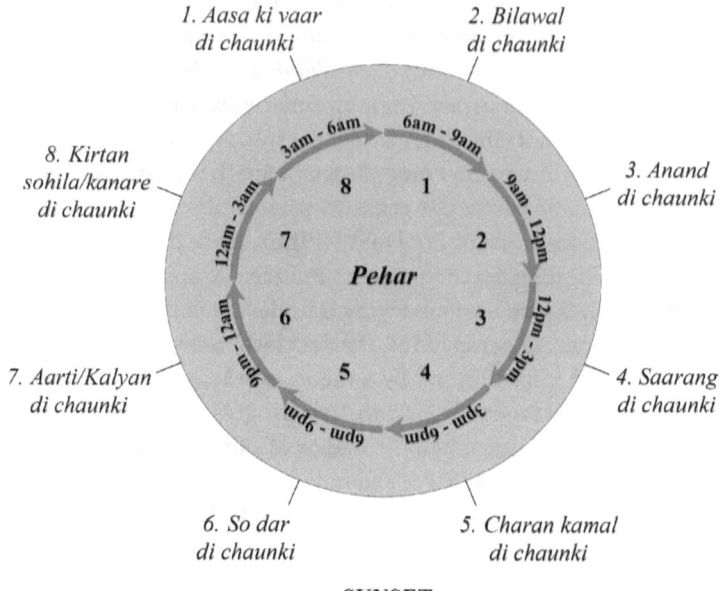

FIGURE 1.4 The division of a twenty-four-hour period into *pehar* and their intersection with the musical sittings (*chaunki*) established by Guru Arjan.

the devotional spirit of *Gurbani* at a distance from contemporaneous courtly musical conventions, where associations between *rāg* and time theory were hardening. The association between *rāg* and time theory was firmly in place by the seventeenth century, according to Persian sources.[34]

From a recitation perspective, journeying might be experienced more deeply across a temporal plane, given the psychological progression from dusk to dawn over the long span of *SGGS*. The impact of the latter is lasting and psychically transformative as experienced by devotees who undertake an unbroken recitation (*akhand paath*), where the entire *SGGS* is read from start to finish without a break, as a rite to mark life-cycle events or as a gesture of gratitude to the divine. On one level, the association of *pada* (stanza) with *rāg* creates an analogue with prevailing poetic and oral practices of music performance. On another level, emphasis on the overarching design of the *Adi Granth* as one series of *rāg* gives way to the next, marks a critical distance from prevailing oral culture: By fixing the association of *rāg* with a particular poem and by tracing a unique sequence of *rāg* over a larger span, Guru Arjan clearly breaks away from the fluid practices of poet-musicians, preferring an exploration of the divine word rooted in an organized experience of music and affect that unfolds over a longer temporal span.

For example, when *rāg Sri* (pp. 14–93) shifts to the folk-based *rāg Majh* (p. 94), accompanied by a turn to the topic of yearning and separation in the verses, a palpable change of mood and feeling is immediately discernible. And again, when there is a shift to *rāg Gauri* on page 151, there is another significant change in narrative tone and mood. Worth noting is that *rāg Gauri* endures for the longest stretch among all the *rāg* of *SGGS* (pp. 151–346) and that entry into this new *rāg* domain is made through the *mishrat* (hybrid/compound) *rāg Gauri Guareri*. Several other versions of *Gauri* precede and follow its sustained stretch from pages 244 to 323. After a contemplative foundation has been established through long stretches of somber reflection (*rāg Sri*), yearning (*rāg Majh*), striving for deeper understanding (*rāg Gauri* and its various *mishrat* forms), and exulted praise (*rāg Aasa*), the rate of *rāg* changes is not as slow. Only *rāg Ramkali* and *rāg Maru* occupy durations comparable to those of *Sri*, *Majh*, *Gauri*, or *Aasa*.

Rāg is not only an organization tool or a means to intensify certain topics and moods. The duration of a devotee's immersion in a particular *rāg* is also essential to shaping their overall spiritual journey. In his organization of *rāg* in accordance with their respective narrative components, Guru Arjan may have had in mind the pace and trajectory of the spiritual journey. To this end there is no backtracking: Once a *rāg* region has been established, it is never repeated. The devotee progresses from one *rāg* to another, always moving ahead and never turning back.

These musings raise the issue of how to interpret information about *rāg* in titles while keeping in mind the three vocal registers in which *SGGS* is approached: silent recitation, intoned declamation with metrical emphasis, and singing. This topic is particularly charged in current discussions around the practices of *kirtan*. Is mention of the *rāg* merely an indicator of the musical spirit in which the verse was conceived by Guru Arjan? Does *rāg* serve as a suggestion for *kirtaniye*, leaving them free to musically interpret the poem as they see fit? Or, in keeping with the understanding of *SGGS* as the sovereign guru, does *rāg* serve as an authoritative instruction (*hukam*, divine command) to undertake *nirdharit kirtan*?

Answering these questions requires returning to the concept of *nād* (divine sound), specifically the intertwining states of *ahat* (struck) and *anahad* (unstruck) *nād* (discussed in chap. 3). At those moments when the gurus criticize *rāg*, they are pointing to the intent and sincerity of the practitioner, not to the musical technique itself. In *rāg Maru* Guru

Amardas explains that *rāg* can inspire love for the divine, as seen with *Kedara* and *Sri*; *rāg Gauri* is auspicious if it brings the divine one into focus.[35] The ideal delivery of *Gurbani* in *rāg* must be oriented toward deepening an inward contemplation of the verses. In other words, music is primarily a vessel for *Gurbani*, which originates in the realm of *ahat nād* but whose emotional rendering of verse enables a sympathetic sounding of *anahad nād* within the devotee. Music that stays in the realm of *ahat* as mere virtuosity with no attunement to the divine word is in vain, as Guru Amardas and Guru Ramdas observe.[36] In *rāg Aasa* Guru Ramdas chastises those who absentmindedly sing *rāg* and play instruments without focusing on the divine: "Your mind is playing a game. / You work the well and irrigate the fields, but the oxen have already left to graze. / In the field of the body, plant the divine name, and divinity will sprout there, like a lush green field."[37] Guru Arjan's musical organization of *SGGS* is rooted in ancient music theory. Narada's efforts to establish a time theory of *rāg* in his *Sangita Makaranda* were rooted in the belief that listening to *rāg*, and enjoining oneself to it, allows auditors to rid themselves of their sins.[38] Guru Arjan made a similar point for hearing *kirtan* in *rāg Gauri Guareri*: "The mind becomes peaceful upon doing *kirtan*. / The sins of countless incarnations are washed away."[39]

In the practice of a style of *kirtan* called *Gurmat Sangeet*, failure to deliver verses in the assigned *rāg* is considered a form of disobedience and disrespect, with some critics going so far as to claim that such renditions cannot be called *kirtan*. Meanwhile, others argue that a clear rendering of *SGGS* in any *rāg*, or no *rāg*, is just as valid as long as the music prioritizes the divine word. My book engages with the full spectrum of musical practices and viewpoints, keeping in mind the historical roots of *kirtan* in the *prabandha* style that we saw with Jaidev and its gradual emergence in the style of *dhurpad* alongside many other styles of singing. In this respect, I engage with a question that is difficult to answer in the absence of archival documentation for *bhakti* musical practices: Did the organization of poems under specific *rāg*, as we see for Bhagat Kabir, Bhagat Surdas, and Mira Bai, somehow fix the poem in that particular *rāg*, thereby limiting the creative freedom of musicians? As cited above, Callewaert argues that musicians continued oral conventions of singing poems in their *rāg* of choice, and Sinha, too, draws on gramophone recordings in observing how "singers hardly make a habit of following the ragas indicated on the page as they prepare to render the compositions of *bhakti* poets."[40] I found a similar situation at play when examining early gramophone recordings of *kirtan*, where some singers offered renderings of a verse in a different *rāg*.

This discrepancy leads me to ask what singers made of the literary impulse to associate a poem with a specific *rāg* during the time of Guru Arjan and, specifically, how this pairing of poetry and *rāg* was perceived within the emerging context of Sikh devotional practice, compared with *bhakti* musical practice. While musicians operating outside the Sikh context may have interpreted this new literary practice as merely suggesting a melodic mode for a verse, the sovereignty of Guru Arjan could have led some musicians to view it as a divine command (*hukam*), an ordained instruction essential to grasping the essence of *Gurbani*. As I now explore, it is the latter argument that continues to fuel debates about *kirtan*, as practitioners offer a variety of viewpoints on the relationship between *rāg* and *Gurbani*.

OTHER MUSICAL DETAILS IN VERSE TITLES:
PARTĀL AND AASA KI VĀR

Why study verse titles? Do these section headings merely provide prefatory material that signals a textual change of sorts? As seen with Sur Das's *Sur Sagar* in figure 1.3, verse titles can be simple in how they convey basic details about *rāg* and, sometimes, *tāl*. In SGGS, however, verse titles are considerably expansive, and they are conceived in a manner that gives devotees adequate information about what they are about to encounter regardless of their chosen mode of engagement (whether silent reading, intoned recitation, or *kirtan*). Titles range from simple declamations — listing only *rāg* and author, using the term *mahala* for the gurus — to more complex groupings of information.[41] Certainly, verse titles indicate a textual change of sorts in the narrative, and scribes used titles as placeholders to convey important details about the upcoming verse or larger section, sometimes even articulating a new section through colorful illumination, an ornate calligraphic design, or the insertion of a *sirlek* (invocative inscription such as *Ek Onkar Satgurprasad*, "By the grace of the guru," as shown through an ornate flourish in fig. 1.1). Titles are not mere sources of information. During worship, these titles are read aloud or sometimes sung in the designated *rāg*, since the information contained within them is considered necessary for how the practitioner and devotee enter into their spiritual connections with *Gurbani*.

In addition to indicating a specific *rāg*, verse titles convey information about poetic structure, poetic meter, musical genre, melodic template, and musical style, among other details. Poetic structure refers to the number of *pade* (sing. *pada*), with common groupings consisting of two stanzas (*dupade*), three stanzas (*tipade*), four stanzas (*chaupade*), five stanzas (*panchpade*), and eight stanzas (*astapade*). Another term, *rahao*, is associated with *pade* because of its placement after the opening sentence or opening *pada* to urge reflection on what has just been stated. For this reason, it is often translated as "pause."[42] The *rahao-pada* relationship is similar to the *asthayi-antara* pairing common to several vocal forms of Hindustani music, but it also plays a unique role in *kirtan* (discussed below).

Pade can be broken down into shorter, sentence-like constituents called *tuke* (sing. *tuk*), including *iktuke* (one sentence), *dutuke* (two sentences), *tituke* (three sentences), *chartuke* (four sentences), *panjtuke* (five sentences), *chhaetuke* (six sentences), and *sattuke* (seven sentences). *Salok*, verses that vary in length from a single line to twenty-six lines, are also prominent in titles, and these are often paired with alternating *pauri* (stanzas). Other poetic forms mentioned in titles include poems structured around the concepts of twelve months (*barah maha*) and quarters of a twenty-four-hour period (*pehar* [pl. *peharay*], shown in fig. 1.4), verses organized along the fifty-two letters of the Sanskrit alphabet (*bavan akhri*), verses arranged into an acrostic (*patti*), songs linked to seasons (*ruti*), songs associated with the division of a twenty-four-hour period into day and night (*din raini*), songs associated with lunar days (*thitee*), and dialogues with holy figures (*siddh goshti*). In addition to indicating poetic structure, titles can convey information about vernacular poetic meters, including *doha* (rhymed couplets), *chaupai* (rhymed quatrains), and *savaiya* (four-line metered verses).

Other musical information given in titles concerns relationships of metric proportion (*partāl*) and melody types (*vār* and *dhuni*). Turning first to *partāl*, it must be noted that these are a distinct feature of Sikh *kirtan*—practitioners generally maintain that *partāl* are not found in any other tradition of Hindustani classical music, and this is corroborated by Tara Singh's close study of *partāl*.[43] There are seventeen verse titles that contain this term, although scholars and practitioners count up to fifty-five *partāl* in total after considering compositions that are listed under verse titles.[44] Only the fourth and fifth gurus (Guru Ramdas and Guru Arjan) have authored *partāl*, which suggests that this practice was specific to their courts and that their *kirtaniye* were highly skilled, given that the rendition of *partāl* involves considerable rhythmic/metric complexity and coordination between instruments and singing.[45] We can only speculate as to whether the absence of this term with regard to the compositions of Guru Tegh Bahadur implies that the practice of *partāl* was in decline by the late seventeenth century or whether the overall topic of his verses—given their emphasis on remembrance and mortality—asks for a somber musical rendition that requires rhythmic simplicity and metric stability.

The evolution of *partāl* as a musical practice in North India is difficult to trace, but Sikh practitioners and scholars maintain that its origins lie in the court of Guru Ramdas.[46] Tara Singh argues that the guru's development of *partāl* kept in mind the vocal traditions (*shailly*) of Amir Khusrau's *drut/chota khyal*, Sultan Hussain Sharki of Jaunpur's *vilambit khyal*, and Maan Singh Tomar of Gwalior's *dhurpad*.[47] Pashaura Singh reminds us that the practice of *partāl* in the Sikh courts of Guru Ramdas and Guru Arjan coincided with the reign of Emperor Akbar, a time when the arts were flourishing in the Mughal court. Akbar, as we know from his visits to Guru Amardas in 1565 and to Guru Arjan in 1598, had his eye on the growing Sikh community, as did his heirs to the throne. The rise of *partāl* took place during a moment when "*raga*-based music" was understood by the Mughals as "richly aestheticised objects of erudite connoisseurship associated with India's courtly arts and literature," as noted by Katherine Butler Schofield.[48] The musical sophistication of *partāl* points to the importance of looking beyond elite Mughal spaces to consider other sites where the arts were flourishing. In the Sikh domain *partāl* may have stemmed from the practice of singing the four sections of *dhurpad* (*asthayi, antara, sanchari,* and *abhog*) in different *tāl*, as Bhai Baldeep Singh proposes.[49]

SGGS titles do not feature information about metric cycles except in relation to *partāl*, albeit with no specificity about the exact metric designation. This term indicates a relationship of metric proportion where part of the composition (the *rahao/asthayi*) is presented in one *tāl* while another (the *pada/antara*) is offered in a different *tāl*. Transfer between *tāl* is facilitated through subdivision of the underlying beat into two or three beats. The tempo (*lay*) may also change between *tāl*. It is not easy to deliver a verse in *partāl* and *kirtaniye* require considerable skill to coordinate shifts between different tempi and *tāl* while singing the verse. The changing number of syllables between the *rahao* and *pada* guides *kirtaniye* in their choice of *partāl*, although many make their decision according to existing conventions of oral transmission. Based on hereditary knowledge, Tara Singh's notation of fifty-four *partāl* draws attention to the considerable sophistication of *partāl* compositions, where sometimes each *pada/antara* will require a different *tāl*.

Audio example 1.1 presents a composition in *partāl* by Bhai Avtar Singh and Bhai Gurcharan Singh, who are revered by practitioners and devotees as being among the most knowledgeable and skillful *kirtaniye*.

This example features the following format: The *rahao* is presented in *teental* and ends with a *tihai* (a thrice-repeating rhythmic pattern) to signal a turn to the *pada*. The closing text of the *pada* merges with the beginning of the *rahao* to ensure a smooth return. This pattern of rotation between the different *tāl* of the *rahao* and *pada* is quickly established, and the *shabad* alternates between these sections to create an ebb and flow of departure and return. This circular motion is an integral structural feature of most compositions, and it plays an important role: It allows for a gradual unfolding and deepening of the *shabad*'s message. As the *rahao* unravels into the *pada*, which again folds into the *rahao*, the devotee develops and connects the ideas of the *shabad* in a meaningful way.

Guru Arjan adopts the literary technique of a feminine persona to intensify the theme of yearning and separation in this verse. The beautiful, adorned woman awaits her divine beloved and is unable to sleep—she exclaims, "Udeeni, udeeni, udeeni" (I desperately wait).[50] While the *rahao* signals her sense of longing, each *pada* emphasizes the spiritual journey of the female protagonist. The switch between different *tāl* from the *rahao* to the *pada* also contributes to this sense of growth: In the first *pada* (*ektāl*, a twelve-beat metric cycle) she implores those who have already witnessed the divine (the blessed brides, *suhagan*) to unite her with her beloved; in the second *pada* (*ektāl*) she speaks to these women as her friends, pleading again with them to tell her how to relinquish her egotism so that she may experience the divine; and in the final *pada* (*rupak tāl*, a seven-beat metric cycle) she completes her spiritual journey and finally witnesses the divine such that sleep now feels sweet to her.

"Mohan needh ne aavai haavai" (*rāg Bilawal*, 830-3) begins with a slow-tempo (*vilambit*) introductory invocation (*manglacharan*) in *ektāl* followed by a lengthy repetition and improvisation on the *rahao* itself, "Mohan needh ne aavai haavai" beginning at 07:26 in *Punjabi theka* (a sixteen-beat cycle). A *tihai* at 14:55 signals the end of the first presentation of the *rahao* and a metric shift to *ektāl* for the first *pada* at 15:02 ("*Saran suhagan charan seess dhar*"), after which there is a transition back to the *rahao* at 15:41. A *tihai* beginning at 16:21 ends the *rahao* and signals a shift to the next *pada*, "*Sunho saheri milan baat* . . . ," also in *ektāl*. At the completion of this second *antara* at 18:16, the *kirtaniye* join the end of the *antara* to the end of the *rahao*, thereby initiating a return to *teentāl*. Another *tihai* at 18:50 signals the end of the *rahao* and a turn to the third section, which expands on the theme of the opening *rahao* and is thus called a second *rahao*, "*Mohan roop dikhavai*," in a new *tāl* (*rupak*). At 20:31 the *shabad* turns back to the opening *rahao* in *Punjabi theka* to complete the composition. As discussed below, this circular motion mirrors a larger approach to listening that flows into and out of two experiences of sound: *ahat nād* and *anahad nād*.

Turning now to melody types, the twenty-two *vār* of *SGGS* are conceived as ballads in a folk style. These exist alongside several other popular folk genres in *SGGS*, including *chhant* (a lyrical composition comprising four or six stanzas in any poetic meter), *ghorian* (wedding songs), *alahanian* (songs of loss or mourning), *birahare* (songs of separation), *arti* (devotional worship), *anjuli* (supplication), *sadd* (elegy), *sohila* (songs of praise), *karahale* (melodies of camel riders), *vanjara* (songs of the trader), *pehare* (songs associated with times of the day), *mangal* (songs of celebration), *chaubole* (four poetic meters or four languages or dialects), and *dakkhane* (music of the south).⁵¹ *Vār* are traditionally performed by folk musicians, as Guru Nanak described himself in a gesture of humility, since folk musicians occupied a low social class and caste during his time. This particular genre occupies a prominent place in *SGGS*.

Comprising stanzas called *salok* and *pauri*, *vār* were traditionally sung by musicians who recounted historical tales of war, valor, and virtue. A well-known *vār* forms the basis of *Aasa ki vār*, a composition of twenty-four stanzas by Guru Nanak, which includes additional verses by Guru Angad, Guru Amardas, Guru Ramdas, and Guru Arjan (see **video ex. 1.1**).⁵² I single out this *vār* not only for its use in early morning daily devotional worship—during the first sitting (*chaunki*) of the day—but also for its historical significance: *Aasa ki vār* opens with a verse (*chhant*) by Guru Ramdas, "Har amrit bhinnai loinna . . ." (448-17), and it is one of the few compositions that is set to a surviving folk melody (*dhuni*). This folk melody is linked to a *vār* that follows immediately about King Asraj, who injured his hand, earning the nickname *tunde* (maimed or one-armed, 462-18).⁵³ Although this *vār* itself is usually delivered through metrical intonation, the other melodies and overall structure of *Aasa ki vār* have survived through oral transmission (unlike many other *dhuni* associated with *vār* in *SGGS*).

Aasa ki vār is a distinctive devotional practice in the Sikh tradition that is offered every morning at Harmandir Sahib and other historic places of worship during the last *pehar* (quarter of the night), beginning at 3:30 a.m. and ending at 6:30 a.m. at Harmandir Sahib (see **fig. 1.4**).⁵⁴ **Video example 1.1** shows thousands of devotees lined up to enter the inner *darbar* (court) in time for when the *kiwad* (portals) open, at 2:30 a.m. during the month of *chet* according to the *Nanakshahi* (Sikh) calendar. The opening time varies slightly from month to month.⁵⁵

The performance of this *vār* is highly distinctive in that all members of the *ragi jatha* (ensemble) are involved in declaiming the text, including the percussionist. The drummer's traditional role as keeper of *tāl* is considerably broadened in *Aasa ki vār* to include playing unmetered strokes and excerpted *tihai* (a thrice-repeated rhythmic pattern), while the primary *kirtaniye* alternate singing *salok* and *pauri*, sometimes interpolating their own choice of *shabad* (sung verse). While many details about *kirtan* from the time of the gurus have been lost, there is broad agreement that the format for *Aasa ki vār* preserves past approaches. The listening guide for **video example 1.1** provides a time-stamped analysis of a single instance of *Aasa ki vār*.[56] Despite broad stylistic similarities in how *Aasa ki vār* is delivered daily, every *ragi jatha* (ensemble) will have slight differences in their rendition of the *dhuni*, the ordering of verses, and the choice of interpolated *shabad*.

The instance that I study begins with a *shabad* chosen by the *jatha*. Typically, the topic of this *shabad* is intertwined with the ritual of receiving *SGGS* into the *darbar* soon after this *chaunki* begins; here, the verse conveys a yearning to feel the presence of the divine beloved. At the assigned moment devotees hear a striking intermingling of *kirtan* with the resounding fanfare of a *ransingha* (brass horn) to announce the arrival of *SGGS*, carried in a gold, ornately carved *palki sahib* (palanquin), draped with richly embroidered fabrics and garlands of fresh flowers from the *Akal Takht* (throne of the timeless one), along the walkway that crosses the *sarovar* (pool of immortality) toward the inner *darbar*. The ceremonial retinue comprises many devotees, and hundreds more are lined up along the walkway to catch a glimpse as they engage in *darshan* (a sensing of divine presence). This journey is marked as a grand occasion, which is duly fit for divine sovereignty, with devotees stopping to bow in reverence as the procession passes. *Aasa ki vār* pauses as soon as the *ransingha* is sounded and resumes only after *SGGS* is fully installed in the *darbar*.

This ceremony is both reverential and jubilant. Several aspects of this *chaunki* emphasize its unique structure. In terms of the sacred verses themselves, the *salok* and *pauri* address a wide variety of topics that explore the inner journey toward self-realization, as well as social, cultural, political, moral, and religious issues.[57] The accompanying *kirtan* has a distinct format that alternates between short sections of sung intonation (which is different from the recited intonation used for the oral delivery of *Gurbani* known as *paath*) accompanied by the harmonium and *rabab* without *tabla* and other short sections where the entire *jatha* plays. Because the choice of *rāg* often changes from one large section to another, there are pauses for retuning instruments, particularly the *rabab* and *tabla*. These sections alternate with longer stretches where different *shabad* are interpolated in various *rāg*; these *shabad* deepen the meaning of a particular *salok* or *pauri*.

One might imagine that the changing lengths of sections, shifting *tāl* and tempi, and pauses to tune instruments between different *rāg* create a discontinuous temporal experience for the devotee. This is not the case, since the *ragi* end each section on the starting pitch of the next section—this technique creates continuity despite the stop-and-start flow. Also, the slow unfolding of Aasa ki vār over a long span of time accommodates flux and change. It is worth noting the physical stamina needed to undertake Aasa ki vār, which stretches over the course of three hours. When devotees enter the *darbar*, often after a long wait, they do so in complete darkness, during the last *pehar* (quarter) of the night. When they emerge, they do so after sunrise, during the first *pehar* of the morning. The experience of hearing Aasa ki vār during the last *pehar* is truly transformational, given how it ties the spiritual journey to the passing of time and the beginning of a new day.

A MYSTERY TERM: *GHAR*

Despite my long research on this topic, the meaning of *ghar* evades me and I tend to side with Gurnam Singh, who claims, "*Ghar* is a mystery and it is yet to be decided whether it denotes Taala or Gram Murchana [intervallic structure]."[58] Or, might I add, something else. What follows is some context on how scholars have grappled with this term and what I have noticed about *ghar* through my own digital analysis of *SGGS*. In the absence of concrete answers, I hope that, in combination with what has already been observed, this data can provide additional guidance for future researchers. Readers who are less interested in entering the murky territory of *ghar* can skip this section and go to "How Should *Kirtan* Be Listened to and What Does *Kirtan* Do?"

We see approximately 378 instances of *ghar* in verse titles.[59] The majority of these occurrences are numerical and indicate up to seventeen *ghar*. For example, the first appearance of *ghar* occurs on page 14, where the title reads "*Rāg Sirirāg, Mahala* 1 [Guru Nanak], *ghar* 1." Although the introduction of a new *rāg* is often accompanied by *ghar* 1, this association is not hard and fast. The placement of *ghar* in the title also varies—sometimes appearing straight after the indication of *rāg*, sometimes at the end of the title, and sometimes interpolated in between the two *rāg* that make up a *mishrat* (hybrid/compound) *rāg*, as we see on 365-4, where the two *rāg*, Aasa and Kafi, are separated: "*Aasa, ghar* 8, *Kafi, Mahala* 3" (a similar phrasing is seen on 369-1 with an added preposition, *ke*). While *ghar* 1 is often followed by *ghar* 2, the sequence of *ghar* doesn't always follow all the way through to seventeen. In *rāg Suhi*, for instance, the progression of *ghar* is 1, 2, 6, 7, 1. Sometimes *ghar* is not linked to a type, as suggested by a numerical designation such as *ghar* 1 or *ghar* 8, but possibly to a proportion or section, as seen on 368-1: "*ghar* 6 ke 3" — "the third part of *ghar* 6." And again on 369-11: "*rāg Aasawari ghar* 16 ke 2 *Mahala* 4 *Sudhang*" — "*rāg Aasawari Sudhang* with the second part of *ghar* 16." Finally, *ghar* is used in some instances to suggest a known melody, a folk style, or a prosodic meter.

One long-held view of *ghar* equates it with *tāl*, as we see with the seventeenth-generation descendant of Bhai Mardana, the hereditary *rababi*, Bhai Lal.[60] Others, looking for more metric nuance, understand the term as designating metric *matra* (unit) in relation to metric cycle.[61] Recently, Charan Kamal Singh has linked *ghar* with syllable structure, phrasing patterns, and semantics.[62] Several scholars have argued that *ghar* is the equivalent of the Sanskrit term *graha*, which indicates the starting pitch for singing and the starting point for playing meter.[63] Others maintain that *ghar* indicates a *rāg* variant, is a form of microtonality, or is equivalent to *dastgah* and thus indicates a relationship to Persian systems of metric patterns.[64]

In an ideal world my data analysis would be coupled with a study of early Sikh manuscripts, but access to these sources is restricted. While I have studied a few documents, I also rely on the observations of those who have had the opportunity to consult manuscripts close-up. Pashaura Singh, Gurinder Singh Mann, and Jeevan Deol are among the few scholars who have been given access to early Sikh manuscripts, and they have all noted that *ghar* is not mentioned in the early manuscript of the *Goindval Pothi* but that it appears at certain points in a later source known as MS 1245 (held at Guru Nanak Dev University) and that this term is developed further in the *Kartarpur Pothi*, which is the copy that Guru Arjan was working on with Bhai Gurdas.[65] Pashaura Singh reminds us that Guru Arjan and Bhai Gurdas were well versed in the various conventions of Sanskrit literature, Braj Bhasha, and contemporaneous regional literary traditions and that Guru Arjan's visits to Varanasi and Agra were "intended to study the various conventions of Sanskritic learning."[66] Their deep knowledge of languages and dialects urges reflection on whether *ghar* is a term that is more literary in spirit, referring perhaps to a poetic form or poetic meter rather than a musical feature.

Alternatively, given the absence of *ghar* in the earlier *Goindval Pothi* and its presence in the later *Kartarpur MS*, it must be asked whether Guru

Arjan and Bhai Gurdas were responding to a musical characteristic heard among singers of these verses. My sense is that the inclusion of *ghar* is likely an original notation in the *Adi Granth*, since *bhakti* scholars have yet to observe song notebooks or anthologies carrying *ghar* in their titles.⁶⁷

One clue that emerges from *bhakti* scholarship brings us back to the link between *ghar* and meter. Barbara Stoler Miller observes that Jaidev was using vernacular meters to broaden the appeal of his Sanskrit poetry.⁶⁸ Thus, when we read *"Ek suan ke ghar gaavna"* (to sing in the *ghar* of *ek suan*) in part of the title of Kabir's verse in *rāg Sri* (91-18), we might ask whether this refers to a known melody, *ek suan*, or a familiar poetic meter.⁶⁹ A similar question emerges for Bhagat Baynee's verse a few pages later, *"Re nar garab kundal"* in *rāg Sri* (93-1), where the appearance of the phrase *"Peharia ke ghar gaavna"* as part of the titular instructions leaves devotees guessing, as does the title, *"Yaanriye ke ghar gaavna"* (802-7), of Guru Arjan's verse in *rāg Bilawal*, *"Mai munn teri tek."* A title from Guru Arjan's verse in *rāg Gauri Bairagan* (203-12), *"Hai koi raam pyaro gaavai,"* invokes a folk style of singing wedding songs by women called *rahoe*. In this instance it is unclear as to whether *"rahoe ke chhant ke ghar"* refers to a specific melody that this verse should be sung to or a poetic meter associated with these wedding songs.⁷⁰ Another title recalls *birahare* (songs of separation) in combination with *ghar* (431-11). The invocation of *ghar* with reference to *ek suan, yaanriye, peharia,* and *birahare* suggests that further research on folk music might also yield information about the meaning of *ghar*.

To aid future study, I present four tables based on digital analysis. **Table 1.1** shows which *rāg* are associated with *ghar* in descending order and specifically which *ghar* appear in each *rāg*. We can make a few observations on the basis of this data. The second-longest *rāg*, *Aasa*, has the highest number of *ghar*, whereas several other *rāg*, including the longest, *Gauri*, have no *ghar*. Might the reason that *ghar* are not assigned to *Gauri* have to do with the mood of the *rāg* themselves or the themes and topics of the verses?

Table 1.2 shows the number of occurrences of each *ghar*. The number declines from *ghar* 1 through *ghar* 9, picks up briefly for *ghar* 10, then declines rapidly, with *ghar* 14–17 receiving only one mention each.

Table 1.3 focuses on authorship and shows how many and which *ghar* are assigned to verses by gurus and bhagats. Guru Arjan's compositions are the most comprehensive in their use of *ghar* (missing only *ghar* 16). In comparison, the compositions of Guru Angad and Guru Tegh Bahadur, and several bhagats, are not associated with any *ghar*.

Finally, **table 1.4** explores the links between author, *rāg*, *ghar*, and

TABLE 1.1 Occurrences of specific *ghar* in each *rāg*

RĀG	TOTAL GHAR	SPECIFIC GHAR
Aasa	46	1, 2, 3, 4, 5, 6, 7, 8, 9, 10, 11, 12, 13, 14, 15, 16, 17
Suhi	37	1, 2, 3, 4, 5, 6, 7, 9, 10
Sri	26	1, 2, 3, 4, 5, 6, 7
Gujri	24	1, 2, 3, 4
Sorath	24	1, 2, 3, 4
Bilawal	21	1, 2, 3, 4, 5, 6, 7, 8, 9, 10, 11, 12, 13
Bhairao	18	1, 2, 3
Dhanasri	17	1, 2, 3, 4, 5, 6, 7, 8, 9, 12
Maru	17	1, 2, 3, 4, 5, 6, 7, 8
Basant	16	1, 2
Kanra	14	1, 2, 3, 4, 5, 6, 7, 8, 9, 10, 11
Malar	14	1, 2, 3
Sarang	14	1, 2, 3, 4, 5, 6
Ramkali	10	1, 2, 3
Gaund	9	1, 2
Tilang	9	1, 2, 3
Wadhans	9	1, 2, 4, 5
Majh	8	1, 2, 3, 4
Devgandhari	7	1, 2, 3, 4, 5, 6, 7
Jaitsri	7	1, 2, 3, 4
Todi	7	1, 2, 3, 4, 5
Kedara	6	1, 2, 3, 4, 5
Aasa Kafi	5	8
Bihagra	4	1, 2
Bairari	2	1
Bibhas	2	1, 2
Kalyan	2	1, 2
Suhi Kafi	2	10
Maru Kafi	1	2

Note: In the following *rāg*, *ghar* was not mentioned: *Aasawari, Aasawari Sudhang, Bilawal Dakhni, Bilawal Gaund, Bilawal Mangal, Dakhni, Gauri, Gauri Bairagan, Gauri Cheti, Gauri Dakhni, Gauri Deepaki, Gauri Guareri, Gauri Majh, Gauri Mala, Gauri Malwa, Gauri Purbi, Gauri Purbi Deepaki, Gauri Sorath, Basant Hindol, Jaijawanti, Kalyan Bhopali, Malligaura, Maru Dakhni, Nat, Natnarayan, Prabhati, Prabhati Bibhas, Prabhati Dakhni, Ramkali Dakhni, Suhi Lalit, Tilang Kafi, Tukhari,* and *Wadhans Dakhni.*

TABLE 1.2 *Ghar* types and number of occurrences

GHAR	NUMBER OF OCCURRENCES
1	119
2	96
3	44
4	30
5	21
6	16
7	12
8	10
9	7
10	10
11	3
12	3
13	3
14	1
15	1
16	1
17	1
Total	378

TABLE 1.3 **Authors' use of *ghar***

AUTHOR	OCCURRENCES OF *GHAR*	SPECIFIC *GHAR*
Guru Nanak	80	1, 2, 3, 4, 5, 6, 7, 8, 9, 10
Guru Amardas	39	1, 2, 3, 4, 5, 8, 10
Guru Ramdas	61	1, 2, 3, 4, 5, 6, 7, 8, 10, 11, 13, 16
Guru Arjan	169	1, 2, 3, 4, 5, 6, 7, 8, 9, 10, 11, 12, 13, 14, 15, 17
Bhagat Kabir	11	1, 2, 3
Bhagat Namdev	12	1, 2, 3, 4
Bhagat Ravidas	3	2, 3
Bhagat Trilochan	1	1
Bhagat Jaidev	1	4
Bhagat Ramanand	1	1

TABLE 1.4 Author, *rāg*, and *ghar* type in *partāl* compositions

AUTHOR	RĀG	GHAR
Guru Arjan	Aasa	15
Guru Arjan	Dhanasri	9
Guru Arjan	Suhi	5
Guru Ramdas	Bilawal	13
Guru Arjan	Bilawal	13
Guru Arjan	Ramkali	3
Guru Ramdas	Natnarayan	0
Guru Arjan	Nat	0
Guru Arjan	Bhairao	3
Guru Ramdas	Sarang	5
Guru Ramdas	Sarang	0
Guru Arjan	Sarang	6
Guru Ramdas	Malar	3
Guru Arjan	Malar	3
Guru Ramdas	Kanra	5
Guru Ramdas	Prabhati Bibhas	0
Guru Arjan	Prabhati Bibhas	0

partāl (as listed in verse titles). It is intriguing that *partāl* did not involve *ghar* 1 or 2, which are the most frequently used in *SGGS*. This preliminary analysis explores interrelationships between the various constituents of verse titles—such as *rāg*, author, and *partāl*—and probes what the role of *ghar* might be for the practitioner and devotee.

Several fundamental questions remain to be answered. Are there only seventeen *ghar* or did Guru Arjan choose seventeen out of many more? How were the seventeen *ghar* that Guru Arjan indicated different from one another? Why are there so few compositions in the higher-number *ghar*? Why are no *vār* linked to *ghar*, whereas *ghar* is linked to the poetic structures of *dupada*, *chaupada*, *panchpada*, and *astapadi*, as well as to the poetic genres of *chhant*, *alahanian*, *anjuli*, *peharia* and *birharai*? What was Guru Arjan trying to convey to his devotees in using this term? Given his efforts toward social inclusivity, whatever this title meant, it was likely something that could be understood by all, not only by experienced musicians or the educated elite. Thus, *ghar* must have communicated necessary information clearly and with little complexity. Although I offer few answers on the meaning of *ghar*, one way that scholars might start making progress on understanding this term is by studying early manuscripts to see where and how it is used—in relation to which poetic structures and genres, in relation to which *rāg* and *partāl*, and in which succession of types.

Since the meaning of *ghar* remains opaque, it's not clear what information devotees are missing. Having acknowledged this missing piece of the puzzle, I now turn to the practice of *kirtan* to explore the following questions: Why do devotees listen to *kirtan* and how? What does *kirtan* do for those who experience it? What ethical responsibilities are bestowed upon devotees when they engage with *kirtan* through their bodies, minds, and consciousness? What journeys can we observe in the experience of *kirtan*?

HOW SHOULD *KIRTAN* BE LISTENED TO AND WHAT DOES *KIRTAN* DO?

Kirtan is characterized by the intertwining motion of sacred poetry and devotional sonic expression. As we have seen in the previous section, *kirtan* is an offering before it is music. There is no hierarchy in this practice—everyone involved in singing and hearing receives and generates the vibrations of *kirtan*.

Kirtan shifts the consciousness toward a meditative state by touching the deepest recesses of the body. Ajit Singh Paintal explains that the gurus "completely eschewed the dance performed by Vaishnava and Shaiva devotees and by the Sufis in their *Sama* gatherings. The Sikh Gurus also rejected the rhythmical clapping with the hands with which the Sufis accompanied their singing."[71] Thus, it is a still body, not one that is moving through dancing, clapping, or excessive swaying, that is seen as taking devotees to a blissful state. Guru Amardas states, "Devotion doesn't happen through dancing and jumping."[72] When Guru Ramdas speaks of "the mind dancing before the guru while the *tura* plays the unstruck melody," this metaphorical dance takes place at the deepest level of meditation accompanied by the mystical sound of the *tura*, a brass instrument. At a moment of self-realization in *rāg Ramkali*, Guru Arjan similarly observes a metaphorical dance, "*niratkari*," accompanied by the internal sounding and sensation of playing several instruments, including the *kainsi* (hand cymbals), *pakhawaj* (double-headed drum), *rabab*, and *bansuri* (bamboo flute).[73] At these moments, dance and music are not aligned with *ahat nād* but with *anahad nād*, since they manifest without cause and effort in the absence of moving bodies and vibrating musical instruments.

These attitudes do not speak to a denial of corporeal involvement in *kirtan*. A remarkable feature of *Gurbani* is the attention given to bodily organs that participate in processing *kirtan*, especially the ears (*kann, sravan, karnahu*) and the tongue (*rasna, jihva, jihba*). We take it for granted that sound is primarily perceived through the ears, but when the gurus emphasize the importance of listening to the divine word, they are careful to invoke the organ that is involved in this process. Devotees are not assumed to listen or to hear—they are instructed to engage in this activity through their ears. Sometimes, two ears are not enough: Guru Arjan asks, in *rāg Suhi*, to be blessed with "millions of ears" with which to hear divine praise.[74]

Listening to slander is considered not using one's ears effectively. In comparison, hearing the divine word through the ears allows the devotee to become self-aware (Guru Nanak, *rāg Majh*, 138-9) and infused with contentment (*sukh*) (Guru Angad, *rāg Gauri*, 200-4). Using the ears for hearing the divine word is considered vital to daily life by Guru Ramdas (*rāg Asawari*, 369-13). Guru Ramdas even praises ears that listen to *kirtan* as "splendid and beautiful" (*rāg Bihagra*, 540-2). Guru Amardas explains that those who listen to the gurus' teachings through their ears are blessed (*rāg Wadhans*, 590-18). There is another reason why the gurus emphasized the importance of listening through the ears. In the absence of amplifying technology, the act of hearing the divine word required proximity and closeness within the *sangat* (community). To reiterate a point I made earlier, listening together generates stronger corporeal vibration, which contributes to social bonding and the impulse to engage in positive social action.

Hearing goes with singing, but it is not the voice that is involved in divine praise. Rather, it is the organ of the tongue that articulates the divine word to render the mind and body pure (*nirmal*) (Guru Arjan, *rāg Sri*, 49-6). In *rāg Sorath* Guru Tegh Bahadur instructs, "Listen to the praises of the divine one [*Gobind*] with your ears and sing songs of praise with your tongue" (631-11). Guru Arjan conveys similar sentiments in *rāg Jaitsri*: "With my tongue, I recite the divine name; with my ears I hear the sweet [*amrita*] divine word" (709-2). The cross-modal experience of tasting through the ears is typical of the divine experience in *SGGS*. Just as the ears taste nectar (*amrit*), so does the tongue, whose sole purpose is to recite the divine name in pursuit of this flavorful essence (*ras*).[75] The taste of the divine name is thus elevated above the finest delicacies so that even the words that are spoken by the tongue will be like nectar (Guru Arjan, *rāg Gauri, Sukhmani*, 269-1 and 270-13) and the music played by the tongue on the flute (*bayn*) will taste sweet (Guru Nanak, *rāg Maru*, 1039-5). Guru Arjan describes the taste (*swad*) of *anahad dhuni* (the unstruck melody) as wondrous.[76]

The vibrant red (*laal*) color of the tongue is attributed to its role in singing divine praise.[77] Bhagat Kabir imagines his tongue as a rosary (*simrani*).[78] In contrast, Bhagat Namdev declares in *rāg Bhairo* that he will cut his own tongue into several pieces if it doesn't speak of divinity (*Gobind*), a point also made by Guru Arjan.[79] In his composition *Sukhmani Sahib*, Guru Arjan mentions that a single tongue can offer much praise (*rāg Gauri*, 287-8). However, in *rāg Dhanasri* he points to the limitations of having only one tongue: "I have one tongue—which of your many virtues can I speak of?"[80] Similarly, in *Japji Sahib* Guru Nanak yearns for more: "If I had one hundred thousand tongues, and these were then multiplied twenty times more, I would repeat with each tongue, hundreds of thousands of times, the name of the ruler of the universe [*Jagdis*]."[81]

The central role of the tongue in Sikh devotion is exemplified by the composition "*Rasna Japti Tuhi Tuhi*" ("My tongue recites, only you, only you," Guru Arjan, *rāg Sarang*). "*Rasna Japti*" is one of the most recorded *shabad* by *kirtaniye* across a range of styles including the *rāg*-based practice of *Gurmat Sangeet* (**audio ex. 1.2**, Bhai Maninder Singh), the *Namdhari* classical tradition (**audio ex. 1.3**, Bhai Balwant Singh), *AKJ* (**audio ex. 1.4**, Bhai Anantvir Singh), commercial style (**audio exs. 1.5** and **1.6**, Bhai Satvinder Singh and Bhai Harvinder Singh, and Bibi Ashupreet Kaur), and digital reinterpretation (**audio exs. 1.7** and **1.8**, Veer Manpreet Singh and Bhai Gurpreet Singh, starting at 39:50). This *shabad* has also crossed over into *qawwali*, a Sufi devotional tradition with which Sikh *kirtan* shares several commonalities that are worthy of in-depth study. Rahat Fateh Ali Khan's recording is particularly well known (**audio ex. 1.9**).

With these examples in our ears, let us begin to explore the practice of listening to *kirtan*. The gurus and bhagats held *kirtan* in high regard—hearing, playing, and singing *kirtan* are devotional activities that they saw as being equally important, as Guru Nanak states in the opening composition of *SGGS*, *Japji Sahib*.[82] Especially notable in the Sikh context is the overlap between these actions: Hearing, playing, and singing can be carried out by an individual in the same moment, with no one action being privileged over another. **Figure 1.5** shows two schemata for how *kirtan* might be listened to according to the long-standing Vedic division of sound into two categories: struck sound, music that is made using effort through musical instruments and the voice (*ahat nād*); and unstruck sound, music that manifests within the body without effort as a form of internal, corporeal timbral vibration (*anahad nād*). The first schema indicates a "flat" sonic landscape where there is no flow of vibrational energy: *Kirtan* is made by *kirtaniye*, and devotees observe their music as (mere) performance. The second schema captures a "live" auditory experience where both the *kirtaniye* and devotees imbibe *kirtan* to facilitate corporeal

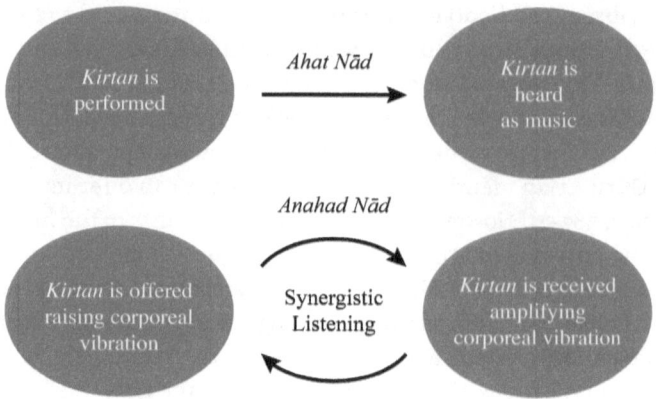

FIGURE 1.5 Schemata showing how *kirtan* can be heard.

vibration, contributing to a synergistic flow of vibrational energy between them. The auditory experience is thus nondualistic and processual, as *kirtan* is initiated in an external realm and becomes transformed into corporeal vibration when it begins to resound—*bhajna*—in the body. Guru Arjan explains in *rāg Aasa*, "I sing inwardly, I sing outwardly, I sing day and night."[83] Devotees aspire to an ideal state of listening where *kirtan* erases the boundary between inner and outer (*antar/baahar*).

Devotees are versatile listeners who switch registers between participation, appreciation, and peaceful meditation: They know when to participate, when to pause their singing while the *kirtaniye* improvise, and when to stop toward the end of a *shabad* as *kirtaniye* might increase the tempo and introduce virtuosic elements such as extensive *taan* (rapidly ascending or descending vocal patterns) to intensify a feeling of ecstatic bliss. Devotees listen simultaneously, which is to defy a differentiated model of listening explored (and subsequently dismantled) in the Buddhist context by Bethany Lowe: "To experience music most directly it is necessary to devote our attention to auditory consciousness and resist going into processing mode until later."[84] Simultaneous listening involves actively processing and shifting between modes of bliss and reflection as *kirtaniye* gently switch between modes of *kirtan* (sung devotion) and *viyakhia/katha* (spoken exegesis). *Kirtan* demands a fluid approach to listening that dismantles an experience of *ahat nād* and *anahad nād* as opposing categories. My discussion refers to the experience of hearing a single *shabad*. In their treatise *Gurbani Sangeet Prachin Reet Ratnavali*, Bhai Avtar Singh and Bhai Gurcharan Singh outline the five-stage format of a typical presentation, involving an introductory *shaan* (instrumental piece), a *manglacharan* (invocation), a *dhurpad* or another composition based on a long *tāl*, a lighter composition that incorporates exegesis, and a closing verse in the same *rāg*.[85]

The *rahao/pada* (*asthayi/antara*) structure that characterizes most *kirtan* contributes to the spiritual journey. Repetition of the *rahao* portion as a refrain invites participation while allowing the central theme of the *shabad* (verse) to be internalized through every occurrence. The *rahao* opens the *shabad* and is repeated several times to give the *sangat* an opportunity to learn the words, to memorize the melody and rhythm, and to become attuned to the verse; the latter is also facilitated through short instrumental interludes that provide time and space to contemplate the meaning of the words that have been sung.[86] A *shabad* is often known by its *rahao* rather than its opening line, which is usually the first *antara*. In some instances, such as "*Rasna Japti Tuhi Tuhi*," the verse begins with the *rahao*. **Figure 1.6** captures the flow of energy behind vibrational listening. Every rotation outward toward a new *pada*, and rotation inward toward a repetition of the *rahao*, allows the devotee to gradually grasp the meaning of the *shabad* over time. Through reflection, as devotees become immersed deeper into a meditative state, the central message of the *rahao* is intensified (indicated here through progressive shading).

What is the purpose of this intensely vibrating body? The pursuit of this blissful state is not a goal in and of itself, and as I stated in my introduction, this is where the practice of *kirtan* stands at a distance from *rasa* theory, where there is a focus on how *rāg* catalyzes individual liberation. The goal of heightened corporeal vibration is to facilitate a focused sense of awareness (*chitt* or *surat/surti*). In turn, self-awareness forms the basis of *seva*, which is understood as service to divinity and holy figures, and community-facing social responsibility and activism, as explained by Guru Amardas in *rāg Majh, Sri, Bihagra*, and *Malar*.[87] Guru Arjan instructs in *rāg Majh* that meditating upon and hearing the divine name is a *daan*

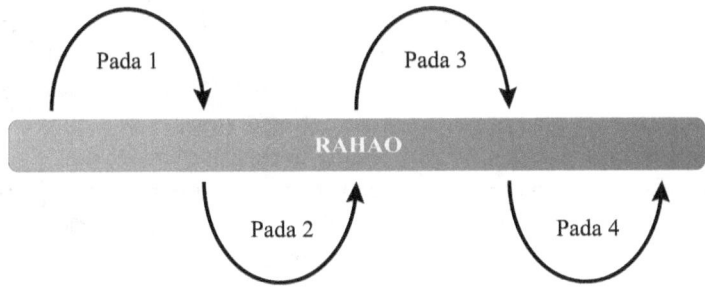

FIGURE 1.6 **How to listen to *kirtan*.**

(gift) that must be shared with all.[88] Moreover, he explains in *rāg Todi*, it is *kirtan* that motivates social action.[89] As with the offering of *kirtan*, it is not the body that initiates and directs *seva* but the consciousness.[90] Bhagat Kabir makes a similar point in *rāg Bilawal*.[91] There are many types of *seva* that involve taking care of the physical body through providing food and maintaining cleanliness, and the metaphysical body must also be nourished through *kirtan* and recitation.[92]

Given the importance of *kirtan* in Sikh devotion, it is not surprising that Guru Nanak views this practice as the highest form of *seva* for divinity. In *rāg Malar* Guru Nanak speaks to the importance of undertaking *seva* through conscious awareness (*surat*) while joyfully singing divine praise.[93] The importance of *kirtan* as a form of *seva* is once again seen in *rāg Maru*: "Service to the [divine] guru brings liberation. Sing *kirtan* night and day."[94] All types of service, including *kirtan*, should be performed without ego.[95] A life without service is wasted away, Guru Amardas states in *rāg Majh*.[96] Furthermore, he explains in *rāg Gujri*, one cannot call oneself a devotee without engaging in *seva*.[97] Sincere *seva* removes the devotee from the cycle of rebirth.

As with listening to *kirtan*, the flow of vibrational energy when undertaking *seva* is cyclic, since heightened corporeal vibration facilitates service that, in turn, sustains inner bliss. In *rāg Gauri Guareri*, Guru Arjan points to the connection between *seva* and corporeal vibration, and Guru Amardas views undertaking *seva* as equivalent to drinking *amrit* (ambrosial nectar), which nourishes the enlightened body.[98] Guru Arjan says in *rāg Aasa* that *seva* renders the mind pure (*nirmal*), allowing one to internally hear the divine name.[99] In *rāg Suhi* Guru Arjan explains how serving the divine guru day and night will allow the consciousness to experience "*sukh, sehaj, . . . shaant*" (contentment, equipoise, peace).[100]

Guru Arjan emphasizes the importance of one human being (*maanukh*) serving another in *rāg Bilawal*.[101] But why is it important to serve others in Sikh devotional practice? One reason has to do with the belief that the divine guru becomes present in the midst of the *sangat* through being remembered: "The true guru is found among the true gatherings of devotees [*sat sangat*]" (Guru Nanak, *rāg Sri*).[102] Guru Ramdas writes specifically about the importance of singing divine praise as part of the *sat sangat*, as does Guru Arjan.[103] Being in the company of holy figures is considered especially conducive to generating inner music (*dhun*) of peace, contentment, and equipoise, as Guru Arjan conveys in *rāg Majh*.[104] In *rāg Sorath*, he writes, "Singing *kirtan* in the company of holy figures is the highest of all actions."[105]

Other reasons for serving others have to do with the benefits of amplified corporeal vibration and how this can work toward transforming the self.[106] The gurus were sharply attuned to the rigid social hierarchy and casteism of their time, and thus constant emphasis on communal devotion contributed to the creation of social equality and social bonds (as underscored by Guru Arjan's emphasis on sharing wealth in 135-19). Engaging in kirtan as part of a sangat was directly linked to bettering one's spiritual and psychological well-being and facilitating the same for others through vibrating together (bhajna). Being one of many, and being part of a larger vibration, also brings about a loss of ego, which is essential to devotional practice and living as a Gurmukh (someone who is oriented toward the teachings of the divine guru).[107] Guru Arjan explains that liberation (mukti) and the celestial domain (baikunth) are found in the company of the sangat.[108] In the sangat the devotee should vibrate (bhajiae) with the divine name (gopal).[109] This state allows the devotee to inwardly hear the divine word, "anahad shabad," as noted by Bhai Gurdas and described as "nirmal nād" (pure divine sound) by Guru Amardas in rāg Majh.[110]

To close this section, I will briefly pose the question What does kirtan do? again to summarize the larger points and make some new ones. I have explained that kirtan mediates between the domains of ahat nād and anahad nād: Guru Arjan explains in rāg Basant, "The ultimate [unstruck] melody resides in kirtan."[111] Devotees can only experience anahad nād through the strengthened vibrations of a sangat, and once attained, this feeling of bliss is nourished and sustained through constantly hearing kirtan, engaging in recitation, and undertaking seva.

At several moments, the gurus speak of singing kirtan throughout the eight pehar (twenty-four-hour period). In rāg Majh Guru Arjan instructs, "Sing kirtan day and night; this is the most fruitful occupation."[112] He describes constant kirtan as akhand (unbroken) and as a kind of bhojan (food) that nourishes the body.[113] In rāg Sarang he explains that the unstruck divine sound (pooran nād) will resound when devotees savor the sweet taste (ras) of kirtan.[114] This connection between struck and unstruck sound can only be sustained when a synergistic relationship has been established between ahat nād and anahad nād so that the effort of making and hearing music in the realm of ahat becomes effortless in the realm of anahad. Guru Arjan makes this point in rāg Aasa: "I sing inwardly, I sing outwardly, I sing when awake and asleep."[115] The feeling of lasting bliss achieved through kirtan allows for the munn (consciousness), rather than the tunn (body), to sing.[116] The true kirtan, thus, is that which is made by the consciousness.[117] This is why kirtan is described as a nirmolak hira, an invaluable diamond.[118]

This is the larger ecosystem in which kirtan operates, and I underscore again the distinctive nature of cyclic auditory attention where corporeal vibration, attunement to divinity, and collective resonance reverberate through one another. In this context, music, if we think of *kirtan* as such, is tied directly to social action, which is sustained through sonic resonance. Guru Arjan urges devotees to live their lives immersed in the color (*rangg*, the joyous spirit) of *kirtan*.[119]

There are numerous other benefits to hearing and singing *kirtan* that are physical and mental, affecting one's body, mind, and consciousness. In *rāg Gauri Guareri* Guru Arjan explains that by doing *kirtan* (*kar kirtan*), one's mind (*munn*) is cooled or rendered peaceful (*seetal*).[120] In this state the mind is fully awakened, and one becomes a true yogi (*jog*).[121] In *rāg Aasa*, Guru Arjan says, "Multitudes of contentment, equipoise, and bliss [*sukh, sehaj, anand*] are obtained by singing *kirtan*."[122] Singing and listening to *kirtan* can bring great peace and bliss (*maha anand*), Guru Arjan states in *rāg Todi* and *Dhanasri*.[123] In *rāg Gujri* Guru Arjan tells us that multiple illnesses vanish upon singing divine praise.[124] The practice of *rāg* itself has physical ramifications. Guru Arjan writes that *rāg* has the capacity to quench one's thirst.[125] Meanwhile, singing *rāg Malar*, associated with the rainy season, renders the mind and body cool and calm.[126]

Corporeal health is paralleled by psychic health, as Guru Amardas explains in *rāg Sorath*: "Singing divine praise, one tastes divine sweetness [*ras*], the consciousness is satisfied, the inner lotus blossoms forth, the unstruck word [*anahad shabad*] resounds within."[127] Guru Arjan also describes the act of singing *kirtan* as allowing the inner lotus to blossom.[128] There is considerable emphasis on tasting *ras* through *kirtan*, which keeps in view the multisensory experience of engaging with sound in Sikh devotion.[129] Singing *kirtan* in a *sangat* facilitates a fully sensory experience where the devotee not only tastes *ras* but also experiences the intense fragrance of fruit.[130] The sensory abundance associated with spring—sight, smell, touch, sound, taste—is linked to *kirtan*. The body is often conceived as a *ghar* (home) in *Gurbani*, and in *rāg Basant* Guru Arjan observes the feeling of spring as arriving within that home where the "divine melody [*dhuni*] of *kirtan* resounds."[131]

A devotee engaged with *kirtan* as listener and singer is protected from negative energy, situations, and thoughts. Guru Nanak explains in *rāg Aasa*, "Enemies [*doot*] won't be able to touch those who sing of divine virtues [*gunn*]."[132] Guru Arjan composes in *rāg Aasa*, "By singing *kirtan*, all pain is dissolved, and the cycle of rebirth ends."[133] In *rāg Gujri* Guru Arjan mentions that singing *kirtan* can help the devotee evade death, allowing sorrow, fear, and doubt to also dissipate. One who listens to and sings *kirtan* is protected from pain and misfortune.[134] Listening to *katha* (discourse) and *kirtan* also eliminates negative thoughts, the feeling of being trapped in anxiety, and overthinking.[135] All in all, through *kirtan* and recitation the devotee experiences happiness, lasting bliss, and fulfilled hopes.[136] In the age of *kaljug* (destruction), *kirtan* is described as a true support (*adhaar*) and as the most exalted (*pardhana*).[137]

LISTENING EXPANSIVELY TO THE *KIRTAN* OF THE COSMOS

SGGS is filled with vibrant soundscapes where nature (through an emphasis on animal calls or meteorological elements such as wind and rain), the cosmos (as conveyed by resonating planets, galaxies, and universes), and the celestial plane (in the songs of deities and other celestial beings) participate synchronously in offering divine praise. Having laid a foundation for sustained engagement with the topic of *kirtan*, I highlight in this final section the broad conception of sound in *Gurbani*—a more in-depth study of this topic is provided elsewhere.[138]

Sonic gestures thicken the narrative texture in two ways: The mere mention of an elephant, a donkey, a horse, or a dog, to cite a few animals, encourages the devotee to picture their appearance and internally hear their calls. At other instances *Gurbani* describes and mimics the unique timbres of animal species. Sonic expressions of the animal kingdom merge with those of the elements and other natural and celestial phenomena. In the opening composition of *SGGS*, *Japji Sahib*, Guru Nanak celebrates a cosmological worship of the divine where planets and universes, deities and mortals, animals and meteorological elements, and flora and fauna all participate in offering divine praise through their unique songs.

When Sikhs recite *Japji Sahib* during their morning prayers, Guru Nanak's verses remind them how the entire matter of the cosmos—whether divine, human, animal, plant, or elemental—sings and hears each entity's personal offering of divine praise. As devotees heed *Gurbani*'s instruction to sing and listen to devotional music, do they also honor Guru Nanak's expansive approach to listening by attending to the cosmological song of divine praise that holds all of existence in a balanced state of vibration? How does an ability to listen expansively impact a person's connection to other forces of life in their daily surroundings? How can this type of listening heighten our sensitivity to hearing sonic gestures in our physical and metaphysical environments as an expression of balance and harmony between all living matter?

The central act of hearing, listening, and audition in the epistemological framework of *Gurbani* is highlighted in the vast sonic expanse articulated by Guru Nanak in *Japji Sahib*. Although this composition has been a part of my daily meditation since I was a child, I acknowledge the growing body of research in the field of ecomusicology over the last few decades—and its many adjacent subfields spanning ethnomusicology, anthropology, and sound studies—for helping me hear the vivid, multilayered soundscapes of *SGGS* in a new way. Ana María Ochoa Gautier's remark that "whether a sound is produced by humans or animals depends on the ear that hears it" serves as a guiding light as I study the vast terrain of Sikh soundscapes.[139]

Also inspirational is an essay by Andrew Hicks about philosophies of audition in medieval Persian Sufism. The distinctions that he draws between ancient Persian and ancient Greek thought on the topic of cosmological sound and its impact on the human body jolted me toward rethinking the sonic expanse of *Japji Sahib*: I see more clearly how Guru Nanak places singing and listening on an equal level and how both activities are directed toward the attainment of an inwardly heard perception of sonic bliss (*anahad nād*). I understand that listening is not a passive or superficial activity, nor is it something that Guru Nanak takes for granted: The guru asks the devotee to resonate with, and to be attuned to, the many divine songs of the cosmos. This kind of listening is not directed outward toward the planets, as the ancient Greek philosopher Pythagoras had envisioned.[140] In contrast, the approach to listening that Guru Nanak outlines is directed inward so that a perception of one's inner vibration, a form of unstruck sound (*anahad nād*), links the devotee to the cosmic vibration of *nirankar* (a manifestation of the divine as formless and beyond time and space). Hicks shows that ancient Greek and Sufi scholars were receptive to ideas about harmony and vibration in the cosmos. These perspectives can be broadened to include the insights of Sikh gurus and bhagats while conceiving of sound as an expression that exists across physical and metaphysical planes at a synchronous moment. Within the framework of *Gurbani*, sonic unity and vibration are the basis of creation, as well as the epistemological foundation for a worldview where all aspects of existence are suspended in a state of equilibrium. The intertwining songs that span the metaphysical and the physical dimensions are presented in *Japji Sahib* as vibrating in a unified harmony.

Japji Sahib forms the basis of Sikh epistemology, where a cosmic vibration of sound is given due prominence. These verses invite the devotee to experience a multiversal, heterogeneous resonance: Celestial, animate, and inanimate forms all vibrate sound and perceive sound in a cyclic relationship that outlines the ideal state of equipoise between *ahat nād* and *anahad nād*. In *Japji Sahib* the act of producing sound by singing or playing instruments is just as important as the act of hearing, since both actions, when they feed into one another, engender an inward experience of devotional love: "Sing, listen, and keep devotional love close to your heart." After the *mool mantar* (opening invocation) and the first two verses, Guru Nanak turns in verse 3 to the important act of *gaaviye* (singing) without specifying which entities offer song. The many sources of song—animate and inanimate—blend into one, ultimately contributing to the cosmic reverberation of the divine breath/word: "Gurmukh nādang."[141]

The act of listening gives an insight into the source of divine song because it is when Guru Nanak lists who is listening that we begin to grasp who is also singing. Listening is explored in four successive stanzas (numbers 8 through 11) through the active form, *suniye*: Spiritual figures and immortalized warriors—as well as the earth; Dhaval (the mythological bull that carries the earth); the sky; oceans; many worlds and underworlds; the deities Shiva, Brahma, and Indra; yogis; sheikhs; seers; and emperors—they all hear cosmic vibration.[142] Listening is given an especially high status since it allows the devotee to evade death, to erase suffering and negativity from their lives, and to obtain contentment and wisdom.[143] Through hearing divine vibration, even the blind find their path, and what lies beyond one's reach becomes attainable. To reiterate, hearing the divine word and feeling its vibration facilitate an inner cleansing (87-8); they bring about a feeling of great peace (715-10); they offer sustenance (749-14); they rejuvenate the mind and body (781-16); they eliminate pain, disease, and suffering (922-18); they bring about inner illumination (113-13); and they offer inner joy (174-5). In *rāg Aasa* Guru Arjan observes that "humans, forests, blades of grass, animals, and birds are all involved in meditation."[144]

Stanza 27 is especially evocative in how it speaks to the continuous plenitude of sound and music vibrating across the cosmos. An infinite variety of *nād*, played by a multitude of musicians, resounds at the place where the divine one is encountered. A multitude of *rāg* are sung by many singers. The natural elements of air, water, and fire also sing divine praise, as do all manner of adorned celestial beings, saints deep in meditation and contemplation, warriors, scholars, beautiful celestial nymphs and jewels, places of pilgrimage, continents, constellations, and universes.[145] The sonic expanse that Guru Nanak evokes is immense, diverse, and boundless. Human beings are just one of many life-forms that vibrate divine sound in tandem with animals, plant life, natural elements, celestial beings, and the entire cosmos. In his humility Guru Nanak acknowledges in this verse that he may have forgotten to mention many other entities who sing; he asks, "How could I possibly recount them all?" As I see it, these other sonic expressions include the contributions of animals, particularly birds, whose song serves as the basis for the topic of yearning in *SGGS*.

What does *Japji Sahib* tell us about how Guru Nanak listened? How does the emphasis on listening in these verses instruct devotees on how to live their lives in sonic harmony with physical and metaphysical vibration? Listening lies at the heart of self-transformation and self-realization.[146] It is not only humans who listen to and attune themselves to divine vibration; so do the earth, its oceans, and multiple lands. Bhagat Kabir also observes a dog hearing the divine name.[147] As the opening composition of *SGGS*, *Japji Sahib* establishes a paradigm for listening that is capacious in keeping with Guru Nanak's vision of divine creation: The act of singing divine praise is not limited to human beings. A willingness to hear *kirtan* coming from all forms of life, across multiple planes, reminds the devotee to hear the divine song that keeps all expressions of life connected to one another. To listen in this way lies at the heart of the devotional experience in *Gurbani*.

Guru Nanak's vast experience of sonic vibration positions the act of listening in humans on an equal footing with how other phenomena engage with sound. My emphasis on a cosmic approach to listening works toward expanding the sonic preoccupations of ecomusicology to include the metaphysical domain. Gautier similarly sought to reinstate the cosmological dimension in her study of vocality in the nineteenth-century Colombian archive, where "Colombia's many different peoples, nonhuman animals, and entities of nature—rivers, volcanoes, the wind"— speak to one another.[148] In her study of Vodou ecological metaphysics in Haiti, Rebecca Dirksen also observes how "ethnomusicologists have infrequently considered the metaphysical conceptions of the bonds between humanity and the environment," inspiring her to redress this imbalance in scholarship that attends to the convergence of the divine, the human, and the natural in sacred ritual.[149] My focus on Sikh metaphysics in *Japji Sahib* contributes to these conversations by highlighting a way of listening that stretches beyond the boundaries that separate tangible from intangible matter and works toward uncovering a sympathetic vibration that holds all entities in a delicate balance. This awareness forms the basis of what Nikky-Guninder Kaur Singh identifies as Guru Nanak's "biophilial ideology and poetics," which establish a relationship between animate and inanimate phenomena on the basis of equality and love rather than hierarchy and domination.[150]

AVIAN YEARNINGS FOR THE DIVINE IN BIRDSONG

Nature—broadly conceived as encompassing animal and plant life—participates directly in the act of singing divine praise. Research in biomusicology, zoomusicology, evolutionary musicology, ecomusicology, ecocriticism, and other fields that pay attention to the sonic expressions of animal and plant worlds finds a rich counterpart in the lively soundscapes of *SGGS*. It is a relatively new approach for scholars to consider the sound production of humans on an equal basis with that of other organic matter, as Holly Watkins does when she sees "human musicking as a subset of the cultural activities and 'biotic arts' of other animals."[151] In parallel, the foundational role of reincarnation in Sikh metaphysics presents animal and human life as deeply intertwined: Past lives as various animals are embedded deep in the consciousness when human life is finally attained. Bhagat Kabir speaks directly to the topic of reincarnation in *rāg Gujri*, where he chides the human for not engaging in remembrance of the divine. He asks, "How will you sing divine praise with four feet, two horns, and a mute mouth?"[152] Against these contexts *Gurbani*'s emphasis on engaging with *kirtan* through singing and listening acquires an even greater urgency: Humans traverse 8.4 million lifetimes (*lakh chaurasi joon*) before attaining the human body, so the opportunity to sing *kirtan* should not be wasted, as Bhagat Kabir captures through his characteristically striking imagery of an inarticulate bull (*bael*). All of creation—human, celestial, animate, inanimate, and elemental—is viewed as having equal status. Nonetheless, the human form is valued above the animal form in *Gurbani* because the tongue (and its role in speech) allows the human to recite the divine word (*shabad*) while the ears allow the body to internalize *shabad* in connecting the self to the divine vibration of *nād*.

Still, there are moments in *Gurbani* when an innermost yearning for the divine brings the human into close alignment with certain other animal species—this intense emotion is often projected through the cultivation of empathy for animal instincts. At several junctures humans are asked to imagine their relationship to divinity in its most basic form: as a means for survival. The comparison to animals through metaphors and similes highlights the topic of survival while encouraging devotees to engage affectively with *Gurbani* through contemplating their emotional and bodily needs. Guru Nanak composes in *rāg Sri*, "Love the divine just as the fish loves water."[153] Bhagat Kabir reminds the devotee in *rāg Gauri* to "meditate and vibrate on the divine name with the same intensity as the *saaring* [bird] yearning for water."[154] Guru Arjan instructs devotees in *rāg Aasa* to love the divine one just as the *kokil* (cuckoo) loves the mango.[155]

In a synesthetic moment with Bhagat Namdev in *rāg Dhanasri*, sound and fragrance merge together as the *kokil's* love for the mango tree blends its sweet birdcalls with the beautiful appearance and aroma of this tree.[156]

Sukhbir Kapoor observes twelve varieties of birds in *SGGS*.[157] Some types are used to deepen the narrative texture, and thus species like the swan, hawk, and heron are not heard. A range of birdcalls—from avian varieties including the *babiha/papiha/saaring/chaatrik*, the *kokil* (cuckoo), and the *mōr* (peacock)—populates *Gurbani*.[158] These sonic gestures are logically equivalent to language when it comes to communicating love and yearning. Gurus and bhagats imagine themselves through zoomorphic (where humans assume animal qualities) and anthropomorphic (where animals assume human qualities) literary techniques as birds yearning for *darshan* (a sensing of divine presence).

Eschewing the primacy of the *shabad*, there are a few heightened moments in *Gurbani* where the plaintive calls of birdsong itself are heard by the divine as an expression of prayer (*bani*); such is their emotional purity.[159] Just as birds are capable of singing *bani*, humans are capable of uttering birdsong as divine praise: In an inversion, in *rāg Tukhari* Guru Ramdas sees the spiritually attained devotee as expressing their inner bliss through birdcalls: "My inner being is illuminated—I continually chirrup '*prio prio*.'"[160] Thus, devotees are instructed to imagine themselves as birds, and birds are considered to be a mere step away from human and divine forms: Guru Nanak composes in *rāg Maru*, "The divine one is neither a woman, nor a man, nor a bird; the true one appears wise and beautiful."[161]

Drawing on the notion of the "animal sublime," Balbinder S. Bhogal explains that these kinds of techniques highlight the "literary and metaphorical interconnectedness that animals are assumed to share with the Gurmukh [one who is oriented toward the guru]." His attention to how "the animal serves as a counterpoint to the human . . . and indeed as a necessary corollary in that the human cannot be thought without the animal" guides the following discussion.[162] *Gurbani* uses metaphor, simile, zoomorphism, and anthropomorphism to create organic and psychological connections between the human and the recurring motif of the bird (*pankhee*).

The *saaring/chaatrik* is always characterized as being thirsty for the first drop of rain (called *swanti boond*) to fall from the clouds—these birds do not wish to consume water in any other way.[163] Their birdcalls are made directly to the clouds as they plead to have water released into their beaks. The thirsty *chaatrik* is invoked at several moments to emphasize that a human's longing for the divine should have the same intense focus.¹⁶⁴ A yearning for the first raindrops is compared at several moments to the ardent love of the devotee for a sensory experience of *darshan* (a sensing of divine presence).¹⁶⁵ Guru Arjan conveys the intensity of this longing in *rāg Majh*, where he anthropomorphizes the bird through emphasis on its emotional cries (*bilap karay*).¹⁶⁶ Guru Ramdas evokes a similar affect in *rāg Dhanasri*, where an anthropomorphized bird cries, desperately, for *darshan* and union with the divine.¹⁶⁷

There are many moments when the gurus incorporate the language of the birdcall itself to convey a heightened emotion. Guru Nanak observes in *rāg Tukhari* how the *babiha* chirrups (*chavai*) "*prio prio*" to express its yearning for the divine beloved.¹⁶⁸ When the clouds have burst forth, Guru Amardas explains in *rāg Malar*, the *babiha*'s thirst for water is appeased and its frantic birdcalls (*kook pukar*) fade away to be replaced by feelings of contentment (*sukh*).¹⁶⁹ In *rāg Tukhari* Guru Nanak also hears the *babiha* cry "*prio*," while the *kokil* sings the divine utterance itself (*bani*).¹⁷⁰ Similarly, Guru Arjan in *rāg Malar* perceives the playing of *anahad mridang* in tandem with the *kokil* reciting the divine name (*raam*) in its sweet, flutelike *kirtan*.¹⁷¹ Again, anthropomorphic techniques intensify the emotion of a scene that Guru Ramdas composes in *rāg Tukhari*: "Night and day, day and night, I cry out '*prio prio*'; without my beloved, my thirst is not quenched."¹⁷² Using captivating imagery in *rāg Sarang*, Guru Arjan compares the anthropomorphized bird crying "*prio prio*" with the longing of the bumblebee for the lotus flower.¹⁷³

A pursuit of proximity to the divine, and experiencing divine presence through *darshan*, erases the incarnational hierarchy between humans and animals. Guru Amardas describes in *rāg Malar* that the *babiha*'s call, which sounds during *amritvela* (the early hours of the morning), is heard by the divine one; at this sacred hour, a simple birdsong is transformed into prayer.¹⁷⁴ Furthermore, the presentation of all animal forms yearning for closeness does not exclude divinity, which, like humans, also takes the form of the *saaring*.¹⁷⁵

How do these literary techniques serve the soundscapes of *Gurbani*? Why are devotees asked to imagine themselves as birds after having gone through 8.4 million reincarnations to reach the highest state of the human being? What does the human lack that the bird does not? Why is it that the true pangs of yearning and devotion expressed through birdsong can only be experienced when one imagines the self in the form of a nonverbal animal?¹⁷⁶

One answer looks to the important role of metaphors and similes in early modern *bhakti* literary conventions. Linda Hess interprets the *cātaka/chaatrik* in Bhagat Kabir's verses as "a touching symbol of longing and devotion."[177] A different answer by Jagjit S. Grewal interprets these literary techniques as ultimately serving a didactic purpose through the evocation of vibrant and affective poetic imagery; imagery also readies the mind for spiritual contemplation.[178] Both approaches coalesce in Balbinder S. Bhogal's Nietzschean notion of the "animal sublime," where a horizontal understanding of the relationship between animal and human reveals the two forms to be intertwined with the other: "The human cannot be thought without the animal."[179]

My own interpretation of zoomorphism and anthropomorphism in *SGGS* focuses on the topic of humility. In having us imagine ourselves in the fragile form of the bird, and embody the bird's yearning song for the divine, gurus and bhagats ask us to lose our ego to adopt an animal identity where we render our plea through nonverbal sonic communication and not through socialized and civilized forms of poetic speech. Because of its association with a basic instinct for biological survival, this desire for the material raindrop and the immaterial divine presence (*darshan*) is portrayed as authentic and direct. An emotional intensity of yearning is carried by birdsong in *Gurbani*, and by expressing this longing through comparison to ardent desire, the devotee engages with the guru in a way that doesn't require emotional or intellectual sophistication. Guru Amardas explains in *rāg Malar*, "This rainbird is an animal; it has no understanding at all."[180] Using remarkable imagery, Guru Amardas goes one step further in rendering the entire earth in the form of the *babiha* that thirsts for the ambrosial divine name.[181]

Darshan is not gained through virtuosity of speech or music but by the desperation of one's need and the sincerity of one's longing. In the epistemological framework of *Gurbani*, emphasis on an animal's instinct for survival portrays their sincerity despite their lower status within the life cycle. Humans are reminded to stay attuned to these same instincts that lie deep within them, connecting them to their former lives. Christopher Chapple observes, "For Sikhs, observation of the natural world and reflection on one's own deep memory of past lives convinces one of the sense of kinship we hold with all living beings."[182]

The compositions of *SGGS* emphasize a yearning for proximity to divinity through imagining the human self in the form of animals, particularly the bird. The use of metaphor, simile, and corporeal relativism through zoomorphism and anthropomorphism has a clear spiritual purpose: These techniques ask devotees to strip away complexity from their human selves in the form of *maya* to focus on their simplest needs. The *chaatrik*'s desperation to taste *swanti boond* translates into the human's deep desire to savor the divine name—*boond* (drop) in this instance has two meanings: The sweetness of the raindrop for the *chaatrik* manifests in the form of *amrit* (ambrosial nectar) for the devotee. These literary techniques are powerful in sending the ultimate message of the gurus and bhagats: Cultivate a closeness to divinity.

Many other animals and plants populate *SGGS*, not to mention realms, worlds, galaxies, and universes. For devotees the rich textures and timbres of slithering snakes, croaking frogs, humming bees, buzzing flies, biting mosquitoes, chirruping crickets, shrieking cranes, chirruping sparrows, deer, elephants, and parrots contribute to a sonic tapestry. The vibrant soundscape of *Gurbani* is at once human, animal, vegetal, elemental, and celestial. To experience *anahad nād* is also to hear the vast sonic resonance of animate and inanimate forms in their contributions to a cosmic *kirtan*.

CHAPTER SUMMARY

From Guru Arjan's meditating blade of grass to Guru Nanak's vibrating cosmos, this chapter charts a journey that takes the reader from the level of detail to a level of abstraction. Sikh sacred verse is idiosyncratically manifested through silent recitation, intoned delivery, and devotional song. *Rāg* contributes to the structural organization of *SGGS* and, through close study of verse titles, we see how *rāg* informs the content and expressive delivery of the verse. Verse titles also point to information about the author, poetic meter and form, melody, musical genre and style, and metric proportion to prepare devotees for their engagement with sacred verse. Ultimately *kirtan* is characterized by the intertwining motion of sacred poetry and devotional sonic expression. *Kirtan* is an offering before it is music. There is no hierarchy in this practice — everyone involved in singing and hearing receives and generates the vibrations of *kirtan*.

The question of how to listen to *kirtan* and what this listening achieves helps us understand how the organs of the ears and tongue are involved. The act of listening, hearing, and audition highlights a cyclic, processual model where an externally produced music (*ahat nād*) generates an internally experienced vibration (*anahad nād*) that attunes the listener to divinity and promotes social activism oriented toward helping others through service (*seva*). *Kirtan* produces a meaningful impact on the mind, body, and consciousness; *Gurbani* is thus beyond human praxis, given that Guru Nanak's vision of humanity is tied to a delicate balance of the cosmos.

To understand the vast soundscapes of *Gurbani* is to see human beings as coexisting with all manner of biological forms—animate and inanimate, celestial and mortal—without hierarchy or attempts at domination. Achieved through recitation, *kirtan*, and hearing the divine name, the ideal Sikh states of *sukh-sehaj-anand* (contentment-equipoise-bliss) emphasize an ease of mutual and respectful existence where every entity is reverberant with the vibration of divine *nād*.

| 2

Tracking the Harmonium from Christian Missionary Hymns to Sikh *Kirtan*

The examples of *kirtan* heard thus far showcase one instrument in particular: the harmonium. Quite unexpectedly, in May 2022 the current leader of the *Akal Takht* (five seats of Sikh spiritual power), Giani Harpreet Singh, made an official proclamation banning the harmonium at the holiest Sikh temple, Harmandir Sahib (Golden Temple), and returning to traditional Sikh instruments categorized as *tanti sāz* (including the *rabab, saranda, sarangi, taus,* and *dilruba*). For the last century or so, the harmonium has been the dominant accompanying instrument in *kirtan jatha* (ensembles). Following his criticism of the "foreign" harmonium, which came to India from Western Europe and America, intense debates began to rage among practitioners and devotees, with arguments being offered on all sides. Against this context, my interest in exploring the journeys of the harmonium across Punjab was transformed into a politically charged project, carrying significant cultural weight.

As we have seen, the harmonium is a small, box-shaped, free-reed portable organ, which is played sitting down; air is pumped through the bellows by one hand while the other hand plays the keyboard.[1] This instrument has been attacked before for reasons that have to do with anticolonial sentiment and nationalist efforts to preserve musical timbres, tuning, and repertoires. All India Radio (AIR) issued a ban in 1940, which was eventually lifted in 1971.² Despite sharing an anticolonial stance, the current attempt at a ban feels markedly different. It comes on the heels of several decades of Sikh scholarly debate about the role of *rāg* in *kirtan*, decolonizing pedagogical reform, and an increasing production of historically informed string instruments. Put simply, the sensitive tuning (to twenty-two *shruti*, or microtonal intervals) of *tanti sāz*, unlike the Western equal temperament (division of an octave into twelve equidistant intervals) of the harmonium, makes it possible to convey *Gurbani* in *nirdharit rāg*. Given growing interest in the practice of *Gurmat Sangeet* and its commitment to *nirdharit rāg*, Giani Harpreet Singh's statement is poised to have lasting impact. The *Akal Takht* proclaims that phasing out the harmonium over a period of three years is the only way to ensure a return to the primordial sound world of *tanti sāz*. The figures of Guru Nanak and Bhai Mardana permeate these debates. Their "original" *kirtan* remains indelible in the Sikh cultural imagination, and proponents of the ban continue to harness Bhai Mardana's "divine" *rabab* to bolster their arguments.

Tanti sāz refers to two traditions: that of the *rababi* (Muslim descendants of Bhai Mardana) and that of performers of string instruments linked to the Sikh *darbar* (court). My struggle to locate primary sources that detail the history of Sikh musical instruments has led me to rely on oral history and secondary sources in concluding that the *rabab* was likely played alongside the bowed *saranda* in the *darbar* of Guru Amardas, Guru Ramdas, and Guru Arjan.³ Guru Hargobind was an esteemed performer in the folk tradition of *dhaadhi vār* (heroic ballads), and his *darbar* is also associated with the peacock-shaped *taus* and the folk *sarangi*. The court of Guru Gobind Singh is linked with the *tanpura*, *taus*, and *dilruba* (although it is possible that the *dilruba* developed later in the nineteenth century).⁴ Other string instruments, such as the *dotara*, *vina*, and later *sitar*, were featured in the Sikh *darbar*, as were percussion instruments like the *pakhawaj* (sometimes called *mridang*), *dhadh*, *jori*, and later *tabla*. The term *tanti sāz* is frequently used to group all manner of string instruments as I do here. **Figure 2.1** shows some of these instruments in a photograph from an early twentieth-century Sikh encyclopedia by Kahn Singh Nabha, representing one of the first modern efforts to reify the timbres of the Sikh courts. This well-known image undergirds the ban, given how it fuels the Sikh imagination while providing a sonic ideal to which *kirtan* should aspire. It's difficult to speculate on why a widely played instrument of this period, the *dilruba*, is missing. Nowadays, the *dilruba* is central to pedagogical reform and the most mass-produced instrument among *tanti sāz*.

The term *tanti sāz* is especially powerful given how it invokes the

FIGURE 2.1 A photograph probably taken in the 1920s showing the different instruments that were played in kirtan at the time: (1) *sitar*, (2) *dotara*, (3) *taus*, (4) *tanpura*, (5) *saranda*, (6) *rabab*, and (7) *jori*. Kahn Singh Nabha, *Gur Shabad Ratanakar Mahankosh* (1930), 179.

twinned notions of sonic authenticity and sonic purity in the context of the ban. These concepts have been widely examined by scholars across various contexts and cultures in the Euro-North American academy. In prevailing Sikh discourse, sonic authenticity refers to instruments associated with the Sikh *darbar* of the fifteenth to the eighteenth centuries. Sonic purity refers to the manifestation of timbre within the space of the *darbar* as pure because it carries the sacred word (*shabad*).[5] Sikh practitioners and spiritual figures of authority of varying perspectives continue to venerate sonic authenticity and sonic purity. Their debates idealize the timbres of *tanti sāz* as "pure" and "authentic," labels that bring into focus the specter of A. H. Fox Strangways's warning from 1914 that the harmonium, a "serious menace," would "before long . . . , if it does not already, desecrate the temple." Over a century later the sentiment behind his statement is considerably amplified within certain Sikh circles, although no one has quite put it like Strangways, who sought to "dismiss from India these foreign instruments" in order to "prune away an unnatural growth."[6]

This chapter interrogates decolonizing attempts to purge Sikh *kirtan* of the harmonium. A critical examination of rarely studied missionary sources (including newspapers, magazines, journals, census reports, gazettes, and encyclopedias) addresses misconceptions about the arrival and history of this instrument that continue to circulate in the Indian press and in social media. This engagement clarifies how the harmonium was taken up by local musicians, while considering how it was developed by Indian instrument makers and manufacturers in response to Western European and American models. Philipp Stockhammer's notion of entanglement offers a helpful conceptual frame for understanding how Indian musicians encountered and manipulated the harmonium. The first stage of engaging with the harmonium shows a "relational entanglement"—"when the object is appropriated and thus integrated into local practices, systems of meaning and worldviews." The second stage signals a "material entanglement"—"which signifies the creation of something new that is more than just the sum of its parts and combines the familiar with the previously foreign. This object is more than just a sum of the entities from which it originated and clearly not the result of local continuities. It can be taken as a representative of a new taxonomic entity."[7] My methodology is constrained by a limitation: An absence of written documentation in the Indian archive has resulted in overreliance on Euro-American accounts, which I read critically in uncovering how the harmonium entered native domains of music-making.

The second half of this chapter changes the dynamics of this imbalance by shifting from the printed word to recorded sound, since that medium allows us to track the "dynamics and processuality" of transcultural entanglement, as noted by Stockhammer.[8] My narrative is guided by another colonial project: Early recordings of Sikh *kirtan* made by the Gramophone Company capture the first steps taken by practitioners of *kirtan* toward making recordings for the purposes of documentation and commercial consumption. The Sikh recording industry has grown substantially since those early days, and it is now supplemented by nonstop broadcasting of *kirtan* on radio and TV, live streaming from historical *Gurudware* online, and extensive libraries of recordings available on apps and through such platforms as YouTube and Spotify. The harmonium remains integral to these practices. Despite this wide availability, the consumption of *kirtan* tends to occur largely within the Sikh community. This is one reason why Sikh *kirtan* has remained peripheral in relation to more dominant forms of Hindustani music; during my research on the harmonium, it was rare to encounter mention of this instrument's role in Sikh *kirtan* beyond a cursory comment. Select recordings are used to analyze idiosyncratic techniques of harmonium playing to highlight this instrument's unique contributions to *kirtan*.

Matthew Rahaim and Cleveland Johnson have offered valuable studies of the harmonium in India, which are the point of departure for all new research, including my own.[9] However, my vantage point is different:

I explore how this instrument proliferated within a missionary context, a perspective that offers insights on how the harmonium was able to stake a presence across the north and in remote regions, which is where missionary outposts were often located. The focus on cities like Calcutta and Bombay (now Kolkata and Mumbai) by Rahaim and Johnson, where British society rubbed shoulders with the Indian elite, has tended to obscure the social networks through which the harmonium entered and flourished in Sikh *kirtan*. Given the close relationship between Muslim *rababi* and Sikh *ragi* (professionally trained male practitioners), we will see that the harmonium entered the space of *kirtan* via *mirasi*. These hereditary musicians negotiated musical performance across a variety of sites and social contexts, including sacred and popular spaces, and held immense musical knowledge. Even as I observe the environments in which Indian converts to Christianity began to play the harmonium, we will see how this instrument came to coexist with and (temporarily) displace local instruments. This shift was on its way by the turn of the twentieth century, as observed by Ananda Coomaraswamy.[10] Although the partition is usually blamed for the disappearance of instruments such as the *rabab* and *sarangi* from Punjab, missionary literature reveals the impact of the imported harmonium on the local scene several decades prior to the separation of India and the creation of Pakistan.

Against the backdrop of heated political and scholarly debates, I offer an empathetic analysis of the entry and development of the harmonium in Sikh devotional worship. Part of this empathy stems from my gendered experience of learning *kirtan* on the harmonium from amateur female teachers as a young girl in a new immigrant East African Sikh community in the United Kingdom during the 1970s, a time when parents were wary of sending their daughters to learn from unknown male teachers who were visiting from India and other diasporic Sikh communities. The penultimate section expands on the discussion of gender inequality raised in the introduction by noting the rising numbers of women and girls involved in learning *kirtan* on *tanti sāz* today. Even as the harmonium is deeply intertwined with the sociocultural fabric of Punjab, as well as the region's political history, only time will tell whether this instrument is here to stay or whether *tanti sāz* will eventually displace it altogether.

DESTINATION PUNJAB: THE HARMONIUM ARRIVES IN INDIA

Some Indian and Euro-American historical accounts trace the invention of the harmonium's predecessor, the free-reed organ, to various German and French instrument makers, while several others ascribe the origins of the free reed itself, one of the harmonium's constituent components, to Asia (specifically China but also India).[11] It is understood that the earliest version of the harmonium as we know it landed in India along with British and American missionaries. But what happened next? And what are the events that led to the first encounter of the instrument by Indigenous musicians and listeners? Seen in relation to the evolving nature of the harmonium—as it shifted from the heavier variety of the upright pedal harmonium to the more portable forms of table and lap harmoniums—this section fills in a crucial gap in our knowledge surrounding the arrival and dissemination of the harmonium across the subcontinent (particularly Punjab), while considering why such scholars as Strangways expressed surprise at the harmonium's presence in the most remote parts of the country as early as 1914.[12] The following discussion considers a cultural shift that has tended to evade the scholarly eye: the emergence of the harmonium in small towns and villages and its gradual migration toward and assimilation across central sites of patronage.

A precursor to the harmonium, the pipe organ, reached India's shores in the sixteenth century with the arrival of the first Portuguese vessels.[13] At the time, the organ was largely restricted to Goa and Portuguese areas of settlement, where it was used in liturgical music-making.[14] Although Portuguese Jesuits were aware of the power of music for the purpose of religious conversion, they also used instruments such as the portable organ for cultural diplomacy as they expanded their empire through India. Among those who encountered this instrument during the sixteenth century were King Krishna Deva Raya of Vijaynagar (in 1520) and Emperor Akbar (in 1579).[15] The organ was used in church services in India by the end of the seventeenth century. All manner of keyboard instruments were still being offered as diplomatic gifts by the Portuguese, Dutch, and English during the early eighteenth century.[16] As noted by Ian Woodfield, the missionary efforts of these years were not as effective or as long-lasting as those of the nineteenth century.[17]

The vulnerable state of the Sikh empire by the middle of the nineteenth century was viewed as an invitation to enter Punjab by church leaders who saw this moment as opportune for conversion.[18] Beyond Portuguese India, it was only with the arrival of Christian missionaries from other parts of the world during the early nineteenth century that the harmonium began to travel through the country before eventually securing a footing in the north (Lahore and Amritsar) and in the east (Calcutta).[19] Great Britain and the United States were especially involved in the distribution of this instrument during the nineteenth century since these nations were both regarded as innovators when it came to the development and production of keyboard instruments. Whereas the influx of keyboard instruments from the sixteenth to the eighteenth centuries was more focused on establishing political relations between Western European (Portuguese, Dutch, and English) powers and Indian monarchies, the entry of the hand-pumped portable harmonium during the nineteenth century was oriented toward religious conversion within lower-class communities. Primary missionary literature reveals the socioreligious circumstances under which this instrument passed into Indian hands.

Central to the practice of conversion in and around Punjab was the establishment of the Christian Missionary Society, which was headquartered in Amritsar, the holy city of the Sikhs, by the middle of the nineteenth century (in 1851). British occupation of this region meant that, as reported in *The Christian Missionary Review* in 1866, "it is just the time to work amongst them [the Sikhs], for the prestige of their own system is broken, and many are disposed to detach themselves from it."[20] A year earlier, in 1865, another missionary account explained why Sikhs were targeted as potential converts: "their manliness of character, so that they frankly avow their convictions, and, if brought under the influence of Christianity, appear well adapted to supply a valuable native agency."[21] Reverend Robert Clark observed in 1877 that Sikhism "has accustomed men to acknowledge and discuss their religious differences, and where conflict of words, as well as of courageous deeds, has trained men to independence of thought and action." These traits lent themselves well to religious conversion: "What missionaries and evangelists, what pioneers, what pastors and bishops too, these Sikhs . . . will make, when once they are converted to Christ!"[22]

Missionaries seemed united in their belief that "even before conversion, music does much to prepare the way."[23] We can grasp the essential role played by accompanying instruments like the harmonium in accounts such as this: "In all the preliminary evangelistic work in missions, music, singing especially, is of prime importance in finding a way to the heart of heathen, old or young."[24] By the middle of the nineteenth century, the harmonium was not yet being played at Harmandir Sahib, as suggested by traveler accounts. Charles Wentworth Dilke noticed that the ensemble consisted of *tanti sāz* and a percussion instrument (either *jori* or *tabla*): "You are met by a bewildering din, for under the inner dome sit worshippers by the score, singing with vigour the grandest of barbaric airs to the accompaniment of lyre, harp, and tomtom."[25] Similarly, in 1882

Frank Vincent Jr. described hearing *kirtan* performed by "three priests . . . to the accompaniment of the sitar, lyre, and tom-tom."[26]

Understanding how the harmonium entered Harmandir Sahib requires taking a deeper dive into missionary sources. Before I undertake this inquiry, I want to emphasize that the encounter between local communities and this instrument was not one of docile acceptance. In parallel with Stockhammer's dual notions of entanglement, Anilkumar Belvadi's concept of "mimicry as rivalry" provides a useful frame for understanding the conceptual and expressive jostle that surrounded the harmonium as it enjoined native communities to the prayer and music of the church.[27] As with Belvadi, I adopt an empathetic mode of critical reading that draws attention to how native congregants actively reworked how this instrument was used in worship as they endeavored to make it their own. It would be an error to assume that the first Indian harmonium players merely mimicked the posture, playing style, and music of their Christian teachers. While many intellectuals—Indian and British—cast suspicion on the harmonium because they feared it would wipe out native instruments, it is worth noting that the harmonium was initially forced to adapt to the soundscape of local instruments, thereby taking on a new role and purpose that was likely unforeseen by Christian missionaries and that manifested as rivalry, as observed by Belvadi. Taking the concept of rivalry even further, I wonder whether the full potential of the harmonium was really only realized once it had fallen into the hands of Indian musicians: Whereas the missionaries tended to use this instrument to accompany hymn singing in a simple, chordal arrangement or by doubling the hymn melody, Indian musicians subjected the harmonium to a complete rehaul in terms of how it was played and, eventually, how it was constructed.

Another observation prepares my study of the significant role played by the harmonium in missionary work. Even though this instrument and its close relative, the handheld concertina, were used in missionary work across Africa, Asia, and the Caribbean, the harmonium really only endured and developed in South Asia (and among the South Asian diaspora), where it is still subject to continued innovation and technical refinement.[28] It is worth contemplating whether this instrument filled a void: Although India was home to many types of string, brass, percussion, woodwind, and idiophonic instruments, a mechanically operated keyboard instrument was not part of its timbral landscape.[29] The novelty of the harmonium is one feature that helped it become a powerful agent of cultural change while contributing to the growth of Christianity and colonial agendas keen to industrialize and modernize India.

"CIVILIZING THE HEATHEN": HOW FEMALE MISSIONARIES USED THE HARMONIUM TO SIGNAL MODERNITY AND SPIRITUAL PROGRESS

Primary sources indicate that the harmonium was first encountered in social contexts where missionary women presented this instrument as civilized and modern to Indian girls and women.[30] Central to this message was equal temperament, whose efficiency signaled modernity and industrial progress given that the instrument could be played at a moment's notice without the need for tuning and adjustment. Indeed, an advertisement in *The Freemason* (1870) selling both English harmoniums, such as the "Oberon," and instruments specifically made for India with "mahogany sound-boards," highlights the "get-at-able-ness" of the latter (likely referring to the option for immediate playing). Interestingly, this advertisement also speaks to the different timbres of the English and Indian harmonium, where the former is characterized by a more full-bodied "diapason character" that supports solo and choral singing.[31] Presumably, this timbre would have been overpowering in an Indian context, where the harmonium needed to blend with the timbres of other local instruments. Similarly, an English advertisement from 1871 speaks to continued improvements in harmonium construction in terms of better voicing for the treble, which was likely important for Indian musical practices given the tendency for instruments to support the melody.[32]

Another instrument maker, W. E. Evans, advertised in 1866 five models of instruments varying from one to nineteen stops and up to two rows of keys.[33] This last feature signals that some of these instruments were not the familiar box harmoniums popular today but larger, stand-up harmoniums that were also taken to India, as seen in an 1878 letter from a missionary worker, Charlotte Maria Tucker, who complained about damage from rats or mice that had entered her harmonium from the pedals despite her use of traps bought in Batala and Amritsar.[34] Other versions of this instrument may have been light enough to carry around, as we see in an account that describes how a church harmonium was used to attract devotees visiting Harmandir Sahib: "As we do not possess a portable harmonium, we brought out the church harmonium, and took our stand not far from the city gate, through which most of the pilgrims pass on their way to and from the golden temple. The music soon attracted large crowds."[35] One can only imagine the striking timbral contrasts between *kirtan* taking place on string instruments at Harmandir Sahib and hymns and psalms being sung in its vicinity on the church harmonium.

Descriptions of imported European instruments as "very respectable," as seen in a letter by Lady Muir's son in response to a service at a "Native Christian Village Church," reveal the powerful ways in which missionary work impinged on local musical values. The pursuit of respectability was likely appealing to hereditary musicians (known as *mirasi*) who otherwise felt tied to subordinate social positions.[36] The case of *sarangi* players is the most obvious example that comes to mind, given their role as accompanists for dancers and singers whose position as accomplished courtesans (so-called nautch girls) was often cast in a negative light in colonial accounts. British India vilified Indian dance in the late nineteenth century. In comparison their religious music was perceived as "having a refining and Christianizing influence" upon rural Indian society.[37]

Missionary workers thought carefully about the efficacy of their pedagogical methods, given that "native Christians hear the indigenous music day and night, and their minds become accustomed to its peculiar accent, cadence and rhythm, so that they are unable, for the time being, to displace the beautiful melodic rhythm of their everyday life by foreign rhythm and melody." They realized the process of conversion cannot be hurried: "Gradually the native Christian community is assimilated to European models and largely loses touch with the best models and methods of its native land."[38] Missionaries were thus mindful about how to transform musical taste. Some found it useful to adapt hymns into the form of work songs: "The girls in the Bareilly orphanage, after the Oriental custom, sit on the floor and grind their grain, and, as they turn the mill, keep time by singing some Christian hymn."[39] Missionary women often intertwined musical worship with daily work, as seen in the numerous letters and advertisements requesting help with procuring new or secondhand harmoniums and sewing machines, two prominent products of the Industrial Revolution that brought about standardization and efficiency, and both chiefly operated by women.[40]

Euro-North American primary sources suggest it was mainly women who played and taught this instrument. A "parlor" harmonium was often placed alongside the piano in public spaces and in living rooms constructed along Victorian lines, where these instruments continued to augment the "genteel performance" of an idealized femininity, as observed by Dianne Lawrence and Dennis Waring.[41] Missionary women taught the harmonium to children (chiefly girls) within the context of their church or in schools that were dedicated to this purpose, as seen with the establishment of the Multan Harmonium School.[42] As early as 1873 we read that "one of the school girls played the harmonium correctly and well."[43] Missionary publications of the 1880s speak to how the instrument is played

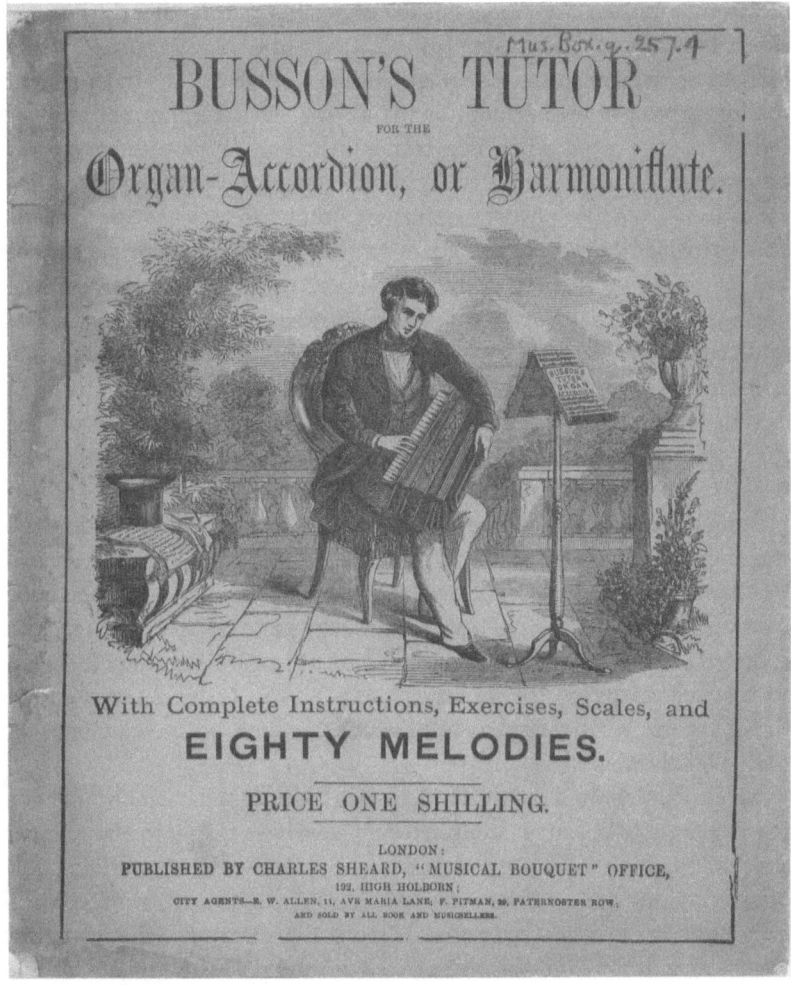

FIGURE 2.2 Tutor for Harmoniflûte (circa 1855).

standing up by young girls, presumably alluding to a table harmonium. Table or lap harmoniums were being made in the United States in the 1830s and in France by the middle of the nineteenth century by Maurice Kasriel and, in the form of the *Harmoniflûte*, by Constant Busson (see **fig. 2.2**). These instruments were likely precursors for the box harmonium that facilitated what Ashok Ranade calls "a baithak [sitting on the floor] version" and whose invention is often ascribed to Bengali instrument maker Dwarkanath Ghose and the manufacturer Harold & Co.[44]

Indeed, this claim has gained considerable momentum in the context of the current ban. Supporters of the instrument argue that the harmonium as we know it has been fully "indigenized" and is quite distinct from its colonial ancestor. As evidence, they point to Ghose's independent manufacturing of the harmonium in Calcutta and his technical improvements (adding stops to produce drones and the ability to alter pitches to accommodate *shruti* [microtones] in different *rāg*). While the particular innovations by Ghose and other Indian manufacturers made considerable strides toward adapting the instrument for use across various genres of Indian music, the claim that Ghose invented the "sitting" version of the harmonium needs to be contextualized. European makers such as Kasriel and Busson were already making small, hand-pumped harmoniums by the middle of the nineteenth century, which could be played sitting on a chair (as shown in **fig. 2.2**).[45] Ghose would likely have been aware of these models, and it should be remembered that he only produced his first hand-operated harmonium in 1887.[46] Certainly, the *baithak* style of playing the harmonium seems to have been in place by the end of the nineteenth century. An account from 1880 describing a Christian service in Amritsar mentions a harmonium that was likely played on the floor by the girls who sat "in native fashion on the ground." Interestingly, the observation that a "native instrument (something like a guitar) is played to keep the voices in time, and the Baboo . . . beats on his drum to add to the effect" shows that the harmonium, at this time, coexisted alongside native instruments.[47]

What music would the first Indian musicians of the harmonium have played? At schools, young children would have been taught to play hymns, as well as British folk songs, marches, the British national anthem, and other patriotic songs. For example, upon Prince Albert's visit to Jaunpur, Uttar Pradesh, we hear of girls from Sigra Normal School singing while "accompanied by a harmonium, an Urdu version of the hymn, 'God Bless the Prince of Wales.'"[48] In a similar way, Indian women were also taught the harmonium by missionaries who worked in the *zenana* (women's residential quarters). Rosemary Seton gives an insight into the power of the harmonium for the purposes of conversion: "Indian women found Western forms exotic, or at least novel. Requests to be taught fancy [embroidery] work or to play the harmonium were frequently the first indications that a *zenana* might be open to Christian agency."[49]

Especially interesting is the process by which hymns were learned. Missionary accounts reveal that Indian Christians tended to translate hymns into local languages, such as Hindi, Urdu, and Punjabi, and sing them with European tunes or familiar melodies from (Indian) regional folk music or devotional songs.[50] For example, in an account from 1852, the writer observes that a hymn was sung following a baptism "by the congregation to the accompaniment of a harmonium, played by one of the members of the Mission: The chant was from the Hindustani hymnbook, possessing apparently but slight poetical merit, but well suited to the place, and well sung, showing that the natives of the country have a full appreciation of the system of European music."[51] Another primary account emphasizes that hymns were translated into local languages and familiar melodies and that these hymns were played on harmoniums during conversion ceremonies. With regard to a "new Christian" recruited in Batala, Punjab, we read in an 1882 article for a women's magazine that a missionary gave them "the unusual treat of hearing the harmonium" as they "sang together the very familiar bhajan [devotional song] which helped to convert Amba—'Jesus Christ has saved my soul.'"[52] In Jhandiala, Punjab, a missionary speaks of playing a newly received portable harmonium for "Mohammedans . . . we sang first a beautiful hymn on 'Victory to Christ' . . . and Urdu versions of our own well-known hymns, 'Lo, He comes!' and 'Let there be light.'"[53] A report from 1882 shows how the harmonium gained traction among communities of new converts in Lahore during the late nineteenth century:

> The young student who now plays the harmonium in the Church Missionary Society's Mission Church in Lahore was taught music by a lady. He in his turn taught his sister, and together they again taught all their younger brothers and sisters to sing, and recently when I was with a friend in Lahore, they were all collected together, and they gave us a little family concert. The father has again and again thanked me for helping his son to learn music, and he told me with delight how his children played and sang hymns to him in the evenings.[54]

By 1898 harmoniums were still not widely observed in Christian worship in some regions of Punjab (Lahore and Clarkabad). This account shows the writer moved to tears—not through emotion but by means of sonic assault, which brings into focus Belvadi's notion of rivalry, as Indian instruments actively rework the traditional timbral soundscape of the hymn:

> One of the features of our six mission services here was the "bhajan" (pronounced "budgeon") or native music. Only about a tenth part of the men and women could read. They had come from different parts of the Punjab, after they had professed Christianity by baptism, and had settled down either as landowners or workers, but they had no chance of learning, so

that a hymn could only be sung by the few. Consequently these simple choruses had been learnt, and sung to four native instruments. Don't ask me to explain how they were played or what was the musical result! Tears rolled down my cheeks at first, and I would gladly have run out into the vestry, but one soon got used to it."[55]

In a similar vein, an account from 1897 observes an informal gathering supervised by a "band of lay brethren" and speaks of Christian *bhajans* and *ghazals* that are accompanied by "the thrumming of a tambourine, or small drum, struck by the fingers, and sometimes by small brass cymbals, or even by a native violin or guitar."[56]

One particularly insightful source about Lahore describes the establishment of "*Sat Sangat Sabha*"—possibly appropriated from Sikh notions of *sat sangat* (true or blessed congregants)—conducted by missionary men for Indian men "after the native fashion." This account describes how they "all sit cross-legged on a carpet. The exercises consist of reading, prayer, short addresses, and *bhajans* and *ghazals*. These last are vernacular hymns set to popular native tunes, and sung to the accompaniment of a flute-harmonium or of a *sitar* and small native drums (kettle-drums)."[57] On the basis of the success of Emma Moore Scott's *The Hindustani Tune Book* (1889), a harmonized collection of transcribed Indian melodies, some missionaries professed a preference for harmonized hymns: "The bhajans sound so much smoother when played on a piano or organ, than when sung by a native choir to native accompaniment."[58]

On occasion we do read of missionaries admiring the transcription of hymns for native instruments, as seen in a rendition of the Psalms of David by a choir in Ludhiana: "The Psalms of David [were] translated into Indian poetic form and set to Indian tunes. The choir has a tobola, a small drum-shaped instrument, beaten with the fingers and hand, two tambourines, one castanet and a stringed instrument like a violin. With this band there was no need of the staid old Mason and Hamlin organ, which stood meekly by under its cover."[59] Rivalry, in this instance, seems to have resulted in the subjugation of the very instrument that had brought psalms and hymns to locals in the first place.

Here, both the texts and melodies of the psalms are reimagined, but it should be noted that some new Indian converts rejected this practice altogether: "Some years ago, when she [Mrs. M. M. McKelvey] was engaged in helping to gather unwritten Punjabee airs for a new book of songs, a blind old pastor poet, himself a convert from Mohammedanism, rejected one of the most attractive airs. 'Yes, it is beautiful to you,' he said, 'but not to me, because I remember the old vile words.'"[60] Frederick and

Margaret Stock suggest an opposing viewpoint with regard to efforts made in 1895 to prepare a Punjabi Psalter "set to local tunes" based on what they heard being played by hereditary musicians (*mirasi*): "Several missionaries gifted in music spent long hours in market places and cafes listening to current Indian tunes and writing them down." Despite the initial opposition of new converts to obtaining musical material in this way, they explained that "it was not long before the former words faded from memory."[61] A similar process is likely behind the adaptation of popular melodies from film and folk music to *kirtan*, a practice that has been the subject of considerable critique within Sikh circles.[62]

A MISSING LINK? MISSIONARY DEPENDENCE ON *MIRASI* AS AN ENTRYWAY TO SIKH *KIRTAN*

After examining the socioreligious contexts in which the harmonium was first played and heard by Indian communities, a question remains: How did this instrument, within a short space of time, come to coexist with and, in certain cases, replace instruments that had been played in India for hundreds of years? Certainly, this could not have happened without the assistance of *mirasi*, broadly defined as local hereditary musicians. Following Suhail Yusuf, Gibb Schreffler, and others, I understand *mirasi* as an umbrella term that refers to groups of hereditary professional musicians, often Muslim, whose lifestyles were tied to folk, popular, and devotional musical practices.[63] A missionary worker, Anne C. Wilson, observed, "Musicians were our neighbors wherever we went, as every village in the Punjab contains some of the Mirasi caste to which these men belong. For, as we now learnt the people of India are essentially a musical race. . . . Mirasis wander about the Punjab like the bards and minstrels of the middle ages."[64] Time and again, missionary sources state their work would have been more difficult, and not half as effective, had they not received the support of *mirasi* who helped spread the message of Christianity among local communities while preparing the stage for conversion.[65] The mood of Wilson's description is captured in a vivid painting (possibly by Kehar Singh) from 1875, *Two Wandering Jogis*, of a *sarangi* player (Allahditta, the Rawal) and his brother, who plays the *ektara* (Ghulam Ali). The *sarangi* and *ektara* are two instruments associated with *mirasi* (see **fig. 2.3**).[66] While it is unclear whether the painting's attributions (title, creator, and musicians' names) are correct, the figure of the *jogi* (both Hindu and Muslim) is not to be confused with the *mirasi* (Muslim) — the former having mostly chosen their path as

FIGURE 2.3 *Two Wandering Jogis*, Government Museum and Art Gallery, Chandigarh.

spiritual devotees, while the latter are born into their roles.⁶⁷ It is not clear whether Wilson was differentiating between the two in her description of bards and minstrels in Punjab.⁶⁸

Mirasi who were employed to play Sikh *kirtan* might also have performed other kinds of music outside of sacred spaces, just as certain folk ensembles, known as *dhaadhi jatha*, were also welcome within Sikh

Gurudware. Awareness of this fluidity broadens the association of *mirasi* beyond their socially stigmatized accompaniment of "dancing girls" in courtly and public spaces and works toward demonstrating the vital role played by this knowledgeable community across a wide range of musical practices.[69]

The *mirasi* community was categorized within British missionary accounts as low caste. Reverend J. Welland states, "It should be remembered that in India music belongs to the lowest of the low."[70] Nonetheless, these professional, skilled musicians were indispensable to Indian society, given their varying roles as genealogists, historians, entertainers, markers of life-cycle events such as births and weddings, and mediators of devotional worship. Their perceived low socioeconomic standing and highly valued professional skills meant that *mirasi* were helpful to missionaries in two ways: as facilitators of a two-way transfer of musical knowledge (from missionaries to locals and vice versa) and as potential converts. For example, an American source from 1890 describes the conversion of a family of *mirasi* ("miyasi") and their essential role in missionary work: "The *Miyasi* is a singer by hereditary profession. Among the four is a bright lad of fourteen, who plays the *sarangi*, or fiddle, beautifully. In a few days he learned to sing and play two of our most popular Bhajans. He is of great use to us in our work."[71] Missionaries seemed unequipped to address the vital sociocultural function of *mirasi*, many of whom continued to participate in Hindu musical practices for their income after conversion: "One section of these Christian village servants, and that the larger, obtain their perquisites for the performance of service to idolatry—they continue to play musical instruments in processions and before the idols, and share in other heathen rites as before they were Christians. They have no industry by the means of which they can support themselves apart from these duties."[72]

My interest in the role of *mirasi* as possible carriers of the harmonium into Sikh sacred spaces takes into consideration the porous spaces surrounding the public *bazaar*, a critical meeting ground where the first missionaries gathered to give their sermons and where musicians themselves would have been present to earn their keep.[73] Raj Bahadur Sharma reminds us about the frequency of "bazar preachings" as a method of reaching potential converts, and missionary literature documents how *mirasi* introduced Christian music to local residents through transcription on local instruments such as the *chikara, sarangi, dutara, dholak*, and others.[74] The process was threefold: "Native musicians" would help the missionaries with their musical endeavors; their close contact would also offer an opportunity for proselytization and conversion, after which new converts would themselves become musical leaders within the church.[75] Help would take a variety of forms:

> In more than one part of the great Indian mission field, native poets have arisen, who have composed Christian hymns in the meters of Hindu prosody and have adapted them to such Hindu melodies as seemed best fitted for the purpose. In many churches of Indian Christians these hymns and tunes are now used with most excellent effect. Preachers and street evangelists in the bazars and villages find many of these native tunes with Christian words most useful in gaining the ear of the people for the proclamation of Christian truth. This conversation of Indian poetry and song to the uses of Indian Christianity was a decided step of progress in the work of naturalizing Christianity.[76]

Mirasi would have had the opportunity to use their musical skills for the purpose of adapting the language and music of hymns as a critical first step. Their role as composers and arrangers was also significant. Christopher Harding observes that the original composition of *bhajan* contributed to "a canon of rural Christian devotional works."[77] Some missions organized these compositions into compiled collections.

We see similar efforts in the case of Mary Rachel Martin. She secured

> an elderly Punjabi musician and hour after hour for months she listened while he played on his sitar—seven-stringed instrument—and she picked out the notes and put them in place so they could be sung by Westerners. The Indians knew the tunes. In this tremendous labor of love Miss Martin was ably assisted by Henrietta Cowden, Mrs. William Mc-Kelvey, and her sister, Josephine Martin. Soon, instead of objectionable songs, indecent love songs, the Psalms were taking their place and calling on all peoples to praise God.[78]

Mention of a seven-stringed *sitar*, a predecessor of the lavishly strung version with sympathetic strings played today, supports Peter Manuel's hunch that the *sitar* was used "as an essentially folk-based accompaniment instrument . . . prior to the spread of the harmonium."[79] Martin's musical exercise was undertaken after a recent convert, Imam-ud-Din Shahbaz, had "reduced the Psalms in Urdu into metric version to be sung to Western music. This was fairly satisfactory for those who were Western trained, but it was not until he translated them into Punjabi to be sung to the soulful Punjabi, or oriental, music that they captured the hearts of all the people of North India." Martin observed that, through

FIGURE 2.4 A group of minstrels at Peshawar. Ashiqullah (*left*) is seen with the *dilruba*. His brother Alladiya (*right*) plays the *sitar*. From "A Mohammedan Minstrel," *Church Missionary Gleaner* (December 1890): 185.

these kinds of musical collaborations, "city streets and village lanes began reverberating praises to God. Christian and non-Christian were singing the sweet Psalms of the Shepherd King."[80]

An important primary source that illuminates how the harmonium may have traveled into Sikh places of worship is the account of Ashiqullah, described as "a Mohammedan Minstrel," in a letter by Reverend Worthington Jukes in 1890 (see **fig. 2.4**). He explains that Ashiqullah was actively employed by Sikhs:

> Sikhs who are fond of music ... always have some [music] at their devotional services every morning if they can secure the services of a capable man. Ashiqullah, with his nephew Alladiya (Eng., Theodore), were accordingly invited to help the Sikhs at their matutinal devotions, the former with his stringed instrument called *dilruba* (literally, heart-ravishing), a kind of guitar; and the latter with another stringed instrument called *sitar*, played with a plectrum. Ashiqullah certainly has the knack of captivating his audience, for I have never heard any Native play and sing with so much enthusiasm and clear articulation, with so much soul thrown into

his spiritual songs, chiefly of his own composition, in praise of God, and condemnatory of religious hypocrisy, and of the pleasures of the world."⁸¹

Ashiqullah, dressed in white and seen with the *dilruba* in **figure 2.4**, was brought to the attention of Jukes by an Indian Christian, and soon Ashiqullah's musical services were enlisted in the singing of Christian hymns. It was only a matter of time before he, and members of his family, including the *sitar* player Alladiya, converted to Christianity and became one of the mission's most valuable assets: "As soon as he began to play a few chords and sing heart-stirring strains, the remainder used to sit quietly and listen with the greatest interest, as he begged them to give their hearts to Christ. In more than one place the people were so impressed with his singing, that tears came into many eyes, and, since then, a work of grace has gone on in their hearts as well."⁸²

Interestingly, the adaptation of Ashiqullah's musical skills for the purposes of evangelizing are seen in another article about the challenges of bazaar preaching, given the tendency to be shut down by locals and the difficulties of engaging natives: "Music is one of our helps in the Anjaman; there is a harmonium which my wife sometimes plays, and we have very well-known hymns. Then we have our musical evangelist, Ashiq Ullah, who plays the sitar and sings Gospel bhajans. It is real Gospel-singing, and many who would not listen to preaching listen to him as he gives the Message in the music and poetry of his country."⁸³ The missionaries adapted the musical structure of hymns to the *asthayi/ antara* (refrain/verse) alternation characteristic of *bhajan* and *kirtan*, as described during a gathering in Amritsar in 1894:

> Two or three long *bhajans* (Native hymns) were sung, Miss Wauton accompanying on a concertina. These strange musical compositions seemed to "begin at both ends and leave off in the middle." If my readers will just sing a verse of the familiar tune St. Ann, and when they get to the end of it go back to the *first line* and *sing half of it* and then stop abruptly, they will get an imperfect idea of what the tune of a Punjabi *bhajan* is like.⁸⁴

Even as missionaries observed formal differences between hymns and *bhajans*, they understood the instructive value of adapting to local musical tastes: "Often we commence with a hymn, a native *bhajan* as they call it, very much longer than our English hymns are. Once or twice we have known it to take from ten to fifteen minutes to sing one, but the people do not tire in the least. These *bhajans* are a great help in the service, as the heathen around are very fond of hearing them."⁸⁵ Whereas

Sikhs describe their devotional music as *kirtan* because of the emphasis on *kirat*, the act of praising divinity, missionary literature tends to use the terms *kirtan* and *bhajan* as though they are interchangeable.[86]

Focusing now on instrumentation, we see how one writer described a combination of European (concertina) and Indian instruments as "marvellously plaintive"; they commented, "Strange was the blending of native instruments and voices."[87] In another missionary narrative that describes the coexistence of free-reed instruments related to the harmonium, such as the concertina, and local string instruments, we hear mention of the *taus* (a Persian term that captures this instrument's graceful peacock appearance).[88] One account recalls "the voice of the dear old Indian preacher minstrel who had just sung for us on his long Indian guitar, decked with peacock feathers, of the Saviour whose salvation is free and whose messengers are offering it with an ever larger freedom to India."[89] The *taus* was an instrument of the Sikh court, and it is worth considering whether this musician, like Ashiqullah, also used his instrument in Sikh devotion.

Another description emphasizes a similar combination of the harmonium and local instruments:

> At the morning service English tunes are used to the Hindustani hymns, but in the afternoon it is native music and Punjabi bhajans. A bhajan is a cross between a cathedral anthem in its many repetitions and a negro minstrel ditty in its quaint music. I can see the church now when I close my eyes. In front sit the musicians. The instruments are a sort of mandoline with a very long handle and many pegs, an accordion, and a pair of drums.[90]

While the unfamiliar timbres, tuning, and playing style of the harmonium were likely greeted with curiosity by local musicians, these accounts are important in that they show how the instrument was initially made to adapt—to invoke the concept of rivalry—alongside local instruments, even as it went on to gradually displace some of them.

Certainly, the 1890s are a critical juncture. While certain parts of Punjab saw the gradual marriage of the harmonium to local instruments, *kirtan* at Harmandir Sahib was still performed on string instruments, as noted by Samuel A. Mutchmore, whose observation offers a deliberate negative slant: "As the journey was first made around the Lake of Immortality on its beautiful pavement surrounded by arcaded buildings, with balconies overlooking, extending three and four stories, we hear a strange hum-drum kind of music from orchestras of stringed instruments, no doubt a part of the complicated temple performances." He continues, "The religious service consisted of shrill music made by a group of musicians squatting upon the floor, who accompanied their atrocious vocal discords with the confusion of inharmonious stringed instruments."[91] The emphasis on *tanti sāz* was certainly in place a decade prior, during the 1880s, as we see in Anthony George Shiell's comments on his visit to Harmandir Sahib: "An Akalee [Sikh] sang and strummed upon a banjo, in all but melody like a Christy minstrel."[92]

The turning point seems to hinge on the early twentieth century. In 1901 Irene Petrie heard "quaint-looking drums and fiddles" during her visit, but only a few years later, a historical Sikh account in English from 1903 by Sardar Sundar Singh Ramgarhia mentions the use of a "diminutive *harmonium*: the only wind instrument employed" at Harmandir Sahib. Emphasis on its small size implies its subservience to prevailing instruments played by Muslim *rabābi* (*rabab*, *dutara*, and *chautara*) and Sikh *ragi* (*saranda*, *taus*, *sitar*, *tambura*, and *tabla*), as noted by Ramgarhia.[93] Missionary literature also reveals that the harmonium had been taken up by Sikh *ragi* by 1905:

> The Sodhis of Anandpur style themselves princes, the descendants of Gobind Singh. . . . Basant Singh, a man prominent among them, never loses an opportunity to help the writer in preaching, whenever he visits Anandpur with his band of workers. He takes his harmonium and other musical instruments to the most conspicuous place in the city. He then plays the harmonium and asks his companions to help him with their instruments. Our blind music and singer, Narain Singh, and our other workers join them.[94]

We see that Sikh musicians, like Muslim musicians, were in contact with missionaries at Anandpur and, on the basis of this practice, it is possible that Sikh musicians aided missionaries at other centers as well, including Amritsar, Tarn Taran, Ludhiana, and Jallandar. These interactions likely facilitated religious conversion in some instances, but they also provided opportunities for *ragi* to hear and play the harmonium while exercising their skills in musical transcription, arrangement, and original composition, as we have seen with Ashiqullah and other professional musicians that missionaries met.[95] Meanwhile, Sikh oral history recalls the *rababi* Bhai Wadhava, who accompanied the eminent *rababi* Bhai Atra at Harmandir Sahib during the late nineteenth and early twentieth centuries, as being the first to use the harmonium in Sikh *kirtan*.[96]

Certainly, by 1926 the harmonium had staked out a presence in the inner sanctum of Harmandir Sahib. British writer Aldous Huxley recounts, "Three magnificent old men were chanting ecstatically to the accompaniment of a small portable harmonium, which was being played with one finger by a fourth, yet more superbly patriarchal."[97] This vivid description highlights the size of a typical *kirtan jatha* (ensemble) of three musicians (including the percussionist), which remains the norm today, while the emphasis on a "one-finger" technique implies that Sikh *ragi* were still figuring out how to navigate this keyboard instrument. Even though Indian and British newspapers and magazines ran advertisements for harmonium tutors (pedagogical books) available for purchase among the British and Indian elite, the harmonium was likely being taught through oral means among local Sikh and Muslim musicians at the time. As reflected in the virtuosic harmonium playing of early recordings, it is clear that *kirtaniye* quickly developed a nuanced system of fingering. Indeed, they probably had to, in keeping with the agility of their vocal improvisation. After the partition, given the emigration of many Muslim *rababi* to Pakistan, harmonium tutors filled a musical void and became more geared toward the Indian lay person rather than Western European upper classes, for whom this instrument used to be a status symbol and a means of entertainment (there are now countless paper and digital resources for teaching *kirtan* on the harmonium, including free YouTube courses).

Even though the harmonium had entered Sikh *kirtan* by the 1920s, there was some resistance within the community. *The "Spokesman" Weekly*, a newspaper operating in New Delhi and Jallandar, urges in an article from 1920, "*Kirtan* in Sikh Gurdwaras must be vitalized. Bhai Sahib Randhir Singh's Jathas should serve as an example. Professional ragis cannot give us much inspiring performances. The Sangat must take up this sacred work. And the Rabab and Sitar must replace the harmonium." Clearly, the harmonium, and a rudimentary mastery of this instrument by ragi, was already posing a threat to the practice of *tanti sāz*, as was amplifying technology: "Gurbani must be clear and the accompanying music sweet and soothing, without the ear-splitting blare of loudspeakers."[98] As will be discussed in chapters 5 and 6, this last point remains relevant today.

Additional resistance toward the harmonium came from outside the Sikh community for reasons that had to do with political strategy. A missionary account from 1921 suggested that "for musical accompaniment Indian instruments may displace the harmonium" to manage waves of rising nationalism across the country in the wake of the Jallianwalan Bagh massacre in Amritsar in 1919, a premeditated killing of hundreds of civilians led by the British army. Maybe it was already too late to advocate for a turnaround: American missionaries had begun to describe the harmonium as an "Indian" instrument, along with the *sitar*, as early as 1922.[99]

Given the turmoil surrounding the current ban, it is important to reflect broadly on the ramifications of the missionary literature presented here. Against renewed attempts to cast out the so-called colonial harmonium, missionary sources provide valuable historical context for understanding how the harmonium entered the domain of Sikh *kirtan*. I also emphasize that its impact on the decline of string instruments in terms of their players and manufacturing did not lead to extinction. In their dedication to string instruments, stalwarts such as Bhai Makhan Singh (who reportedly never used the harmonium), Bhai Sham Singh, Bhai Sunder Singh Atta Mundi, and many more *ragi* kept the fire burning such that the resurgence of *tanti sāz*, now fueled by young *kirtaniye* keen to revive their musical heritage, can continue.[100] Certainly, the harmonium led to a decline in the use of string instruments. But this hand-pumped reed organ also contributed to the expansion of India's orchestra, an entity that is used to assimilating newcomers in the spirit of Belvadi's rivalry, as witnessed centuries earlier with several instruments, including the Persian *rabab*.

For the purposes of tracing the journeys of the harmonium within Punjab, missionary accounts become less useful after the first decade of the twentieth century, a moment that coincides with a colonial turn toward making recordings. In steering our attention toward recorded sound for the remainder of this chapter, I briefly consider the earliest Sikh recordings that were made by the Gramophone Company.[101] Michael Kinnear documents several legendary practitioners of Sikh *kirtan*: Bhai Mehroo, Bhai Uttam Singh Hakim, Bhai Roora, Bhai Moti, Bhai Mool Singh, Bhai Hira Singh, Sant Gulab Singh, and Bhai Sain Ditta are among those who recorded in a wide range of *rāg*. Many recordings are not available for consultation, although a handful belonging to private collectors has been digitized and made available. Notably, we have some recordings by Bhai Uttam Singh Hakim and Bhai Sain Ditta.[102] The latter was a renowned vocalist and teacher, who taught several respected *kirtaniye* at the Central Khalsa Orphanage (*Yatimkhana*) from 1914 to 1932. Despite their poor quality, these recordings have value: We can grasp the *tāl*, the overall shape of the melody, and its *alankar* (ornamentation), as well as aspects of musical structure, pronunciation, and presentation of *rāg*. The limitations of early recording technology mean that the tempo that emerges is likely faster than the original tempo, while constraints of timing made it impossible to capture lengthy improvisation. Gerry Farrell reminds us that the first discs offered a maximum duration of two to three minutes.[103] This is especially lamentable in the case of Bhai Ditta, whose introductory improvisation (*dandaut/manglacharan*) is renowned in oral history. Bhai Ditta is also remembered as a virtuoso of the harmonium, and this is evident in recordings where it is used as a drone and as doubling support for his voice.

How are we to interpret the observation that the earliest recordings of Sikh *kirtan* by Bhai Ditta and Bhai Hakim feature the harmonium? Missionary literature reveals the harmonium had emerged as a focal accompanying instrument by the turn of the twentieth century. However, there is insufficient historical data in print and in sound to conclude whether other accompanying instruments, such as *sarangi* and *dilruba*, had been eliminated or whether these *tanti sāz* were becoming increasingly subservient to the harmonium, resulting in a tiered organization.

Beyond harmonium tutors, which provide valuable insights into the history of the pedagogy of the harmonium, very little material has been published in English, Punjabi, and Hindi about the history and changing role of this instrument in *kirtan*. Yousuf Saeed's research in Urdu musicology suggests that postpartition publications by musicians who emigrated to Pakistan might be an untapped source for learning about the harmonium.[104] It is with this lacuna in mind that I now use specific case studies to analyze the harmonium's role in Sikh *kirtan*, keeping Belvadi's concept of rivalry close to show how *kirtaniye* saw in the harmonium an opportunity to cultivate a greater degree of expressive control over their accompaniment and an exemplary vocal style. It should be remembered that *kirtaniye* were not only soloists in the traditional sense; they were also part of a *jatha* (ensemble) and expected to demonstrate vocal fluency and accompanying skill during one and the same moment (much as we see in the parallel genres of *qawwali* and *ghazal*). Returning to the ban, I will briefly summarize key points of the debate as preparation for grasping the nuances of how the harmonium is played in *kirtan*.

THE ISSUES AT STAKE

Wide-ranging coverage of the proposed ban in the Punjabi and Indian press, and on social media platforms, has seen three types of responses. Some who have long rejected the harmonium, such as the esteemed musical representative of the Namdhari tradition, Bhai Balwant Singh, and practitioner-artisan-scholar Bhai Baldeep Singh, are keen for this ban to take effect.[105] Those who want to dispense with the harmonium are particularly critical of its limitations with regard to pitch. Proponents consider equal temperament detrimental for two interrelated reasons. First, because *rāg* are characterized by microtonal movement, they cannot be played well (if at all) on the harmonium.[106] Second, a constrained pitch palette seems to have encouraged certain *kirtaniye* to incorporate melodies better suited to equal temperament from popular and folk idioms. Those who wish to banish the harmonium argue that it has displaced traditional instruments and pushed into oblivion the precious repertoire that those instruments carried: specific melodies, turns of phrase, and, especially important, ornamentation, which relies heavily on nuances of *shruti* for its expressive effect.

At the other end of the spectrum is the impassioned response of hundreds of *ragi* who rely on *kirtan* for their livelihoods. They have embraced the relatively inexpensive and widely available harmonium because it can be learned quickly without a teacher by using harmonium tutors or (more recently) online tutorials. The prospect of spending several years mastering a string instrument, coupled with the challenges of finding a dedicated teacher and the costs of purchasing and maintaining an instrument, has proven to be worrisome for those who earn a living through performing and teaching *kirtan*, a profession that often requires travel and hence a robust instrument. For amateurs, too, who may not have access to training, the ban is unsettling because it limits the extent to which they can engage in *kirtan* as part of their devotional practice, an activity that is given great importance in *SGGS*. Thus the harmonium appeals to people across the board. The instrument is pretuned and easily withstands the challenges of extreme temperatures and changes of climate. It can provide both a drone and a simultaneous doubling for the voice, as well as adequate melodic support for communal singing, which is essential to the practice of *kirtan*. Finally, the harmonium offers complete independence: *Kirtaniye* control the volume of their instrument while they sing, and they can also accompany themselves. There is no need for any other accompanist.

Bhai Harjinder Singh (Srinagar Wale), who is a practitioner of *nirol kirtan* (a lyrical, call-and-response-based style that privileges the divine word over the use of *nirdharit rāg*), has emerged as a spokesperson for professional *ragi*.[107] A highly respected *hazuri ragi* (a designation that indicates his elevated status as someone who has performed at Harmandir Sahib), Bhai Harjinder Singh has always played *kirtan* on the harmonium, and his argument for retaining this instrument despite its colonial past hinges on the idea of sonic purity. He describes the harmonium as the "instrument of beggars" (*bhikariyon da sāz*), a term he rescues from negative characterization. The phrase *bhikariyon da sāz* reveals historical awareness given that this instrument was first played by *mirasi*. It also shows cultural awareness because *kirtaniye* are taught to deliver *kirtan* as a form of supplication that is undertaken with the utmost humility. An absence of ego is associated with the idealized figure of the beggar in Sikh consciousness. Immediately after hearing about the ban, *ragi* implored Bhai Harjinder Singh to address his *sangat* (gathering of devotees) and to explain that, since *tanti sāz* are traditional instruments associated with the gurus, they should be known and respected. However, the harmonium has also been a part of the gurus' courts since the nineteenth century. Over time, Bhai Harjinder Singh explains, the impure (*apavitar*) harmonium has become pure (*pavitar*) through its use in *kirtan*, a point that he underscores by comparing it with another "foreign" instrument, the "Irani" (Persian) *rabab*.[108]

Along with Giani Harpreet Singh and other practitioners, Bhai Harjinder Singh views the musical practice of *Gurmat Sangeet* (which emphasizes playing *nirdharit rāg* on traditional instruments) as being distinct from the category of *Shastriya Sangeet* (referring to Hindustani classical music more broadly). He maintains that the choice of instrument is less important than attunement to *shabad* (sacred word), which remains foremost.[109] Like Bhagat Namdev, who is remembered as playing the simple one-stringed *ektara*, the *kirtaniya* must be drenched (*bhinna/bhijna*) in *Gurbani*, a sentiment that is known to Sikhs from their daily hearing of *Aasa ki vār*, whose opening stanzas capture this ecstatic state.

A third reaction travels the middle road. This position was articulated by Harjinder Singh Lallie in 2016, when he stated that the harmonium "is now a fully pledged Sikh instrument and is here to stay. It is a mainstay in the modern Sikh musical experience." At the same time he suggested that preference might be given to "traditional Indian instruments [that] provide a richer and more orthodox musical experience which better captures and presents the emotional sensitivities of the sabad."[110] Similarly, Bhai Harjinder Singh's suggestion to use *tanti sāz* in addition to the harmonium is what the governing body of *Gurudware* (the Shiromani Gurudwara Prabandhak Committee [SGPC]) has said it will implement. Although the revival of *tanti sāz* is necessary, the SGPC argues, these instruments will not altogether displace the harmonium, which will continue to be a part of *kirtan jatha* (for now).[111]

Instrument repairers and manufacturers, some of whom have been in this business for over fifty years, are also pleading for a hybrid solution because they don't want to lose their livelihoods and see the collapse of an industry that sources materials from various parts of India.[112] When

Sikh musicians turned to the harmonium in the early twentieth century, artisans, woodworkers, and carpenters invested considerable effort in engineering a type of instrument that was more suited to *kirtan* than the instruments brought into the country by missionaries. Craftsmen had to consider the specific timbres, textural balance, and tuning of *kirtan jatha* (ensembles). The robust wood industries of Punjab were easily able to expand to include harmonium workshops and manufacturing companies through the first decade of the twentieth century (such as Mohkam Singh and Sons, Gujranwala).[113] In the wake of the ban, it is likely that these artisans will need sufficient time and training to regain the lost craft of making historically informed string instruments.[114]

Another motivation for retaining the harmonium is due to its sustaining power. The size of the *sangat* in the Harmandir Sahib complex has increased substantially since its completion in 1601. The amplification of voices and instruments using an extensive network of microphones and speakers helps to disperse *kirtan* through the complex. The ability to sustain sound and control the volume of the harmonium through pumping the bellows, especially during interim moments when string instruments and *tabla* are being tuned, ensures the continuous presence of sacred music, which was important to Guru Ramdas. In a verse in *rāg Aasa*, he laments the lost opportunity to sing divine praise during the time taken to choose singers and tune instruments.[115]

The "hybrid" efforts that I outline here have been at the forefront of *kirtan* reform over the last decade or so. On any given day, *kirtan* at Harmandir Sahib incorporates a *jatha* comprising *tanti sāz* and the harmonium. By now, the *sangat* is used to seeing these kinds of ensembles, as well as *jatha* comprised entirely of *tanti sāz*. Thus, the shock value of Giani Harpreet Singh's statement has to do with his official, publicized commitment to a process that has been underway, slowly but certainly in plain sight. Virinder Kalra reminds us that the SGPC announced in 1999 that "there would be a gradual introduction of traditional stringed instruments at the *Harimandir* and phased withdrawal of the harmonium (which by 2013 had still not occurred)."[116] Since the proclamation of the ban, I notice that a "phased withdrawal" has indeed taken place at Harmandir Sahib, and central to this shift is pedagogical reform, which has been occurring both within India (notably in Amritsar through the Central Khalsa Orphanage and the Shaheed Sikh Missionary College) and, with equal verve, in diaspora over the last few decades. Recent reports by the SGPC mention that only one in five *jatha* is trained on string instruments.[117] This ratio is already better than what Coomaraswamy had observed at the turn of the twentieth century when he visited the

Gandharva Maha Vidyalaya in Lahore (a school established in 1901 by Maharashtrian music scholar and reformist Vishnu Digambar Paluskar): "fourteen boys learning the harmonium, and one the *vina.*" He sighed, "I cannot think how any college professing to teach Indian music can permit a harmonium to be heard within its doors."[118] Current goals, as stated by Dr. Alankar Singh (professor of vocal music at Punjabi University, Patiala), need to focus on altering this ratio in favor of string instruments rather than banning the harmonium altogether.[119]

In parallel with programs supported by the SGPC that prioritize training in *Gurbani Sangeet*, several institutions across the world emphasize historical continuity through the revival of *kirtan* in *rāg* on *tanti sāz*. Based in the United Kingdom, Raj Academy publicizes the relatively quick ability to learn and perform compositions on string instruments.[120] Similarly, in their efforts to expedite reform, the Delhi Sikh Gurudwara Management Committee has asked professional *ragi* to master a string instrument in just six months.[121] These kinds of aims speak to a huge shift in perspective with regard to approaches for teaching and learning: Although some students have the opportunity to study at a slower pace with an ustad/guru over several years in *Guru-Shishya Parampara* (the master-student tradition), teachers in India and the diaspora are responding in agile ways to students, both senior and junior, who want to learn about the musical practices of the Sikh gurus' *darbar* within a time frame that is amenable to their busy lives. Despite my own initial training on the harmonium as a child, my turn to the *dilruba* in recent years speaks directly to this pedagogical shift, as I see my classmates learning how to quickly get around this instrument while being encouraged to participate in weekly *diwan* (worship). This is no mean feat since performing *kirtan* involves both playing and singing, and the linguistic plurality of *SGGS* provides an additional challenge when it comes to putting text and music together.[122]

I resume the discussion of pedagogy in my closing section, but it is important to mention here another concern that lurks among these debates: that of female *kirtaniye* who are still not permitted to offer *kirtan* at Harmandir Sahib. Several critics of the ban have asked SGPC and the *Akal Takht* to prioritize this serious problem of discrimination rather than the issue of musical instruments.[123] No efforts have been made to remedy this inequity thus far.[124] I will pick this thread up again when considering the leading presence of women in pedagogical reforms that center *tanti sāz* and the revival of *Gurmat Sangeet*. The following section must first tackle an important question: How is the harmonium used in Sikh *kirtan*?

SHOWCASING THE HARMONIUM IN SIKH *KIRTAN*

The lesson of Bhai Satta and Bhai Balwand, and Guru Arjan's subsequent encouragement of all Sikhs to participate in *kirtan*, unintentionally paved the way for the harmonium to quickly establish itself in *kirtan* centuries later. Surinder Singh Bakhshi captures the outlook of many: "The harmonium liberated Kirtan. It is easy to learn. A novice learns to play and sing basic tunes with just a little training. In fact, that is the most common level of achievement in amateur players. However, it does take years of learning and practice to become proficient at it."[125] Aside from the troubling use of "liberated" to describe a Euro-American instrument, the sentiment that the harmonium allows amateurs to participate in *kirtan* almost on an equal footing with professionals is well taken, as is the observation that although one can learn to play the harmonium quickly, fluency takes time and training. Indeed, as musicians have begun to master the harmonium over time, whatever expectations the missionaries had for this instrument have long been surpassed both in terms of its construction and in terms of how it is played. Furthermore, harmonium playing in South Asia can no longer be understood as an undifferentiated musical practice. We see the emergence of *gharana*-like lineages, given the rise of the harmonium as a solo instrument, and variations in instrument design and performance technique.[126]

Given the strong assimilation of this instrument in *kirtan*, it is astonishing that Sikh musicians rarely feature on lists of notable harmonium players. The reason for this omission reveals a defining trait of Sikh devotional practice: Although *kirtan* is initiated in the realm of *kan ras* (aesthetic appreciation through the ears), its rendering facilitates auditory engagement in a peaceful realm of inner contemplation, *sookham ras*, as described by the Sikh intellectual Bhai Vir Singh.[127] Thus, while several *kirtaniye* are respected for their harmonium playing, they are rarely identified as virtuosos because that kind of demonstration is used sparingly within *kirtan* so that it doesn't detract from the *shabad* (sacred word). To be sure, recordings of *rababi* and *ragi* trained within the traditions of *Gurmat Sangeet* reveal an incredible musical prowess. While their improvisations ask to be listened to *as music*, their musical exuberance is subordinate to the spiritual import of the *shabad*.

Drawing on Belvadi's concept of rivalry and Stockhammer's notion of material entanglement, the following analysis of select recordings shows the distinctive use of the harmonium in *kirtan*, where it has two main functions: to provide support for the *kirtaniya* in the form of a drone, as well as doubling, echoing, or developing sung material in the form of improvisation; and to provide melodic support for the *sangat*. In this respect, Strangways's lament that the harmonium "has a unique power of making an unharmonized melody sound invincibly commonplace" points to another reason why this instrument became popular in *kirtan*: "Commonplace" is exactly what is required for a style of music that encourages participation.[128]

To briefly restate the cyclic approach to hearing *kirtan*, as discussed in chapter 1, a *sangat* is typically comprised of multifaceted and versatile listeners: *Kirtaniye* and devotees are bound together in their nonhierarchical and nonlinear experience of *kirtan*. The *sangat* is aware that *kirtan* facilitates an inner experience of divinity, a vibrational connection among its members, and a dispersal of resonant energy through social responsibility and service (*seva*). Devotees are attuned listeners whose auditory behaviors are complex. An appreciation of *kirtan* draws their attention to the *shabad*. The *shabad* embodies *kirtan* in the form of *rāg*, just as *kirtan* permeates the *shabad*. As this intertwined relationship between music and sacred word draws devotees toward inner contemplation, they also attune themselves to certain behavioral patterns: when to join in during the repetition of a *rahao/asthayi* (refrain) or *pada/antara* (verse) or when to stop singing while the *kirtaniya* improvises. The social dynamics of this learned behavior are imbibed from a young age, and interactions between *kirtaniye* and the *sangat* take place without conversation and in a state of meditative reflection and corporeal repose. While *kan ras* (aesthetic appreciation) is an important starting point, virtuosity should never detract from the goal of *kirat*—praising divinity. Certainly, there is no place in *kirtan* for applause as an indicator of personal appreciation.

Sikh *ragi* are trained to play the harmonium in a specific way, although there is undoubtedly overlap with other musical traditions (such as *ghazal*). I will focus on the following techniques: fingering, the use of a drone, playing chords and triads, and ornamentation. Beginning with fingering, given Huxley's comment about playing with one finger, we see a formalized approach to fingering in harmonium tutors (and in online tutorials) where the thumb connects pitches to facilitate movement between different sections of the register (*saptak*).[129] This is a standard method of fingering for keyboard instruments.

The recording I choose to demonstrate this technique is by a faculty member at the Kanya Maha Vidyalaya (Jallandar), Bibi Ashupreet Kaur, and her sisters: "*Mera Baid Guru Govinda*," *rāg Sorath* (**audio ex. 2.1**). The melodies of the *rahao* and *pada*, and the vocal improvisations, incorporate swift movement between pitches at different parts of the vocal register, while the harmonium provides close doubling to ensure sufficient support of pitch and volume—not that these vocalists require reinforcement, given their *buland* (robust) voices. In the first interlude, 00:57–01:02, the octave coupler has been enabled on the harmonium; this allows pitches to be doubled an octave above (as we hear here) or below. The result is a rich sonority whose volume is amplified by increasing the bellow power through faster pumping. In general one rarely hears large variations of dynamics within *rahao* and *pada*, but a surge in volume is often heard during musical interludes to prolong the *bhaav* (devotional mood).

My interpretation of the role of musical interludes in *kirtan* is quite different from that described by Ustad Vilayat Hussain. Bigamudre Chaitanya Deva recounts an instance:

> Once, in the forties I had gone to a concert of Ustad Vilayat Hussain in Pune and the redoubtable Ustad Ghulam Rasul was accompanying him on the harmonium. During the interval, some of us met Vilayat Hussain and I made bold to ask him: "Ustad, how do you tolerate this instrument?" Pat came the reply, "Are beta, *usko kon sunta hai!*" [Oh, my son, who listens to the harmonium?!]. For him it was more of a breather between improvisations.[130]

In *kirtan* interludes indeed give the singer a break. More importantly, though, interludes intensify the mood that has been created by *kirtaniye* as they repeat *asthayi* to embed the message of *Gurbani* deep within the listener. In *SGGS* the specific term *rahao* (pause, reflect) is placed directly after the *asthayi*, instructing devotees to reflect on the significance of the refrain. The interlude allows the music or *rāg* to shape the space of contemplation.

I now turn to the technique of playing against a drone, which is the only role the missionary Reverend Herbert A. Popley described as being fit for the harmonium: "If the small Indian harmonium is used at all, it should only be used for playing the tonic note and its fifth. No attempt should be made to try and fit harmony to Indian music, as this is quite foreign to the melodic structure of Indian music."[131] I address Popley's point about harmony below. Regarding drones, most *ragi* either use drone stops via knobs, which are pulled out at the front of the instrument, or they intermittently play the principal drone pitch and associated pitches, such as *ma*, *pa*, and *ni*, in between phrases. **Audio example 2.2** features a *dandaut/manglacharan* (invocation) by Bhai Shamsher Singh Zakhmi where the principal pitches (*sa* and *pa*) are heard as a drone ("*So Kat Jaane Peer Parayi*," *rāg Madhuvanti*). The *kirtaniya* was taught by Darshan Singh

Komal, who was a student of Bhai Ditta, so we might catch a glimpse of what Bhai Ditta's renowned *dandaut* was like. Bhai Zakhmi's expansive improvisation is offered in the spirit of supplication while demonstrating considerable skill and knowledge in terms of the development of *rāg*. Bhai Ditta's influence may also be apparent in Bhai Zakhmi's rendition of verses in *rāg* not used in *SGGS*: *Madhuvanti* does not appear and neither do *Kaushi Dhani* or *Kaushi Todi*, other *rāg* that Bhai Zakhmi sang in. As seen in early recordings made by Bhai Ditta, Bhai Hakim, and others, the practice of performing in *rāg* other than those designated in *Gurbani* may have been in place at the turn of the twentieth century. Indeed, Bhai Vir Singh's essay from 1906, "Ragi, Dhaadhi te Giani," laments this practice.[132]

The third technique I discuss is the use of chords to create harmony in two ways. First, through the accentuation of the drone, and its associated pitches and overtones, by producing chord clusters (closely spaced pitches played simultaneously). This effect is likely an Indian innovation that approximates the sound of a *tanpura* drone or a *swarmandal*. For example, Bhai Nirmal Singh Khalsa creates chord clusters at various moments in his *manglacharan* in *"Jog Baneya Tera Kirtan Gayee"* (**audio ex. 2.3**)—listen, in particular, at 00:30–00:40, 00:57–01:02, and so on. This technique is a common feature of *manglacharan* and can be heard across a range of recordings that feature the harmonium (either alone or in combination with *tanti sāz*). Clusters are perceived as immensely moving, given how they superimpose and yield pitches to the principal phrases of the *rāg*.

Second, chords can be used to punctuate a vocal phrase. It is possible that this technique was adapted from missionaries or from musicians who were in contact with missionaries since hymns were often harmonized. In keeping with this reasoning, Popley observed, "There is however a present tendency for the harmonium to be introduced and these beautiful melodies are often played on the harmonium, which spoils their beauty and robs them of their real Indian characteristics: This also leads to the use of some form of harmony for the Indian music which ill accords with the melodic character of the music."[133] Sikh *ragi* are judicious with regard to their use of chords. For example, Bhai Nirmal Singh Khalsa introduces triads in the first interlude after the presentation of the *rahao/asthayi* in *"Jog Baneya Tera Kirtan Gayee"* (*rāg Aasa*) (listen at 05:05–05:11). **Audio example 2.4** offers a more recent use of this practice by Bhai Gagandeep Singh (Sri Ganganagar Wale), in *"Har Kirtan Sunai Har Kirtan Gavai,"* where triads punctuate the phrase: The first triad is heard after "gavai" at 00:07 and then at several musical interludes (00:21, 00:26, 00:47, 00:50, and 00:56–00:58).

This observation points to a divide that emerged during the 1980s: Younger *ragi* who incorporate triads, as well as occasional instrumental interludes and vocal harmonization, tend to incorporate stylistic influences from musical traditions outside of *kirtan*. In contrast, senior *ragi* prefer to use the harmonium in two ways. First, to create a drone. Second, to double the melody to provide additional vocal support. Short musical interludes can be heard, but these often serve the function of introducing the melody of the following *pada* rather than of offering melodic variety and development. Two stalwarts of *Gurmat Sangeet*, Bhai Avtar Singh (1926-2006) and Bhai Gurcharan Singh (1915-2017) can be heard playing in this manner in *"Jagat Mein Jhooti Dekhi Preet"* (*rāg Devgandhari*, **audio ex. 2.5**). This way of playing also characterizes the *kirtan* of Bhai Harjinder Singh (Srinagar Wale), whose musical style focuses on conveying *nirol* (pure) *Gurbani*, as he describes it in his defense of the harmonium, and whose expressive lyricism can be heard in *"Prabh Dori Haath Tumare"* (**audio ex. 2.6**).

Another stalwart without whom any account of Sikh *kirtan* would be incomplete is Bibi Jaswant Kaur (1921-2010), who is among the few female *kirtaniye* of her generation to receive serious musical training.[134] Her contributions to *Gurmat Sangeet* are especially valued because she was one of the last surviving students of a notable *rababi*, Bhai Tabba. In *"Dhan Dhan O Ram Bin Bajai"* (*rāg Malligaura*, **audio ex. 2.7**), Bibi Jaswant Kaur uses the harmonium to provide a drone and to support her voice through doubling. The musical interludes are not extensive and thus do not offer an opportunity for the harmonium to emerge as soloistic.

The next audio example demonstrates another facet of the triad technique by Bhai Anantvir Singh, who has attained celebrity status as a practitioner of the *AKJ* style for his rendition of *"Madho Hum Aise Tu Aisaa"* (**audio ex. 2.8**).[135] *AKJ kirtan* is characterized, above all, by three features: an ecstatic delivery of a lyrical, simple melody; the participation of the *sangat*; and a strong percussion section. These work together to create a feeling of *bairaag/vairaag*, a sense of detachment from the material world coupled with an intensely emotional longing for union with the divine. Bhai Anantvir Singh's soaring voice needs no additional instrumental support, but he incorporates triads to produce a rich sonority for his large *sangat*, who carry the *shabad* with great feeling (at 00:09–00:10, 00:13–00:15, and 00:17–00:18, for example). Chords provide metric emphasis along with the *tabla* and *chhainay* (steel tongs overlaid with small cymbals) as soon as those instruments enter (at 00:44).

The final topic I address is ornamentation (*alankar/harkat*), which, along with tuning, is probably among the most contentious issues when it comes to demonstrating the value of the harmonium in Indian classical music in general and in Sikh *kirtan* in particular.[136] Deva speaks directly to the challenge of producing ornamentation on this instrument: "Gamakas such as *meend* (Glide), *andolana* (swing) cannot be played on it, at best one can get trills and flicks (*khatka, kan,* etc.) on it."[137] Even with the vast technical innovations that have taken place, it is still not possible to play *meend* (slide) or *andolan* (oscillation) on the harmonium, although *ragi* have tended to mask this deficiency by using their voices to create the desired effect. In the *manglacharan* for "*Ab Mohe Ram Apna Kar Janea*" (*rāg Malkauns*), Bhai Beant Singh Bijli can be heard creating a vocal *meend* at 00:05–00:06, 00:32–00:33, 00:46–00:47, and 01:47–01:50 (**audio ex. 2.9**). He combines *meend* with another type of ornamentation, *murki*, at 01:05–01:07 (also at 03:07–03:11 and 03:13–03:17). At best, these ornaments can be approximated on the harmonium, much like the *taan* (rapid rising and falling scales) that we hear throughout this *manglacharan* both on the harmonium and in the voice. Drawing on *khatka* and *murki* (similar to mordents in Western classical music), this particular *kirtan* is virtuosic, and a *ragi* even demonstrates aesthetic appreciation at 02:19 with "wah wah." The expressive effect of this *managalacharan* is conveyed through the wonderful *tabla* playing of the renowned Bhai Ajit Singh Mutlashi, who plays a slow tempo (*vilambit laya*) rhythmic pattern characteristic of *manglacharan*. The resonating timbre of his strokes (*bol*) suggests his technique of playing with open, flat palms, which is also used for playing *jori* (paired drums). A more recent example shows how vocal ornamentation requires the harmonium to take on a harmonic role where it plays chords or serves almost as a drone rather than closely doubling the voice (**audio ex. 2.10**). In this instance, Bhai Dilbagh Singh is vocally agile and does not need to rely on the harmonium for pitch support.[138]

When heard in relation to missionary accounts of the harmonium in Punjab and the recent ban, these examples illustrate the range of innovations developed by Sikh musicians over the last century or so. We see that it is challenging to play the harmonium well. *Kirtaniye* must master the effect of a *tanpura* through freely timed cluster chords while playing exactly in time with the voice (as heard with Bhai Nirmal Singh Khalsa). Musicians are required to play in a sustained manner that is rhythmically synchronized to their voices (as heard with Bibi Ashupreet Kaur and Bibi Jaswant Kaur) and in a way that can accommodate detached triads (as heard with Bhai Anantvir Singh) as well as fast *taan* and light *murki* (as heard with Bhai Beant Singh Bijli). The ideal *kirtaniye* offer their musical devotion on the harmonium in a manner that does not, primarily, invoke admiration but rather contemplation.

PEDAGOGICAL REFORM AND THE RISE OF FEMALE *KIRTANIYE*

There has been a strong surge in recent decades—notably among second- and third-generation diasporic Sikhs—to hear and play *kirtan* on *tanti sāz*. Efforts to re-create the music of the Sikh courts are riddled with challenges: The rise of harmonium manufacturing since the second decade of the twentieth century, coupled with the decline of instrument makers knowledgeable in the production of *tanti sāz*, remains a hurdle, given the rising demand for historically informed, well-made instruments. A related obstacle concerns finding teachers who are conversant with techniques for playing *tanti sāz* in *Gurmat Sangeet*.

The attempt to replace the harmonium with string instruments is not straightforward since this act involves many moving parts: Instrument manufacturers and traders, practitioners, pedagogues, scholars, students, and the *sangat* all need to be on board and synchronized in their efforts for this initiative to take root. Furthermore, the flip-flopping nature of the current debate has created considerable confusion among these entities, given that authorities sometimes seem committed to a phased ban and at other times appear less concerned. Questions remain: Is it possible for *kirtaniye* to discard the harmonium? Or will a hybrid model be in place until the various factions agree with one another—or possibly, even, for the long term? Looking back at radio programming, as reported in *The Indian Listener* in the years prior to the partition, we see frequent recitals on the *sarangi*, harmonium, and *tabla*, which indicate that soloists were not quite ready to let their string accompanists go but preferred them to share the stage with the harmonium, thereby creating a tiered system of accompanists.[139] Maybe the tables will be turned, and the harmonium will similarly drift toward becoming a support instrument for other support instruments, such as the *dilruba* or *rabab*, thereby taking on a subordinate role where its presence is felt as no more than a relic of its bygone glory days.

It is difficult to determine exactly when the tide began to turn away from the harmonium and toward *tanti sāz*. The eleventh-generation practitioner Bhai Avtar Singh reclaimed the *taus* and *dilruba* as his main instruments during the last years of his life, but change had been underway for several decades, notably in his own circles, as seen in the revivalist efforts of his descendant, Bhai Baldeep Singh, in the 1980s and early 1990s.

Meanwhile, the Namdhari Sikh community continued to craft and play *tanti sāz* through the late nineteenth and early twentieth centuries. Their reputation for consolidating a sacred musical heritage throughout this period of political turbulence has resulted in Namdhari spiritual leaders being viewed as custodians of *nirdharit rāg kirtan* and *Gurmat Sangeet*. Satguru Ram Singh (1816–72) promoted a classical (*shastriya*) style of singing as well as the offering of *Aasa ki vār* (early morning *kirtan*) using *tanti sāz*.[140] He also employed *dhaadhi* (folk musicians or ballad singers) and *ragi jatha* (ensembles of professionally trained *kirtaniye*) from his community across Punjab, as did his successor, Satguru Hari Singh (1819–1906).[141] Next in line, Satguru Partap Singh (1890–1959) was trained in Hindustani classical music by Mahant Gajja Singh (a master player of the *taus* and *dilruba* who had served under Maharaja Bhupinder Singh at his court in Patiala) and his disciple, Sant Mastan Singh.[142] Satguru Partap Singh established the Namdhari Mahavidyalaya in 1928, employing Bhai Harnam Singh (Chavinda Wale) to teach Hindustani classical music. The Namdhari community valued learning from eminent *rababi* (such as Bhai Taba and Bhai Naseer) at their *Gurudwara* (Bhaini Sahib, Ludhiana) until these *rababi* emigrated to Pakistan after the partition of Punjab in 1947.[143] Under the spiritual and musical leadership of Satguru Partap Singh and his son and successor Satguru Jagjit Singh (1920–2012), Bhaini Sahib grew its reputation as a center for *Gurmat Sangeet* in the twentieth century. A particularly important event in this regard was the establishment of the *Gurmat Sangeet Samelan* at Bhaini Sahib in 1933, soon after the arrival of the musicians of the *Talwandi gharana*, Ustad Udho Khan and his son Ustad Rahim Bakhsh, who taught at Bhaini Sahib. This music festival continues to attract eminent musicians at its annual gatherings to this day.

I focus on Namdhari musicians because they continue to be sought out as performers and teachers of *Gurmat Sangeet* and Hindustani classical music. In particular, their approach to teaching children provides a template for other institutions that have arisen in recent decades with a similar goal. These include programs attached to *Gurudware* in India, such as the Gurmat Sangeet Academy (Anandpur Sahib) and Akal Academy (Baru Sahib), as well as various others in the Sikh diaspora. They also include programs linked with Indian universities and colleges, including Punjabi University (Patiala), Guru Nanak Dev University (Amritsar), and Gurmat Gian Missionary College (Ludhiana). Also significant are independent music conservatories, such as Bhai Baldeep Singh's Anād Foundation and others in the diaspora, including some that partner with Punjabi University (Patiala), such as Sikh Garden State (New Jersey) and the Sikh Centre of the Gulf Coast Area (Houston). Stand-alone programs also serve a thriving community of *kirtaniye*—Tanti Saaj Sri Gurmat Academy (California), Gurmat Sangeet Academy and Raj Academy (United

Kingdom), and Guru Nanak Institute of Global Studies (Canada) are just a handful of examples.

Curricula, workshops, seminars, camps, and online tutorials are frequently organized by institutions and individual practitioners to provide education on playing *nirdharit kirtan* on *tanti sāz*. Typically, these are open to everyone, regardless of age and ability, and it is often the case that women and girls are eager to participate. A particularly effective push has come from the SGPC-supported reality TV show *Gavo Sachi Baani*, which aired on PTC Punjab Gold in 2016 and whose evolution speaks to major issues facing the future of *kirtan*: offering *Gurbani* in *nirdharit rāg*, increasing the use of *tanti sāz*, and growing the presence of women as contestants and judges. At present this show offers auditions to contestants who come from various parts of Punjab, but there are plans to open its doors to the wider diasporic *sangat*.

Speaking as part of the diasporic community, I see how increasing interest in learning string instruments has pushed practitioners toward facilitating the purchase of instruments and providing instruction that encourages participation across the *sangat*. Students often find themselves playing in front of the *sangat* early on in their education, and because it is frowned upon to critique *kirtan*, given its associations with divine praise, these types of opportunities are generally supportive and confidence building. What makes the process of performing less daunting is, in my experience, that *kirtan* is not a primarily soloistic endeavor, as discussed above. Of course, this is not to say that there are no virtuosos.

Although the numbers are still small, there are currently several *kirtaniye* who, by performing only on *tanti sāz*, indicate that it is possible to eliminate the harmonium. Bhai Siripal Singh plays *taus/dilruba*, while his companion, Bhai Mahaveer Singh, plays the (Afghani) *rabab* (as opposed to another type of *rabab* used in *kirtan* called *dhrupadi* or *Nanakshahi*, discussed in chapter 4). Another *jatha*, headed by Bhai Navjodh Singh, comprises the *saranda*, *rabab*, and *dilruba*. Administrative leaders are also using commemorative events to raise awareness of how the sonic and visual profile of *kirtan* is changing. For example, an event commemorating the 550th birth anniversary of Guru Nanak at Sultanpur Lodhi in 2019 was headlined as featuring "550 *rababi*" who traveled from *Gurudwara* Rababsar in Bharoana village (the hometown of Bhai Firanda, who made Bhai Mardana's *rabab* at the request of Guru Nanak) to *Gurudwara* Ber Sahib in Sultanpur Lodhi, where they performed *kirtan* using only *tanti sāz* (see fig. 2.5).[144] Similarly, *tanti sāz* featured prominently in a performance by hundreds of young *kirtaniye* at the four hundredth birth anniversary of Guru Tegh Bahadur in 2021 at Red Fort in Delhi, close to where he was beheaded by order of Emperor

FIGURE 2.5 550 *Rababi* commemorating the 550th birth anniversary of Guru Nanak at Sultanpur Lodhi in 2019.

Aurangzeb in 1675. Some harmoniums were played by children, but they were not as amplified as the strings.[145]

Today, many young *kirtaniye* are involved in learning *Gurmat Sangeet* on new instruments whose historical predecessors were played by the Sikh gurus. These cultural events serve an important role in shaping the musical tastes of the *sangat* and in orienting a global Sikh consciousness around issues of heritage and historical continuity. As instrument manufacturing works in lockstep with pedagogical efforts to prioritize string instruments, it is to be seen whether the harmonium will disappear or whether it will retain a pedagogical role as a first instrument for children who are learning *kirtan* and don't have access to small *tanti sāz*. The harmonium is also useful for adults who want to learn *kirtan* later in life and whose physical limitations prevent them from playing *tanti sāz* in a low seated position.

As I look at these videos and images, I see the instruments and their players, but I also notice many girls and women who are active participants in revivalist efforts. Why, then, aren't more women visible at the professional level? Even though I tackle this question in greater depth in my final chapter, this seems like an opportune moment to argue that it is essential for girls and women to find supportive environments to deepen their training and to receive opportunities for teaching and mentoring. The relatively large number of girls and young women who compete on *Gavo Sachi Baani* indicates a strong desire to learn and perform. As they progress, these *kirtaniye* should be encouraged to take on positions of musical and spiritual leadership.

The elephant in the room is why women are still banned from offering *kirtan* at Harmandir Sahib.¹⁴⁶ Women have been excluded on various grounds, including an alleged lack of musical technique, knowledge of *rāg*, and skill in playing *tanti sāz*. These hurdles have been crossed, as seen in the accomplishments of contestants on *Gavo Sachi Baani*, the *kirtaniye* of Bhaini Sahib, and many other women who perform using the harmonium or *tanti sāz* at *Adutti Gurmat Sangeet Samelan* and other high-profile gatherings of Sikh musicians. If room is not made for these skilled *kirtaniye*, they will likely choose to build their careers outside of official Sikh institutions, which is already proving to be a tremendous loss. Chapter 6 explores how many women have been turning to the digital realm as a safe space that offers uncensored, limitless opportunities for innovation. In an ideal world these women would also have an equal opportunity to offer *kirtan* live in the sacred space of the *Gurudwara*.

Even if the harmonium's supreme reign for over a century is drawing to a close, it will be difficult to erase the instrument, given that its sounds and moods have become embedded deep within the memories of several generations. Musician-poet Madan Gopal Singh recently published a poetic appreciation of the instrument where he anthropomorphizes the harmonium as an immigrant to expose the trauma that underlies its banishment:

> It is a bit like a shadow without the body. It is a cultural remnant of an unfinished colony where the original home is lost and disowned in history by both the coloniser and colonised. It cannot go back to Europe. It has learnt to live with its own relative nonpresence, its homelessness, and its unending anonymity.¹⁴⁷

Given how many other instruments from neighboring lands have been accommodated within India's large musical family, my sense is that the harmonium might continue to eke out a presence in Sikh *kirtan* to some degree, whether as a first instrument for learning or as a secondary supporting accompaniment. Whatever its fate, it is important to at least remember the instrument's journeys, how local musicians altered its construction while changing how it was played, and the many hands it passed through as it was repurposed to fit the devotional soundscapes of Punjab.

CHAPTER SUMMARY

Against the backdrop of a recently declared ban, this chapter provides historical and cultural context for understanding how the harmonium made its way into Sikh *kirtan*. As a range of primary sources from missionary literature show, native musicians adapted this instrument to suit their expressive needs, while using it alongside existing instruments. Female missionaries, in particular, were involved in the dissemination of this instrument among native women and girls. *Mirasi* also played a central role in bringing this instrument into the Indian soundscape and into *kirtan*.

A detailed analysis of various audio recordings further highlights the distinctive way the harmonium is used by Sikh *kirtaniye*. These analyses draw attention to the idiosyncratic manner of playing the harmonium in *kirtan*, showing how its mechanics and expressions have been modified to suit the specific purposes of Sikh devotional worship. The larger issue that grounds this chapter points to a growing tension between practitioners who seek to banish the harmonium in attempts to revive and restore traditional instruments (*tanti sāz*) and those who see a more inclusive future that acknowledges the important contributions of the harmonium to *kirtan*.

| 3

Anahad Nād and the Sonic Embodiment of Divinity

While previous chapters focused on the historical dimensions and music-theoretical foundation of *kirtan*, here I hone my focus on the spiritual conception of sound around which this devotional practice is organized. An understanding of *anahad nād* is crucial to gaining a full appreciation of *kirtan*. Pronounced "un-hud," "un-hut," or "un-aa-hud," *anahad nād* references the sonic dimension. This phrase is woven into *Sri Guru Granth Sahib* (*SGGS*) through several formulations. A few of these serve as synonyms, such as *anahad dhuni* (divine melody). Some formulations point to a qualitative aspect of sound through emphasis on its status as immaculate or pure (*nirmal nād*) or to associations of divine sound with the primal word or utterance (*anahad shabad* and *anahad bani*). Other phrases place emphasis on the accompanying idealized states of bliss and equipoise: *sehaj aanad* and *sehaj dhun*. Meanwhile, the expression *anhat sunn* captures another aspect of the sonic field: silence.

The different verbal shadings of *anahad nād* reveal the poetic flair and spiritual discernment of the gurus and bhagats who drew on this concept to illustrate an elevated spiritual consciousness. This intensely synesthetic moment is felt inwardly, and it is marked by a confluence of timbres that mingle with the gentle trickle of ambrosial nectar (*amrit*) and a dazzling aura of light. A lyrical rendition of this experience is composed in *rāg Dhanasri* by Guru Nanak, whose evocative description of daily evening *aarti* (ritual worship with candles and flowers) is abundant with sensory opulence:

> The sky is our platter, the sun and moon our lamps, pearls of starry galaxies shimmer around us,
> wafting sandal infuses our incense, the breeze is our flywhisk, all vegetation our flower offerings to you.
> What a beautiful worship takes place.
> This is your worship, oh destroyer of fear.
> Unstruck sound [*anahad shabad*] vibrates through the *bheri* [kettledrums].[1]

Guru Nanak maps an externally observed cosmic symphony onto an internally felt bliss. These sights and sensations mark a corporeal experience of *anahad nād* within the Sikh body. To be clear, this is not a Pythagorean situation where the harmony of the spheres becomes suddenly perceptible to "a mortal listener," as discussed by Andrew Hicks.[2] Whereas the ancient Greeks located celestial music outside the body, using planetary motions to calculate the mathematical ratios that form the basis of musical principles, *anahad nād* is encountered within the body when awareness of the material world has been rendered immaterial.

Anahad nād functions as a leitmotif in *Gurbani*. It reminds devotees that the purpose of their lives is to hear, to listen to, and to become attuned to the celestial music of the divine word (*shabad*) that is constantly resounding within the body, which is rendered, quite literally, as vibrating matter, a *corps sonore*, to adapt a term coined by eighteenth-century music theorist Jean-Philippe Rameau.[3] Another phrase, used by Bhagat Singh Thind within a Sikh epistemological framework, is *Dhunnatmic*, which is especially nuanced in the way that it aligns divine melody—*dhun*—with one's "own inexpressible primal sound" (referring to that of the human spirit, *atma*).[4] It is through embodied attunement to these variegated sounds and timbres that one can become detached from worldly preoccupations and experience the resplendence of divinity that resides within, thereby reaching the pinnacle of human existence, *nirbaan*, which ends the cycle of birth and death to which the Sikh body is otherwise bound. This is the purpose of human life as explained by Guru Arjan in *rāg Majh*.[5]

A primary focus of this discussion concerns a quandary: For devotees the ability to hear *anahad nād* is a much yearned-for state that signals spiritual attainment and union with the divine. Yet, they are reminded that few (*virlai*) will ever experience this heightened divine ecstasy in their minds and bodies. Guru Nanak observes in *rāg Maru*, "How rare is that person for whom the word of the guru makes itself heard."[6] Bhai Gurdas, the revered poet and scribe, points to two types of listening: one oriented toward externally made music and another toward internally generated timbres. "Everyone listens to the music of *rāg*, but those whose consciousness attunes to the divine word [*shabad*] are rare."[7] It is only the Gurmukh—those oriented toward the teachings of the divine guru—who receive this sonic abundance.[8]

The driving forces behind this chapter come from the issue of how to hear *anahad nād* in relation to the timbral complexity through which divine sound manifests. Given the spiritual weight of this question, I realize it can only begin to be answered through dialogue with the sacred verses of the gurus and bhagats, which I engage with while charting the emergence of a uniquely Sikh understanding of *nād* through its alignment with—from the broadest to the most specific aspects of the sonic dimension—a preexisting, primordial sound; a form of made music that includes the practice of recitation; and an array of differentiated timbres as referenced in *Gurbani*.

Rooted in Vedic thought, the division of sound into two categories was an important starting point for the gurus, who inherited a dualistic framework for thinking about *nād*. Put simply, *nād* was characterized as either struck (*ahat*) or unstruck (*anahat*), heard or unheard, temporary or permanent, and materializing through the corporeal effort of singing and playing instruments or existing beyond bodily exertion. By elevating *kirtan*, the gurus brought an element of dynamism to this seemingly static dualistic framework. In *SGGS kirtan* is, above all, a catalyst, a mediating agent, that attunes the mind and body to hearing *anahad nād*.[9] The recasting of *kirtan* in this role marks a crucial difference between Vedic and Sikh notions of *anahad nād*, which explains, to some extent, why *kirtan* is given such a high status in *Gurbani*.[10] Without *kirtan* the human body remains earthbound. Through *kirtan*, as Guru Ramdas explains in *rāg Aasa*, "One attains the supreme status."[11]

The spiritual journey toward hearing *anahad nād* begins in the outer sphere with the perception of *kirtan*: Contemplation of the divine word (*shabad*), as carried through music, shifts one's concentration to an inner sphere. Gurus and bhagats alluded to this process through recourse to the contemporaneous practices of yoga, which were often subject to trenchant criticism. What emerges through this criticism is a distinctive configuration of the Sikh body and mind, whose ideal state of contentment, equipoise, and bliss (*sukh*, *sehaj*, and *anand*) is facilitated through the transformation of *kirtan*: An outwardly facing form of a cohesive, structured music merges into an inwardly attuned multitude of discrete timbres as *rāg* is transformed into the timbral vibration of *nād* at the deepest state of meditation (*samadhi*), described as the fourth state in *SGGS*.[12] The specific tone colors of a variety of instruments—including the *bheri, rabab, kinguri, tura,* and *sinyi,* among others—signal the moment when the tenth door (*dasam dwar,* located toward the crown of the head) opens, allowing the self to merge with the divine. The timbres and instruments associated with the five primal sounds (*panch shabad*) sound simultaneously within the mind and body to signal an inwardly experienced sonic ecstasy.

This wide array of instruments highlights that the gurus thought carefully about timbre and that they were attentive to the specific kinds of timbres that mark the moment of a heightened inner sensory awakening. For readers who have not encountered timbre within a musical context, I see it as pointing to the unique sound profile of an instrument or voice, which contributes to its defining character or quality. I use the term when comparing specific sounds that issue from instruments—the timbre of a plucked *rabab* is different from that of a struck *pakhawaj,* for instance. When these instruments play together, we hear a timbral blend or a fusion of heterogeneous (contrasting) timbres.

Euro-North American scholars emphasize a considerably more nuanced definition of timbre that points to its paradoxical condition, while using metaphors to indicate its sonic manifestation as color (light/dark), texture (soft/harsh), and mood (joyful/gloomy), to name just a few formulations. In contrast, when the notion of timbre is approached from the epistemological framework of Indian metaphysics, it is not intertwined with the traumas of paradox, ontology, taxonomy, and selfhood, which emerge as key qualities when examining timbre from the standpoints of Western European psychology and philosophy, as we see most recently in the work of Zachary Wallmark and Isabella van Elferen. While Wallmark pays attention to "the higher levels of cognition," I orient the focus toward higher levels of consciousness to consider situations where the timbre of an instrument is felt to reverberate throughout the body in the absence of an identifiable source.[13] Critical attention has yet to be given to the distinct timbral properties of *anahad* instruments and sounds, and this chapter takes a first step in moving timbral studies in that direction, preparing readers for the in-depth study of *anahad* musical instruments in chapter 4.

There are few moments in the literature (in Punjabi and in English) where *anahad nād* has been examined with the kind of focus and scrutiny offered here.¹⁴ I honed my understanding of *nād* in conversation with intellectual companions across a range of fields, including Indigenous studies, sound studies, voice studies, sensory studies, ecomusicology, and global transfer and hybridity. This wide-ranging body of work has served as a cross-cultural, critical sounding board. In turn, my expansion of familiar concepts into the relatively unfamiliar Sikh sonic domain broadens prevailing discussions, particularly given my emphasis on timbre as a variegated and divinely attuned inner experience. Although it took music scholars several years to respond to Cornelia Fales's complaint that they had "no language to describe" timbre, the notion of *anahad nād* presents a cogent language for describing timbre whose metaphysical basis extends beyond a preoccupation with the auditory system. Sikh epistemology also posits clear correlations between "the *acoustic world*" and "the *perceived world*," as discussed by Fales.¹⁵ Until now scholars have tended to focus on the issue of knowing timbre by paying attention to how it is produced, perceived, understood, and verbalized.¹⁶ Sikh auditors are beyond such concerns: When hearing sound in an idealized state of *sehaj* (equipoise), they not only have full awareness of its source and journey. They are also indifferent to them.

TOWARD A THEORY OF *ANAHAD NĀD*: THE CASE OF BHAI HIRA SINGH (1879–1926)

Bhai Hira Singh was a highly respected *kirtaniya* who lived in Punjab during the late nineteenth and early twentieth centuries.¹⁷ I begin with an anecdote about his life because it draws into focus the close relationship between *ahat* and *anahad nād* in the Sikh philosophical tradition while reminding us that *anahad nād* cannot be equated with silence despite its frequent characterization as "unheard." This rings especially true for those who are attuned to the immensity of sonic reverberance that marks *anahad nād* as a moment of sensory saturation in the mind and body.

Bhai Hira Singh was renowned for the *ras* (sweet taste) of his early morning *kirtan*, which took place during *amritvela*, which roughly corresponds to the period between 3 a.m. and 6 a.m., a time considered sacred in the Sikh tradition. This time frame is understood as the last of the eight watches, a division of the twenty-four-hour period according to the concept of *pehar* (see **fig. 1.4** above). Nikky-Guninder Kaur Singh explains that "*amrit velā* . . . is the time of day most conducive to reflection," and many devotees and practitioners view *amritvela* as a special moment when the entire universe is reverberant with recitation of the divine name; it is understood that prayer at any other time of day is not as potent.[18] Referring to *amritvela* as *pichhal raat*, the last watch of the night, Sheikh Farid offers a striking description of this temporal phase: "Farid, if you do not awaken in the early hours before dawn, you are dead while still alive."[19] Sheikh Farid does not mince his words when it comes to affirming the validity of human existence through remembrance of the divine name within this time frame.

It was customary for Bhai Hira Singh to undertake tours of *kirtan* for *sangat* in remote areas.[20] During a tour in Shimla, one of the organizers (*sevadaar*) heard a faint voice coming from the mountains at around midnight. He had heard tales of Bhai Hira Singh keeping a small, portable harmonium with him at all times. The *sevadaar* made his way into the mountains and, from a distance, noticed Bhai Hira Singh sitting with his eyes closed and performing *kirtan* through poems of supplication and others that expressed a longing for union with the divine. The *sevadaar* listened from afar for a few hours, as Bhai Hira Singh remained immersed in *Gurbani*. Around 2 a.m. he tied up his harmonium, went back to his room as quietly as possible so that no one would be aware of his absence, and lay down for a few minutes, after which he awoke his companions, reminding them to bathe in preparation for the morning recitation of *Aasa ki vār*. Afterward, the *sevadaar* approached Bhai Hira Singh and asked him two questions: Why had he retreated into the mountains to sing *kirtan* in the middle of the night all alone, and why, in the midst of singing, did he sometimes stop for long periods of time? Bhai Hira Singh explained that the *kirtan* he does during the day is for the *sangat* who give him love and money but that the *kirtan* he does at night, at the feet of Guru Nanak, is for Guru Nanak. Whatever the Guru gives to him at that moment is his own wealth, which allows him to perform *kirtan* for the *sangat*. With regard to his silences, the moments when the *sevadaar* said that Bhai Hira Singh had stopped singing, he wasn't quiet. *Gurbani* had brought him to a state of intense focus and awareness (*surti*) where his outward silence was answered inwardly for many hours by the loving sounds of the divine one's conversations, which are so different from anything in this world.

This story highlights a uniquely Sikh notion of *anahad nād* where *kirtan* mediates between an outward and an inward experience of sound. As seen in **figure 3.1**, *kirtan* has the potential to shift one's *surti* (focus or awareness) from the earthly domain, where music is actively made and heard, as signaled by Bhai Sahib's harmonium and voice, to a celestial domain where many other timbres and varieties of sound

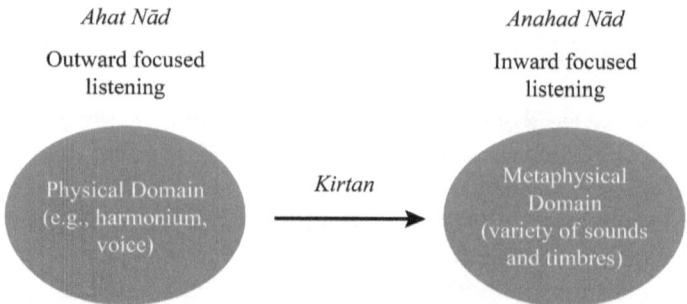

FIGURE 3.1 *Kirtan* mediates between an outward and an inward experience of sound.

can be contemplated. A single phrase from *Japji Sahib* explains how the primordial sacred word resounds and vibrates as *nād* (divine sound): "Gurmukh nādang."[21] *Kirtan* attunes the listener to the word and, through this attunement, offers the possibility of experiencing an even deeper vibrational connection to divine sound. This mediating role is crucial to understanding the immensely high status given to *kirtan* in sacred verse. Playing *kirtan* and hearing *kirtan* are vital to human existence because they allow one's bodily vibrations to be amplified and aligned with those of other community members and with those of divinity. Guru Amardas points to how Sikh bodies are constantly resonating and to how a heightened vibration marks the experience of *anahad nād*.[22] Corporeal resonance in this instance is not a marker of individuality, as we see in Wallmark's comment, informed by Italian philosopher Adriana Cavarero: "Timbre is always unique—it's your body making it."[23] A focus on the unique self that we see with Wallmark and Cavarero is out of place in the Sikh context, where internal timbral resonance merges with surrounding corporeal and material resonance to generate undifferentiated vibration. In fact, the purpose of attuning oneself to and intensifying inner timbral resonance is to lose a sense of self and individuality.

Gobind Singh Mansukhani offers an insightful analysis of this transformational process in his description of the three stages of *kirtan*. To be clear, it is rare within the field of Sikh studies to come across attempts to trace how *kirtan* is perceived and its potential to impact the listener's consciousness. Mansukhani's efforts highlight the inherently fluid mode of listening adopted by devotees, where "the initial impact of *kirtan* may begin as *kan-rasa*, literally 'pleasure of the ears,'" a first stage that is associated with the individual's search for auditory pleasure. Aesthetic enjoyment facilitates "*man-rasa*, that is, 'pleasure of the mind,'" in the second stage, through which "*kirtan* cleanses the mind." In the final stage devotees hear the emergence of *dhuni*, "the echo or resonance of the sacred music within oneself." Mansukhani makes an important distinction at this point and explains how *kirtan* can be internalized and how, in so doing, it enables a form of inner cleansing that allows for a shift in consciousness. He breaks down the process of listening to its constituent parts: "We pick up the tunes and the words... which have appealed to us and begin to sing them to ourselves. Like musicians tuning their instruments, we tune the vibrations of our minds to the *kirtan*. The resonance of melody and rhythm becomes so strong that it holds the mind steadfast. In this way, the mind is being trained and channeled toward calm and repose." Inner cleansing thus brings about an internal "resonance and illumination," and the repetition of this mode of listening facilitates a state of "*sahaj* or divine bliss." From this point on, when devotees crave to hear *kirtan*, it is because of "an inner need," which facilitates a union with the divine ("*surat-sabad-da-mel*").[24]

This nuanced and process-oriented understanding of *anahad nād* is different from formulations that stress a dualistic framework, which are favored by Vedic epistemology. For example, **figure 3.2** shows how an outwardly heard struck sound, *ahat nād*, refers to music of fixed duration that is made through bodily exertion, using musical instruments and the voice. This is opposed to an inwardly experienced sound that is constantly reverberating within the body, *anahad nād*, which has no traceable cause or duration.

At this point it is important to make a clarification: Sometimes the terms "unstruck" and "unheard" are used interchangeably. These terms

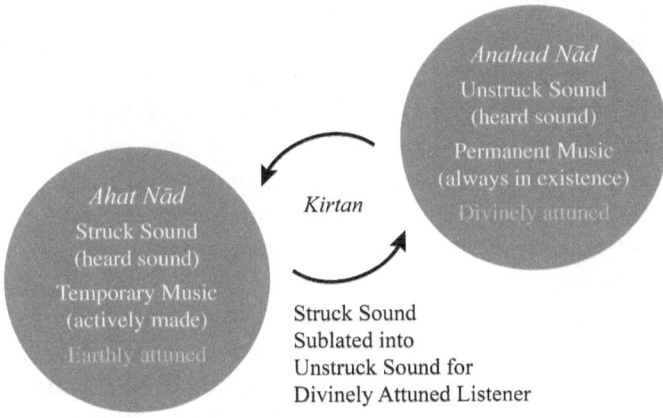

FIGURE 3.2 *Kirtan* sublates *ahat nād* into *anahad nād*.

operate on different levels, however: Unstruck sound is audible to a listener whose senses are fully awakened, but it will be unheard to one who is not thus attuned. Struck sound is easily available to all auditors, although its vibrations may be subsumed into those of unstruck sound for auditors whose senses are inwardly attuned. I will come back to this point about a circular mode of listening.

THE CRITICAL COMMENTARIES OF BHAI VIR SINGH AND BHAI RANDHIR SINGH

My attempts to move beyond the dichotomy of *ahat* and *anahad* will appear rudimentary in comparison with the nuanced efforts of Sikh thinkers. I engage with two scholars in this section, Bhai Vir Singh (1872–1957) and Bhai Randhir Singh (1878–1961), whose perspectives, although contrasting in some ways, are also complementary in that they transform existing discussions of *rāg* and *kirtan* in relation to embodied perceptions of *anahad nād*. I focus on these two figures for several reasons: They are revered for their immense knowledge of *Gurbani*; their literary prowess; and their keen sense of history, politics, place, and identity, living as they did in the decades following the collapse of the Sikh empire in the middle of the nineteenth century and during a period of increasing British colonial violence. Today Bhai Vir Singh is seen as an intellectual and an entrepreneur, a man of letters, who was heavily involved in Sikh religious reform through his mobilization of the print economy in Punjab.[25] Bhai Randhir Singh, widely known as the founder of the *Akhand Kirtani Jatha* (*AKJ*) movement, is revered as a revolutionary figure whose spiritual attainment, intellectual authority, individual courage, and proclivity to protect the vulnerable have established him as a powerful role model for his followers.[26] It is likely that Bhai Vir Singh and Bhai Randhir Singh knew of each other. Even if they didn't meet, it is clear that the two men were kindred spirits who were united in their efforts to end colonial rule, as reflected in the glowing endorsement given by Bhai Vir Singh to the publication of letters written by Bhai Randhir Singh from jail. The latter was imprisoned for his involvement in the Gaddar movement, which aimed to overthrow British power.

Bhai Vir Singh's linguistic versatility (he was educated in Persian, Sanskrit, and Braj, in addition to his native Punjabi and Hindi) fueled a prolific and varied literary output, which included historical fiction, novels, poetry, scholarly editions and annotations, and exegeses, to list a few genres.[27] Against these monumental achievements, it may seem strange to single out his short (but dense) untranslated essay, "Shabad de Bhaav te Raag di Taseer" (The emotion of shabad and the impact of *rāg*). Little known outside of specialist circles, this piece opens a substantial volume of essays about *kirtan*: *Gurmat Sangeet: Par Hun Tak Mili Khoj* (1958). This book's five sections include detailed discussion of topics including pitch, *rāg*, *tāl*, *vār*, and musical style.[28] This volume is among the earliest publications on *Gurmat Sangeet* from the mid-twentieth century, a period during which the impact of colonization had heightened the need among practitioners to document and formalize musical knowledge and share it through publication. The value of Bhai Vir Singh's essay lies in two areas: first, in its original aesthetic evaluation of *kirtan*; second, in how it draws connections between *kirtan* and *anahad nād* through the role of *rāg*. Bhai Vir Singh argued that the *sangat* must alter their taste for *kirtan* that is inspired by the music of popular dramas (*natak*) and folk traditions (*tappe*) to prevent the treasures of *rāg* and melody from becoming hidden away in the chests (*sina*) of *rababi* and *ragi* and thus from becoming lost to future generations.[29]

Bhai Vir Singh points to a strong association between *rāg* and the experience of *anahad nād*. Alluding to his title, he argues that the unique effect (*taseer*) of *rāg* has a powerful impact on the listener in that it can lift the string of consciousness (*surti di taar*) — which "sticks" to *rāg* — upward to the highest spheres of contemplation, where *rāg* is involved in churning ambrosial nectar. *Rāg*, he explains, has this capability because the manifestation of *ras* (essence or flavor of *rāg*) is inherent to its creation and melodic nature, and this *ras* is that of "*anahad dhuni*," which belongs to the sphere where music is made, the divine realm. Thus, *rāg* is of divine origin, which is why it can link consciousness to divinity. His argumentation on this matter is clear: The emotion associated with *nād* and the underlying sentiment of *Gurbani*, as communicated through the *ras* of the *kirtaniya*'s purity of conscience, must all be attuned to one another. To this end, a musical education focused on vocal training and access to high-quality instruments is essential to experiencing the intensity of *nād*.[30]

Especially striking is Bhai Vir Singh's analysis of *nād* as existing along a continuum. He observes a five-stage process where *ahat nād* is transformed into various shades of *anahad nād* (see **fig. 3.3**). Reading **figure 3.3** from right to left: The first *mandal* (sphere) where music is manifest, and aligned with *ahat nād*, is where music is made through labor and effort. This refers to instances where two entities come into contact with one another, such as fingertips plucking the strings of a *rabab*, air passing over vocal cords to create friction, palms and fingers

Bhai Vir Singh, "Shabad de bhaav te rāg di taseer,"
("The emotion of shabad and the impact of rāg") [no date]

NIRANKAR	EK ONKAR	Sphere of *anahat nād*	Sphere of *anahat jhunkar* (tinkling bells)	Sphere of *ahat nād*
		ਅਨਾਹਤ ਨਾਦ ਦਾ ਮੰਡਲ	ਅਨਾਹਤ ਝੁਨਕਾਰ ਦਾ ਮੰਡਲ	ਆਹਤ ਨਾਦ ਦਾ ਮੰਡਲ
ਨਿਰੰਕਾਰ	ਏਕੰਕਾਰ	ONKAR ਓਅੰਕਾਰ	Mediating point	ਦੂਈ (ਵਿਸ਼ਵ ਸੈਸਾਰ)
ਕਲਾ ਰਹਤ ਮੰਡਲ	ਅਕਲ ਕਲਾ ਦਾ ਮੰਡਲ	ਕਲਾ ਧਾਰਨ ਦਾ ਮੰਡਲ		ਕਲਾ ਧਾਰਿਆ ਹੋਇਆ ਮੰਡਲ
Sound is manifest without cause and effort	Sound is manifest	Sound is conceived		Sound is actively made through effort
		Sookham ras – Experience peace and contentment		*Kan ras* – Experience auditory pleasure

FIGURE 3.3 Bhai Vir Singh's theory of *nād* from "Shabad de Bhaav te Rāg di Taseer."

striking the membranes of the *pakhawaj*, a bow passing across the strings of a *kinguri*, and air blowing through a *shankh* (conch). Vibrations are felt by the membranes (*parde*) of the ears, processed by the brain, and perceived in the mind as *ras*. The discussion of *ras* in this context clearly aligns an affective experience of music with the domain of *kan ras* (appreciation through the ears), as mentioned by Mansukhani. Associated with the sphere of *anahad* is the cultivation of *sookham ras*, a state of ease where the *kirtaniya* and the listener lose a sense of self.[31] Bhai Vir Singh's expansion of aesthetic theory beyond the traditional nine *rasa* of Hindustani classical music underscores the point that *amrit ras* and *har ras* are essential to the practice of *kirtan* as articulated in SGGS.

Figure 3.3 shows Bhai Vir Singh's explication of the five stages of *anahad nād*. The dualistic framework of *ahat* and *anahad* initially frames his inquiry, although it is considerably refined. Entry into the realm of *anahad* is marked by a mediating point governed by the timbral effects of small ringing bells (*anahad jhunkar*). Having transitioned into the realm of *anahad*, Bhai Vir Singh draws attention first to the sphere of *anahad nād*, where divinity is manifest as the creative spirit of *onkar*; this is where music (*kala*) is conceived (as opposed to in the realm of *ahat nād*, where music readily comes into being). Moving deeper into the space of meditation (toward *samadhi*, a form of deep, meditative, and ecstatic equilibrium), Bhai Vir Singh indicates a growing perception of the fullness of divinity through manifestation as *ek onkar* (in a realm where music is not yet conceived). Finally, the deepest sphere of meditation (where music does not exist) is associated with *nirankar* (a conception of divinity as pure, abstract form, beyond time and space).³² Bhai Vir Singh's observations are broad and largely concerned with how *rāg* allows the listener's consciousness to be lifted toward higher spheres of contemplation, leading to a sonic encountering of the divine in the form of *nirankar*. His analysis of the different stages of divine encounter (*onkar–ek onkar–nirankar*) along this sonic spectrum is unique in its concern with articulating various junctures of the auditory journey from *ahat nād* to the deepest state of *anahad nād*. On a broader level, this paradigm retains parallels with the Sikh mystical experience (explored in the next section).

When read alongside the writings of Bhai Randhir Singh, his contemporary, Bhai Vir Singh's focus on *anahad nād* can be broadened further to imagine the body as a site where divine sound reverberates. Unlike Bhai Vir Singh, Bhai Randhir Singh did not consider *rāg* to be the only conduit for *amrit ras* or *har ras*. In fact, his outlook on whether sacred verses should be sung specifically in the *rāg* stipulated in *SGGS* is insightful for the way he conceives of this musical knowledge as being hidden (*azgaibi*) within the consciousness: "When we become absorbed in divine color, and when *kirtan* is begun in this realm of divine color, the hidden raag reveal themselves to us (*supharan*) on their own."³³ The link between *rāg* and instinct or consciousness is also clear in an exchange with a member of the *sangat* who praised Bhai Randhir Singh's delivery of *kirtan* in *rāg Bilawal*, saying that he had never experienced such a feeling of bliss (*anand*) upon hearing this *rāg* from other *ragi* (practitioners). Bhai Randhir wrote, "Upon listening, I laughed in my mind and was surprised because I didn't even know which raag is known as Bilawal, how it is sung, or even what time of day."³⁴ In this respect, his emphasis on bodily attunement to the divine *shabad* (through *kirtan* and recitation) as a source of *ras* stands at odds with Bhai Vir Singh's emphasis on pedagogy and training as powerful vehicles for initiating what he called *sookham ras*.

As seen in Bhai Randhir Singh's book *Anhad Shabad Dasam Duar* (Unstruck word tenth door), the act of *nām simran* (recitation and remembrance of the divine name), especially when allied with the *gur-mantar* (mantra) *waheguru*, was considered an important practice for accessing *anahad nād*.³⁵ Along these lines, Bhai Randhir Singh's conception of *anahad nād* is largely corporeal given its emphasis on a cyclic relationship between the tongue—as initiating and sustaining *simran* and *kirtan*—and the navel—the first place where wondrous bliss (*bismaad*) manifests; this practice of recitation and breath opens access to higher, spiritual realms.³⁶ In keeping with *SGGS*, the ecstatic state of *anahad nād* is experienced as multisensory and synesthetic: Touch, taste, and hearing are simultaneously awakened through the haptic sensation of *amrit* (ambrosial nectar) trickling down from the crown of the head toward the navel and the uniquely flavorful taste of *anahad dhuni*, whose multicolored sounds (differentiated timbres) are also savored through hearing.³⁷ It is through *nām simran* that the *Gurmukh* reaches a blissful state of equipoise and heightened sensory sensitivity by losing their sense of self as the consciousness is raised. Arvind-Pal Singh Mandair fruitfully compares this process to "remembrance of one's own mortality," which facilitates an awakening to *nām*.³⁸

As with Bhai Vir Singh's essay, Bhai Randhir Singh's *Anhad Shabad Dasam Duar* is little known outside of specialist circles, even though it stands as an important contribution to literature on *anahad nād*. My brief discussion aims to create connections with the ideas of Bhai Vir Singh while establishing a Sikh conceptual framework for engaging with *anahad nād*. Similarly, Bhai Randhir Singh was keen to establish a conceptual hierarchy where the experience of *anahad nād* produces timbres within the body that he considered superior to those heard in Hatha yoga.³⁹ Here, consideration of his book's title provides critical insight: "Unstruck word tenth door" instructs readers to think of the body through the lens of *sehaj yoga*, as expounded by gurus and bhagats (discussed in more detail below). Bhai Randhir Singh explains, citing Guru Amardas, whose verse in *rāg Majh* I paraphrase here: It is an ease of meditation, rather than challenging *asana* (yogic poses), that facilitates an inner resounding, "as each of the body's nine openings (doors) to the outside world are closed off, allowing pranic energy to be channeled toward the hidden tenth door, located at the crown of the head, where the sonic manifests in abundance."⁴⁰ In other words, an exertion of control over the nine points of contact with the external world—through the openings associated with the reproductive organs, two eyes, two nostrils, two ears, and one mouth—facilitates a sensory experience whose intensity throws open the tenth door, thereby activating a simultaneous inner awakening and alignment of the sensory faculties.⁴¹

Bhai Vir Singh's gradation of different states of *anahad nād* finds an intriguing parallel in Bhai Randhir Singh's focus on hierarchically organized timbres and their association with different states of meditation, the highest being the fourth state, *turiya bivastha/avastha* (as described in *SGGS* and in keeping with Bhai Vir Singh's five stages of *nād*). Citing Guru Arjan, Bhai Randhir Singh maintains that it is thunder that signals *anahad* in the deepest state: "The divine one thunders [*gajai*] and anahad vibrates." To that Bhagat Kabir adds the dazzling aura of lightning: "Lightning blazes and bliss is felt."⁴² Bhai Gurdas also explains in his *kabit* (poems) that thunder and lightning are the signs (*nisaan*) of having reached *dasam dwar*, a moment that is captured through the upturning of the inverted lotus at the position of the navel, whose motion disperses dazzling light throughout the body (I return to the topic of the lotus below).⁴³ One of the best-known verses on this topic is by Guru Nanak, who perceives the breath of divinity as causing the realm of *dasam dwar* to thunder (*garjai*).⁴⁴

In contrast, buzzing sounds (described as "*ghun ghun*" in Punjabi) suggest a lower state of attainment for Bhai Randhir Singh. He goes on to make the point that in the fourth state there is no desire for *ahat nad* in the form of vocal singing or pitch- and rhythm-playing instruments, given the sonic abundance of *anahad nad*, an observation that Guru Nanak puts forth in his description of the awakened state in *rāg Aasa*.⁴⁵ Interestingly, Bhai Randhir Singh relegates the experience of hearing "the sweet voice of a flute" and "the ringing of a bell" to the early stages of entering *samadhi*. The timbres of *chhainay* (steel tongs overlaid with small cymbals, also called *chimta*) and the *shankh* (conch) are not available at this stage, although the devotee might hear the faint, indistinct rumbling of clouds (glimmers of thunder) associated with the deepest state.⁴⁶ A synesthetic experience marks the deepest state of *samadhi* for Bhai Randhir Singh: He is clear that the intensity of *anahad shabad* heard upon the opening of *dasam dwar* (the tenth door) indicates sensory hypersensitivity. Taste, touch, sight, and hearing are fully awakened through cross-modal engagement: "Those who haven't tasted *naam ras*, those who haven't felt the flourishing of the lotus that sits at the navel, those who haven't seen rays of light shine within them; how can they have heard *anahad shabad*?"⁴⁷ Furthermore, once these divine timbres (*anahad dhuni*) have been heard, he argues, lovers of *kirtan* cannot be satisfied by (earthly) instrumental *kirtan*.⁴⁸

Thus, Bhai Randhir Singh clarifies his point that *anahad sunn* or *sehaj sunn* (often translated as "void") is not empty (or, in other words, silent). To the contrary, it marks an especially elevated state signaled by continuous timbral saturation, where one sound that stands out is that of tinkling (*jhunkar*).⁴⁹ In the realm of *dasam dwar*, timbre is disassociated from its source, so one is no longer aware of an instrument (such as a bell or, as he calls it, a bronze instrument) but rather of pure vibration.⁵⁰ We might think of this sound as being equivalent to a drone in that it is always in a state of vibration.

Recitation (*nām simran*) also plays a significant sonic role in its manifestation as continuous intonation. *Ajapa jaap* refers to the constant, automated recitation of such phrases as "guru" and "*waheguru*," which, according to Bhai Randhir Singh, allows *Gurbani* to become embedded and manifest in the consciousness.[51] Indeed, in keeping with the emphasis on "rom rom" in *SGGS*, the closest idiomatic translation into English might be "in every fiber of my being," but in this context it might also be translated as "in every hair of body." This heightened state of recitation facilitates the vibration (thundering, *gararta*) of the divine name throughout the entire body, even on a molecular level, in every nerve and vein, as Bhai Randhir Singh explains.[52] In a letter from 1922, he writes about a similar experience several years earlier: Upon hearing recitation, a key phrase, "*kahao gur vaho*," had such a striking effect on his being that immediately the tingling music of "*waheguru waheguru*" imbued the fibers and hairs of his body. He explained, it was "as if my inner being was being wound by an *anahad* key. As if every hair of my body had acquired a tongue each of which was reciting *waheguru*."[53]

It is understandable that some readers, upon reading this description, might visualize a scene that is in keeping with surrealism or grotesquerie. But these associations couldn't be further from what Bhai Randhir's reflections, and the Sikh context, require. The imaginary of a multitude of sonorous tongues is directly attributed to *Gurbani*, where the sonic manifestation of *kirtan* and recitation enters the porous surface of the body to awaken nerves, fibers, veins, and cells. I must here invoke an intriguing correlation with Wallmark's perception of how "we tend to perceive the behavior of sounding actions in relation to our own corporeal experience. Musical sounds do not just passively enter us through the channels of the flesh: They are actively processed, interpreted, and reenacted through a complex system of intercorporeal mirroring."[54] Bhai Randhir's Singh's reflection points exactly to this transformative potential of timbre by showing how through an awakened state divine sound can also exit the body and, in an unexpected inversion of the unstruck/unheard relationship outlined in **figure 3.2**, become heard as sound, even to those who remain unattuned (see **fig. 3.4**). Guru Arjan clarifies this state in *rāg Aasa*: "Inwardly, I sing divine praise, and outwardly, I sing divine praise; I sing divine praise while awake and asleep."[55] In *rāg Ramkali* Guru Arjan explains that just as recitation takes place in the form of *ajapa jaap*, *kirtan* takes place in that "realm of celestial peace and bliss" where love for the divine one offers nourishment and *kirtan* provides support.[56]

It is in this context that the first *kirtan* sung by Guru Nanak, and recalled in the hagiographical *Janamsakhi* literature, can be understood.

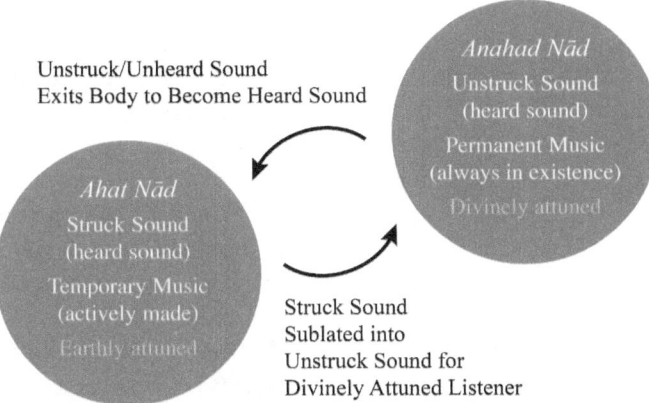

FIGURE 3.4 Divine sound exits the body and becomes heard as sound, even to those who remain unattuned.

The *Puratan Janamsakhi* uses the evocative phrase "the unstruck melody arose" (*dhun anahad uthi*) early on to describe the moment when Guru Nanak was compelled (divinely instructed, one might say) to sing this verse in *rāg Sri*: "If I could live for millions and millions of years with only air for my food and drink . . . I still wouldn't know your value nor how to describe your greatness."[57] Indeed, throughout the *Janamsakhi* corpus, the urgency with which Guru Nanak asks Bhai Mardana to set the mood for his verses through playing *rāg* on his *rabab* suggests his desire to convey the divine one's message as soon as it is uttered in his inner ears. Again, these moments might easily be interpreted as performative— Guru Nanak conveying poetry through song—but their heightened ecstasy (a "state of wonder," *bismaad*) points to the epitome of *kirtan*, an ideal to which all *kirtaniye* should strive as emphasized by both Bhai Vir Singh and Bhai Randhir Singh.[58] Guru Nanak is rarely described at these moments as singing the divine word (*shabad*) in *rāg* but rather as speaking it (*bolna, aakhna*).[59]

I began this section with a *viyakhia* (exegesis) of Bhai Hira Singh, and it seems fitting to close this section with another story, this time about Dattatreya, who is described as a *rishi* or *sanyasi* (a spiritual recluse) in Sikh written and oral accounts (such as the *Janamsakhi* and present-day *kirtan viyakhia*) and as a deity in ancient Hindu texts (such as the Puranas).[60] In the B-40 *Janamsakhi* (1733), Dattatreya (Datta) is mentioned in the episode, "A Visit to Hivanchal."[61] Dattatreya is a spiritually accomplished ascetic whose vow of silence (*muni-vratāh* in Hindi or *maun vrat/ maun dharan* in Punjabi) was questioned by Guru Nanak.[62] My focus is not so much on the philosophical sophistication of their existentialist debate, as recounted in a *viyakhia* by Bhai Gurpreet Singh, but on what Guru Nanak, and his companions, Bhai Mardana and Bhai Bala, experience upon encountering the *rishi*. There are various versions of the meeting between Guru Nanak and Dattatreya, but the version narrated by Bhai Gurpreet Singh is unique for its emphasis on the vow of silence taken by Dattatreya, from which Guru Nanak has received divine command to release him.[63] Most *Janamsakhi* accounts situate Dattatreya among the mountains where he dwells with other yogis, as seen in several well-known paintings.[64] His location in this *viyakhia* shifts to that of a cave (*gufa*), which is heavily symbolic in *SGGS*: The deepest recesses of the consciousness are referred to as *gufa*, and this is where a meeting with the divine one is experienced.

In the story this particular *gufa* is empty, but upon entering they hear a voice echoing through the cave. Bhai Mardana and Bhai Bala are taken aback by this acousmatic *mantra* (*rām rām*) — looking around them, they cannot locate the source of this sound — but Guru Nanak explains that it belongs to a powerful ascetic who has been performing penance, meditation, and prayer for hundreds of years. During this time *rishi* Dattatreya had accumulated such an immense power that he was able to sustain his existence in this cave, in a state of deep meditation, while having taken a vow of silence. This explanation proves to be a sticking point for Bhai Mardana, who is compelled to inquire where the voice is coming from if the *rishi* is, in fact, silent. Guru Nanak replies that the refrain, *rām rām*, issues from Dattatreya's body, from the depths of his inner being (*riddhai*), from his navel (*naabhi*, from which divine sound originates). Furthermore, Guru Nanak explains, even as Dattatreya's *zubaan* (speech) is absent, his *surti* (consciousness) is joined to *nām* (divinity), and it is this connection that allows the *dhuni* (sacred melody) of *rām rām* to reverberate from all four corners of the *gufa*. It is because he does not wish to break this connection (*liv*) that Dattatreya does not respond to Guru Nanak's salutatory greetings upon entering the cave.

But Guru Nanak's visit takes place under divine command (*hukam*), and he has been sent to show Dattatreya how to keep his consciousness connected to divinity while living in the world and engaging with others through speech. The solution, Guru Nanak explains, is to recite the divine name (*jaap*) in such a way that *ajapa jaap* (an internalized, automatic recitation) begins deep within the body, while the *surti* (consciousness) remains attached to *nirankar*, whether one is working, eating, sleeping, or talking: Externally the mouth may be involved in conversation, but internally *nām simran* takes place. It is when *ajapa jaap* begins from the depths of one's being, without the tongue being actively involved in recitation, that a high spiritual status (*bivastha/avastha*) has been attained. Thus, one's inner being becomes imbued with the sacred melody (*dhuni*), and the string of consciousness (*munn ki taar*) becomes joined to *nirankar*. This point is made by Guru Nanak in *rāg Ramkali*: "The *Gurmukh* meditates on the divine one with every hair of the body. Oh Nanak, the *Gurmukh* merges in truth."[65] An approach to sound as something emanating from the smallest level of bodily structure, converging to create an expansive timbral resonance and eventually pouring out of the entire body in a synesthetic wash of light and sound, offers new perspectives for thinking about how sound and body coexist in, as, and through each other.

Having established these broad outlines for thinking about the nuanced relationship between *nād* and the body in dialogue with the writings of two prominent Sikh thinkers, we are well placed to delve deeper into *Gurbani* in a continued effort to understand Sikh notions of *anahad nād*. The primary interlocutors for the writings of Bhai Vir Singh and Bhai Randhir Singh are the Sikh gurus and bhagats. It is to their poetic distillation of divine ecstasy that I now turn in exploring Sikh perspectives on yoga and the manifestation of *anahad nād* in the form of specific musical sonorities. We will linger in Dattatreya's cave a little longer.

FROM HATH YOGA TO RAJ YOGA: ARRIVAL AT THE TENTH DOOR (*DASAM DWAR*) AND BEYOND

Many of the gurus and bhagats referenced the yogi Gorakhnath, and his followers, in making the point that *anahad nād* and the accompanying states of *sukh* (contentment), *sehaj* (equipoise), and *anand* (bliss) are not experienced through prolonged yogic *asana* and abstinence but through *nām simran* and *kirtan*—both of which start out in the external realm through conscious, physical effort and, with attunement, shift to the internal realm in the absence of physical and corporeal exertion.[66] This section traces the journey from *ahat* to *anahad nād* across three stages that are concerned with (a) locating the tenth door (*dasam dwar*) at the crown of the head as corporeal energy ascends through the body's six *chakras*; (b) unlocking and opening *dasam dwar* through the sustained presence of *nām simran* and *kirtan*; and (c) permitting the consciousness to pass through *dasam dwar* in gaining access to the deepest realm of meditation—that of the fourth state (*nirankar*).

This spiritual progression is significant from a synesthetic and sonic perspective since it tracks several sensory transformations including the shift from *ahat* to *anahad* as accompanied by the experience of taste (*amrit*, ambrosial nectar), touch (water, wind, and breeze), fragrance (fruit and flowers), and sight (light). Consideration of the fourth state, as marked by an unaided and untraceable reverberation of sonic timbres, deserves its own, separate discussion, which I take up later in this chapter. In preparation, however, the verses examined in this section continue to refine our understanding of *anahad nād* while offering an opportunity to begin sketching an inventory of musical instruments associated with entry through *dasam dwar*; these instruments are examined more closely in chapter 4.

First, I draw *anahad nād* and yoga into proximity through consideration of the lotus, a motif that is central to all branches of yoga and one that the gurus referenced in their descriptions of *anahad nād*. Alongside significant timbral changes that are experienced inwardly during a shift in consciousness, *SGGS* often seizes on the prominent yogic symbol of the lotus (*kamal*). Its transformation from an inverted position (*oondhau kaval/ult kamal*) to an upright position foregrounds the inner sensation of movement (captured by the term "blossoming," "blooming," or "unfolding"). Guru Nanak observes that for those who care only for their ego (*manmukh*), "the lotus [of the *manmukh*] is upside down."[67] In correcting this, he instructs the devotee to engage in meditative reflection: "The inverted heart-lotus has been turned upright through reflective meditation. / From the sky of the tenth gate, *amrit* trickles down."[68] Indeed, as Guru Arjan observes, those "whose inverted lotus is illuminated [has blossomed] see divinity [*nirankar*] everywhere."[69] Guru Amardas explains how it is through the blossoming of the lotus that "eternal peace is obtained, as one's light merges into the light."[70] Guru Ramdas also describes this remarkable inner transformation in *rāg Sarang*: "The heart-lotus blossoms forth, and the mortal is lovingly absorbed in the state of supreme bliss."[71]

It is worth noting that the lotus is primarily associated with the heart (*hirdai*) in *SGGS*, whereas in yoga it is linked to each *chakra*, with the most abundant form of the lotus, the thousand-petaled *sahasrara-padma*, located at the crown of the head.[72] Thus, Bhagat Baynee, in keeping with a yogic perspective, places the lotus, adorned with jewels, at the crown of the head.[73] Furthermore, in *SGGS* the bodily experience of music as *nād* and *kirtan* is intrinsic to the rotation of the lotus. Guru Amardas specifically links the blossoming lotus with *anahad* in *rāg Gauri Guareri*; he makes a similar point about how blossoming (*kamal pargaas*) is tied to *anahad* in *rāg Sorath*.[74] In *rāg Gauri* Guru Arjan hears *anahad dhun* (melody) as a form of unbroken (continuous) *kirtan* when the inner lotus turns upright.⁷⁵ Thus, *kirtan* initiates the spiritual journey, activating a devotee's internally blossoming lotus. Guru Angad draws on the quintessential figure of Guru Nanak as a *dhaadhi* (folk musician or ballad singer) in conveying this message through *rāg Majh*.⁷⁶ This discussion of the lotus motif in *SGGS* provides just one example of how gurus and bhagats drew on yogic terminology and concepts that were familiar to their *sangat* to convey their spiritual teachings.

Because of their visibility in Punjab and surrounding areas, the followers of Gorakh were often used as a foil in *SGGS* to underscore the importance of recitation and *kirtan*.⁷⁷ Although Nath yogis lived on the fringes of society, gurus and bhagats brought these figures into sharp focus by invoking them as interlocutors for discussions concerning *dasam dwar* and *anahad nād*. The vivid metaphors and descriptions that are woven through these verses reflect a broad familiarity with the habits and practices of yogis in general, and by using this specific community, as well as *udasi sadhu* (holy men) as a focal point, gurus and bhagats crafted a message that would be seen as having sociocultural relevance and be easily understood.

There is debate among scholars as to whether Gorakhnath lived in the eleventh or twelfth century.⁷⁸ Certainly, he was not contemporaneous with Guru Nanak, although frequent mention of Gorakhnath throughout *SGGS* reflects the social visibility of this particular sect during the fifteenth and sixteenth centuries and reveals the zeal with which his followers continued his teachings and practices, revering Gorakh as a deity and leading lives marked by celibacy, isolation, begging for alms, and practicing yoga.⁷⁹ Outside of Sikh studies, the figure of Gorakh and his lineage have attracted some critical attention, although scholars have yet to consider Sikh sacred verse as a valuable vantage point from which to examine the sociohistorical significance of this sect, and other yogic communities, even as some of their practices elicited a critical response in the Sikh context. The extracts that are studied here offer an insight into the spectacle of the yogic lifestyle: Their distinct habits allowed a renewed focus on the dichotomy between the *munn* (mind) and *tunn* (body) to elevate a disciplining of the mind through actions of *nām simran* (remembering the divine name through silent or intoned recitation) and *kirtan*.

A verse by Guru Nanak in *rāg Suhi* offers a fruitful point of entry, given its insightful glimpse into the appearance and practices of the Nath yogi (and no doubt other sects of yogi) through a playful poetics of negation. He divests a yogi's few material possessions of their value and gives us a sense of their physical look by explaining what yoga is not:

> Yoga is not the patched coat. Yoga is not the walking stick. Yoga is not smearing the body with ashes. Yoga is not the earrings and not the shaven head. Yoga is not the blowing of the [animal] horn [*sinyi/singi*]. . . . Yoga is not wandering to the tombs of the dead, yoga is not sitting in trances, yoga is not wandering through foreign lands, yoga is not bathing at sacred shrines of pilgrimages. To remain unblemished in the midst of the filth of the world—this is the way to attain yoga. Meeting with the true guru, doubt is dispelled and the wandering mind is restrained. Nectar rains down, celestial music [*sehaj dhun*] resounds, and deep within, wisdom is obtained.[80]

Guru Arjan also highlights the superficial value of the Nath yogis' distinctive physical appearance—ash-smeared bodies, patched robes, and earrings (*mundra*) that dangle from pierced cartilage—in elevating recitation as a spiritual tool.[81] While the robe was believed to "provide protection from the demons" for the yogis, Guru Arjan, in keeping with Guru Nanak, emphasizes that protection and contentment is conferred only by remembrance of the divine name.[82]

Throughout *SGGS* gurus and bhagats carefully repurpose fundamental aspects of Nath yoga in offering an understanding of the body that is entirely reconfigured to prioritize a sonic inner reverberation of divinity. Kamala Nayar and Jaswinder Sandhu explain that, "according to Indian yogic traditions, there are 72,000 pathways (*nādīs*), which are the arteries of the subtle body." The central pathway, *sushmanaa*, runs "from the base of the spine to the top of the head," linking the six major chakras. Twisting around *sushmanaa*, and interlinking at each *chakra*, are the *ida* and *pingala nadi*, which also originate at the base of the spine. The flow of energy through *ida* creates "a cooling or calming effect," while the force that flows through *pingala* serves to heat and energize the body.[83] The goal, however, is not to alternate but to hold the breath in the central *sushmanaa* pathway, which facilitates the rise of energy toward *dasam dwar*. Bhagat Kabir comments on this practice of bodily control at several moments.[84] During the process of inner cleansing, as managed by the breath, it is the gradual awakening of each *chakra* starting from the base of the spine through to the crown of the head that takes the yogi to the state of *samadhi*. Thus, Bhagat Singh Thind describes *sushmanaa* as "the nadi [neural pathway] which connects the finite with the infinite."[85] The end goal for Nath yogis, as Nayar and Sandhu explain, may include the "acquiring of occult powers and, ultimately, immortality," a point echoed by William Pinch, who observes that the "'yoga' of Nath Yogis was principally about the cultivation of supernormal power. Of particular importance was power over the natural world ... and indeed over death itself."[86] However, this is not the goal of *raj yoga* (royal yoga), which is idealized in SGGS and aligned with the attainment of meditative bliss through introspective reflection on *shabad* (the divine word).[87]

Guru Nanak makes this point in *rāg Ramkali* when he equates *dasam dwar* with a sense of detachment.[88] In "Discourses with the Siddhas" (*Siddh Gost*), a section of SGGS that captures Guru Nanak's debates with "perfected yogis" (yogis who have attained the highest state of contemplation), Guru Nanak specifically draws on aspects of their language and spiritual practice to emphasize the primacy of the word.[89] Addressing the flow of breath and energy through the channels of *sushmanaa, ida,* and *pingala*, he points out that a truly divine corporeal experience lies beyond the yogic control of these energies.[90]

Guru Nanak also emphasizes the importance of *nām simran* by pointing to the futility of yogic breathing techniques for the purposes of spiritual awakening in *rāg Dhanasari*.[91] In another verse, his focus on the recitation of the divine name involves reassigning spiritual value to aspects of yogic attire, such as the musical instrument *sinyi*, an animal horn, which Nath yogis wear around their necks, and their begging bowl.[92] Here Gorakh, who is also mentioned in Guru Nanak's composition *Japji Sahib*, is referred to as the Hindu deity Vishnu, and Guru Nanak implies that the yogi's primary goal is to receive the gift of the divine name, whose internal reverberation sets in motion the external (*ahat*) vibrations of the *sinyi*.

The bhagats were equally conversant with the breathing techniques of the Nath yogis. As seen with Guru Nanak, *rāg Ramkali* is similarly favored for verses on the topic of *anahad* and *samadhi* by Bhagat Baynee and Bhagat Namdev. In an extensive composition, Bhagat Baynee's rhetorical appropriation of yoga is tied to an association of *dasam dwar*, located at the topmost *chakra* of the mind's sky (a pervasive metaphor in SGGS), with *panch shabad*, a confluence of five distinguishing timbres (another recurring concept that is discussed below). This verse speaks directly to the synesthetic experience of *anahad*:

> The energy channels of the *ida, pingala,* and *sushmanaa*: these three dwell in one place. / This is the true place of confluence of the three sacred rivers; this is where my mind takes its cleansing bath. / Oh Saints, the immaculate one dwells there. . . . What is the insignia of the divine one's dwelling? The unstruck word vibrates there. . . . The nucleus of the mind sky is drenched with ambrosial nectar [*amrit*]. . . . The tenth gate is the home of the inaccessible, infinite supreme one. . . . The five primal sounds

[*panch shabad*] resound and vibrate in their purity. / The fly whisks wave, and the *shankh* [conch] blares like thunder.[93]

The sensations of water flowing from sacred rivers and the gentle air currents created by the graceful sweep of fly whisks are accompanied by the taste of *amrit* and the intermingling of discrete timbres with the sound of the conch rising above the rest. This moment clearly signals the multisensory awakening associated with the merging of the self with divinity. Bhagat Namdev's verses further expand our understanding of *anahad nād*. He refers to the unstruck music of the *bayn* (flute) heard in the realm of *nirankar* while acknowledging the state of detachment in which he begins to sing divine praise.[94]

Building on Guru Nanak's perception of the body as a cave (*gufa*) that engulfs a reverberating *anahad nād*, Guru Amardas and Guru Arjan develop especially nuanced reconfigurations of the yogic body in their compositions.[95] In *rāg Maru Dakhni* Guru Nanak offers a sixteen-stanza metaphoric description of the inner journey toward hearing *anahad nād*. In these evocative verses the body is imagined as a village, and the mind's sky, the location of the tenth door (*dasam dwar*), is where the divine one resides. The notion of a door (*dwar*) is borrowed from yoga, whose epistemological framework allows the body to be seen as having nine openings (two for the reproductive organs, two eyes, two nostrils, two ears, and one mouth). *SGGS* places great emphasis on the concealed tenth door (*dasam dwar*), given that this is where divinity resides:

> The hard and heavy doors of the tenth gate are closed and locked. Through the word of the guru's primal word [*shabad*], they are thrown open. / Within the fortress [of the body] is the cave, the home of the self. / The creator established the nine gates of this house by divine command and will. / In the tenth gate, the primal one, the unknowable and infinite dwells; the unseen one is revealed. . . . The wind blowing around like a fly whisk, waving over the divine one. The creator placed the two lamps, the sun and the moon; the sun merges in the house of the moon. . . . The tree of life is fruitful, bearing the fruit of ambrosial nectar. / The one who is attuned to the guru [*Gurmukh*] intuitively sings glorious praises; they eat the food of divine sublime essence. Dazzling light glitters, although neither the moon nor the stars are shining. . . . Unstruck tinkling [*jhunkar*, the timbre of small bells] vibrates continuously in the home of the fearless one.[96]

At this moment of ecstasy, the devotee feels, tastes, smells, sees, and hears in a synesthetic inner acknowledgment of union with the divine.

The metaphor of the body as a *gufa* (cave) is taken up in equally compelling ways by Guru Amardas. In *rāg Majh* he describes the "inexhaustible treasure" that is hidden in the cave, whose divinity is only revealed by subjugating the ego through recitation.⁹⁷ Emphasis on the treasures of the inner cave also furthers the critiques of yogic practices of social isolation made at several other moments of *SGGS*.⁹⁸ Equally striking in Guru Amardas's forty-stanza composition in *rāg Ramkali, Anand Sahib*, are the final verses (38–40), which cast the cavernous body as a musical instrument.⁹⁹ Revered for its description of an ecstatic inner bliss, the daily singing and recitation of this composition reminds devotees that "singing the true song of praise in your true body" (922-16) and listening to *Anand Sahib* facilitate the inner resounding of *shabad* (divine word) and *nād*. These reverberations are voluminous (*shabad ghanayray*, 917-8) and contribute to *panch shabad* (literally "five sounds" but referring to a multitude of musical timbres), where the sound of the *turay* (a brass instrument) bursts forth (922-19). In *rāg Maru*, too, Guru Amardas notes the roles of divinity as a musician and of the body as an instrument. A similar emphasis is made in *rāg Gauri*.¹⁰⁰ The yogi's unabating material desire (*trisna*) becomes the focal point of criticism in *rāg Ramkali* where Guru Amardas points to the futility of playing the *kinguri* (a bowed string instrument associated with folk music) and argues instead for turning the entire body into the vibrating chamber of this instrument in the search for true yoga.¹⁰¹

I will dwell on Guru Amardas's metaphor of the body as a musical instrument for a moment since it signals an important point in the spiritual ascent toward the fourth state, one where divinity channels music through the body, as heard in an attuned state. Guru Ramdas takes up this point in *rāg Gauri Majh*: "Oh, great one, the music of the wind is deep within; as divinity plays this music, so does it vibrate and resound."¹⁰² Guru Arjan also conceives of the body as a vibrating string instrument (*jant*, Braj for *tant*) in *rāg Bhairo*: "I am your string instrument and you are the instrumentalist."¹⁰³ Guru Nanak, the archetypal folk musician, imagines the yogic body specifically as a *kinguri* whose strings (as symbolized by the right and left nostrils) "vibrate the wondrous melody of the *shabad*," while the consciousness vibrates through the timbre of the *sinyi* (animal horn) and the mind through that of the *bayn* (flute).¹⁰⁴

It is primarily to Bhagat Kabir that I now turn in building on an understanding of the body through metaphors that speak to yogic practices, while furthering our understanding of how the anatomy of musical instruments is mapped onto human physiology during spiritual transformation. Kabir's verses are veiled in metaphor, but they never miss their mark, whether they involve praise or critique. Following Guru Nanak, the gurus mainly turned to the popular *bhakti rāg* of Ramkali to convey their commentaries on inner bliss. In contrast, Kabir's vision of a new corporeality comes through in a variety of *rāg*, in relation to which he explores metaphysical allusions to contemporaneous yogic practices alongside an unwavering attention to the pursuit of divine union.[105]

One verse that is particularly striking in this regard is in *rāg Gauri*, where the Nath yogi's few material belongings and preference for isolation are once again reinterpreted to elevate internal meditation. Notably, this verse shows Bhagat Kabir reenvisioning his mind and breath as constituent parts of a *tumba* (a one-stringed folk instrument) that are held in place by divinity. In a state of bliss, the string of the *tumba* (which stands in for the body and refers specifically to *sushmanaa*) "becomes steady and does not break." Once the consciousness ascends to this ecstatic state, it is not the earthly (rustic) strumming of the *tumba* that is heard but the divine strains of the (celestial) *kinguri*, which is linked to the realm of *dasam dwar*.[106]

This state of equipoise finds contrast in a related verse, where the broken string of the body prevents the experience of divine union and thus brings Bhagat Kabir to a state of distress conveyed in *rāg Gauri Purbi*.[107] The frustration he feels at being earthbound—as opposed to in his ideal dwelling in the metaphorical sky of *dasam dwar*—is also expressed in *rāg Aasa*. Here, the metaphor of the body as a broken string signals a troubled mind, which prevents the celestial *rabab* (a plucked chordophone) from being played.[108] In *rāg Ramkali* Kabir reconceives the consciousness and mind as instruments: Kabir instructs the Nath yogi, "Apply the ashes of wisdom to your body; let your *sinyi* [animal horn] be your focused consciousness. / Become detached and wander through the city of your body; play the *kinguri* of your mind."[109] Upon finding the door of liberation (*mukat dwar*), Kabir hears the *tur* (brass instrument) being played in the realm of *nirbhao* (divinity as fearless), where "the unstruck sound current vibrates and resonates forever."[110]

Even as he sometimes questions the integrity of how Nath yogis practice, Kabir also reappropriates key aspects of their behavior to describe how these can be directed toward the attainment of inner bliss. Again, in *rāg Ramkali*, he invokes inner cleansing as taking place through breathing techniques and facilitating spiritual attainment.[111] It is only at a certain moment of his meditation that he becomes aware of the distinct timbre of the *bayn* (flute): "When I was focused and merged into the all-pervading one, the unstruck *bayn* began to play."[112] The implicit suggestion that there are stages to meditation is important to observe, given his insightful comments on accessing the highest realm. Here, too, Kabir reappropriates yogic techniques. In a *tipada* (three-stanza) composition in *rāg Gauri Bairagan*, he explains, "I turned my breath inward and pierced through the six chakras of the body, and my awareness was centered on the primal void [*sunn*] of the absolute one."[113] Kabir establishes an important dualism that situates the primacy of *sunn* in the fourth state.

Whereas bodily labor initiates the meditative process through control of the breath, it is eventually the ceasing of work that marks entry through *dasam dwar*. Beyond this point the state of *sunn* is marked by a quality of stillness and equipoise where there is no exertion of energy; Guru Nanak instructs in *rāg Suhi*, "Practice such a yoga where one is dead while still alive."[114] Thus, Kabir is able to express in *rāg Bhairo*, "Turning away from the world, I have forgotten both my social class and ancestry. / My weaving now is in the most profound celestial stillness [*sunn sehaj*]."[115] It is not only the labor of weaving that finds ease through a lack of effort. Musical instruments whose unique timbres mark arrival at and entry through *dasam dwar* are also sounded in the same way. In *rāg Aasa* Guru Nanak reminds us that *ghungroo* (small bells) are played when the "mind is held steady," while in *rāg Suhi* Guru Nanak says that the timbre of the *sinyi* signals a deeper meditative state: "When the *sinyi* is blown without being blown, then you shall reach the state of fearless dignity."[116] Also in *rāg Aasa* Guru Nanak links the *sinyi* to yogic *asana* and to the first player of this instrument, Shiva.[117]

In the deepest state, other instruments are also sounded without being played. Guru Amardas, in *rāg Ramkali*, says, "Play the *kinguri*, which vibrates without being played, Yogi."[118] Guru Arjan hears the music of the unplayed *kinguri* in the deepest meditative state. In *rāg Ramkali*, he experiences the body as a temple and the devotee as a yogi who wanders past the many windows: "I come to your door after searching and searching; finally, the yogi finds their home. Thus, the formless [*anoop*] *kinguri* plays; in hearing it, the yogi finds it sweet."[119] Bhagat Namdev, also in *rāg Ramkali*, explains that he forgoes singing in the earthly realm, preferring instead the detached form of music-making that occurs in the deepest realm of *nirankar*.[120] Bhagat Kabir implores the devotee to "become detached, wander through the body [city], and play the *kinguri* with the consciousness [*munn*]."[121]

The journey that I trace in this section began in a realm inhabited by tangible phenomena—ranging from instruments to objects from Nath yoga—and marked by corporeal exertion, associated with conscious recitation through articulation of the tongue, awareness of playing and hearing *kirtan* through bodily movement, and auditory and visual stimulation. My observations on a sonic delivery of *shabad* through the means of recitation, remembrance (*nām simran*), and *kirtan* were accompanied by the writings of the gurus and bhagats, which point to the importance of locating the hidden tenth door (*dasam dwar*) within the body. As the consciousness passes through this door, located at the crown of the head, it encounters a realm defined by intangible phenomena, a metaphysical expanse that is beyond materiality and exertion, whose divine status is conveyed through a paradoxical stillness of sound and sensation. In this fourth state recitation takes place without speech (*ajapa jaap*), instruments sound without being played, and a weaver such as Kabir weaves without weaving. These processes are often described as automatic and spontaneous, and while these actions certainly retain this aura, I emphasize a different facet of their manifestation, one that points to a distinct lack of effort since it is the concentration of bodily energy in the mind that activates an intense experience of sound and sensation upon experiencing divine union.

The fourth state is the highest state of spiritual attainment and signals absorption in the deepest realm of *samadhi*. Over the course of my discussion I have signaled various musical timbres that are intrinsic to this journey and might even be seen to punctuate spiritual progress if one were to perceive, as Bhai Randhir Singh did, the timbres of *jhunkar* as a lower-stage timbral sign, the *shankh* as a mid-stage sign, and the thunderous *bheri* as signaling arrival at the pinnacle, the realm of *nirankar*.[122] It is worth mentioning that the timbral trajectory is not fixed in *SGGS*, whereas Vedic texts tend to emphasize a hierarchy of timbres.[123] In *Gurbani* it is sometimes the *bheri* that signals arrival in the fourth state, while at other moments it may be the *kinguri*, *turay*, *sinyi*, *ghungroo*, or a combination thereof. I now pay close attention to the articulation of the fourth state through timbral resonance in continuing to refine Sikh notions of *anahad nād*.

THE FOURTH STATE AND TIMBRAL RESONANCE OF *PANCH SHABAD*

The fourth state is known by a variety of names in *SGGS*, including *turiya avastha* (state of pure consciousness), *chautha pad* (fourth stage or realm), *chauthai sunnai* (fourth void or expanse), *chauthai ghar* (fourth home or body dwelling), *chauthee pauree* (fourth step), and *sunn* (void or expanse). Guru Arjan uses the metaphor of a jewel-filled chamber (*rattan kothri*) to describe this rare and precious region in *rāg Ramkali*, which Bhagat Namdev also perceives as a source of light comparable to the sun; the internalization of solar energy is described as *anhat sur*.[124] Meanwhile, in *rāg Gauri* Bhagat Ravidas refers to this blissful realm with the striking metaphor of *Begam Pura*, "the city without sorrow."[125] Given the many formulations that reference this sphere, including *baikunth* (celestial) and *param pad* (supreme state), I will continue to use "the fourth state" for ease of reference and because it keeps in view a clear identification with the four states of consciousness central to both Vedic and Sikh epistemologies: wakefulness, dream state, deep sleep, and pure consciousness.[126]

Nayar and Sandhu offer a useful explanation of the difference between the third and fourth states: "In the deep-sleep state, the mind is in a state of absolute stillness. As there are no thoughts or dreams, consciousness gradually experiences *Nam* resonating from the core of one's being. The deep-sleep state leads to the fourth state, wherein consciousness is totally immersed in *Ek Oankar*."[127] The "core" is what is interpreted as the navel (*naabh*) in *SGGS* and what plays a central role in elevating the consciousness during yogic breathing techniques and the practices of *nām simran* and *kirtan*. The pinnacle of a devotee's spiritual journey toward the fourth state is reached through overcoming the three *gunas* (qualities or attributes) associated with *maya* (the illusion of materiality): *sattva* (true, pure, luminous), *rajas* (passion, excitement, activity), and *tamas* (dark, inertia).[128]

In preparation for a study of timbral resonance (how different instruments are made to sound) in the deepest stage of meditation, I briefly draw attention to the auditory journey that has been taken thus far. As mediated by *kirtan*, the initial encounter with music and timbre has been associated with an external sounding (*ahat nād*) in the earthly realm whose resonance facilitates a corporeal shift to a place of inner sounding (*anahad nād*) linked to the celestial realm. Several verses from *SGGS* narrate this journey through a physical and metaphysical understanding of the body, capturing the vibration of sound from the level of the cellular to larger neural networks and the depths of pure consciousness (*rom rom*) in search of that place, *dasam dwar*, whose threshold is signaled synesthetically. Along the way close attention has been given to sonic markers that designate arrival at *dasam dwar*: These have included the *bheri, sinyi, shankh, rabab, kinguri, bayn, jhunkar, ghungroo,* and *tur* (see fig. 3.5). My study of the fourth state, where the spiritual potency of the body is felt in its heightened form as vibration, pays close attention to a parallel process where music manifests in the consciousness through its purest form as timbre in the form of *panch shabad*.

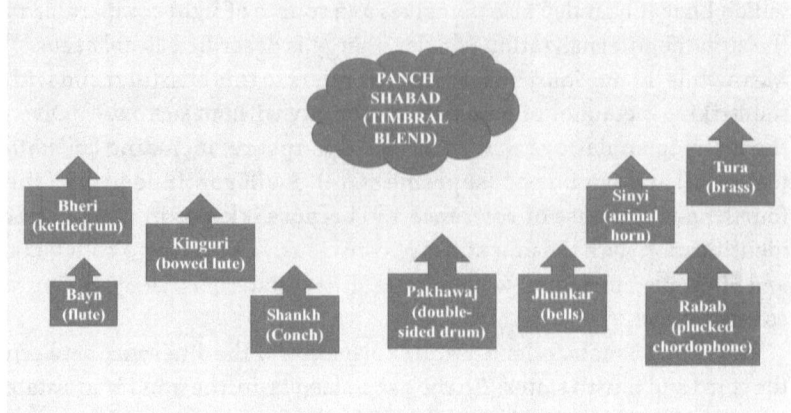

FIGURE 3.5 Individual musical timbres blend to create a heterogenous timbral blend (*panch shabad*) at the deepest state of meditation.

I chart this sonically marked journey in **figure 3.6**, which captures the fourth state as a culminating point reached by overcoming the three qualities (*gunas*). Bhagat Kabir explains in *rāg Kedara*, "Raaj gun, taam gun, and sat gun are all your illusions of maya. / The one who seizes the fourth state, only that person has attained supreme bliss."[129] **Figure 3.6** alludes to another significant conceptual counterpart in *Gurbani* as delineated by Guru Nanak in *Japji Sahib* (particularly verses 34–37), where he outlines five realms: *dharam khand, gyan khand, saram khand, karam khand*, and, finally, *sach khand*.[130] Nikky-Guninder Kaur Singh describes these realms as demonstrating "the quintessential illustration of the Sikh mystical journey," and **figure 3.6** captures this experience across three conceptual planes; the auditory journey from hearing *kirtan* to experiencing *anahad nād* undergirds the entire schema.[131]

Although *panch shabad* is commonly aligned with the fourth state and thus an approximation to the primal word (*shabad*), the notion of "five" (*panch*) has been interpreted in contrasting ways. We see its association with (a) allusions to the sensory domain (Nikky-Guninder Kaur Singh); (b) five types of materials through which musical instruments are made and through which they vibrate (Sukhbir Singh Kapoor, whose approach is in keeping with Bhai Vir Singh's five-pronged conception of *nād* discussed above); (c) five types of musical instruments (Gobind Singh Mansukhani and Pashaura Singh); (d) an indication of timbral blend, "a mixture of all five kinds of sounds" (Christopher Shackle and Arvind-Pal Singh Mandair); and (e) an association with five melodies (Kirpal

Anahad Nād and the Sonic Embodiment of Divinity | 139

TURIYA (Fourth State) Pure consciousness	**SACH KHAND (truth)** "the home of the Ultimate Reality" (N-G. K. Singh)	**NIRANKAR**
THUNDER	"complete resonance with the Ultimate Reality" (Nayar and Sandhu)	
Shankh (Conch shell) Chhainay (steel tongs, cymbals)	**KARAM KHAND (grace & action)** ANAHAD NĀD	**EK ONKAR** Sookham ras (experience peace)
Flute Tinkling bells		**ONKAR** → Anahad Nād Jhunkar (tinkling bells)
	SARAM KHAND (aesthetics)	
	GYAN KHAND (knowledge)	
	DHARAM KHAND (duty & morality)	
KIRTAN/SIMRAN (recitation/remembrance)	**CONTEMPLATION OF KIRTAN/SHABAD**	**KIRTAN - AHAT NĀD** RĀG
	"Five stages by which human beings can ascend toward the Ultimate Reality" (N-G. K. Singh) "Five spheres of spiritual practice" (Nayar and Sandhu)	Kan ras (experience auditory pleasure)
Bhair Randhir Singh's model		Bhai Vir Singh's model

FIGURE 3.6 Bhai Vir Singh's and Bhai Randhir's Singh's models of *nād* set in parallel against the five stages of spiritual ascent outlined in *SGGS*.

Singh).[132] To be sure, these viewpoints are complementary, and they infuse my own reading of *panch shabad* as pointing to distinct, intertwined timbres. The blending of these timbres at a moment of spiritual intensity contributes to a resplendent voluminosity captured by the notions of multiplicity and plenitude inherent to the term *ghanayray* and conveyed through two key verses by Guru Nanak. *Panch* (five) is not to be taken literally, but symbolically, as referring to sonic richness.

For example, stanza 27 of *Japji Sahib* describes the fourth state ("*so ghar*"), the realm that lies beyond *dasam dwar* ("*so dar*"), as one that is reverberant with multiple timbres conveyed through numerous manifestations of *nād* and abundant *rāg* played by countless musicians and singers, including spiritually accomplished *siddha*, ascetics, yogis, pandits, warriors, fairies, enchanting women, gods and goddesses, sixty-eight sacred sites of worship, and nature itself in the form of wind, water, fire, jewels, continents, constellations, and universes. This verse is remarkable for its inimitable description of the reverberant and resonant cosmic song to divinity, whose infinite sonic profusion is fitting for the divine "emperor of emperors."[133]

Another verse in *rāg Malar* by Guru Nanak retains a similar focus on sonic and timbral multiplicity:

The true guru is the all-knowing primal being; the true one shows us our true home within the home of the self. / The five primal sounds [*panch shabad*] resonate and resound within; the insignia of the primal sound [*shabad*] is revealed there, vibrating gloriously. / Worlds and realms, nether regions, solar systems, and galaxies are wondrously revealed. / The strings and harps vibrate and resound; the true throne of the divine one is there. / Listen to the music in the home of the heart. Lovingly tune into the state of celestial ecstasy.[134]

This verse points to an important difference between moments in *Gurbani* where emphasis is placed squarely on timbral fusion, as suggested by the simultaneous sounding of multiple, heterogeneous timbres seen with Guru Arjan in *rāg Aasa*: "rabab, pakhawaj, [rhythmic] *ghungroo* play *anahad shabad*."[135] In contrast, at other moments a specific timbre may be singled out. As outlined above, one might read isolated timbres as articulating points of progression in the journey toward spiritual ascent, while their combination in the fourth state symbolizes arrival in this realm. Rabinder Singh Bhamra notes a similar timbral trajectory: "When the time comes for union . . . *Anhad Sabad* changes to *Toor* . . . followed by *naad*, a loud low frequency humming sound before you are let into *Sach Ghar* [*Sachkhand*] . . . [where] *Anhad Sabad* changes to *Panch Shabad*."[136] The progression from identifiable timbres associated with the external realm of music-making to an awe-inspiring confluence of "mystic sounds," as noted by Pashaura Singh, is significant for how it points to sound and timbre as participating in and guiding the process of spiritual awakening.[137] Along these lines, we see how Guru Arjan, in *rāg Ramkali*, explains the timbral perfection of *panch shabad*: "The five timbres, the five primal sounds, echo the perfect sound current of *nād*. / The wondrous, amazing unstruck melody vibrates. . . . It is the realm of celestial peace and bliss."[138] In this instance, *panch shabad* is manifest as *nād*: a balanced intermingling of undifferentiated timbres. The powerful timbral intensity of *panch shabad* marks the devotee's arrival in the fourth state. In Guru Ramdas's verse in *rāg Kanra* it is the sound of thundering that marks this moment: "*Panch shabad* vibrate with the wisdom of the guru's teachings; by great good fortune, unstruck melody resonates and resounds. / I see the creator, the source of bliss, everywhere; the word of the guru's *shabad* thunders."[139]

It is difficult to parse the variegated nature of *panch shabad* into its constituent timbres — SGGS doesn't explicate the sonic makeup of *panch shabad*, nor is the attuned devotee invited to pick out the unique sounds of individual instruments.[140] Instead, the timbral resonance of *panch shabad* immerses the detached *Gurmukh* into a richly reverberant soundscape where the need to locate the source of sound doesn't even arise. The devotee is beyond such reflexive questioning and concerns, which is why Michel Chion's term "acousmatic" — a way to characterize disembodied sound — has no place here. In the fourth state there is no desire to trace the physical source of sound since the devotee has already perceived the sonic through merging with the divine. In this realm it is divinity itself that is the source of sound rather than a physical, observable finite object like a musical instrument. As we saw in the previous section, this is how instruments like the *kinguri* can vibrate without being played, and this is why the entire body becomes a sonorous instrument played by divinity. Infinite bliss associated with hearing *panch shabad* is conveyed in *rāg Suhi* by Guru Nanak, who compares this moment of divine union to an earthly equivalent, that of marriage.[141] Songs of joy (*mangal*) are also emphasized by Guru Ramdas; for him, earthly *kirtan* sparks this spiritual journey.[142]

There is just one moment associated with *panch shabad* where a single instrument comes to the fore, and this is in the Vedic-oriented description of *anahad nād* by Bhagat Baynee, who emphasizes the immaculate purity of *panch shabad* (described as "*nirmaeel*") while also sensing the thunderous vibrations of the *shankh* (conch), an instrument mentioned mostly by the bhagats and only a handful of times.[143] Otherwise, *panch shabad* is perceived as an unlocatable, uninterrupted, awe-inspiring, voluminous, intensely vibrant timbral blend whose sonic resonance activates a uniquely synesthetic experience of divinity.

| CHAPTER SUMMARY

Having reached the peak of the spiritual journey toward *anahad nād*, I use this cliff-hanger as an opportunity to take stock of the observations made thus far in preparation for an in-depth study of *anahad* instruments in the following chapter. Many devotees, especially those of the diaspora, remain unsure about the meaning of *anahad nād*. I have clarified the meaning of *anahad nād* while highlighting its manifestation as an intensely synesthetic experience of corporeal vibration, where the unique timbres of musical instruments, either heard individually or in the form of a multitudinous blend, signal spiritual attainment. The longstanding duality of *ahat/anahad nād* that underlies a Vedic theory of *nād* does not fully capture the Sikh experience because it doesn't account for the critical role played by *kirtan* in facilitating the devotee's shift of consciousness from an aesthetically engaged appreciation of music to a psychically detached contemplation of timbre.

As I honed my observations about timbre and embodiment in conversation with scholars in the Euro-North American academy, I sensed the urgency of drawing on Sikh notions of *nād* to broaden current discussions and show how timbre can indeed "be simultaneously ineffable, metaphysical, transcendent, *and* physical, corporeal, material," a paradoxical mode that is problematized by Elferen in her emphasis on the binary dimensions of timbre.[144] Similarly, I draw attention to an epistemological framework where timbre has long been considered "a more active phenomenon than we generally give it credit for," as noted by Wallmark; gurus and bhagats are among a long line of thinkers who have viewed timbre as "something we do with our bodies in both production and sympathetically in perception. These bodily, experiential structures of timbre influence how we ultimately derive aesthetic and social meanings from sound."[145] The uniquely embodied experience that I observe points to a convergence between psychological, physiological, and philosophical reflections on timbre, as developed by Wallmark, van Elferen, Eidsheim, and others, and supramundane perspectives that draw into the conversation a focus on the consciousness. My interest in the vibrational force of the subtle body fosters a natural dialogue with Eidsheim's ideas about transduction, in particular. Going one step further, I highlight intersections between the subtle and the gross body to develop an even greater awareness of the *whole* body. Further studies of embodied timbres are thus primed to examine a relatively underexplored area where physical and metaphysical matter converge and coexist.

It is important to take note of an important distinction: Despite the musical rendering of verses in *rāg*, we must keep in view that *kirtan* is not only a mode of musical performance. Or, rather, *kirtan* is only secondarily an opportunity for aesthetic engagement. Although the devotee may start out by appreciating the musical setting of poetic verses, the purpose of *kirtan* is not only to entertain but also to elevate the consciousness in a way that impacts the molecular structure of corporeal matter, allowing even the smallest cellular structures, nerves, and fibers, to vibrate with divine energy, thereby allowing the amplification of the divine name to resonate through the body. I have focused on the individual here, but it is important to note that this resonance extends beyond the body; it is transduced through surrounding matter to resonate in harmony with surrounding phenomena, whether human, animal, vegetal, meteorological, or otherwise.

Musical instruments play a critical role in articulating the phases of spiritual attainment. The label *anahad instruments* gives them due credit, and we will now come to learn more about them as we consider why the *bheri, sinyi, shankh, bayn, tura, kinguri, rabab,* and *ghungroo* were chosen to narrate the inner journey toward divinity.

| 4

Hearing (*Anahad*) Instruments and the *Rabab* in Sikh Art

A changing array of instrumental timbres accompanies the shifting consciousness as it progresses toward the deepest realm of meditation in the fourth state. The instruments referenced in the context of *anahad*—*bheri*, *sinyi*, *shankh*, *bayn*, *tura*, *kinguri*, *rabab*, *ghungroo*, and *kartāl*—are all earthly. However, the activation of their timbres either individually or as part of a timbral blend also confers upon them a divine status. To expand our understanding of these *anahad* instruments, I consider their materials and other historical-cultural associations. The *rabab* receives close attention because it is the first instrument associated with *kirtan*, having been played by Bhai Mardana.

This chapter has three parts. The first lists *anahad* instruments to create an inventory of Sikh instruments (those associated with *kirtan* since the time of the gurus but also played in other contexts and places, as I indicate). Although much literature has been written about *rāg* in relation to Sikh devotional practices, little scholarly attention has been given to musical instruments: what they look like; how they were constructed; how, where, by whom, in what contexts, and for what kinds of listeners and patrons they were played, and so on. Confusion remains on what a *tura* is, for instance, or a *sinyi*, and key instruments such as the *rabab* and *kinguri* continue to be mistranslated (usually as "rebec" or "harp," respectively). The observations that I make are largely based on secondary sources by South Asian and Euro-North American scholars, and these are supplemented as much as possible by details gleaned from discussions of the instruments themselves in SGGS.¹ I continue to deepen the work begun in chapter 3 of noticing how the unique timbres of *anahad* instruments punctuate the spiritual journey.

A study of the *rabab* as an existing instrument—including recent discoveries of *rabab* belonging to Guru Arjan, Guru Hargobind, and Guru Gobind Singh—is productively deepened by examining eighteenth- and nineteenth-century visual materials to uncover more information about this instrument and its status during the time of the gurus. The second section takes an iconographical turn bolstered by my decades-long experience of studying how music and sound inform the techniques and subject matter of painting. By virtue of the *rabab*'s association with Bhai Mardana and the travels (*udasi*) he undertook as the primary companion of Guru Nanak, much of the material studied here relates to the *Janamsakhi* corpus (posthumous literary and visual accounts of Guru Nanak's life). A handful of images highlight the vast, regional variety in depictions of the *rabab*. This artwork was produced across numerous workshops stretching from Lahore, across the Punjab hills and plains, to Murshidabad in the East and the Deccan region in the South. Many of these illustrations were produced by artisans of varying religious and cultural backgrounds; Nikky-Guninder Kaur Singh tells us, "The artists who painted [Guru Nanak] were also Hindu, Muslim, Buddhist, or Jain, and they presented the Sikh Guru through the lens of their respective religious beliefs."² A particularly important source, the B-40 manuscript (1733) housed at the British Library, is described by Surjit Hans as being "doubly Sikh" because it was "painted by a Sikh for the Sikhs but [it] also embod[ies] the basic doctrines of Sikhism." Hans suggests that this manuscript rises to the challenge of creating ideologically oriented pictorial art.³

Hans's criticism of scholars for focusing on the "literary merit of the *Janamsakhi*" has been largely assuaged by the efforts of Nikky-Guninder Kaur Singh, Atsushi Ikeda, and Gurdeep Kour, among others.⁴ In tandem with the research of these authors, this chapter is among the first to trace a musical iconography of the *rabab* in Sikh art, a task I pursue bearing in mind the heavily stylized mode of depiction that characterizes this work, which speaks to the roving nature of the mind's eye and creative freedom (the perils and pitfalls of which are addressed later in the chapter). Despite increasing scholarly study of the *Janamsakhi*, it is surprising that the *rabab*, which features in almost every narrative and frame, has evaded critical analysis. This is a lacuna that I fill by observing aspects of its appearance, variations in its playing style, and its narrative function. Growing out of this discussion in the penultimate section is a brief engagement with the sonic significance of the halo whose amplification of the body's internal vibrations serves as a marker of divinity. A Sikh perspective on the halo draws this visual motif into discourses of *anahad nād* and *dasam dwar*, given its visual correspondence with the *rabab* and its placement at the crown of the head.

ANAHAD INSTRUMENTS

Having established how *panch shabad* (five primal sounds) are tied to the deepest shifts of consciousness in chapter 3, I now trace the timbral trajectory that signals and accompanies this transformation by singling out the instruments that contribute to this blend. In thinking about *panch* symbolically, as indicating sonic plenitude rather than a literal delineation of five instruments, I briefly mention those instruments associated with *anahad*. Gobind Singh Mansukhani's classification of instruments into four types proves useful: (a) *tat vad* (where contact with strings is made by fingers and a plectrum) and *vitat vad* (where contact with strings is made using a bow); (b) *sushir vad* (where sound is created through the vibration of air); (c) *avanad vad* (where contact with a membrane is made using the hands); and (d) *ghan vad* (where sound issues from idiophones, self-sounding instruments).[5]

Other than the primal word (*shabad*), the first instrument to be associated with *anahad* in *SGGS* is *bheri*, which is also listed as one of the upper-level timbres (along with the double-faced drum, *mridang*, and thunder) in the *Hamsa Upanishad*. The *bheri* is a single-headed drum, played standing up, with a tightly bound leather membrane attached to a metal, dome-like base, whose timbre is likely closest to that of the drum known among Sikhs as the *Ranjit nagara* (based on the Persian, *naqqarah*) and which is associated with Guru Gobind Singh (*Ranjit nagara* is typically translated as "the drum of victory in the battlefield").[6] According to Jagtar Singh Grewal, a single drum was prepared in 1679 and struck daily (morning and evening), as well as when the guru was going out to hunt.[7] In *SGGS* Sheikh Farid also mentions the beating of the drum (*naubat*) in the morning.[8] The membrane is usually made of ox or cow hide, with a crisscross looping of leather thongs through its edges, which are secured into a ring that surrounds the circumference of the drum membrane. Its two wooden sticks (*dagga* or *danka*) have small, rounded tops.[9] Another membrane percussion instrument associated with *anahad* is the double-headed *pakhawaj* (also called *mridang* in *SGGS*), which features as part of an ensemble and as a single timbre played by divinity in the form of *mridang anahad*. In *rāg Malar* Guru Arjan instructs the devotee to sing the divine name of *rām* with sweetness and beauty, like a *kokil* bird, against this percussive accompaniment.[10]

Whereas *bheri* and *pakhawaj/mridang* are recognized as *avanad vad*, other *anahad* percussion instruments, such as *ghungroo*, fall into the category of *ghan vad* and assume a divine role at three points. Guru Nanak associates this timbre in *rāg Aasa* with the moment where the "mind is held steady" during meditation. Guru Arjan describes *ghungroo* as one of four instruments that play *anahad shabad*.[11] Finally, during a moment that is not aligned with *anahad* but that nevertheless gives insights into the range of instruments used in *kirtan*, Guru Ramdas mentions *ghungroo* as a rhythm-playing instrument in a verse where he laments the long wait for musicians to gather their instruments and tune them in preparation for *kirtan*.[12]

Mostly though, it is the timbre of *ghungroo*, translated as the vibration of small, tinkling bells described as *jhunkar* or *runn jhunkar*, that is tied to *anahad*, as seen at several moments with Guru Arjan: "In peace and poise, the unstruck vibration of the *shabad* resounds. / In peace and poise, the celestial bells resound" and "Remembering the divine one, one hears unstruck tinkling."[13] Guru Arjan also links this timbre to acts of service: "The unstruck celestial tinkling resounds when one performs acts of true service."[14] Guru Nanak's description in *rāg Maru Dakhni* suggests that bells are a discernible timbre in the fourth state: "An unstruck tinkling [*runn jhunkar*] vibrates continuously in the realm of the fearless one. When unstruck sound resounds, doubt and fear run away."[15] He also says, in *rāg Maru*, "The creator resounds the pure tinkling of the *panch shabad*."[16] Both Guru Nanak and Guru Arjan associate ringing bells (*jhunkar*) with *anahad*. Guru Nanak explains in *rāg Aasa*, "The unstruck melody of the sound current [*runn jhunkar*] resounds with the vibrations of celestial instruments." Guru Arjan in *rāg Sarang* also hears the many timbres associated with *anahad* as ringing (*jhunkar*) with peace.[17] Meanwhile, through his trademark striking imagery, Bhagat Kabir places the timbre of tinkling bells at the lips (*hōt*) where *anahad shabad* is first initiated in the form of recitation and *kirtan*.[18] In *rāg Aasa*, at the deepest state of meditation, he observes that his mind no longer exerts itself to play the handheld cymbals, *mandariya*.[19]

Guru Arjan also associates different parts of the body with the act of playing instruments in a heightened state, and this time we notice another new percussion instrument, the *kartāl* (wooden clappers), sometimes shortened to *tāl* in *SGGS*.[20] Guru Arjan links this idiophone clearly to *anahad* in *rāg Aasa*: "The devotee plays the *rabab*, *pakhawaj*, *tāl*, [and] *ghungroo*, and the unstruck word (*anahad shabad*) resounds."[21]

Moving on to brass instruments, an *anahad* instrument that retained a martial sensibility (like the *bheri*) at the time of the gurus is the *tura* (also known as *turi*, *turava*, or *ran-singha* in other states of India).[22] These are just a few ways to romanize this spelling given the numerous pronunciations that we see in *SGGS*, ranging from *tur* to *turai*, *tura*, and *turahi*. Belonging to the category of *sushir vad*, the *tura* is a heavy, brass or copper instrument. It is mostly thought of as a straight instrument, but it can also be S-shaped, where the two parts slot into one other and are held in place by broad rings of brass (which serve a supportive and decorative function).[23] Bigamudre Deva describes this lip-reed aerophone as ancient, given its appearance in twelfth-century sculpture (and even earlier at the historic site of Sanchi, Madhya Pradesh).[24] An *anahad instrument*, the bright and resonating timbre of the *tura* is associated with jubilation, especially by Guru Arjan, as seen in several verses in a variety of *rāg*:

> Those who have been given the mantra of *nām* [divine name] by the guru shall not be turned away
> They are filled with the ambrosial nectar.
> Oh Nanak, unstruck *tura* vibrates for them. (*rāg Gauri*)

> Says Nanak, those for whom the true guru is perfect, the unstruck *tura* vibrates for them. (*rāg Aasa*)

> I have obtained the nine treasures [abundance], rejoicing prevails, unstruck *tura* resounds. (*rāg Wadhans*)

> Unstruck *tura* vibrates as I chant the divine name in a state of tranquility, equipoise, and peace. (*rāg Sorath*)

> The perfect guru has dispelled inner burning [*taap*]; unstruck *tura* resounds. (*rāg Sorath*)

> By meditating on *hari* [the true one], cross over the ocean of existence [*bhavjal*] and fulfill your wishes.
> Even the worst corruption is taken away, peace wells up, and unstruck *tura* vibrates. (*rāg Suhi*)

> Peace has awakened within me; unstruck *tura* is played. (*rāg Bilawal*)

Such is Guru Arjan's association of *tura* with ecstatic joy that he hears this timbre as activating *panch nād* (a synonym for *panch shabad*): "By pleasing the holy ones, glimpse the beloved one; the unstruck *tura* plays the *panch nād*."[25]

In addition to Guru Arjan, Guru Nanak and Guru Ramdas also associate the timbre of the *tura* with a feeling of inner joy at reaching the tenth door (*dasam dwar*). In *rāg Gauri* Guru Nanak writes, "By practicing control over the nine gates, one attains perfect control over the tenth gate. / There *tura* is played in the realm of *anhat sunn* [void]" and "Following the guru's teachings [*Gurmat*], the perfect humble ones meditate. / Within their hearts, the unstruck *tura* is played." Guru Ramdas explains in *rāg Bilawal*, "This mind dances before the true guru; the melody of the unstruck *tura* plays the primal word [*shabad*]." Among the bhagats Kabir associates *anahad tura* with internal bliss and the realm of *nirbhao* (divinity as fearless), as does Bhagat Namdev in *rāg Sarang*: "You yourself sing, you yourself dance, you yourself play the *tura*."[26]

Older than the *tura*, the *sinyi* is another *sushir vad* aligned with *anahad*, although its participation is slightly different given its firm association with Nath yogis and their adoption of this instrument in reverence of their ultimate deity, Shiva. The reassignment of *sinyi* to the realm of *anahad* shows the gurus and bhagats appropriating a defining sonic marker of the Nath yogis' physical world and transforming it into a divine timbre in support of their teachings (although one might argue that the *sinyi*'s association with Shiva already imbues it with a sacred aura). As we saw with Guru Nanak above, it is the sound of the *sinyi* itself that embodies divine instruction: "Place your awareness on the divine word [*shabad*] and the teachings; my *sinyi* plays, and the people hear the sound of its vibrations."[27] Within India, we see a variety of names for this instrument, which pay tribute to its material derivation from animal horn. A member of the "pipe-horn family," the *sinyi* is also referred to as śringā (Sanskrit), shringa, sīng (Hindi, Punjabi), and shing (Marathi), and in other regions as singā, shingā, narsingha, and ransingha.[28] The body of the instrument is usually made of buffalo horn, but horns of the deer and ox are also used, especially in folk and tribal music. With the Garos of Meghalaya (Northeast region of India), for instance, the mouthpiece is made of bamboo, which allows for the production and variation of timbre. Ganesh Tarlekar and Nalini Tarlekar mention that this mouthpiece could also be made from a bull's horn.[29] Meanwhile, in the sixteenth-century *Ain-i-Akbari*, a Mughal chronicle of Emperor Akbar's time, the historian Abu'l Fazl observes that the *sing* was made of brass.[30]

In *rāg Aasa* Guru Nanak links the *sinyi* directly to Shiva since the sacred timbre (*dhun*) of this horn resounds in his realm (*Shiv nagri*) in its most perfect form: "*poorai nādang.*"³¹ It is "through the unheard vibration of this instrument played by the consciousness that the light of divinity illuminates every heart" (Guru Nanak, *rāg Ramkali*), a point that Guru Amardas also makes in *rāg Ramkali*: "Make meditation your walking stick, yogi, and let your horn sound your consciousness."³² Guru Ramdas explains in *rāg Sorath* that divinity itself is the source of this celestial timbre: "The beloved one is the sound of the *sinyi*, which is played by divinity itself."³³ In his critique of Nath yogis, Guru Arjan explains that the *sinyi* sounds not in the earthly realm but "in that realm [of higher consciousness] where there is no fear; there, I have assumed my *asana* [yogic posture]. The unstruck *sinyi* sounds in the form of *bani* [divine utterance]."³⁴ Meanwhile, Bhagat Kabir's critique in *rāg Gauri* also removes the *sinyi* from the earthly realm. Instead, he hears its resonance through the cosmos (*khand brahmand*, the solar systems and galaxies).³⁵ Finally, I mention another brass instrument, the trumpet, which is referenced in *Gurbani* through a Persian term, *burgoo*, by Guru Nanak and Guru Arjan in conjunction with the Muslim call for prayer.³⁶

I stay with *sushir vad* in examining another *anahad* instrument, the flute, whose appearance in *SGGS* is varied, given the many names by which it is referenced. Just as the *sinyi* retains its associations with its first player, Shiva, the flute is similarly aligned with its divine master musician, Krishna. Thus, the timbre of the flute is often described as sweet in *SGGS* (in keeping with Krishna's sensibility and culinary fondness). In a singular appearance, Guru Arjan alludes to Krishna's flute as *murli*, thereby evoking divinity itself as playing the charming flute.³⁷ Guru Ramdas describes this *anahad* instrument in Sanskrit as *vuns* in his description of how Krishna himself, "the blue one," plays the flute.³⁸ Guru Nanak also uses the Sanskrit term *vuns* in a remarkable verse in *rāg Maru* where he describes the earliest state of the cosmos: "For endless eons, there was only utter darkness." Through the poetic technique of negation, Guru Nanak gradually paints a vivid picture of the vibrant world that surrounds him, and through the deities, people, behaviors, natural phenomena, and processes that progressively populate his world, one by one, we can get a sense of what he may have observed on a daily basis in his own life. Guru Nanak characterizes the silence that pervaded the earliest moments of creation by pointing to the absence of *vuns* during a discussion of cowherds (alluding to Krishna): "No one played the flute."³⁹

In a similar narrative mode, as Guru Arjan observes the expansive, infinite, and endless realm of the divine one — who is described as inaccessible (*agam*) and unfathomable (*agaadh*) — he witnesses the multiplicities that operate within the multiverse. Using betacism — the interchange of *v* with *b*—Guru Arjan shifts to using *bayn*, a name related to another Sanskrit term for flute, *vaynav*. Guru Arjan explains, "Many [Krishnas] play the *bayn*."⁴⁰ Betacism is also seen with Guru Nanak, who uses *bayn* to describe the flute that is played by the consciousness in *rāg Ramkali*; in *rāg Maru*, Guru Nanak explains that it is divinity itself that plays the "sweet flute," while Guru Arjan, describing the beautiful, dark-hued form of Krishna, explains that everyone is mesmerized upon hearing his flute (*bayn*).⁴¹

The bhagats also used this term, and with Namdev it retains its strong associations with Krishna not only through its role as an identifying marker of divinity—"blessed, blessed is that flute which *Rām* plays"—but also through its distinguishing timbre, which is both sweet and thundering, thereby placing Namdev's experience of *anahad* within the Vedic context where the flute retains the highest association with divinity: "The sweet, sweet *anahad* melody thunders."⁴² In another verse in *rāg Ramkali*, Bhagat Namdev rejects singing the divine songs of the "countless Vedas, Puranas, and Shastras" so that he may only play "*anahad bayn* in the imperishable realm of *nirankar*," thereby aligning the flute with the fourth state. It is in this state of detachment (*bairagee*) that he (internally) sings the praises of *Rām*.⁴³ Also in *rāg Ramkali*, Bhagat Kabir points to the fourth state: He hears the "*anahad bayn* play when the consciousness is in a state of *sehaj* [equipoise]."⁴⁴ In terms of etymological development, it is noteworthy that the more familiar term for flute, "*bansuri*," is used just once, and by Guru Arjan, to describe the "sweet [*madh*] timbre that resonates in the ears" during a synesthetic experience of divinity where "the tongue vibrates the divine melody [*dhun*]" and the mind performs an animated dance.⁴⁵

Moving away from *ghan vad* and *sushir vad*, I turn to *vitat vad* (contact with strings through a bow) and to the special instrument of the *kinguri*, which is also associated with an inner music in *Gurbani*, as seen in this verse by Guru Nanak in *rāg Sri*: "The sound of the *kinguri* vibrates in each and every heart, night and day, with sublime love for the divine word [*shabad*]."⁴⁶ This bowed string instrument consisting of one played string and a few resonating strings has tribal and folk associations.⁴⁷ The two string instruments that I discuss in this section, the *kinguri* and *rabab*, are very much instruments of the people, unlike the other instruments mentioned thus far, including the *bheri* and *tura*, which cultivate a royal aura given their connection with the court of Guru Gobind Singh; the *sinyi*, which is linked to the Nath yogis; and the *vuns/bayn*, which is inextricable from divinity in the form of Krishna. In this spirit Joep Bor, while describing the *kinguri* as "a bowed instrument akin to the *sarinda*," emphasizes its broad appeal and accessibility in his observation that the *kinguri* "was also used by the Pathan, Baluchi, Sindhi and Rajput minstrels accompanying the armies."[48] This relatively unsophisticated instrument, made of a hollow gourd, whose animal skin membrane supports just a few strings, is ascribed with celestial status, as captured by Bhagat Kabir: "The divine sovereign plays *anahad kinguri*. / Through the divine glance, we become attuned to *nād*."[49] In parallel with the mention of other folk instruments in *Gurbani*, the *kinguri*'s elevated status reflects an overarching desire to reach the lower classes.

In a Persian account from the late thirteenth and early fourteenth centuries, Amir Khusrau describes the *kinguri* along these lines: "Kingra or Kingri has been a beggar's instrument, very popular in northern India."[50] A verse by Guru Nanak in *rāg Ramkali-Dakhni* suggests that the figure of the beggar in Khusrau's account was likely a yogi who takes on a divine form: "The detached yogi, with whom we have fallen in love, vibrates the *kinguri* in each and every heart."[51] Guru Amardas picks up on the same motif in *rāg Ramkali* when he instructs the yogi to "play that *kinguri*, . . . / which vibrates *anahad* sound and allows us to remain attuned to divinity." Meanwhile, Guru Arjan criticizes the yogi in *rāg Ramkali* for not being able to hear how the immaterial, formless (*anoop*) divine reverberation of the *kinguri* in the fourth state "sounds sweet."[52] The association of the *kinguri* with divinity is also seen with Khusrau, who observes that this instrument is related to the *kinnari vina*; the *kinnari* are celestial beings—their hybrid identities encompassing female bodies combined with wings—who play this instrument while the demigods *gandharva*, their celestial musical counterparts, sing.

THE *RABAB* IN SIKH ART

I save for last the *rabab*, which is the most important instrument in the Sikh cultural imagination because of its association with the first *kirtaniye*, Guru Nanak and Bhai Mardana. It has proved immensely challenging to trace the origins and development of this instrument in Punjab. In the absence of historical documentation that goes back to the time of the gurus, I have relied on Balbir Singh Kanwal's historical examination of *rababi* (players of the *rabab*) and Gurinderpal Singh Josan's recent study, coupled with oral histories where available. Discussions of the *rabab*'s role in Sikh *kirtan* in extant historical sources that cover musical life in North India, such as Persian and Urdu treatises, is also limited. All in all, this lacuna has led to considerable debate and conjecture among practitioners and scholars concerning the beloved *rabab* and its significance for Sikh *kirtan*.

Despite these limitations Sikh iconography remains one area of study that offers considerable insights regarding this instrument's role in the devotional context. Painting produced between the seventeenth and nineteenth centuries serves as a particularly rich resource for understanding the *rabab*'s varying appearances and expressive roles. The discussion that follows contextualizes the prominence of the *rabab* in South Asian art during this three-hundred-year span while gathering clues about this instrument through sketches, paintings, and illustrations associated with the *Janamsakhi* corpus. Despite wide-ranging research on these materials, the visual dimension of the *rabab* and its significance for Sikh *kirtan* remains underexplored. One exception is a recent presentation by art historian Gurdeep Kour, whose work goes beyond the common tendency to merely acknowledge the presence of this string instrument within a scene.[53]

Surprisingly, the categories "Sikh iconography" and "Sikh art" still occasionally raise questions pertaining to notions of identity: How can art be Sikh? That is, given the variety of artisanal techniques, religious influences, and cultural ideas that permeated the production of these artworks, how can it be claimed that the resulting products are distinctively Sikh? These are important, challenging questions, and we see William McLeod addressing them over twenty years ago at the start of his book *Popular Sikh Art*.[54] Even as his answer lies in the adoption of a broad perspective that takes into account the identity of artists, where the artwork was produced, who it was commissioned by, its subject matter, and its style (including important contributions made in folkloric popular art, as well as in courtly Mughal forms), the clearest response to these questions emerges through the sheer range of art that he surveys. More recently, Gurdeep Kour's dissertation provides a rigorous and detailed rationale for the emergence and proliferation of Sikh art and its engagement with a number of elements: "Persian, Indian, Mughal, and European."[55] The first wave of scholarship on Sikh art (roughly corresponding to 1960–80) needed to focus its efforts on building collections through identifying sources and understanding key stylistic differences in the work of painters distributed between the Punjab plains and hills. In contrast, Kour's research builds on this body of work and lends nuance to our understanding of the cultural dynamics between the various workshops, given the complexities in how artists reacted to the flow of ideas and styles across a geographically large and politically active landscape.

These observations notwithstanding, my reason for using this label is based on the acknowledgment that many of the examples I study are now part of a recognizable Sikh canon of painting with its roots in the folkloric dimension seen in the *Janamsakhi*—where "Sikh art was born," as claimed by McLeod—and its continued flourishing through formal techniques of portraiture, the first examples of which Karamjit K. Malhotra traces to the late seventeenth century.[56] The cover of my own book, which shows an acrylic painting by Priyanka Mac, *Waheguru* (2019), is a case in point when it comes to showing how Sikh art continues to innovate through multiple styles, aesthetics, media, and techniques. The topics and signs that I interpret in the following discussion are now firmly aligned with and embedded into narratives of Sikh history and culture, which continue to grow and diversify.

Even as I make observations about the appearance of the *rabab* and how it might have been played, I do so with an element of caution since these paintings were created by artisans and painters trained in traditions associated with a variety of styles (Rajasthani, Kashmiri, Murshidabadi, Deccani) and hired to produce artwork for a range of patrons in workshops that were dotted across the vast region of the Punjab plains and hills. The latter is characterized as the *pahari* style of the mountains and mainly associated with the regions of Guler and Kangra. Nikky-Guninder Kaur Singh makes a similar observation while adding the important point that "the stories . . . [the artists] chose to paint depended on their personal interest, and much was contingent on their individual talent."[57] For some of these painters, pictorial precision may have been a concern—especially for those accustomed to producing Mughal miniatures—but for others it was not always a priority. Quite often, a lack of synchronicity seemed to exist between those who were involved in making preparatory sketches and those charged with creating the final, painted product. In this respect, my approach to tracing an iconography of the *rabab* differs from that of Rohita Sharma and Kour, whose attention to "Sikh fashion" in relation to the forging of Sikh identity following the founding of the Khalsa in 1699 casts a less critical eye when it comes to evaluating pictorial exactness.[58]

There are several challenges with reading images for musical clues, as seen in the comparison between a late eighteenth-century *pahari* sketch from Guler and the final painting for *Guru Nanak Subdues Kaliyuga*.[59] Three critical differences are noted: The shape of the *rabab*'s sounding chamber is pear-shaped in the sketch and oval in the final version, a subtle yet significant change that obscures the lineage of this instrument and how it relates to existing Indian, Persian, and Mughal forms of the *rabab*. Also missing in the final painting is the supportive "M" bridge for the strings, which is distinctly visible in the sketch. Finally, the painter has reinterpreted the sitting position, giving Bhai Mardana an unusually wide stance for supporting the relatively small sound chamber. We see other kinds of discrepancies, too. An emphasis on flatness, a two-dimensional perspective, might lead some painters to distort the appearance of the instrument and the grip of the hand on the fingerboard (as we see in a nineteenth-century Kashmiri painting, *Guru Nanak with Followers*).[60] Furthermore, the number of strings are sometimes visible in an image, but this count may not always tally with the number of pegs (visible or inferred). These types of observations complicate the act of critical reading at moments when there is organological coherence between a detail and an aspect of structure: Can we accept as accurate those instances where the number of strings and pegs are in accordance, for instance?

My study of scenes relating to *Janamsakhi* narratives ultimately reveals that verisimilitude was not as important to the makers and viewers of these images as the cultivation of, and affective engagement with, the devotional mood or *bhaav* of the scene.[61] Central to the portrayal of affect is hand gesture (*mudra*), and I therefore play close attention to how the *rabab* is held by the hands in relation to the body, the position of the fingers when holding a plectrum, the action of plucking strings, and when the player is at rest (caveats about pictorial accuracy notwithstanding).[62] The main challenge of reading iconographical sources for musical clues resides in being able to distinguish between the kind of details that veer toward stylization versus those that are rooted in concerns with verisimilitude. To be sure, a critical and informed eye and ear are crucial for this type of visual analysis. Preparatory sketches, where available, prove immensely helpful for understanding the artistic process. In reflecting on the manuscripts of the Kapany Collection, for instance, I wonder whether portrayals of the *rabab*—showing the size and shape of its sounding chamber and its waist, the presence of carved notches, the shape of its peg box, the style of decorative paintings on the membrane, the inclusion of precious inlay, and the presence of elaborate carvings on the stand located behind the peg box—can shed light on issues of dating and provenance where these kinds of facts are ambiguous. Certainly, visual artists were clear on who Bhai Mardana was and his firm association with the *rabab*. While regional variations of this instrument result in notable differences between the shape of his *rabab* from one illustration to another, his instrument is consistently depicted as a plucked chordophone, not to be confused with other types of string instruments that entered the sphere of devotional expression, as we see in the inclusion of a bowed *saranda* accompanied by a *dhadh* (a small, double-faced, handheld drum) in the mid-nineteenth-century watercolor *A Meeting Between Two Saintly Men*.⁶³ The *saranda* can also be seen in *Mian Mir and Mulla Shah with Devotees* (Sheesh Mahal Museum, Patiala, early nineteenth century).⁶⁴

It is also worth pointing out the predominantly soloistic pictorial treatment of the *rabab*, particularly in illustrations connected to the *Janamsakhi*; it is rare that this instrument encounters a sonic competitor. The nearest we hear is in a scene from the B-40 *Janamsakhi* (*Baba Nanak and Mardana with Dancing Pathans*) where a compartmentalized picture — with Guru Nanak and Bhai Mardana occupying a higher spiritual plane than a group of dancing men who are placed directly beneath them — brings additional instruments into our view, including a mirror image of Bhai Mardana's own *rabab*.⁶⁵ Bhai Mardana's *rabab*, which is played in a half-kneeling position (*ardha padmasana*), and Guru Nanak's lyrical effusions transport them to a realm of bliss, while a group of men who dance to the music of cymbals and *rabab* represent something quite different, as captured by Nikky-Guninder Kaur Singh: "While Mardana's rebab raises empathy and human connections, the rebab and cymbals in the lower frame promote selfish indulgence."⁶⁶

Another rare moment when Bhai Mardana's *rabab* is brought into conversation with a different instrument is in the previously mentioned late eighteenth-century watercolor from Guler, *Guru Nanak Subdues Kaliyuga*. Here, Bhai Mardana's *rabab* accompanies Guru Nanak's words as they subdue Kaliyuga. In a playful stroke, the painter inserts into the frame another instrument and its master musician, the ancient *vina* and Narada. Goswamy's analysis is apt: The painter "brings in, entirely on his own, Narada, the divine sage, who transcends all barriers of time and space, and appears everywhere at will, especially where the sacred name of God is to be heard. The sage has no direct role to play in the exchange . . . one hand held up, [he is] clearly amazed at the Guru's fearlessness or the beauty of his utterances."⁶⁷ While the preparatory sketch presents the *vina* as only half visible, its fully rendered, detailed presence in the painting brings two string instruments into conversation: The long-standing divine aura of the ancient *vina* looks to engage with the newly emerging capacity of the *rabab* in this role under the hands of Bhai Mardana.

This juxtaposition of instruments evokes Kahn Singh Nabha's description of the *rabab* in his *Mahan Kosh* (encyclopedia) as a *vina*, specifically *Ravan Vina*, by which Nabha may have been referring to a type of bowed instrument called *ravanhasta vina*, also known as *ravanastra* and *ravanhatho*.⁶⁸ This designation also brings into focus Deva's observation regarding the broad category of *vina*: "This term, in Sanskrit and other Indian languages, till recently, seems to have been applied to any instrument except, perhaps, the drums."⁶⁹ Curiously, *vina* is a term that Deva uses for discussing an instrument that resembles the *rabab*, the ancestor of which Bharat may have encountered in the form of *kacchapī* as early as 200 BCE, as claimed by Deva in his dating of the *Natyashastra*. Deva's description of this type of *vina*—comprising a pear-shaped wooden body covered with leather, with a convex resonator and a body extending into a neck attached to a fretless fingerboard, sometimes bent backward—strongly resembles a type of *rabab* identified with Bhai Mardana. This traces a lineage to the *citra-vīnā*, "the short-necked ovoid lute type," as described by Margaret Kartomi.⁷⁰ Finally, an unusual juxtaposition of the *rabab* played alongside a bowed *sarangi* can be seen in two Mughal portraits of Guru Nanak from 1680 and 1685.⁷¹ And, in an even more unusual pairing, we see the *rabab* being played alongside the *kansia* (hand cymbals) in an eighteenth-century *pahari* painting, *Guru Nanak with Followers*.⁷²

The following discussion, then, is a call to listen as we view. To be spectators who look with their ears. When the *rabab* is present, as it often is in depictions of Guru Nanak, the viewer is being asked to listen intently: to the imagined sound of Guru Nanak's *shabad* and Bhai Mardana's improvisation as these mingle with the sonic vibrations of nature. Like all Sikh *kirtan*, the first singing by Guru Nanak and Bhai Mardana was ultimately for divinity rather than for those other entities—human, animal, vegetal, or meteorological—that populate visual scenes. The question of how the humble *rabab* was elevated to a divine position is now explored in relation to the origins and development of this instrument.

THE RISE AND FLOWS OF THE *RABAB*

It is difficult to trace the origins of the *rabab* despite dominant narratives that view the plucked chordophone as emerging in a region generally identified as the Middle East and probably referring to Mesopotamia, as this vast area was known in the past.⁷³ As K. Krishna Murthy observes in his study of ancient sculptural representations of musical instruments, "Around 2000 B.C. some country in or near Asia Minor produced the lute."⁷⁴ Movement of this instrument along trade routes through and around central Asia and the Mediterranean has led to a wide proliferation of names: *rubāb*, *rebāb*, *rabob*, and *rhubob*, to name just a few. To be sure, questions regarding this instrument's origins, development, structure, naming, tuning, and playing open onto a vibrant and heterogeneous vista, although recent research on global music histories — focusing on social and cultural interactions along the complicated routes of the Silk Road — has been vital in shedding light on some of these issues.

Within India some art historians have observed the earliest visual references to the *rabab* (or, rather, its chordophone ancestor) in sculpture from Sanchi and Bharhut around the third and second centuries BCE and from Gandhara around 1 BCE. Although the *rabab* is widely thought of as a Persian import to India, Claudie Marcel-Dubois is among the first Western European scholars to have observed two types of indigenous *rabab* in Indian temple art dating back to the first century CE: the short neck, three-stringed *Gandhara* (in the north) and the long-neck, five-stringed *Amaravati* (in the south).[75] Subrahmanyam Krishnaswami conjectures that the "Gandhara instrument could be a precursor of the modern *sarod* and perhaps it was not imported from the Middle East at all."[76] With regard to his own excavations at Harappa and Mohenjodaro, Kailash Nath Dikshit also observes pictographs representing a "crude stringed instrument, a prototype of the modern *vina*."[77] Later, a fretless lute instrument, described as *kacchapi veena* by Deva, can be seen in a fifth-century Gupta-period sculpture from Pawaya.[78]

Gabriela Currie's research offers a rigorous assessment of various types of early chordophones in the lute family in Gandharan art against the backdrop of the complicated paths of Eurasian trade routes.[79] To link these observations to James Willward's study of migration and influence along the Silk Road, it is entirely plausible that "most musical instruments have always been hybrids, nodes in wide cultural networks extending over regions and continents and reaching back in time." In this respect, Willward's perception of the history of the *sitar* as being indebted to "multiple Central Asian and Indian lineages, combining in themselves Hindu, Muslim, Persian, and Turko-Mongol Central Asian cultural elements and historical traditions," provides a helpful template for thinking about the cultural influences that shaped the development of the *rabab* from the twelfth century onward.[80] Beyond these invaluable studies of ancient sculptural panels, a handful of scholars has undertaken a study of the instrument in relation to early modern Persian sources; the large, intervening gap when this chordophone wasn't as noticeable in visual representation has been interpreted by scholars as a time when the instrument was no longer being actively played and developed in India but had instead started to travel further East.[81]

It is against this context of flow and exchange — wherein the early portable version of the *rabab* emerges as "the transcultural musical instrument par excellence," as described by Currie — that we should read Allyn Miner's suggestion that the development of the Indian *rabab* occurred in dialogue with its newly arrived Persian counterpart, starting around the eleventh century. Lal Mani Misra also claims that the *seniya rabab* (discussed below) was "the developed and modified version of Indian string instruments, although in later stages it acquired some of the foreign traits in association with Persian and Afghani rababs."[82] These viewpoints offer a more nuanced observation than the popular claim that the Indian *rabab* as we know it is a "foreign" instrument, although the dynamics of contact between these instruments remain difficult to measure.[83] Iconographical differences — albeit scrutinized with a somewhat circumspect eye — are perhaps the closest we are able to get in being able to distinguish between different types of *rabab* during the early modern era.[84]

Andrew Greig made a rather sensible point thirty years earlier concerning the assimilation of instruments in the early modern period:

There were often variants in a type of musical instrument, performing approximately the same musical function, in the contiguous musical cultures of the Eurasian continent. For instance, in the fourteenth to sixteenth centuries, there was a variety of instruments named Rabāb to be found from India in the East and as far west as Europe. Undoubtedly, some common ancestor inspired a terminological continuum, if not a morphological one, early on.[85]

This morphological continuum underlies the subtle differences in the visual portrayal of this instrument across Persian, Indian, and Mughal iconography, which are the primary driving forces behind Greig's identification of four types of *rabab* in sixteenth-century India.[86] The *Persian rabab*, known as *sen-e-rabab*, was named after the late sixteenth-century musical legend Tansen, who was described as a virtuoso of this instrument in the court of Akbar.[87] Other notable court musicians of this instrument include Qasim Kohabar (in the court of Akbar), Kalawant Sukhsen (in the court of Shahjahan), and Hasan Khan (in the court of Muhammad Shah II, Rangila).[88] There is also the *Indian rabab*, sometimes called *seniya rabab* in a modification of the Persian term, which, according to Lal Mani Misra, was an instrument that Tansen modified from its earlier version of the *chitra veena*.[89] Greig identifies a third type, the *Mughal rabab*, but this likely referred to an instrument that was modeled on Persian and existing Indian instruments. Finally, the *Afghani rabab*, also called *Kabuli* and *Pathan* and regarded today as the precursor to the *sarod*, is clearly distinguishable from the other types.[90]

Even within each of these varieties, there are notable regional differences, which is to say that there was considerable variety in the appearance of *rabab*. Not all Persian *rabab* look the same, and the same goes for Mughal, Indian, and Afghani *rabab*.[91] There is also the question of whether *rabab* are primarily plucked or bowed instruments. Greig postulates that the Arab and Central Asian *rabab* (broadly speaking) may have been a precursor to the European bowed *rebec*, while several scholars observe the mention of a bowed *rabab* in Arabic texts by al-Fārābī (872–950 CE) and Ibn Sīnā (also known as Avicenna, 980–1037 CE): *Kitāb al-mūsīkī al-kabīr* (The great book of music) and *Kitāb al-sifa* (The book of healing), respectively.[92] Murthy observes a bowed chordophone even earlier in fifth-century sculpture at Ajanta.[93] Krishnawami, on the other hand, maintains that the *rabab* "remained a plucked instrument for a long time but subsequently began to be used as a bowed instrument."[94] Although it is difficult to trace the evolution of bowed and unbowed *rabab* across this vast region, it may not be too far-fetched to imagine that the two types coexisted, even within the same region. Today, the *kamaicha* of the Manganiyar community based in Rajasthan, a state neighboring Punjab, bears witness to the dual development of the *rabab*, especially given the resemblance between the *dhrupad rabab* and the *kamaicha*.[95]

(ANAHAD) RABAB AS SEEN THROUGH SIKH ICONOGRAPHY

Greig observes two types of Indian *rabab* in miniatures produced by Mughal, Rajasthani, and Deccani artists during the fifteenth, sixteenth, and seventeenth centuries. The Indian *rabab* is depicted as short necked, with a face covered by animal (typically goat) skin; a hollowed-out, spherical sounding chamber (usually made of *tun* [mahogany] or *shahtoot* [mulberry]); a fretless fingerboard; and typically six gut strings stretching across two bridges. One bridge is gently curved and placed toward the bottom of the instrument, while a flat second bridge is placed at the top of the peg box (the bridges are not always visible in paintings nor is the exact number of strings). As we can see with Bhai Mardana in **figure 4.1**, these *rabab* were often played with a plectrum (which he holds in his right hand) and had gently tapering sides known as a collar, notch, or barb (hence the Western European designation, barbed lute).[96]

Figure 4.2 shows Greig's second type of Indian *rabab*, which had only four strings, as mentioned in the *Kitāb-i-Nauras* (by Ibrahim Adil

FIGURE 4.1 *Bhai Mardana Ji Playing Rabab to Accompany Guru Nanak in Song.* Early- to mid-nineteenth century, Lahore or Amritsar (Punjab). Watercolor on paper. Object number M.2006.2.31, Williams College.

Shah II).[97] Greig suggests that this type was the instrument that Emperor Akbar's chief historian, Abu'l Fazl, called *Dakhanī Rabāb*, a designation that confirms oral accounts of Guru Nanak and Bhai Mardana's visit to Golkonda, a Bahmani sultanate, during the second of their five *udasi* (around 1511).[98] This painting was produced around 1660–70, well after

FIGURE 4.2 Barbed *rubab* (lute), 1660–70, Golkonda.

this *udasi*, during the Qutb Shahi dynasty (1518–1687), and emphasizes a Sufi stylization of Guru Nanak and Bhai Mardana, as indicated primarily by their style of turbans, beards, and clothing. The *rabab* shown here might well be a Mughal *rabab*, which seems to have had a similar appearance to Indian *rabab* in that it was also characterized by a hollowed-out, spherical sound chamber, covered by a skin face, with a collar that tapers between the body and neck of the instrument to give its characteristic elegant curved shape. Greig and Miner observe additional connections between the Mughal and Persian *rabab* in the long peg box, which in the case of the Persian *rabab*, Miner notes, is "bent back at an angle at the end of the neck."[99] The distinctive angled neck was generally not seen in conjunction with Indian and *Afghani rabab*. For example, in **figure 4.2** the pronounced vertical (not an angular, bent-back) peg box, with three gleaming pegs, appears behind Guru Nanak's left shoulder; presumably the fourth peg is out of sight, blocked by the back of the guru's head.

While the Persian *rabab* tends to favor a smaller, trapezoidal face and a longer, slender neck, reminiscent of a *tambura*, it only occasionally appears in Sikh iconography (see **fig. 4.3**).[100] In contrast, the Mughal *rabab* appears more frequently in the form of the smaller Indian *dhrupad rabab* (also called *dhurpad/dhrupadi/dhrupati*). Sometimes, its portrayal features the Persian angled peg box, as we see in a late eighteenth-century watercolor of a *Janamsakhi* episode (from Guler), a detail that is suggestive when it comes to evaluating the ways in which the Persian *rabab* impacted the development of the Indian instrument.[101] The treatment of perspective in some depictions raises the question of whether the neck is truly bent back or whether Indian painting techniques — with their emphasis on the flatness of perspective due to which the ornate carved stand on which the *rabab* rests sometimes bulges into view — cause the peg box to be seen as such. However, my observation that the Mughal/Indian *rabab* was frequently depicted holds for these particular Guler

FIGURE 4.3 *Guru Nanak with Followers and Other Holy Men*. Watercolor and gold on paper. Kashmir/Punjab, first quarter of the nineteenth century. Himachal Pradesh Museum, Shimla.

watercolors because of one curious detail: In some scenes the instrument is shown covered by a protective plain, red cloth during travel, and the outline of the instrument, with its bent peg box (which is consistent between the preparatory sketch and final painting), is unmistakable.[102]

An early rendition of *dhrupad rabab* can be seen in a watercolor painting held in the Kapany Collection (*Guru Nanak and His Companions Mardana and Bhai Bala*, 1700–1800), as well as in three late nineteenth-century images: an anonymous colored woodcut (1875) of Guru Nanak, Bhai Mardana, and their additional companion, Bhai Bala, who was added to later eighteenth-century accounts of the *Janamsakhi*; a painting made in the Punjab hills (around 1895) of Guru Nanak in conversation with the Sri Lankan king Raja Shivanabh; and in an early nineteenth-century painting of Guru Nanak dressed in the patchwork robe characteristic of dervishes (with whom his association is also captured by the shape of his turban). The *rabab* takes on a unique teardrop shape for its sounding chamber in this painting.[103]

Miner notes the *dhrupad rabab*'s frequent depiction in "late Mughal, provincial and Pahadi miniature painting, [where] it is characterized by its large round skin-covered body and a distinctive and pronounced turned-back collar around the base of the neck."[104] Additional representations of this instrument, with the more common vertical neck and peg box, can be seen across a large number of paintings, many of which relate to the *Janamsakhi*. In **figure 4.4**, a mid- to late eighteenth-century Mughal gouache miniature, Guru Nanak appears again in the Sufi dervish garb of a multihued patchwork robe and conical turban, while Bhai Mardana is shown playing his charmingly decorated instrument (*Guru Nanak and Bhai Mardana in a Landscape*, ca. 1750–99).[105] The (anonymous) painter allows us to catch a glimpse of the ornately carved stand, which sits behind the peg box; the exquisite fingerboard; and the elaborately decorated resonating chamber, whose floral design is continuous with the embroidery of Bhai Mardana's cloth waistband (*patka*). Given the Mughal propensity for detail, it is worth speculating whether there is correspondence between the three pegs and the three visible strings that are strung over a clearly delineated curved bridge and whether the one string that is darker in appearance is in fact made of a different material than gut (such as metal).

This feature is of interest since it was more common for *rabab* to have between four and six strings rather than just three. We can clearly see six strings in a detailed *pahari* painting of a *Janamsakhi* episode from 1830 where Bhai Mardana's *rabab* lies propped up on its carved stand while he makes *roti* (bread) without fire or water (**fig. 4.5**).[106] Taking advantage of

Hearing (Anahad) Instruments and the Rabab in Sikh Art | 165

FIGURE 4.4 *Guru Nanak and Bhai Mardana in a Landscape* (1750–99). Gouache with gold on paper.

an unobstructed view of the *rabab*, the painter draws the gaze toward this decorated instrument, particularly its fingerboard, the ornate carving at the waist, and the beautifully painted periphery of the face and underside of the instrument through the simple repetition of small white dots, which contrast against the brown wood. Similarly decorative are two

FIGURE 4.5 *A Leaf from a Series of Janam Sakhi*. Accession no. 63.1321, National Museum, New Delhi.

nineteenth-century watercolor paintings, which showcase the intricate floral designs painted onto the skin membrane: *Guru Nanak's Meeting with Dhru Bhagat on Mount Kailasha* and *Guru Nanak's Meeting with Praladh*.[107] In the latter, we also catch a glimpse of the elaborate floral design on the underside of the instrument (on the large resonating chamber), which is painted in a contrasting shade of yellow that ties into the clothing of the holy figures, Praladh and Guru Nanak, thereby also suggesting a divine status for this instrument itself.

The playing style is also intriguing in *Guru Nanak's Meeting with Praladh*, where Bhai Mardana holds the *rabab* upright against his left shoulder while he plays, a position that we see in other visual settings, too. In various versions of the *Janamsakhi* Bhai Mardana is often shown waiting for Guru Nanak's instruction to play, and thus two types of sound are suggested: ambient, in the sense that the *rabab* is perceived as functioning passively in the perceptual background of a listener's attention, somewhat like a drone; and intrinsic, where Bhai Mardana is actively involved in playing his instrument to accompany Guru Nanak's singing. Ambient *rabab* is perceived in *Guru Nanak's Meeting with Praladh*, where the *rabab* rests against the left shoulder and Mardana's left hand sits in his lap while the right hand strums the strings almost to suggest a dronelike accompaniment for this divine encounter.[108] Similar depictions in this vein include *Guru Nanak Meets Nath Siddhas at the Village of Achal Batala*, a nineteenth-century watercolor attributed to Murshidabad, where Bhai Mardana holds a decorated *rabab*, painted in vibrant yellow and ocher; and in an eighteenth-century watercolor, *Guru Nanak's Visit to Bhai Lalo the Carpenter*, where Guru Nanak is engaged in conversation with Bhai Lalo.[109]

While it is compelling, I hesitate, slightly, in using the term "drone" since it is unlikely that this *rabab* had additional strings that were assigned a droning function (in the manner of *chikari* or *tarab* strings). In addition, it is difficult to determine how the open (unstopped) strings of the *rabab* were tuned. Thus, I speculate as to whether open strings are played in a manner that emulates a droning function, a musical technique that would have been familiar to painters from the practices of both folk music — Amir Khusrau observes a drone performed by two strings of the *kinguri* — and courtly music, where a continuous drone was likely to have been in place as a musical feature by the seventeenth century.[110] What these paintings suggest is not the *rabab*'s functioning as an instrument that provides a continuous drone, in the manner of a *tanpura* today, but a certain flexibility in its role as an instrument that provides melodic and rhythmic accompaniment for the voice, while also being able to offer some stabilizing pitches in the form of a drone (what Bonnie Wade calls an "intermittent pitch reference").[111]

Another way of playing the *rabab* is seen in *Guru Nanak Debates with a Group of Yogis*, an early nineteenth-century *pahari* painting from Guler where the *rabab* sits against Bhai Mardana's right shoulder. Since his hands venture nowhere near the strings, one might conclude that he is at rest.¹¹² We see a similar gesture of rest in an eighteenth-century watercolor, *Guru Nanak and the Cannibal Kauda*.¹¹³ Bhai Mardana is again shown waiting for the guru's command (*hukam*) to play in an early nineteenth-century watercolor, *Nanak the First Teacher* (1800–1810), this time with his right hand gently resting in an unlikely place: the crevice of the *rabab*'s carefully carved notch.¹¹⁴

Even as I draw attention to how Bhai Mardana holds his instrument, it is worth commenting on playing position, given the variety of ways the instrument is placed against Bhai Mardana's torso and legs. Sometimes, he kneels in full (*bharadvajasana/vajrasana*), as when he holds the *rabab* upright; we see precursors for this position in the work of Mughal portrait painter Govardhan in *Prince and Ascetics* (1630) and *A Rustic Concert* (1625).¹¹⁵ We also see a variation on *bharadvajasana/vajrasana* in a half-kneeling position (*ardha padmasana*), where only the right leg kneels while the left is raised as the left foot is placed on the floor, thereby creating a wedge for placement of the *rabab*'s large resonating chamber. Occasionally, Bhai Mardana sits fully cross-legged (*sukhasana*) or with the right leg folded over the left (*gomukhasana*) to play the *rabab* in the manner of a *sitar*, as seen in *Guru Nanak Seated on a Terrace in Discourse with Raja Shivanabh*. Here, a modification that involves the slight raising of the left leg allows for a wedge to be created.¹¹⁶ Even though painters and illustrators were not observing their subjects in the manner of still life, they seemed to be sensitive to the different playing positions of the *rabab*.

We see a number of variations on playing the *rabab* while standing up. For example, in *Guru Nanak's Meeting with Sajan the Thug*, a nineteenth-century *Janamsakhi* watercolor from Lahore, Bhai Mardana is engaged in conversation with his *rabab* nestled in the crook of his left elbow.¹¹⁷ In *Guru Nanak Visiting His Sister Bibi Nanaki*, Bhai Mardana provides a drone while standing and cupping his *rabab* with his left hand, a position that we also see in another image from this series, *Guru Nanak's Discourse with Datatre on Mount Byar*.¹¹⁸ We see a standing position in the nineteenth-century watercolor *Bhai Mardana Ji Playing Rabab to Accompany Guru Nanak in Song* and in an eighteenth-century Deccani painting, *Guru Nanak (1469–1539) The First Guru of the Sikhs*.¹¹⁹ In the latter, as seen in the B-40 *Janamsakhi*, painters play with the size of figures to indicate a difference in spiritual status. This particular painting veers quite far in this direction, relegating Bhai Mardana to a minor position in the background, while Guru Nanak is placed squarely within the foreground. All in all, these standing-position portraits are reminiscent of *seniya rababi*, who may have had a strap attached to the back of their *rabab* for exactly the purpose of playing while standing up, as seen in an earlier Mughal watercolor by Hunhar, *A Mughal Prince with a Musician* (1650–60).[120] In the courtly context Adrian McNeil observes that playing while standing up is a position that is respectful of the patron.[121]

There is another bodily gesture that appears in representations of the upright *rabab* in the nineteenth century and that suggests a significant shift in the rendition of *kirtan* (at least, as suggested through iconography). In earlier *Janamsakhi* Bhai Mardana was often placed at a distance from Guru Nanak and was rarely depicted as performing music for the guru, whose inspired verses were intended for a different kind of listener, divinity itself. Two courtly representations transform this ideal *kirtan* into one that is rendered as performance in the way that a subject might perform for their patron. For example, in a late nineteenth-century woodcut (1870), *Guru Nanak with Followers*, the *rabab* is held as a contemporary *tanpura* might be, while Bhai Mardana gestures with his left hand, suggesting a manner of courtly deportment.[122] Meanwhile, Guru Nanak engages in *katha* (oral exegesis) for his two sons seated in front of him (as interpreted by McLeod). A similar visual allusion to courtly musical embodiment can be seen in an earlier nineteenth-century *pahari* representation of the upright position, which again brings the topic of the drone and its accompaniment of a stylized vocal form into view.[123] A courtly portrayal of Guru Harkrishan as *patshah* (emperor) exudes from the elaborate setting—the ornate rug, bolster, and *palki* (throne), not to mention his opulent attire, which is complete with royal plumage, *kalghi* (aigrette), in the turban. The equally decorated musician adopts courtly musical affect as seen in his raising of the left hand while strumming the strings of his instrument with the right. A lack of distinction between a skin membrane and wooden sounding chamber creates ambiguity as to whether this instrument is indeed a *rabab* or whether, given the continued development of chordophones during the times of the gurus, the *rabab* has been replaced by a fretted melody-playing *tambur* or drone-creating *tambura*, as discussed by Wade and Miner; these instruments were all familiar to courtly settings and are visible in Mughal and *pahari* painting.[124]

It is noticeable that despite the changing depiction of string instruments, *pahari* painters are not consistent in including a percussion accompaniment at this point, which raises the question of whether, in keeping with Guru Nanak's and Bhai Mardana's imagined musical practice during their *udasi*, rhythm was maintained through strumming the strings (or, even, through hand gestures) and whether the consistent incorporation of percussion instruments such as the *pakhawaj* is something that became common as the style of *kirtan* became aligned with *dhurpad* by the seventeenth century.[125] A late-eighteenth/early nineteenth-century painting held at Lahore's Chughtai Museum incorporates the *pakhawaj*, while a nineteenth-century watercolor, *Guru Nanak with the Other Nine Gurus* shows Bhai Mardana accompanied by a *jori* player.[126] Another contemporaneous watercolor, *Guru Nanak, with Bhai Mardana Singing*, also features the *jori*.[127] Outside of the courtly sphere, we see a similar combination of instruments in a seventeenth-century Rajasthani drawing, *Three Musicians*, where the *rabab* serves as a melody-playing instrument, the *tambur* provides a drone for the gesticulating singer, and the *pakhawaj (mridang)* fills a percussive role.[128]

Many eighteenth- and nineteenth-century depictions of the *rabab* tended to favor a horizontal playing style accommodated by smaller proportions of the *dhrupad rabab*, as we see in the eighteenth-century watercolor *Guru Nanak and His Companions Mardana and Bhai Bala*, which serves as a template for many similar depictions.[129] A horizontal playing style carries over into other media as seen in the *mohrakashi* (frescoes) that adorn Harmandir Sahib (Golden Temple) and that Madanjit Kaur sees as being related to wall paintings found in the Kangra valley.[130]

Even as the *dhrupad rabab* gained momentum in its use from the sixteenth to nineteenth centuries, especially with Tansen in the court of Akbar, Miner notes its disappearance as instruments such as the *been*, *sursingar*, and *sitar* stepped forward to take its place in the sphere of Hindustani classical music by the late nineteenth century.[131] McNeil also observes that the influence of *seniya rababi* "began to wane around the same time that Mughal hegemony lost its own paramountcy at the beginning of the eighteenth century."[132] This decline in the Mughal court may not have been mirrored within the context of the Sikh court given the tenth guru, Guru Gobind Singh's, active use of *tanti sāz* (string instruments) in *kirtan* and his continued innovations with regard to instrument building, as he adapted their use for the battlefield. There is little scholarship on this topic, but Sikh oral history maintains that the *taus* was modified to become the *dilruba* for this very purpose.[133] In this regard, an interesting parallel emerges between the adaptation of the *Afghani/Kabuli rabab* in India as an instrument that accompanied soldiers in war and the continued modification of instruments for the purposes of travel and mobility in the Sikh military context.

Whereas Greig speculates as to the origins of the *Afghani rabab* in India, Miner argues that its emergence in Afghanistan and establishment in India took place by the middle of the eighteenth century. As with Miner, McNeil draws on oral histories and twentieth-century secondary materials in exploring the association between Afghani "rabab-playing musicians on foot or horseback, leading kings in procession or troops into battle," while noting its appearance in India from at least the time of the Lodi dynasty (thirteenth to fifteenth centuries) if not earlier.[134] Miner notes this instrument was used for military purposes "because of the fervor and heat that it creates."[135]

Even as Peter Manuel and Brian Bond indicate the parallel traditions of Mughal court *dhurpad* and *kirtan*, it is worth speculating on the potential convergence of Mughal and Sikh courtly musical practices, given McNeil's observation of how, after their decline, the musical expertise of *seniya rababi* "was in great demand by musicians outside their family and, through their indirect means of teaching nonrelated disciples, *seniyas* continued to stamp their impression on the development of music in North India."[136] With the collapse of the Mughal empire during the eighteenth century, these *rababi* turned to other Hindu, Muslim, and Sikh patrons, as noted by Katherine Schofield.[137] Harish Dhillon mentions that several of Emperor Aurangzeb's court musicians sought employment at Guru Gobind Singh's court in Paonta Sahib after the emperor "banned music from his court," a story whose nuances are explored by Schofield.[138] As emphasized by Kanwal, several important *rababi* in the Sikh tradition traced their lineage to Akbar's court musician, Tansen. Thus, even though *dhurpad* was not as conspicuous following the decline of Mughal power, one might imagine its continued presence in the less visible centers of the Sikh devotional context, along with many other vocal genres and styles of the court, as Mughal *rababi* allied their arts with those of Bhai Mardana's descendants and Sikh *ragi*, thereby keeping these traditions alive outside of the Mughal court and in the thriving spaces of the Sikh *darbar*. It is important to note the coexistence of Mughal and Sikh courtly practices within the same spaces during these decades. Today, when I learn a *puratan reet* (an orally transmitted melody) based on a *thumri* (a "light" vocal composition aligned with courtesan artistry) or when I hear a *guldusta* of *shabad*, as *rāg* are interwoven one after another into a fragrant bouquet or a scintillating *tarana*, I continue to witness a still thriving dialogue between Mughal and Sikh courtly expressions.

Kanwal is among a handful of scholars to have explored how Muslim *rababi* and Sikh *ragi* continued to undertake Sikh *kirtan* on the *rabab* and other *tanti sāz* through the early twentieth century (and earlier).[139] His study mentions some notable musicians who made substantial contributions to *kirtan* on *tanti sāz*, including Sham Singh, who played the *saranda* at Harmandir Sahib during his long life (1803–1926).[140] Kanwal also draws attention to the robust activity of teaching and learning that was taking place at the court centers of Kapurthala, Patiala, and Nabha.[141] For example, Mahant Gajja Singh (1850–1914), a student of Mir Rahmat Ali at Kapurthala, is known to have been a virtuoso on the *dilruba* and *taus*, and his esteemed contemporaries included Bhai Moti, Bhai Lal, Bhai Taba, and Bhai Chand, to name a few stalwarts of Sikh *kirtan*. As discussed in the introduction, we know that Mahant Gajja Singh was an important teacher for the Namdhari community.[142] While Bor suggests that the *saranda* and *sarangi* took the place of the *rabab* after their assimilation into the Sikh *darbar* (court), I wonder whether the introduction of additional string instruments brought about a more inclusive, rather than a competitive, environment where instruments were used to amplify sound rather than replace one another.[143]

Specifically, within the Sikh tradition, it is also worth noting the emergence of another type of *rabab* made with six silk (as opposed to gut) strings and later called the *rabab sikandari* (thereby paying reference to its supposed creator, Sikander, Alexander the Great). This instrument was associated with Guru Nanak, as noted by Miner, who observes a later reference to his instrument in Sadiq Ali Khan's *Sarmāya-i 'ishrat* (also known as *Qānūn-i-mūsīqī*) (1875).[144] I have not found historical mention of the *rabab sikandari* prior to Khan's text, although it is relatively well known among practitioners. Nor has it been possible to trace historical documentation of another *rabab* that is important to Sikhs, the *Firanda rabab* (also called the *Firandia* or *Phiranda rabab*), beyond its mention in the *Janamsakhi* corpus.

The literature points to Bhai Firanda of Bhairoana, Sultanpur, being asked to make a specific type of *rabab* for Bhai Mardana, which Bhai Firanda gladly hand-delivered to Guru Nanak. This episode is narrated in a nineteenth-century watercolor, *Guru Nanak Meets Firanda the Rabab Maker*.[145] We witness a rare opportunity to see the frontal perspective of a *rabab* lying on its side without being held. One might speculate that a smaller-sized, compact instrument was necessary for the arduous long journeys that Guru Nanak was planning to take with Bhai Mardana. This point seems to be emphasized by the painter, who draws attention to the smaller size of this instrument in relation to the human figures that occupy this scene.

At the same time that the painter shows some concern for accuracy, it is confusing that they paint over the distinctive skin membrane, complementing its darker shade with the light brown of the supportive wooden frame; this feels like a moment where the painter is likely concerned with stylization over accuracy. We see a similar effort toward stylization and a coloring over the skin membrane in *Guru Nanak's Meeting with the Jeweler*

Salas Rai, as well as in *Guru Nanak in Kamarupa, the Land Ruled by Women*, a playful scene where Bhai Mardana is transformed into a goat, leaving his *rabab* sitting unaccompanied among the animals.¹⁴⁶ There are other possibilities: Might the use of brown for the *rabab*'s face suggest a fully wooden sounding chamber in keeping with that of the newly emerging *sursingar* or the *tambur*? Wade explains that, with the latter, "the face of the bowl was of wood, with a contrasting dark color of wood edging either side of the front and continuing on the other side."¹⁴⁷ Other aspects of the painted *rabab* tend to counter this possibility: its lack of a metal plate on the fingerboard and its relatively petite frame, for instance.¹⁴⁸ What is more compelling is that the painters had observed—whether through illustration or in person—a variety of string instruments and playing styles and that these may have influenced certain artistic choices.

Although the *Firanda rabab* is thought to be related to the pear-shaped *Afghani rabab* by some, others emphasize a distance between the two. Certainly, there is a notable difference in appearance: The *Afghani rabab* has a "deep narrow body with a sharply indented waist ... carved from a single piece of wood," as noted by Miner, whereas Sikh iconography presents the *Firanda rabab* as an Indian/Mughal instrument, especially given the frequent depiction of a large, spherical sounding chamber—shown in the eighteenth-century painting *Guru Nanak Meets the Poet Kabir*—and sometimes a notched waist, as shown in *Guru Nanak's Meeting with Dev Loot and Other Demons* and other *Janamsakhi* paintings.¹⁴⁹

A range of *rabab* are depicted in a series of watercolor miniature paintings currently held at the Royal Collection Trust showing the first nine Sikh gurus listening attentively to *kirtan*.¹⁵⁰ These portraits convey a curious mix of reality and idealization steeped in local cultural knowledge about the gurus and their defining qualities. Guru Nanak is shown in his characteristic multicolored patchwork Sufi robe, while Guru Hargobind appears with an important Sikh symbol of prestige and authority, the hawk; Guru Harkrishan, who died in his youth, is portrayed as a young boy. The presence of *kirtan* seems to be sanctioned by the gesture of *vitarka mudra* with Guru Nanak, Guru Angad, Guru Ramdas, and Guru Harkrishan.¹⁵¹

Kirtan resounds in these portraits, particularly in those where the *kirtaniya* is actively singing with his mouth pursed, as evident in the scenes with Guru Ramdas and Guru Harkrishan. *Tanti sāz* are actively incorporated into these images. We see differently shaped sounding chambers: a unique teardrop shape for the scene with Guru Nanak, which is not repeated, and then the classic round shape of the *seniya rabab* for the other gurus, except for Guru Amardas, who hears *kirtan* on a bowed instrument likely because he developed the bowed *saranda* for this purpose.¹⁵² The instrument that we observe here looks more like a *sarangi*, however, since it is missing the characteristic notches of the *saranda*. Except for this single bowed instrument, all the other instruments shown in this series are plucked, but it is curious that the artists paint over the defining skin membrane of the *rabab* in their idealized portrayals. Several aspects of these portraits—from the opulent borders to the heavily stylized, ornate setting of the scenes themselves—show a preoccupation with evoking the splendor of the Sikh gurus and their courts, as presided upon by an immaculate rendering of the natural environment.

THE EXTANT SIKH *RABAB* AND ITS STORIES

We see two historical instruments, both of which conform to the Indian style. J. S. Bhatia conjectures that a *rabab* he discovered while undertaking doctoral research on Sikh portrait paintings at Gurudwara Dera Baba Nattha Singh in Kapurgarh was probably made in the sixteenth century and given by a Rajput king to Guru Arjan.¹⁵³ The ornate paintings on the instrument are identified by Bhatia as being made by Rajasthani artists working in the early sixteenth century.¹⁵⁴ A second *rabab*, believed to have belonged to Guru Gobind Singh, is currently held at Sri Padal Sahib Gurudwara Mandi (in Himanchal Pradesh).¹⁵⁵ A striking feature of these instruments is the considerably large resonating chamber and the beautifully carved stands and peg boxes. The six pegs of Guru Arjan's instrument—I assume three pegs are also present on the unphotographed side—suggest six strings, while Guru Gobind Singh's instrument suggests eight strings, as noted by Gurinderpal Singh Josan.¹⁵⁶ A third extant *rabab*, belonging to Guru Hargobind and currently held in a private collection, has been photographed in a publication by Daljeet [Kaur].¹⁵⁷ The natural beauty of these instruments—where the mulberry wood (*shahtoot*) takes center stage—is admirable and leads to the question of how Bhai Mardana would have transported such a large instrument during his travels with Guru Nanak.¹⁵⁸ Bhai Firanda's *rabab* is thought to have addressed this issue with its smaller size and its convenient protective cloth. Certainly, these extant instruments are considerably bigger than the scale suggested in manuscripts, and I wonder whether they were intended for a nomadic lifestyle.

The *rabab* played a vital role as an accompanying instrument to Guru Nanak's vocal compositions during his travels. One can only speculate as to whether, by including this instrument, Guru Nanak's concerns were primarily practical: The *rabab* is relatively easy to transport on challenging hikes and long journeys compared with the *vina*, for example. Also worth mentioning are the practicalities surrounding the playing of the *rabab*, given the urgency with which Guru Nanak would implore Bhai Mardana to take up his instrument when divine inspiration struck (as documented in the *Janamsakhi*). I would imagine there is no time to undertake extensive tuning of an instrument at such moments, hence the fewer the strings, the better.[159] I also draw attention to the supposed ease of playing the *rabab* in comparison with an instrument like the *vina*, a point that is foregrounded in oral historical accounts around Bhai Mardana's initial attempts to play the instrument and Guru Nanak's subsequent affirmation that the melodies will play themselves. Indeed, as oral history holds, the first melody to emerge from Bhai Mardana's *rabab* uttered, "Tu hi *nirankar* [you are *nirankar*, the divine]."[160] The possibility of an amateur being the musician of choice for Guru Nanak's vocal compositions is powerful in that it reinforces the message, which was articulated with special vehemence by Guru Arjan, that all Sikhs can and must participate in *kirtan*.[161] Of course, this is not to downplay the proficiency of those who have mastered the *rabab* and who established themselves as virtuosos.

Going back to Govardhan's evocation of *bhaav* (a heightened devotional mood), other reasons emerge for why Guru Nanak chose the *rabab* over, say, the *kinguri* or *sarangi*—vocal-supporting folk instruments that were accustomed to the itinerant lifestyle. As suggested by Govardhan in *A Rustic Concert*, might the *rabab*'s association with the practice of *bhajan* within the context of *bhakti* (devotional expression) participate in an established tradition that easily allowed his audiences to become affectively attuned to this instrument's timbres when coupled with verse? To this end, maybe Guru Nanak's choice of instrument was also connected to the musical versatility of the *rabab*: Unlike the *kinguri* or *sarangi*, it can provide a clear rhythm in the form of strumming patterns and melody through plucked individual notes, thereby offering a perfect counterpart to Guru Nanak's vocal compositions (sometimes, small bells are attached to the bow of a *kinguri* or *sarangi* to create a percussive rhythm synchronized with the changing direction of the bow). There is no need for a musical ensemble. And despite its limited resonance, which we tend to overlook today, given amplifying and sound enhancing technologies, the lightweight and structurally simple *rabab* proved ideal for the first creators of Sikh *kirtan*.

Finally, the history that I trace of the *rabab* in this chapter points to the symbolism behind Guru Nanak's choice: Like the Guru's teachings, this instrument has a cosmopolitan background that incorporates Indian, Persian, and Mughal influences while being rooted in the daily lives of the people and not only the formalized spaces of elite courts. Faqirullah, a nobleman associated with Aurangzeb's court, observes in his *Rag Darpan* (1666) that the timbre of the *rabab* and its overtones make this instrument suitable for singing genres of the *chautukla* and *khayal*, "with a voice laden with pathos."[162] During their travels Guru Nanak and Bhai Mardana transported the *rabab* from the realms of the Mughal court and the battlefield into the sphere of divine contemplation. Courtly genres like the *chautukla* and *khayal*, and many others, made their way into *kirtan* when *rababi* dispersed from the Mughal courts after their fall and found new patronage among the Sikhs.

We are accustomed to thinking of courtly culture as being the site of intellectual and philosophical debate, but as Greig reminds us, *bhakti* poets and Sikh gurus seated far from these elite institutions were deeply involved in rigorous reflection and the production of knowledge: "In the countryside, religious, aesthetic, and intellectual ideals were freely shared and interchanged by devotionalists of both religions: Bhaktis and Sūfīs alike. They traded songs and styles, practices and poetry, meditations and music; what was important was the result: ecstatic union with God." He adds that the Indian *rabab* was used "in both court and countryside in the sixteenth century," which explains its regular appearance in Mughal paintings of Sufis and holy men (such as those concerning Guru Nanak).[163] We know that Emperor Akbar traveled to see Tansen's guru, Swami Haridas; he also met Guru Amardas at Goindwal, making the gift of land after hearing about "teachings of equality and the institution of *langar* (free community meal) . . . on which the Guru's successor, Guru Ramdas, built the town of Ramdaspur, later known as Amritsar," as explained by Mohinder Singh.[164] Pashaura Singh reminds us that Akbar also met Guru Arjan in 1598.[165] Emperor Akbar was aware that a myriad of lives and ideologies existed beyond those formalized by his court. With the *rabab*, an instrument that occupied both spheres of courtly entertainment and devotional practice, we see how one aspect of its structural development was also tied to its ability to speak across social, cultural, and religious registers.

The illustrations discussed in this chapter show how the *rabab* accrued over time a dual affiliation with devotional music and with a broad variety of people that Guru Nanak encountered. The guru had a clear affection for this instrument, also seen in his comparison of the lonely self, separated from the divine guru, to the broken string of the *rabab*.[166] It was not only an instrument for entertainment but also one for edification.

Certainly, whatever it may have been in the past, the Sikh *rabab* is today an instrument that is firmly and forever aligned with Guru Nanak's praises for divinity. This is why some practitioners still refer to this instrument, with reverence, as the *Nanakshahi rabab*—the *rabab* of divine sovereign Guru Nanak.

There is a story that permeates Sikh oral traditions and brings the courtly realm of Akbar into direct alignment with that of Sikh *kirtan*. Suneera Kasliwal reminds us that "during the reign of Akbar we also find that a never-before Bhakti movement took place. It is just about impossible that the saint poets of Mathura and Vrindavan and the court singers of Akbar were alien to each other."[167] It is known that Akbar was keen to hear the voice of Tansen's guru, Swami Haridas, who is seen holding a four-stringed tambura in *Swami Haridasa with Tansen and Akbar at Vrindavana*.[168] When Tansen is unable to reproduce the same intensity of devotional fervor (*bhaav*) as his guru, Akbar chides him. Tansen responds, "I sing for you whereas my Guruji sings for the divine one." When it comes to the discussion of *bhaav*, Sikh oral commentary offers an important narrative interpolation: Who had taught Swami Haridas that his song will only have significance if it is sung not for a person but for divinity? The answer, Sikh oral history holds, is Bhai Mardana, which is not impossible given that they were contemporaries.[169] And who had taught Bhai Mardana that true *kirtan* is that which is sung for divinity? Guru Nanak. Tansen upheld the status of the *rabab* in the earthly domain, and Bhai Mardana did the same for this instrument in the celestial realm.

THE *RABAB* IN THE B-40 *JANAMSAKHI* MANUSCRIPT

The B-40 *Janamsakhi* manuscript (1733) is a fully illustrated bound set, which I examined at the British Library several years ago and which is an enormously valuable resource for Sikh studies given its importance as an early manuscript written in the Punjabi language (using Gurmukhi script) and containing fifty-seven color gouache illustrations.[170] To my eyes and ears, the golden yellow color of the *rabab*'s goatskin face, which echoes the tone of Guru Nanak's robe in every image, cements the association between this instrument and divinity.

This kind of symbolism is explored in unusual ways by illustrator Alam Chand Raj, whose technique, as Nikky-Guninder Kaur Singh notes, combines a "strong Punjabi rural impulse" with "the charming folk arts style from the Rajasthani Malwa School."[171] Raj offers us several angles from which to consider both the larger symbolic significance of the instrument, as well as its specific characterization in the form of a *Firanda rabab*. As characteristic of "religious painting," Hans observes the division of scenes into distinct planes where the world (*lok*) and transcendental reality (*parmarth*) exist across two different spheres: The supramundane is inhabited by Guru Nanak and the mundane is inhabited by Bhai Mardana.[172] The *rabab*, often perceived as a third companion in commentaries on the *Janamsakhi*, has a complex role to play: Tying in with the discussion of *ahat nād* in chapter 3, the *rabab* establishes itself as the source of *kirtan*. Even as it is often relegated to the realm of the mundane, as we see in *Kaliyuga Baba Nanak and Mardana* and *Baba Nanak and Mardana with a Robber Landlord*, its sounds carry over into the realm of the supramundane especially when conversation with divinity and about divinity takes place, as we see in these scenes and others including *Baba Nanak, Shaikh Ibrahim, Shaikh Kamal and Mardana, Angad and His Companions Visit Baba Nanak, Baba Nanak and Mardana with Siddhas at Achal Batala, Baba Nanak and Bhagat Kabir, Baba Nanak and Mardana with a Sikh, Baba Nanak and Mardana with a Philosopher, Baba Nanak, Gorakh, Kala and Mardana*, and *Baba Nanak, Guru Angad and Mardana*.[173] At other moments of spiritual elevation, as seen in *A Revenue-Collector, Baba Nanak and Mardana*, where Guru Nanak is seated with his eyes closed, Bhai Mardana occupies the same plane: Here he no longer plays, and the implication is that his *kirtan* has already taken the guru to a place of deep meditation where he hears *anahad rabab*.

There are two illustrations, in particular, that speak to the topic of *anahad nād*: *Baba Nanak Practices Austerities* (image 24 of the B-40 manuscript), where the commentary explains, "Wherever Baba Nanak sat in meditation, there the *rabab* played *kirtan*." Guru Nanak is in deep bliss, his head tilted gently to one side, his eyes softly open in a distant gaze as he inhabits the fourth state, drawing just one breath a year to stay alive. Bhai Mardana looks on patiently as Guru Nanak draws this breath through his open mouth. It is intriguing that he does not actively play the *rabab*; the *kirtan* issuing from the *rabab* is thus of the *anahad* variety, heard only to Guru Nanak. *Baba Nanak in the Presence of God* (image 28) retains the symbolic division of mundane/supramundane as Guru Nanak, hands raised upward and with eyes half closed in meditation, converses directly with divinity, while Bhai Mardana actively plays his *rabab* in mediating this engagement.

At other moments, such as *Baba Nanak and Mardana with Fakirs on Their Way to Mecca* (image 30), Bhai Mardana joins Guru Nanak on a higher plane when new figures enter the narrative, such as the fakirs in this scene and the yogis in *Baba Nanak and Mardana, Three Jogeshwaras* with Kamla (image 57). Meanwhile, the narratives of other scenes place Bhai Mardana on the same plane, but behind Guru Nanak, to indicate a lower spiritual status as observed in *Baba Nanak and Mardana with a Gardener, Baba Nanak and Mardana with Temptresses Sent by King Shivanabh, Baba Nanak and Mardana with King Shivanabh, Baba Nanak and Mardana with Dattatreya and His Sannyasis, A Magnate, Baba Nanak and Mardana, Baba Nanak and Mardana with Thugs*, and *Baba Nanak, Guru Angad and Mardana*.[174]

Although rare, there are instances where the illustrator is compelled to isolate the instrument, which allows our attention to be given entirely to the physiognomy of the *rabab*. In *Guru Nanak Practices Austerities* (image 18) the focus is on the recitation of *Japji Sahib* (emphasized by the verb "reading" [*parhan*] in the commentary), and hence the *rabab* sits on its stand close to Bhai Mardana, who is lost in meditation. We see the turned-back peg box, beautifully carved and decorated stand, fingerboard, neck, and face, whose contrasting golden yellow echoes Guru Nanak's clothing throughout the B-40 manuscript, suggesting an indelible bond between the two while investing this instrument with a divine aura. A playful painting where Bhai Mardana is turned into a ram through sorcery, *Baba Nanak in a Country Ruled by Women* (image 19), offers another chance to see the instrument placed on the floor as a lone observer to events. Outside of the B-40 manuscript, there is another eighteenth-century *Janamsakhi* gouache miniature that positions the *rabab* as an independent observer in an episode where Guru Nanak and Bhai Mardana meet Bhagat Kabir. We see a concern with verisimilitude, as captured by tonal contrast between the pale skin membrane and the brown wooden structure, while the characteristic bent neck speaks to the influence of the Persian *rabab*.[175]

Going back to B-40, other opportunities to see the *rabab* close up are offered in a painting that Hans marks incomplete, *Guru Nanak Gave Boons to the Visitors* (image 25). Here, we see five gleaming pegs, which are otherwise not clearly visible in the other portraits and which suggest five principal strings for the *rabab*. Throughout the B-40, whether Bhai Mardana is actively playing his instrument or whether he is at rest, *kirtan* having transported Guru Nanak to an inner state of bliss, one detail that Alam Chand Raj seems to have paid particular attention to is the triangular plectrum. This could be made from wood as well as other materials such as horn, ivory, or coconut shell, and Bhai Mardana always has it grasped between his right thumb and forefinger, ready to play at the command of the guru.[176]

Through a small selection of paintings, I have given some insights into the wide variety of *rabab* that were placed into Bhai Mardana's hands to accompany Guru Nanak by painters working across a two-hundred-year span. We have seen the different ways the *rabab* was held as it was played, as it rested against Bhai Mardana's body, or as it traveled, as an essential third companion on their journeys—heard and seen. It is worth adopting a critical eye and ear toward this instrument not only for the variation that underlies its appearance, as it speaks to the vivid imaginations of the painters who attended to its material and sonic nuances, but also for the important connection that its vibrations make between the spheres of human activity, the vegetal and animal domains, and the celestial realm.

ANAHAD NĀD AND PICTORIAL RESONANCE: THE HALO AND SONIC VIBRATION IN SIKH ART

In closing, I highlight a neglected visual marker of Sikh iconography that is present in many of the images studied above and that is suggestive for its connection with sound: the halo.[177] I have been drawn to the sonic properties of the halo since my earliest study of the *Janamsakhi* corpus and Sikh portraits. In spite of my conscious focus on stylized depictions of the *rabab*, my senses were also subconsciously attuning to a potent symbol of these illustrations, what Som Prakash Verma observes as "a large radiating halo" in Mughal art, whose solar luminosity alludes to divinity, a quality that is immediately conferred upon those who are adorned with the halo whether Sikh gurus and kings, faqirs, swamis, or Mughal emperors.[178]

When the halo is viewed in relation to Sikh imagery and its philosophical traditions, this symbol is immediately drawn into existing discourses concerning *dasam dwar* and the resounding of *anahad nād*. As informed by theories of aura, corporeal frequency, and scholarship in sound studies and vibration studies, the symbolic function of the halo makes evident that which cannot be seen but only felt: In other words, it projects outward the intensity of light and sonic expression that are perceived within the mind and body as the consciousness shifts to its highest state at the pinnacle of the spiritual experience of *anahad nād*.[179] Against this context, the halo emerges as an external marker of an internal attunement to the divine one, an idealized state of unceasing corporeal vibration. A vibrating body asks the spectator to attune to the latent sonic frequencies of the halo as it extends the powerful auras and vibrational energy of Sikh gurus and other holy figures outward into the physical world, while marking their unwavering existence as spiritually realized beings.

Sikh art allows the inner/outer dialectic of the halo to come into view: To our eyes, the halo signals spiritual attainment, while to our ears it invites us to contemplate the intensity of sonic vibration that resounds through and emits from the body: Devotional music, in the form of Bhai Mardana's *kirtan*, is absorbed into the body and transformed into the vibrational energy of *anahad nād* upon the opening of *dasam dwar*, whose intense resonance breaks through the crown of the head and the body's pores to become manifest in the vibrational form of the halo. This cyclic motion shows that corporeal aura is only heard by those who are acutely perceptive of its resonance, as Ernest B. Havell explains: "The aura represents the subtle, luminous envelope, by which ... the bodies of all human beings, animals, and even trees, plants, and stones are surrounded, though to those without a developed psychic sense it is invisible."[180]

This chapter's visual examples invite readers to experience the sonic dimension through the unique positioning of the halo in relation to the *rabab* and enlightened figures. The prominence of the *rabab* intensifies an underlying sonic resplendence; whether its strings are actively being plucked or not, reverberations that issue from the halo and *rabab* float through the image. My critical focus on sonic vibration as suggested by a symbolic connection between halo and *anahad nād* allows a concentration at the head in Sikh art to offer a new vantage point from which to consider the iconographical significance of this symbol and its external amplification of an inner *anahad nād*. Also important is the pictorial significance of a distant gaze, often conferred upon Guru Nanak, as indicating a type of listening that is inwardly attuned.

Despite its prominence in Mughal art of the sixteenth century, the halo began to emerge in Sikh art of the eighteenth century, becoming even more prominent during the nineteenth century, when it was associated with portraits of the Sikh gurus and key nobility such as Maharaja Ranjit Singh and Maharaja Karam Singh of Patiala. There are many instances where allusions to sound in the form of vibrations that issue from the *rabab* reverberate through the visual frame and are amplified through the halo when it is present. In the eighteenth-century painting *Guru Nanak and Bhai Mardana in a Landscape*, we see the typically Mughal style of halo presented as a solid, gold, flat disk in keeping with portrayals of emperors and "rare pictures of holy men," as Verma explains (see **fig. 4.4** above).[181] The divine aura of Guru Nanak is conveyed through the golden halo's allusion to a dazzling solar energy whose potent vibration is conveyed through the image, especially given that the *rabab* is in view—or, maybe, *because* the *rabab* is in view.

Here, we should note the placement of the halo: While beckoning to Bhai Mardana in *vitarka mudra*, Guru Nanak kneels in *bharadvajasana/*

vajrasana, thereby allowing the halo to be positioned lower in the frame and not within the same plane as the sun. A connection between *kirtan* and divinity is brought clearly into view. The halo's indication of individual spiritual attainment — in contrast to Guru Nanak, Bhai Mardana does not wear a halo — points to an elevated consciousness whose transformed state is captured sonically, as the *rāg* of Bhai Mardana's *rabab* finds a parallel resonance in the form of divine, *anahad nād*, which echoes through the golden hues of the halo across the painting. It is not only an externally made music that is being shown but also a heightened experience of an internally heard music that is captured, above all, in Guru Nanak's glance — his inwardly attuned gaze does not fall on the source of external sound, Bhai Mardana's *rabab*, but reaches far into the distance, accompanied by the sound of divinity as it reverberates through the universe.

At moments like these we witness the transformation of *rāg* into *nād*. While Bhai Mardana actively plays his *rabab* at Guru Nanak's bidding, an externally made *kirtan* facilitates and intensifies an internally experienced *anahad nād*. As the *rabab* and halo occupy the same frame, we also see how a larger cultural understanding of *kirtan* as a catalyst for an experience of divinity was in place and understood as a defining trait of Sikh spiritual practices, as shown in eighteenth-century paintings. Indeed, depictions of Guru Nanak and Bhai Mardana, whether produced in the plains or the hills, often establish a link between *kirtan*, the experience of *anahad nād* as conveyed through a distant gaze, and a vibrating, reverberant halo.

Whether the halo is depicted in its simplest form as a circle stretching from the base of the shoulders to encircle the entire head, or in its most elaborate form as a strikingly colored solid disk that is articulated by a dark border and radiating flames, it is ultimately a symbol that has a long history in different visual traditions around the world and that is universally understood as extending into the exterior realm an internally vibrant, pure energy. The significance of this vibration is ultimately determined by the wearer of the halo.[182]

With Guru Nanak the halo has multiple functions: It speaks to his spiritual attainment while allowing the resonances of his voice and of Bhai Mardana's *rabab* to infuse each scene with an endearing devotional *kirtan*. Resonating music casts into the physical realm that which is metaphysical. In this instance, a richly resplendent *anahad nād*, which is reverberating through Guru Nanak's interior through the opening of *dasam dwar* facilitates the experience of spiritual peace/bliss (*anand*). It is because these scenes are saturated with divine music in its manifestation as *ahat nād* and *anahad nād* that the halo in Sikh art stands apart from its precursors in Mughal art. Even though the colors, textures, sizes, and luminosity of the halo may be similar, the halo in Sikh art has a different vibrational aura because it is inflected through *kirtan* and the divine word.

CHAPTER SUMMARY

This chapter has provided an extended exploration of instruments associated with the spiritual journey that *kirtan* facilitates and enacts. Very particular instruments have been endowed with divine status given their emergence as *anahad*: *bheri, ghungroo, kartāl, mridang/pakhawaj, tura, sinyi, bayn, kinguri,* and *rabab*. When these instruments are played by the mind rather than the body, they indicate an elevated consciousness and a critical shift from an aesthetic appreciation of *rāg* to a sensory perception of *nād*. Among these instruments the *rabab* merits particularly close attention given its status as the first instrument of Sikh *kirtan* and its pervasive presence across all manner of Sikh visual media. These visual media invite a close study of its history and evolution. A focus on Sikh art allows the relationship between *ahat* and *anahad nād* to be examined from the new vantage point of the halo, which is tied to the notion of *dasam dwar* in the Sikh context.

Paired together, chapters 3 and 4 work toward clarifying the emergence of *anahad nād* as an internally embodied sensation. The following two chapters turn once again to the material realm in examining how technology mediates and intensifies this experience.

| 5

Engineering *Anahad Nād* as Digital Bliss

The Case of Amritvela Trust

Technology mediates how *kirtan* is performed, produced, consumed, and shared. A common goal of these innovations is to create cohesion among an in-person *sangat* and with a virtual *sangat* (gathering of devotees), thereby uniting Sikhs who are scattered across India and other parts of the world. The final two chapters address the topic of technology directly, keeping in view the myriad ways through which devotees use various media — audio and video recordings, streaming services, radio and TV broadcasting, translation websites, social media platforms, and other apps designed for mobile phones and tablets — to consume, disseminate, and appreciate *kirtan* as part of their daily worship. Just as the vibrational energy of devotees helps them feel connected to one another in a live gathering, the digital realm offers a parallel space where they can contribute to the formation of a global *sangat* while participating in the production of knowledge and the crafting of a personal Sikh identity.

The multimedia *kirtan* of Amritvela Trust, an organization based in Ulhasnagar (Maharashtra), is used as a case study to explore how technology mediates an experience of spiritual bliss. As discussed previously, the term *amritvela* refers to a sacred period of the early morning considered especially conducive for perceiving heightened vibration (3 a.m. to 6 a.m.). Amritvela Trust is renowned for offering recitation and *kirtan* during this time frame. This practice offers an original standpoint for engaging with the concept of *anahad nād*. Whereas chapter 3 outlined an understanding of *anahad nād* that was rooted in *Gurbani* and pointed to an inner experience of bliss, the unique efforts of Amritvela Trust complicate this definition by posing a different question: How can *anahad nād* be experienced by the distracted, digitally overstimulated minds and bodies of the twenty-first century?

My focus on *kirtan* as a sensorially heightened, cross-modal, digitized experience is unusual.[1] Within Sikh studies only a handful of scholars have been curious to explore the effects of technology and media on devotional practice.[2] Until now most scholarly focus on technology and media has been oriented toward issues that concern the construction of lived identities in relation to aspects of cultural and political history. In contrast, attention to the underexplored topic of acoustics shows how media and technology converge around emerging devotional practices related to *kirtan*. My investigation has benefited from being in dialogue with two insightful interlocutors working in the fields of religion (Jasjit Singh) and film and visual studies (Thomas Brandon Evans). Jasjit Singh's research offers valuable data and observations about how British Sikhs navigate media to harness knowledge that helps them take control over their cultural and religious lives as a social minority.[3] Evans's deep study of Sikh media and the soundscapes of the Harmandir Sahib (Golden Temple) complex in Amritsar using methodologies from German media theory introduces a new theoretical apparatus for engaging with Sikh digital worship. His attention to such Sikh media as specialty doorbells, sonic air fresheners, and digital ring counters (to help devotees keep track of their daily recitation) shows how quotidian sonic cues sustain a devotional impulse throughout the day.[4]

Outside of Sikh studies research on digital religion and media has only recently begun to include Sikh perspectives. Heidi Campbell's earlier work focuses on how Jewish, Muslim, and Christian groups respond to different forms of media. In particular she draws attention to the complex dynamics surrounding some religious communities who "take a highly critical view of many forms of mass media" while others are "embracing the dominant media technologies of their day," as I demonstrate for the Sikh context.[5] Her case studies find points of contact in South Asian studies on media and technology, particularly in the work of Annette Wilke and Murali Balaji, who examine the formation of modern Hindu identities in relation to topics of nationhood, political freedom, knowledge production, and sonic mediation.[6] This chapter engages in silent conversation with Wilke's and Balaji's extensive scholarship, as well as with valuable research about Islam and media studies, including Taha Kazi's study of "the impact of religious [TV] shows on the social, political, and religious lives of Pakistanis," which has a close correlate in the Sikh world that has yet to be explored. Patrick Eisenlohr's focus on "the technical reproduction of voice in Islam," another topic that I have long wondered about, begs further research in Sikh studies.[7] Naveeda Khan's historical study of the use of loudspeakers at mosques overlaps with a concern of my project, which, along with Evans's doctoral dissertation, is a starting point for future research on the use of audio technology at *Gurudware*.[8]

How do these topics — loudspeakers, Sikh media, and digital bliss — relate to Amritvela Trust and the goals of this chapter? My initial introduction to Amritvela Trust via YouTube was quite by chance. Around 2018, I watched thousands of devotees listening to the *kirtan* of Bhai Gurpreet Singh (Rinku Veer Ji) while wearing large, black headphones during — what seemed to me — the middle of the night. A sea of colorfully dressed, gently swaying bodies, sang *kirtan* along with Bhai Gurpreet Singh, with their eyes closed and their headphones wrapped around turbans, *dupattas* (scarves), and other head coverings (see **fig. 5.1**). Around this time, I had been reading various articles about the ban on loudspeakers and issues of noise abatement in the Indian press, and I was also aware of scholarship across a range of fields that addressed the use of loudspeakers and amplification in religious worship.[9] My own tendency to use good quality headphones when listening to music directed my initial thoughts about what I was witnessing at Amritvela Trust to issues of sound quality: Devotees clearly prefer the clarity and focus of hearing *kirtan* through headphones, I assumed. It was only after

FIGURE 5.1 **Amritvela Trust,** *Chaliya* **2021.**

I spoke with members of the *sangat* and the administration of Amritvela Trust a few years later that I learned the real reason. The introduction of Bluetooth headphones, an initiative taken by Bhai Gurpreet Singh, was in response to government and local bans on the use of loudspeakers, which were part of the efforts to reduce noise pollution during early morning hours following residential complaints.[10] In this instance, a practical solution also had the unintended consequence of heightening a devotee's experience of sonic vibration during the early morning period of *amritvela*. Around the same time that Bhai Gurpreet Singh implemented this technology, it was also being used by Indian partygoers: In Mumbai Bluetooth headphones had been in use at late-night dance celebrations of *garba* during the festival of *Navratri*, inspired by the silent disco scene in the Bollywood film *Ae Dil Hai Mushkil* (2016).[11] Although the same technology is put to use in tackling the problem of noise pollution in Maharashtra, the corporeal experiences of hearing *kirtan*, *garba*, and disco are very different.

Beginning with a consideration of how technology is used to acoustically manipulate the sounds of *kirtan*, the discussion goes on to consider how diasporic Sikh communities, in particular, rely on technology and media to inform their worship. The central effort of this chapter examines the impact of Bhai Gurpreet Singh's intervention on the experience of listening to *kirtan* in a heavily mediatized setting: Several LED projection screens, laser lighting, ambient fragrance, textured fabrics, decorative flowers, an ornate structure housing *Sri Guru Granth Sahib* (*palki sahib*), multiple drones, video cameras for recording and live streaming, and blessed food (*langar*) come together to create an experience of *kirtan* that is sensorially vibrant and resplendent. The case study of Amritvela Trust shows how *kirtan* can make use of technology and media in ways that build community and facilitate service. My observations speak to the main theme of the book, which traces the digital journeys of *kirtan* across media and between devotees.

KIRTAN AND ACOUSTICS

In the Sikh imagination *kirtan* often intertwines with the natural environment, as we have seen in earlier chapters. The *Janamsakhi* corpus portrays Guru Nanak singing outdoors in the mountains, by lakes and rivers, and in forests. Other paintings that capture *bhaav* (devotional mood or sentiment), such as Govardhan's *Prince and Ascetics* (1630) and *A Rustic Concert* (1625), show how devotional music often took place in small, informal groups outdoors. The term *dharamsala* was used during the seventeenth and eighteenth centuries to describe informal gatherings that took place outdoors or indoors.[12] A ballad by Bhai Gurdas mentions that every home becomes a *dharamsaal* when *kirtan* is sung there.[13]

Over time, the term *Gurudwara* became more commonplace to describe the indoor and outdoor spaces where devotees gathered to sing and recite together. The topic of acoustics comes into the foreground with the development of the historic Harmandir Sahib at Amritsar, which was conceived by Guru Amardas; initiated in 1577 by Guru Ramdas, who also excavated the *amrit saras* (pool of nectar/immortality); and completed, in terms of the space now described as the inner sanctum, in 1601 by Guru Arjan.[14] Harmandir Sahib has grown into a complex of buildings over the years, and this extensive sacred site, which holds at its center the aquamarine *amrit saras*, is popularly and affectionately called the Golden Temple on account of the glorious gold plating added by Maharaja Ranjit Singh during the nineteenth century, the reflection of which glimmers in the sparkling water of the pool.[15] The Mughal-inspired marble architecture of Harmandir Sahib incorporates the use of high domes in the inner sanctum, and it is commonly held that this was a deliberate architectural feature that allowed the voices and rhythms of the *kirtaniye*, who sat directly beneath the highest dome, to receive the greatest level of natural sound amplification. This mid-nineteenth-century orientalist watercolor by English painter William Carpenter is one of the few visual artifacts that shows *kirtan* being offered on *rabab* and *jori* in the inner sanctum and presumably under the main dome (see **fig. 5.2**). The audio engineer Davwinder (Dindae) Sheena also explained how the hard marble surfaces of the complex participate acoustically to reflect and distribute sound. The tranquil waters of *amrit saras* play a similarly reflective role, "like a piece of mirror," Dindae noted.[16]

With growing numbers of devotees and tourists, the Golden Temple complex now draws on a sophisticated system of sound-amplifying and sound-processing technology, which includes the use of microphones by *kirtaniye* in the inner sanctum whose sound is carried and dispersed through a vast network of Bose speakers throughout the temple complex.[17] It's not only that sound is amplified in order to reach the thousands of daily visitors but also that the sound is deliberately manipulated so as to cultivate "cues for . . . liveness," as noted by Evans in his conversations with the chief audio engineer at Harmandir Sahib. Evans explains that efforts to keep away from the "clean, even sanitized, material produced in the studio or with editing" means intentionally creating effects of "peaking, crackling, and echoing," which are so common (sometimes

FIGURE 5.2 William Carpenter, *Interior of the Golden Temple, Amritsar* (1854). Watercolor on paper.

unintentionally so) in *Gurudwara* spaces.[18] William Mason's research on audio-engineering techniques also speaks to how audio equalization (EQ) and compression work toward changing "timbral features of a sound that correspond to qualitative perceptions of material, space, and exertion."[19] Similar considerations are at play for audio engineers at Harmandir Sahib whose efforts to manipulate sound are applied toward affective ends — that is, to evoke a feeling of *bhaav* and *anand* (bliss) among devotees and visitors. In exploring the affective dimension of audio equalization, Mason draws our attention to decisions that are made by audio engineers around the selection of microphones, their placement, and the cultivation of balance between instruments.

Important for the audio and mixing engineers at Harmandir Sahib is the addition of reverberation techniques. These deepen the spiritual affect of *kirtan* by dispersing a robust resonant sound throughout the temple complex, allowing sonic reverberations to envelop and enter the body while simultaneously keeping devotees attached to *kirtan* through the deliberate enhancement of liveness effects: peaking and crackling, as Evans mentions, but also the short breaks that *kirtaniye* take between each *shabad* to retune their instruments (and cough, an effective way to check microphone liveness). Paul Théberge's attention to how reverberation functions as "an acoustic phenomenon almost exclusively connected to interior spaces and built environments" illuminates acoustic engineering concerns at Harmandir Sahib.[20] Also relevant is Mason's study of the "transcendental potential" of technologies of augmentation, EQ, and compression in present-day recording studios. It is striking that audio engineers at a vast, sacred site such as Harmandir Sahib rely on similar kinds of techniques to evoke the spiritual transcendental in combination with the awe-inspiring beauty of Harmandir Sahib itself. Sound and sight inspire devotees while "the radiant sunlight sweeps the visitor into a sensory swirl" at this temple complex, as Nikky-Guninder Kaur Singh observes.[21]

Nowadays, the intervention of technology facilitates the incorporation of engineering techniques that enhance the natural resonance of the *Gurudwara*'s primary architectural materials—such as marble and wood—to create an even stronger reverberation. The sound that issues through the Bose speakers is also transduced through marble, wood, water, fabric, metal, flowers, human and animal bodies, vegetation, and other materials to create a vibrating temple complex. The careful and deliberate manipulation of sound at Harmandir Sahib adds a valuable perspective to current discussions about architectural acoustics in sacred spaces.[22]

CURRENT MEDIATIONS OF TECHNOLOGY IN SIKH *GURUDWARE*

Given the resistance to technology that Heidi Campbell reports in her research on religious communities, I am struck by the extent to which technology has been embraced in the Sikh world in a way that speaks to the phenomenon of "hypermobility," as discussed by Catherine Gomes, Lily Kong, and Orlando Woods.[23] My own mediatized daily habits include morning *darshan* at Harmandir Sahib via 360-degree virtual reality broadcast by the PTC Punjabi network and accessed on YouTube.[24] Contrary to Jasjit Singh's observation that "the Internet may not be acting as a 'worship space,'" I find that live *kirtan* broadcast from Harmandir Sahib with 360-degree virtual reality, where I can see the intricate architectural features of the inner sanctum while witnessing the decorated presence of *SGGS* in high-density detail, facilitates a sensorially vibrant worship space.[25] At moments when I am drawn to a particular verse, voice, or musical instrument, it is hard not to feel that I am, at that very instant, seated in the inner sanctum close to the *ragi* who offer their *kirtan* to the right of *SGGS* and the women who are seated opposite them, to the left of *SGGS*. Through my iPad I watch devotees pay their respects by bowing down in front of the sovereign guru, while others sing along to *kirtan*, their eyes closed in blissful meditation. My digital *darshan* makes it possible for me to dwell inside the inner sanctum for as long as I wish, an opportunity that is not always available in real life, given the large crowds. Despite the ease of access granted by technology, daily digital *darshan* is not something I take for granted, and I cherish the immersive experience afforded by technology to both observe and participate in daily ritual from the distance of another continent.[26]

Like many Sikhs, I actively consume *kirtan* throughout the day via my Khoj Gurbani app, SikhNet Play (formerly Gurbani Media Center), radio, social media platforms such as YouTube, and streaming platforms such as Spotify (although I own many cassettes and CDs, I no longer listen to *kirtan* through those media).[27] I am not on Facebook, but colleagues, friends, and family routinely send me recordings via WhatsApp, and I am able to access Punjabi-language cable networks (PTC Punjabi, Akaal Channel, Sangat TV, and Sikh Channel) online. Finally, accompanying me at the end of the day, when I undertake my *riyaaz* (practice) on my *dilruba*, is a digital *tanpura* (drone) accessed via my iTablaPro app. There are many more technological interventions that I don't make use of, such as *Gurbani*-inspired ringtones or "caller/hello tunes" (music that callers hear while they wait for the call to be answered, popular in India). Not only am I aware that my daily existence is marked by an avid consumption of live and recorded *kirtan* through various media; I also know that I am not alone in the ways that I access and bring *kirtan* into my daily routine.

Every *Gurudwara* will have its own relationship to technology based on the needs of the regional *sangat* and the capabilities of the *sevadaar* (volunteers who manage and run the *Gurudwara*). Perhaps the most obvious place to explore the role played by technology in Sikh devotional practice is in the kitchen: Many *Gurudware* around the world are used to feeding large numbers of devotees and visitors in their free, community-led (vegetarian) kitchens. As I have seen firsthand at multiple *Gurudware* across Kenya, India, the United Kingdom, and the United States, the opportunity to receive meals at a local *Gurudwara* is a boon for individuals and families who are food vulnerable. News articles routinely publish on the kinds of machinery that have been created for the purpose of feeding up to one hundred thousand people at popular sacred sites, such as Bangla Sahib in New Delhi and Harmandir Sahib, including *roti* (wheat flatbread) machines that can make up to four thousand *roti* in one hour.²⁸ Even in these kitchens, as shown in the video of the automatic *roti* machine, devotees hear live *kirtan* through speakers that channel sound from the main *darbar* (space of worship). The link between *kirtan* and *seva* (social responsibility and service) is thus palpable—devotees listen, recite, and sing as they undertake service for the community.

In diasporic contexts, *Gurudware* have been leaning toward embracing technology to secure participation and help first-generation immigrant devotees stay connected to their faith and culture, while guiding second, third, and fourth generations toward opportunities to deepen awareness of their spiritual heritage. This observation speaks directly to a point made by Gomes, Kong, and Woods, who note that "digitised religion plays a particularly important role amongst migratory and mobile population groups. It enables them to not only be able to connect to their faith . . . wherever they are physically located, but also to interpret and engage with their physical, social and cultural surroundings through the lenses of digital media."²⁹ Around the last quarter of the twentieth century, many diasporic *Gurudware* found themselves in a state of crisis: *Giani* (religious knowledge bearers) and *kirtaniye* who were visiting from India began to realize that later generations didn't always have the language skills to understand *kirtan*, their exegetical commentaries, or prayer. As a reminder, although *SGGS* is written in Gurmukhi script throughout, it makes use of a variety of languages and dialects, including Punjabi, Apabhramsha, Braj, Hindi, and Persian.³⁰ Although there are some overlaps of vocabulary and grammar, vernacular spoken Punjabi is quite different from the linguistic complexity of *SGGS*. Even if a native speaker can read and write Punjabi, this does not indicate that they can understand the multilingual poetic nuances of sacred verses. Recognition of this challenge meant that emphasis was placed on encouraging native-language speakers to speak Punjabi and to read Gurmukhi, and to pass these skills on to Sikh youth. Over time schools and camps were established that taught Gurmukhi script, spoken Punjabi, Sikh history, daily prayer, and basic skills to undertake *kirtan*. But technology also played a critical role in helping young Sikhs understand their cultural and religious heritage and forge a connection for themselves.

Gurudware worldwide have responded to the crisis of language, comprehension, and participation by installing projection screens inside the main *darbar* (hall) where the *sangat* can read the *shabad* that is sung. Typically, the translation is taken from SikhiToTheMax.org or Srigranth.org, and the projected material will include the original Gurmukhi along with a transliteration and translation into English. Some *shabad* are well known among the *sangat* and thus invite participation. For example, "*Deh*

Shiva Bar Mohe Ehai," with its jubilant call, "Bole So Nihaal Sat Sri Akaal," is a popular *shabad* sung during the spring season of *Vaisakhi*, which is celebrated with great joy to mark the founding of the Sikh *panth* (community), the Khalsa, by Guru Gobind Singh in 1699 (**audio exs. 5.1** and **5.2**). Another popular *shabad* sung during a celebration (such as a birth, birthday, or wedding) is "*Lakh Khushiyan Patshaaiyan*" (also known by its *rahao* [refrain], "*Mere munn ekas sio chitt layai*," **audio exs. 5.3** and **5.4**). For daily *kirtan*, a *sevadaar* typically puts the *shabad* on the projection screen once the *ragi* have sung the opening *rahao* (refrain). The *sangat* is thus able to join in for the remainder of the *kirtan* and to grasp an understanding of the verse (translation limitations permitting). Typically, *shabad* are chosen by *ragi* or the *sangat* on the basis of the season — compositions in *rāg Basant* are often sung during the spring, for instance — or historical events, including birth anniversaries of the gurus (*gurpurab*), installations and anointments of Sikh gurus (*gur gaddi diwas*), and death and martyrdom commemorations.

In addition, some *Gurudware* install a screen to project the *hukam nama* (the divine command of the guru) retrieved by opening SGGS to a random page during morning and evening prayers — the *hukam nama* is read from the left-hand side of the page in the morning and from the right-hand side of the page in the evening. The practice of metrically intoning the *hukam nama* slowly and clearly so that its meaning may be contemplated and absorbed by devotees is an important aspect of daily worship that is not to be confused with bibliomancy or forms of book divination that predict the future. *Hukam nama* steers the devotees' thoughts throughout the day, and to this end, some individuals will subscribe to apps such as Hukamnama Sahib Daily Mukhwak, which delivers the *hukam nama* from the five *takht* (seats of Sikh spiritual authority) and Nankana Sahib directly to their mobile phone, while websites such as SikhNet.com offer the possibility of taking a personal "cyber hukam."[31] Finally, screens may also be used in the *langar* hall to give information about meals, upcoming events, donations, or how to sign up for *seva* opportunities. Unfortunately, we live in a moment when *Gurudware* in some parts of the world are vulnerable to hate crimes, and thus CCTV cameras and other security devices are also part of the digital terrain.

Alongside projection screens, the use of technology in worship can be seen in a variety of ways. Mobile phones are especially noticeable: *Ragi* will sometimes tune their instruments according to pitch frequencies retrieved from the iTablaPro app, and in cases where speakers are available, some *ragi* will choose to play a *tanpura* (drone) and *swarmandal* (plucked box zither) through this app. Mobile phones have also become an indispensable technology for accessing *shabad* through such apps as iGurbani or through websites; *ragi* often keep their phones propped up on the harmonium cover or close to their instruments as they follow the lines of the verse, and the *sangat* might prefer to access *shabad* on their mobile phones, too.

Outside of *Gurudwara*, devotees can access *kirtan* and other related features—such as *katha/viyakhia* (exegetical commentary), *nitnem* (daily prayers), recitation of *SGGS*, and stories about the Sikh gurus and Sikh history—through several means, including websites, blogs, podcasts, apps, social media, and video games. I have a strong intellectual interest in how sound reinforces and subverts stereotyped representations of gender, culture, and race in video games.[32] Although Heidi Campbell and Gregory Grieve do not explore Sikh perspectives in their edited volume, their observation that "digital games are an important site of exploration into the intersection of religion and contemporary culture that helps us understand what religion is, does, and means in a changing contemporary society" is hopefully sufficient to prod researchers of Sikh media to explore how the ludic dimension contributes to the production of knowledge surrounding Sikh identity, history, and culture.[33]

There is constant innovation and development with regard to how *kirtan* is disseminated, and the earlier anxieties that were seen around the mediatization and commercialization of *kirtan* have almost fallen to the wayside. These concerns pointed to two factors related to the act of sonic reproduction. The first had to do with the shift in the musical style of *kirtan* from one that was *rāg*-based and devotional in spirit to one that was oriented toward popular tastes and the commercial marketplace by the 1980s. The second factor saw practitioners draw attention to the problems of performing *kirtan* in a recording studio, a space that is not sanctified or sacrosanct and where artists and engineers might consume alcohol and other intoxicants that are not permitted.

As discussed in the introduction, Sikh recording culture emerged under the auspices of the Gramophone Company at the turn of the twentieth century through the HMV label, and it continued to develop over radio and in the context of the Indian recording studio with the ascent of Indian cinema through the 1930s.[34] The close match between these first recordings of *kirtan* and early Indian cinema in terms of voice timbre, musical style (including the addition of extensive instrumental introductions and interludes), orchestration, and overall mood is remarkable: It's easy to see why some *kirtaniye* balked at the transgression of the sacred into the space of the commercial. At the same time, some listeners saw the presentation of *Gurbani* through the popular style of *filmi sangeet* as affording accessibility—the generation of Sikhs who grew up with this style of *kirtan* is often nostalgic for it in the same way that earlier generations lament the loss of the golden era of early Indian cinema.³⁵

The Sikh recording industry consists of a complicated network of agents, processes, and materials that awaits further research by students and scholars. As I see it, a historical-statistical study of the recording industry's intervention into Sikh *kirtan* and the concomitant proliferation of recording companies and studios across Punjab and the diaspora is both urgent and vital to understanding the pedagogical motivations and musical efforts of *kirtaniye* today. Jayson Beaster-Jones's research provides a suitable model for the kind of inquiry that is much needed in Sikh studies, especially given the nature of this type of research to exclude the unique market dynamics of Sikh *kirtan* by folding this music into the broad, undifferentiated, and subordinate category of "devotional."³⁶ Picking up from the introduction, this quick gloss orients our focus toward the main topic of this chapter: how a heavily mediatized experience of *kirtan* participates in the experience of individual and collective bliss. A reminder of how *kirtan* has long been brought into the fold of audio technology since the turn of the twentieth century through LPs, radio and TV broadcasting, cassettes, CDs, DVDs, websites, streaming services, and film paves the way for our study of the efforts of Amritvela Trust: The sensory richness of this *kirtan* transforms audio technology into a device imbued with divine power.

Evans suggests as much in his concept of "theophanic media," which refers to an understanding of media "not as channels to transcendent elsewheres, but [as] live instantiations of an eternal processual 'here.'" He argues, "Media *are* where they are *activated*," an observation that rings true for Amritvela Trust, given the extent to which the external environment is a source of sensory stimulation during devotional practice — listening to *kirtan* through headphones over a multi-hour-long period grounds devotees in this uniquely mediatized environment, even as some report feeling being transported to heaven (*jannat*) through *kirtan*.³⁷ Théberge's observations have an uncanny parallel in the experience of attendees at Amritvela: "When we listen with headphones, we do not immerse ourselves in the spaces created by stereo so much as we wear them, like a halo, over our heads." This divine aura, so to speak, "may have a profound impact on how we perceive acoustic space in music recordings."³⁸ Théberge is tentative in the conclusions that he draws, but my interviewees confirm his belief that embodying sound through headphones alters not only how they situate themselves within their surroundings but also the stable nature of the environment itself, leading me to ask, How did the earthly transform into the celestial?

Evans's use of media theory to capture a uniquely "Sikh distribution of audiovisuality" finds a stimulating analogue in Mack Hagood's study of headphones as a tool of personal control over one's environment.[39] Hagood shows how headphones help users "sonically fabricat[e] microspaces of freedom for the pursuit of happiness," thereby functioning as a form of "orphic media" that, in my context, might be thought of as a form of *divine media*. Although his study does not deal with devotional concerns, Hagood's nuanced analysis of behaviors around wearing headphones offers insights that are entirely in keeping with those of this chapter: "Understanding orphic mediation—the control of how we allow ourselves to resonate, especially where the vibrations of others are concerned—has important sociopolitical potentials." While Hagood draws attention to how headphones give users a choice as to whether they want to connect their selves with their environment, my observation of headphone use in the context of Amritvela Trust shows how wearing headphones allows devotees to feel connected as part of a larger *sangat* with each other and their common environment. Personal isolation and individual protection are not coveted in this space although receiving *kirtan* through headphones, without contributing to noise pollution, relates to Hagood's perception of how people use orphic media "to sonically *re*mediate uninhabitable relations that emerge between ... heterogenous elements." Hagood's discussion of affect as "accumulat[ing] slowly over time, gradually conditioning the range of possibility for future action," also speaks to the experience of hearing *kirtan* over a period of several hours and to how the increased amplification of inner bodily vibration is manifested through various forms of *seva* (social responsibility and service).[40]

ESTABLISHING AMRITVELA TRUST IN ULHASNAGAR (MAHARASHTRA)

In preparation for a closer study of mediatized *kirtan* at Amritvela Trust, I now sketch a brief biography of the chair of this organization, Bhai Gurpreet Singh, which I obtained through an interview with his close aide and treasurer, Gurmukh Singh, in 2021. Bhai Gurpreet Singh was sent to Ulhasnagar by Baba Kundan Singh during the mid-1980s with his parents. As a young child he expressed an interest in learning *tabla* from *ragi jatha* (professionally trained *kirtaniye*) that visited the local Gurudwara. One day he decided to approach the harmonium—he played it very naturally, and everyone noticed that he was very gifted. By the age of fifteen he had learned *tabla* and harmonium and expressed a desire to sing film songs for Bollywood. His mother dissuaded him and told him to use his musical gifts to offer *kirtan*. At the time he was reading books about Baba Nand Singh, and Bhai Gurpreet Singh learned in particular about the importance of doing *kirtan* during *amritvela*. He began to undertake *kirtan* from 4:00 a.m. to 5:30 a.m. every day at two *Gurudware* in Ulhasnagar: He spent two years offering *kirtan* at one *Gurudwara* and then two years at another.

Over time the *sangat* became very attached to his *kirtan*, and Amritvela Trust was founded in 2013. The goal was to join people to the practice of offering *kirtan* during *amritvela* within each home. This attachment to early morning *kirtan* could only be formed through habit, and so Bhai Gurpreet Singh drew on the Sindhi tradition of *chaliya* (also known as *chaliha* or *chaliho*) that involves undertaking a spiritual activity for forty days to help his *sangat* make this change in their lives.[41] At Amritvela Trust *chaliya* first began in 2014, and it has since been occurring every year, including in 2020 when it was virtual. Since 2015 it has taken place in a large circular field (*gol maidan*) located near a water tank (see **fig. 5.3**). Although *chaliya* initially took place in the lead-up to the celebration of Guru Nanak's birth anniversary (*Prakash Purab/Gurpurab*) every year (a date determined by the lunar calendar), *chaliya* now happens twice a year: in October–November for *Gurpurab* and during the summer

FIGURE 5.3 Author's photograph of *gol maidan*, Ulhasnagar, Maharashtra.

(April–June). The concept of summer camps during school vacation is uncommon in India—summer vacation *chaliya* is oriented toward children to teach them how to read and write in Gurmukhi, learn *kirtan* on the harmonium, begin recitation, and participate in *seva* while gaining spiritual knowledge and awareness of how to be an engaged member of their family and community. In this chapter, *chaliya* refers to the period preceding *Gurpurab* and not summer vacation *chaliya*.

When resident complaints about noise pollution started to increase, Bhai Gurpreet Singh looked to Bluetooth headphones as a solution. He had noticed how these were being used in *dandiya ras* (a folk-inspired dance using wooden sticks and performed in groups) during *Navratri* celebrations, so he ordered two pairs of headphones from the United States and began his research into how they are made and how they might be used effectively for the purposes of multi-hour-long "silent *kirtan*," as Amritvela Trust calls it. After deciding to pursue the matter further, he followed a lead from Dindae Sheena for a contact in China and traveled there along with four trustees of Amritvela Trust to inquire about manufacturing customized headphones that met their specific requirements.

Amritvela Trust purchased twenty thousand battery-powered headsets in 2017 and then another five thousand the following year. Anticipating large crowds during *chaliya*, Bhai Gurpreet Singh ensured that the adapters for headsets could be shared between two people. At the time of my conversation with Gurmukh Singh in 2021, he reported that *chaliya* have been attended by up to fifty thousand people in person. Every year they order more headsets. I have focused only on the impact of Amritvela Trust in Ulhasnagar, the city in which it was founded, but the Trust has in recent years established centers across India and diasporic hubs with large Sindhi Sikh populations like Dubai (five hundred centers were reported in India during *chaliya* 2022, although the number is larger now, with new centers established across Gujarat and Maharashtra). The *sangat* that attends *chaliya* comes from considerable distances: Mumbai, Chembur, Mulund, Ahmedabad, Pune, Kolapur, Bhopal, Pimpri, and other towns. The diasporic *sangat* is situated across several countries, including the United Kingdom, Germany, Canada, Australia, the United Arab Emirates, Oman, Singapore, and the United States.

During our conversation Gurmukh Singh emphasized how wearing headphones creates and enhances vibrations among members of the *sangat*. I was also struck by his remark that the main goal of Amritvela Trust is to join devotees to *shabad* (the utterance of the guru): "*Gurbani* stresses a link to *shabad*. The *sangat* is not supposed to be interested in anything else except for the guru's word [*shabad*]." He explained that their purpose is to encourage and motivate people to join Amritvela Trust, and *chaliya* is one way they achieve that goal. Drawing on another long-standing tradition, Bhai Gurpreet Singh organizes an annual *prabhat pheri* (a two-kilometer walk), a practice that dates back to at least the seventeenth century if not earlier, where the *sangat* moves through town singing devotional music during the early morning to awaken residents and have them join in. Amritvela Trust's *prabhat pheri* in 2018 gathered up to 250,000 people in the streets of Ulhasnagar, all wearing headphones. Bhai Gurpreet Singh's efforts to create the largest *prabhat pheri* and silent *kirtan* in 2018 were recorded in the World Book of Records in 2019. In 2023 the *prabhat pheri* was expanded to a period of thirteen days and drew even more crowds—headphones had been dispensed with, given the extra large volume of people.

It is clear that Bhai Gurpreet Singh is one of the most popular *ragi* today, amassing millions of views on YouTube and thousands of devotees in person in India or when he is on tour. In 2022 he observed that up to 7.5 million devotees were participating in live *chaliya* via projection screens and TV screens that had been set up across 1,500 locations (up to 5,000 people were gathering at each of these locations), and this number increased in 2023. Across the numerous sites in India where projection screens are set up for live streaming, up to 20,000 members of the *sangat* gather as early as 1:45 a.m.[42] One woman I interviewed said that she was based in Sangli (Western Maharashtra) and that although she had never visited Ulhasnagar, she tuned in to hear *kirtan* at *chaliya*; she explained that the broadcast is delayed to 5:30 a.m. because it is not safe for women to travel out in the middle of the night in Sangli. Meanwhile, another woman who travels to *chaliya* using her motorcycle in Ulhasnagar mentioned the sheer number of people on the road at that time: "It's like peak hour." In 2023 up to 40,000 people attended *chaliya* on the final day.

Let us recall that Baba Kundan Singh sent Bhai Gurpreet Singh to Ulhasnagar. This small city, located on the outskirts of Mumbai and named after the nearby Ulhas river, served as a military transit camp, established as army barracks by the British government during World War II.[43] After Indian independence, the camp was turned into a refugee camp for thousands of displaced migrants from West Pakistan, mainly from the state of Sindh. Many within this community were business owners, and thus Bombay (as Mumbai was then called) was an appropriate destination. By the 1970s the entrepreneurial spirit of the Sindhi business community was seen in Ulhasnagar's renown as an industrial center; Tarini Bedi and Ka-Kin Cheuk note that this city became known as "an industrial center for a wide range of counterfeit commodity manufacture; the products were often made with low budgets and sold with the mimicking label 'Made in U.S.A.' standing for 'Ulhasnagar Sindhi Association,' for the local Sindhis were at the center of this trade."[44]

Despite my lack of insight into Baba Kundan Singh's motivations for sending Bhai Gurpreet Singh to Ulhasnagar, Himadri Banerjee's detailed study of Sindhi Sikhs gives a clue, given the challenging experiences faced by this community following their resettlement after Indian independence.[45] Banerjee's attention to how Sindhis practiced as Sikhs before the partition suggests that the strengthening of Sikh faith among this displaced and fragmented community was seen as vital by Baba Kundan Singh. Bhai Gurpreet Singh was likely seen as someone who could communicate the central thoughts of *Gurbani*—much of which had been forgotten through the generational struggles of adapting to a new life—in a way that could strike a chord with the unique syncretic religious identities of the Sindhis who were forging a new existence in a new town in a newly born nation.[46]

It is remarkable how over a period of a few years, this city has become a place where "everyone has started to resonate with his [Bhai Gurpreet Singh's] *kirtan*," one interviewee explained to me: It is broadcast widely through television and radio networks, and shop owners who form a key part of the *sangat* stream Bhai Sahib's *kirtan* directly from YouTube and Facebook. In case one happens to miss these opportunities, cellphone ringtones, which are frequently shared over WhatsApp, play memorable refrains. A young professional I spoke to described Ulhasnagar as congested and "not such a sophisticated place. . . . But once you come here you feel that bliss." The idea that a city or locale is capable of reverberating with bliss is one that Bhai Gurpreet Singh alluded to in his much-anticipated announcement for summer *chaliya* 2024. In the video he describes the importance, for a *sangat* dispersed across several locations, of gathering together at a single site to benefit from the effects of increased corporeal vibration through recitation and *kirtan*, especially at the closing of *chaliya*.[47]

AMRITVELA TRUST'S *KIRTAN*: MEDIATING *DARSHAN* BETWEEN THE METAPHYSICAL AND THE DIGITAL

Amritvela Trust's creation of a digitally enabled, multisensory experience of *kirtan* that many in the *sangat* describe as facilitating a sense of bliss is wholly unique. There is nothing else like it in current lived practices of Sikh *kirtan*. Gathering together as early as 1:45 a.m. during *chaliya*, thousands of devotees first recite morning prayers (*Japji Sahib, Sukhmani Sahib, Japji Sahib* again, then *Shabad Hazare*) before participating in *kirtan* at 3:30 a.m. Thousands more participate in recitation and *kirtan* through live streaming on YouTube and Facebook — typically members of the *sangat* announce their presence as they join through various spiritual greetings ("*Waheguru ji*" and "*Dhan Guru Nanak Ji*"), gestures of gratitude ("*shukrana*"), and others that request blessings ("*mehar karo*" and "*kirpa karo*"). To be sure, the constant stream of messages can be distracting. At the same time, this participation, and the similar nature of the comments, amplifies the feeling of devotion among a virtual *sangat*. Whereas I used to find the chat function distracting, I now see it as a powerful means toward building and reinforcing a sense of community; I seamlessly become a participant as soon as I log on.

Going back to in-person devotion, an interviewee explained, "All your senses are awakened." Indeed, every sense of the human body is engaged: olfaction, through the *ittar* (fragrance) that is dispersed through the space and the scent of fresh flowers; touch, through the fabrics that meet seated bodies and the vibrations that flow between the closely seated *sangat*; and taste, through the shared *langar* (blessed food) that everyone partakes in. The most actively engaged senses involve sight and sound (see **fig. 5.4**). Placed at the center of the stage is an elaborately constructed and vibrantly decorated *palki* sahib, which holds *SGGS*, attended

FIGURE 5.4 *Chaliya* 2023. Photograph courtesy of Rajee Hazari.

to by a seated *sevadaar* who waves a fly whisk and additional *sevadaar* who stand on either side. Male singers, including Bhai Sahib, sit to one side of the stage with their instruments, and female singers sit on the other side—all wearing headphones. Meanwhile, the vast headphone-clad *sangat*, nestled in the warm colorful glow of gently changing lighting, is greeted by huge LED screens. These project the onstage *kirtan* (along with the sung verse in Gurmukhi and Devanagari scripts), with video cameras regularly panning toward the *sangat* for brief moments. Some *sangat* prefer to keep their eyes closed, while others watch the screen or access the *shabad* that is being sung through apps on their mobile phone; some devotees also post the sung verse in the Amritvela Trust WhatsApp group in real time.

Since *chaliya* draw large crowds of up to fifty thousand devotees in person at Ulhasnagar (with thousands more participating online across India and the diaspora), it was necessary for a location larger than the local *Gurudwara* to be identified. An open field (*gol maidan*) situated a few kilometers away from the *Gurudwara* was selected as a suitable option. At the time it was unimaginable that the large field would prove too small, and yet, during the final days of *chaliya* or during important celebrations such as *Gurpurab* (birth anniversaries of the Sikh gurus), thousands are seated outside *gol maidan* in parking lots, streets, and other designated areas that have been equipped with carpeting, lighting, and projector screens. **Figure 5.3** shows a photo of *gol maidan*, where *chaliya* is set up every year. It was hard for me to imagine that this bare, open field could be transformed into the lavish setting for *chaliya* shown in **figure 5.4**. In the early days of *chaliya*, before they used a tent, the *sangat* used to sit in the unsheltered space of *gol maidan*, even in the heavy monsoon rain. Several *sangat* members reported that no one left when the rains came—everyone would stay and continue to participate in *kirtan*. One explained, a "connection develops [between the *sangat* and *kirtaniye*], so no one wants to get up and leave."

The installation of a tent allowed the decoration of *gol maidan* to become even more extravagant. I can now appreciate why some of my interviewees describe the experience of listening to *kirtan* in this setting as equivalent to reaching *jannat* (derived from the Arabic *jannah*, referring to heaven or paradise) or perceiving the otherworldly bliss of the celestial abode ("*swarag prapat hota hai—anand alag hai*"). One interviewee explained that she feels as though the celestial realm has become manifest on Earth ("*dharti par swarag ho gaya*"), while another has the impression that she has directly reached the celestial abode and is engaging in *darshan* (a felt presence) with the divine guru ("*asaa lag* ta hai jaisai seedha swarag mai pahunch gayi hun aur guru ke darshan ho raha hain"). The transformation of mood and psyche is remarkable and socially impactful: Unless one is invited to a sumptuous wedding, it is a rare opportunity for most residents of Ulhasnagar to experience such magnificent decor, given their socioeconomic circumstances. At *chaliya* they can feel they are part of a local community that nurtures their metaphysical (spiritual) and physical (nutritional) well-being without expecting any form of payment. The expenses of running *chaliya* are covered by donations (local and global) and likely revenue from online platforms such as YouTube and Facebook, although I should mention here that there is no sponsored advertising because that would disrupt the flow of recitation and *kirtan*. On the final day of *chaliya* in 2022, the entire event lasted ten hours—it is remarkable that the full content is available on YouTube without interruptions for advertising. Speaking of length, I should mention that one of the *kirtaniye* typed a message onto his phone nine and a half hours in and passed it through the other *kirtaniye* sitting onstage to Bhai Gurpreet Singh, asking him to end the program because he couldn't physically sing anymore.

As Bhai Gurpreet Singh regularly mentions in his *katha/viyakhia* (commentary), the hardest part of *chaliya* is waking up and making the journey to *gol maidan*. Travel is relatively straightforward for residents of Ulhasnagar, but since many thousands also attend from other parts of Maharashtra—up to four hours away—Amritvela Trust organizes free buses and asks volunteers to undertake *car seva* (bringing and dropping devotees using their own cars). Those who work in Mumbai will arrive by train and travel back to the city in time for the start of their day; a devotee told me that travel timetables are given out and shared via social media during *chaliya*. Bhai Gurpreet Singh is mindful to start and end his program on time (and several interviewees remarked on his punctuality).

Beginning at 1:45 a.m., the recitation of *Japji Sahib* and *Sukhmani Sahib* proceeds in a call-and-response manner (**video ex. 5.1**, 46:45–49:37). Against the drone of an electronic *tanpura*, the leader—who is the mother of Bhai Gurpreet Singh and known as Mata Ji—intones the opening line from the verse, while male and female *kirtaniye* respond with the next line in octave unison in parallel with the *sangat*. This experience is oral, aural, and visual, as demonstrated by the changing camera angles, which alternate between Mata Ji and the *kirtaniye* throughout (occasionally panning to Bhai Gurpreet Singh). The peaceful setting speaks to an experience of digital *darshan*: Mata Ji sits against a dark background, where multicolored lighting emphasizes the Amritvela Trust logo and other features that create a contemporary "lounge" ambience: the soft glow of chandeliers, hanging lighting, ornate *diya* (lamps), and plush carpeting. Meditative prayer is offered in a contemporary chic environment, pointing to the vision of Sikh devotion at Amritvela Trust as a lived practice that speaks to present-day aesthetics and moods.

After recitation has been completed, Bhai Gurpreet Singh and his *ragi jatha* (ensemble of professionally trained *kirtaniye*) begin their *kirtan* at 3:30 a.m. At Amritvela Trust, *kirtan* has a unique format and musical style that is unlike other styles I have examined thus far, given its commitment to situating sound within a carefully woven multimedia web oriented toward devotion. The introduction to my book points to several styles of *kirtan*. Amritvela Trust's *kirtan* presents yet another style that is defined by the following steps: (a) a slow tempo opening section is built around the *gur-mantra*, *waheguru*; (b) this section leads seamlessly into the central *shabad* (sung verses) through the gradual introduction of preparatory *tuke* (a few lines of text from the central *shabad*); (c) these *tuke* prepare the devotee for the main topic of the *shabad*; and (d) the *shabad* is sung and interspersed with *katha/viyakhia* (commentary), which blends exegetical analysis of the *shabad* with historical episodes from Sikh history. The flow of recitation into *kirtan* and *katha* over a period of several hours immerses devotees in a multimedia devotional experience that creates impact on two levels. First, it orients the *sangat* and connects them to divinity. Second, this spiritual practice strengthens ties to a prepartition Sindhi Sikh past for some, while forging a new historical awareness for others.

My conversations with devotees have helped me gauge the extent to which Amritvela Trust's *kirtan* is infused with *bhaav* (a feeling of heightened or ecstatic devotion). This cultivation of devotional mood is not primarily achieved through *rāg* but through careful attention to every nuance of *Gurbani* within a musical context that is defined by a slow temporality. There is no feeling of being rushed to get through several stanzas of a composition, for example. Taking just a few lines at a time, Bhai Gurpreet Singh expands on their meaning in relation to the Sikh historical past and the lived present within a relaxed temporal flow that invites devotees to lose their sense of time and place. To this end, the stabilizing use of an unchanging *tāl* (metric cycle) in the *tabla* and other percussion instruments is almost hypnotic, drawing the devotees into a trancelike state where simple melodies are used to attune the *sangat* to *Gurbani*. I call this style and approach *slow kirtan* and explore it more in chapter 6.

According to Gurmukh Singh, Bhai Gurpreet Singh's style of *kirtan* changed in 2013 when he started to do more *katha/viyakhia* in Hindi as a means to explain the central principles of *Gurbani* to the local Sindhi Sikh community, whose displacement following the India-Pakistan partition resulted in many losing their links to Sikh spiritual practice. One interviewee gave her viewpoint on the Sindhi migration to Ulhasnagar: "We were uneducated and illiterate people. We are Sindhis and we had *Guru Granth Sahib* at home growing up, but we never knew how to read Gurmukhi or how to understand. Rinku Veer Ji [Bhai Gurpreet Singh] has given us so much knowledge and understanding." Although it is largely a Sindhi *sangat* that attends *chaliya*, a local participant informed me that the *sangat* is now comprised equally of Sindhi and Punjabi Sikh attendees, with some of other faiths, too.

Around 2013 or 2014, Bhai Gurpreet Singh's *kirtan* became based on simple melodies. Maybe due to the musical education he received as a child from various *ragi jatha* who visited his local *Gurudware*, his style is a blend of classical and popular idioms, which coalesce into a *dharna* style of performance, modeled on call-and-response. Typically Bhai Gurpreet Singh sings an opening phrase while the male and female *jatha* support the *sangat* in singing the response. His simple melodies usually fall within the range of an octave and sit across a registral span that is comfortable for all voice types. Some melodies unfold in the form of a *rāg*, while others resemble a folk melody, a melody from a well-known *bhajan* (Hindu devotional song), or a Bollywood or TV serial theme. Similarly, rhythms are uncomplicated and the choice of *tāl* is constant and easy to access (a six-beat, eight-beat, or sixteen-beat metric cycle: *dadra*, *keherva*, or *teental*). The instruments that are played by *ragi* onstage, harmonium and *tabla*, are typical of most *kirtan* ensembles. These timbres are enhanced by traditional instruments (*tanti sāz*) such as the *dilruba*, *taus*, and *sarangi* (bowed string instruments). This nostalgic reference is given an inclusive, modern feel through its combination with other acoustic instruments, including the *bansuri* (bamboo flute), the *dholak* (double-faced single drum), the guitar, and a global percussion section including bar chimes, hand bells, shakers, and such.

Despite this sizable ensemble, a synthesizer often serves as the core of the *jatha*. It provides additional rhythms and metric patterns while throwing in the occasional melodic phrase on a variety of synthesized instruments (*sitar*, *swarmandal*, piano, guitar, bass guitar, or violin).[48] As an electronic instrument that participates in an acoustic ensemble, the synthesizer bridges the gap between acoustic and digital dimensions, thereby emphasizing the mediatized presentation of *kirtan*. To my ears it is the conspicuous attempt at harmonization of improvised melodic material in the synthesizer that speaks to the innovation of *kirtan* at

Amritvela Trust. The undiscriminating use of musical vocabularies ranging from pop, jazz, and blues harmonies to Latin American and jazz rhythms reflects the capacious quality of Amritvela Trust's *kirtan*, as it ties musical styles and idioms that are familiar within the Indian commercial sonic landscape to features of Hindustani classical music used as the basis for *kirtan*.

The typical format follows a trajectory that traces an inner journey of spiritual ascent: Preceded by the recitation of *mool mantra*, the initial forty or so minutes of *simran* (meditation on the *gur-mantra*, *waheguru*) takes place at a slow tempo (**video ex. 5.2**, 03:06:22–end). Bhai Gurpreet Singh uses a few lines from a verse by Guru Ramdas in *rāg Gauri Bairagan* (*SGGS* 167-10/11) as his *manglacharan* (invocation), accompanied by arpeggiated harmonization in the synthesizer and shimmer effects in the percussion. The *simran* (sung recitation), based on the *gur-mantra*, *waheguru*, takes place in a six-beat *dadra tāl*, where a simple melody is harmonized by the synthesizer in the middle vocal register (*madhya saptak*, A section, 03:09:38). After a short musical interlude, the *simran* continues in a slightly higher register (B section, 03:14:22) before returning to the opening A and B sections. The predictable structure of sung sections, alternating with instrumental interludes, is designed to enjoin devotees to the *gur-mantra* with ease (*sehaj*). Through each repetition, the *mantra* becomes corporeally embedded and the devotee is drawn deeper into the meditative state.

At the same time that there is repetition and predictability, the musical structure is also slowly evolving in keeping with the shifting state of consciousness. Thus, once the mood of the *simran* has been established, *ragi* begin to intersperse lines (*tuke*) from other verses. At 03:19:00, for instance, we hear part of a *salok* by Guru Arjan (*SGGS* 957-9) in a lightly ornamented vocal style to satisfy an aesthetic appreciation of musical beauty, as divine word combines with melody (03:19:46). The impetus behind this practice is to prepare the *sangat* to grasp the meaning of the main *shabad* ("*Sunn yaar humare sajan ik karo benantiya*"/"Listen, my dear friend, I have just one request," Guru Arjan, *rāg Jaitsri* [703-13]). In this case the *salok*'s opening line, "Day and night I yearn to feel the presence of the divine guru," amplifies the meaning of the *shabad*, which again speaks to a desire to witness the beloved divine. Building toward the *shabad*, Bhai Gurpreet Singh interjects another *tuk*, "Grant me the blessed vision of your glance [*darshan*], take me into your embrace" (Guru Arjan, *rāg Sri* [74-6], 03:21:01). The refrain (*rahao*) of the central *shabad* is woven into the next melodic phrase, "*Sunn yaar humare sajan ik karo benantiya*" (03:22:09). The pacing toward this point has been slow and gradual, without a feeling of being rushed. A sense of ease is prolonged, as *ragi* continue to build on the mood of *tuke* and the *shabad*. At 03:25:49 we hear another *tuk* extending the topic of yearning for *darshan*, this time from Bhagat Kabir in *rāg Bilawal* (856-16), after which Bhai Gurpreet Singh offers a *tuk* that deepens the plea (03:26:48, Guru Amardas, *rāg Dhanasri* [666-11]) and intertwines with the refrain from the *shabad*.

The musical texture continues to expand through vocal improvisation around various *tuke* that explore the theme of yearning for *darshan* (see 03:30:52, Guru Nanak, *rāg Suhi* [764-18]; and 03:32:04, Guru Arjan, *rāg Tukhari* [1117-12]). Having prepared the *sangat* to engage with the topic of the *shabad* in this way, Bhai Gurpreet Singh now melds the final line of his *tuk* with the melody of the *shabad's* refrain (03:32:41), which is repeated for several minutes before returning to the *waheguru simran* to close off this section (03:34:43). A final vocal improvisation at 03:36:31 (Guru Arjan, *rāg Jaitsri* [703-12]) leads the way into the *katha/viyakhia* section of *kirtan* (03:37:32), where Bhai Gurpreet Singh explains the significance of *darshan* in *Gurbani* through speech that is interspersed with short sung phrases that orient the *sangat's* attention toward the *shabad's* refrain as he continues to sing the remaining verses (03:45:08). Another *tuk* at 03:47:16 by Guru Arjan (*rāg Gujri* [520-8]) deepens an understanding of *darshan*, whose true experience is felt by very few, the rare ones (*virlai*). Against a background where the synthesizer and percussion continue to improvise, the *katha/viyakhia* section is one where spoken exegesis is combined with historical stories (*sakhi*) that expand the topic of *darshan* even further to include love for the divine (3:50:10). Putting this association to devotional purposes, Bhai Gurpreet Singh asks the *sangat* to lead the refrain at 03:54:18, giving us a rare chance to hear the *sangat*. In an otherwise "silent *kirtan*," this is the only sound that is heard, and it is not amplified through loudspeakers.[49]

As described here, the *tuke* have an important structural function, where each interjection enriches the *sangat's* understanding of *darshan* while pointing to this term's significance in *Gurbani*. Because *tuke* take the form of vocal improvisation, they often appear as interludes between the main sections of call-and-response. Musical interludes are a characteristic of commercial *kirtan* and have two purposes: to provide vocal relief to the singers and to allow the *sangat* to reflect on the message of what has been sung. Opportunities for vocal improvisation also bring the *ragi* into view. When I asked Gurmukh Singh how *ragi* are selected for Amritvela Trust, he mentioned that many of them are recruited from Jawaddi Taksal, an institution dedicated to teaching *Gurbani* and *Gurmat Sangeet* in Ludhiana, Punjab, after they have completed their training.

As is evident in their abilities to improvise using the syllabus of music notation (*sa, re, ga, ma, pa, dha, ni*) and *akaar* (non-text-based improvisation), *ragi* are clearly highly trained (see, for example, 03:20:25). Like Bhai Gurpreet Singh, they do not showcase their skill through virtuosity but through restraint. The ecstatic ornamental flourishes that we hear toward the end of the *simran*, and at the end of the *kirtan* in a high vocal register at 04:28:58 (*taar saptak*), are not empty gestures of virtuosity for the sake of showmanship. Rather, this jubilant vocal expression indicates the attainment of spiritual bliss following the steady trajectory toward this point that begins in the *madhya saptak* at the start of the *simran*. The devotional affect of this ascent in vocal register is one of exulted joy captured by the term *nihaal*—a devotee explained to me, "*nihaal ho ja thi hai sangat*" ("the *sangat* becomes joyful"). This day's *kirtan* closes with Bhai Gurpreet Singh singing the refrain one final time, with no *tabla*, before introducing an original composition (known as *dharmic geet*, a nonscriptural verse) where he draws the *sangat* in even deeper by addressing the topic of yearning and love directly in his own words: "I have found everything but you" (04:32:30, "*Sab kuchh miliaa, tun nahi miliaa*"). The program ends with a sung recitation of *Chaupai Sahib* (04:40:32), followed by *Anand Sahib* (04:45:04), *Ardas* (04:47:54), and *Hukam nama* (04:58:12).

Admittedly, when I first listened to Amritvela Trust's *kirtan*, I was not drawn to its simplicity and lack of musical sophistication typically expressed through the motions of *rāg*. "*Sun Yaar Humare Sajan*" has a completely different quality when sung in *rāg*, as seen with Bhai Dharam Singh Zakhmi, Bhai Nirmal Singh Khalsa, Dr. Gurnam Singh, and Bhai Kultar Singh, to name a few. However, when I started to experience *chaliya kirtan* in one sitting, without any disturbance, I noticed that the long time frame and deliberately paced slow temporal flow deepened my engagement with the verses of *Gurbani* even in the absence of *rāg*. In my own musical practice I tend to move quickly from once verse to the next. Additionally, as we saw with the practice of *Aasa ki vār* in chapter 1, the *ragi* retune their instruments every time they sing a *shabad* in a new *rāg*. This creates a temporary break in the flow of *Gurbani*. The avoidance of *rāg*-based *kirtan* at Amritvela Trust is likely a way to attract the local community whose musical tastes are shaped by their frequent engagement with Indian commercial TV and film. In this instance, Bhai Gurpreet Singh adapts a version of "*Sunn Yaar Humare Sajan*" that is hugely popular in commercial *kirtan* in a recording made by Bhai Satvinder Singh and Bhai Harjinder Singh (Delhi Wale). Bhai Gurpreet Singh's musical exploration of sacred verse at a slow pace over a long time span forces listeners to slow down and contemplate a few words of *Gurbani* at a time.

These *tuke* are like drops in the ocean—their vast meaning and personal significance sink into our consciousness gradually. It is in this sense that Amritvela Trust's *kirtan* facilitates corporeal and psychical transformation.[50] One devotee revealed to me, "[The] *bani* goes into your body." Another pointed to the lasting effects of this *kirtan*: "*Kirtan* reverberates in your ears through the day" (*kaano mai kirtan bhajta hai*). This is the lasting impact of *slow kirtan*.

HEADPHONES AND ABSORPTION

Bhai Gurpreet Singh's headphones initiative was initially conceived to tackle the obstacle of noise pollution—he reminds those attending *chaliya* to be quiet as they arrive and depart so as not to disturb residents, and this caution extends to the use of vehicle horns, which are vibrant participants in the country's sonic landscape, as any visitor to India knows. In addition to facilitating "silent *kirtan*," the use of headphones at Amritvela Trust also democratizes sound distribution; one interviewee explained to me how, with loudspeakers, the *sangat* at the front gets too much sound, while those seated at the back can't hear much at all. Many interviewees praised the high-quality sound and good range of the headphones, noting the option to adjust the volume (see fig. 5.5). Amritvela Trust's *kirtan* is focused squarely on creating *ras* (a sweet essence or aesthetic and ecstatic delight) through participation. It is not about an individual's experience of bliss but a communal one. To

FIGURE 5.5 Amritvela Trust headphones. Photograph courtesy of Rajee Hazari.

this end, Bluetooth headphones play a critical role, as the main organizer reminded me, "Wearing headphones creates and enhances vibrations among the *sangat*."

Furthermore, Bhai Sahib's use of microphones and the careful mixing of his sound through filters that enhance reverberation and delay play a critical role in engendering a feeling of enveloping, communal bliss. A team of audio engineers is responsible for managing the complicated setup for *chaliya*, which includes maintaining balance between the male and female *kirtaniye* as well as calibrating the microphone for Bhai Gurpreet Singh with his preference for sound delay and reverberation to achieve the sonic effect of a full, resonant vibration. This engineered sound plays an important role in creating a sonic aura conducive for receiving *kirtan*. The experience of liveness is quite different from what Evans describes at Harmandir Sahib, where sound is configured as "a live event with feedback, handling noise, and other auditory media artifacts acting as cues for that liveness."[51] At Amritvela Trust, an immaculate sound is carefully engineered in a multimedia environment geared toward promoting a feeling of transcendence and multisensory bliss.

Sight and sound interact in unexpected ways at Amritvela Trust. In an example of *ahat nād*, the *sangat* can see the *ragi jatha*, their harmoniums, and the musicians with their large variety of musical instruments being played onstage. However, they cannot hear the music except through headphones. If a visitor were to attend without connecting their headphones, they would likely see the actions of instruments being played, but they wouldn't hear much (in keeping with the premise of "silent *kirtan*"). This *kirtan* thus manifests as unheard sound. In a rare inversion of the dynamics of *kirtan*, the only sound one can hear without wearing headphones is that of the *sangat* themselves when they sing (**video ex. 5.3**). Bhai Gurpreet Singh's headphones, on the other hand, are calibrated to capture his own sound as well as the *sangat's*, providing real-time auditory feedback.

Another (unintended) positive outcome of wearing headphones is that it facilitates a deeply immersive, absorptive experience. This feeling attaches devotees to the divine guru, as described by an attendee ("*jurh jaathai hai guru ke saath*"), while heightening a feeling of peace and inner bliss (*sukh-sehaj-anand*). One interviewee noted how everyone appears lost in *kirtan* ("*khoai parai rahtai hain*"); she explained that the consciousness or focus (*munn*) remains joined to *Gurbani* and one feels a sense of peace ("*aap ka munn jorhai ga . . . aap ko anand ayai ga*"). Another devotee shared how wearing headphones allows him to lose himself in *kirtan*, especially since conversation between attendees is limited—he becomes completely absorbed and doesn't miss a word ("*koi shabad miss nahi ho thaa hai*"). Another remarked that the sound goes directly into the ears ("*awaaz direct kanna de vich jaandi hai*"); without headphones, the spiritual link is broken by members of the *sangat* talking among themselves or making a disturbance.

Wearing headphones also affords a feeling of intimacy, which is significant in this devotional practice. One devotee emphasized that while her consciousness stays focused on *Gurbani*, she feels that "Bhai Sahib is speaking to [her] directly.... It feels very intimate, [as though] he is speaking just for [her]" ("*Bhai Sahib ki awaaz humarai liyai hain*"). Another said that she also has that experience: "He's talking only with me.... Whatever question I have, the next *kirtan* he gives the answer ... [or] in the same *kirtan* [that day]." In this way many devotees feel they have cultivated a personal connection with Bhai Gurpreet Sahib through hearing his *kirtan* via the apparatus of headphones.

Many interviewees spoke about the positive impact of *chaliya* on their lives. One woman explained, "So many miracles have happened to me during *chaliya*," one of which involved getting pregnant. She explained, "The vibration of his *kirtan* is so positive." Another interviewee mentioned the healing powers of *kirtan* with regard to her son, whose extended hospitalization was brought to an end when she began to attend *chaliya*—her son doesn't have use of his limbs, so he edits and makes videos of *chaliya* using just his nose.

An immersive experience of listening to *kirtan*, where *Gurbani* is felt to literally enter the body, is both soothing—devotees feel attuned to the positive vibrations—and deeply emotional, leaving some feeling vulnerable in that they are compelled to reveal their inner thoughts and feelings. Several comments reminded me of another aspect of *kirtan*, which is its ability to touch one's emotions by evoking *viraag/bairaag* (anguish brought about through separation from the divine) such that devotees are reduced to tears through contemplation of *Gurbani*. One interviewee told me that "tears will not stop falling from your eyes when you listen in the early morning." Speaking on this issue, another interviewee mentioned how listening through headphones makes her cry ("*rohna bhi aata hai*"); she feels as though she is in the presence of the guru ("*aasai lagta hain ke guru mil gain hain*"). On the topic of *viraag*, another explained that *kirtan* is "not only going into [her] ears, head, brain ... [but it also touches] inner feelings [such that] people start crying." *Chaliya* of 2018 is especially remembered as an event that elicited intense emotion of *viraag* (detachment and yearning) among the *sangat*.

In his study of "the moral problem of headphones" in contemporary society, Thomas Everrett emphasizes the dominant perception of headphone wearers as antisocial, given their deliberate efforts to create a private space.[52] In parallel, several scholars have noted the use of headphones as a way to articulate what Alex Blue V calls "a personal, silent safe zone" in environments from which they seek to escape.[53] Focusing on the technique of auditory flooding, Jacob Downs extends these observations even further into the space of sonic violence and torture, noting situations where headphones are weaponized to invade "the interior phenomenological space of the head."[54] In stark contrast, the practice of wearing headphones at Amritvela Trust reflects a completely different preoccupation: By emphasizing vibrational harmony, this apparatus brings individuals closer together through communal absorption in *kirtan*.

EXPERIENCING DIGITAL *ANAHAD NĀD*

Repeatedly, my interviewees describe the experience of wearing headphones as facilitating an inwardly focused listening, an absorption that enables proximity to a divine realm (*jannat/swarag*), and a witnessing of divine presence in keeping with the ecstatic experiences of *anahad nād* described in *Gurbani*. In reflecting on my own engagement, I wonder how the digital realm expands my understanding of *anahad nād* as a corporeal journey where a gradual shift in consciousness signals spiritual progress. The devotee's awareness of distinct musical timbres during this journey becomes more intense as the pinnacle of the meditative state is reached. At this moment, fully awakened sensory faculties speak through one other: The sweet taste (*amrit ras*) of a voluminous blend of timbres (*panch shabad*) that thunders through the inner body is accompanied by intoxicating fragrance, a gentle breeze, the dazzling sight of brilliant light, and the glimmer of multicolored jewels. *Gurbani* tells us that very few individuals (*virlai*) perceive *anahad nād*. How does this definition relate to my experience of *anahad nād* at Amritvela Trust?

Anahad nād is manifest in three ways. First, the notion of "silent *kirtan*" speaks directly to *anahad nād*, given that intensely vibrating bodies will appear still and quiet to anyone observing from the outside. For this reason, another common translation of *anahad* is "unheard." At Amritvela Trust, you cannot hear Bhai Gurpreet Singh's highly resonant *kirtan* unless you are wearing headphones. If we were to walk into *gol maidan* at 3:30 a.m., we would hear periods of silence followed by moments of singing by the *sangat* and no musical instruments. All this serves the initiative to reduce noise pollution, but it also creates an immersive devotional experience where listeners report feeling as though their spiritual journey toward the divine realm has been expedited: Wearing headphones provides a "direct link to the gurus," and it feels as though one has "directly reached *swarag*," my interviewees explained.

Second, the experience of *anahad nād* can be evoked musically through aspects of tempo, texture, timbre, and audio engineering. For example, during *chaliya* 2021 (day 8), a state of ecstatic bliss is marked by a quickening tempo, which also tightens the call-and-response texture built on the *gur-mantar*, *waheguru*, so that this recitation starts to feel internally automated and corporeally produced, in keeping with the notion of *rom rom* (in every fiber of my being) as discussed in chapter 3. In reaching a Sindhi Sikh population that is attuned to the soundscapes of Hindu devotion, the timbre also privileges instruments that the *Hamsa Upanishad* associates with *anahad nād*, such as the *bansuri* (flute) and the *shankh* (conch). With the inclusion of *manjira/kartāl* (hand cymbals), the *kirtan* becomes timbrally marked for the predominantly Sindhi *sangat*, since the *bansuri*, *shankh*, and *manjira/kartāl* are not typically used in Sikh *kirtan*. Audio manipulation of the sound to create distance, delay, echo, and reverberation creates an otherworldly aura that attunes the *sangat* to the presence of a divine realm (see **video ex. 5.4**, from 02:48:21 to 02:53:04; the tempo starts to pick up at around 02:50:25, and the sound is actively manipulated around 02:51:15).

Finally, there is another way that the ecstatic, synesthetic, blissful experience of *anahad nād* is created at Amritvela Trust. At the close of *chaliya*, or on other festive days, such as birth anniversaries (*Gurpurab*), the vast *sangat* is greeted by a festive display that feeds the senses. For example, the close of *chaliya* in 2022 included a vibrant ceremonial procession of *SGGS* in an exquisitely decorated palanquin accompanied by a retinue of *ransingha* (a large, S-shaped brass horn) players and the beating of large drums (*dhol*), as well as fireworks. As discussed in chapter 1, this fanfare is a distinctive feature of *Aasa ki vār chaunki* (early morning *kirtan*) at Harmandir Sahib, where martial timbres announce the arrival of *SGGS* in the inner sanctum. At Amritvela Trust this royal procession is reserved for the final day of the proceedings, where it is a central feature of a multimedia devotional experience whose decorative opulence knows no bounds. At the start of the *simran*, the *sangat* views an ornately decorated *palki sahib* onstage (projected onto large LED screens within the main tent but also on screens dotted around the area, given the vast *sangat*) accompanied by a changing display of multicolored laser lighting and flowing fabrics that decorate the tent. Gradually, the meditative experience is deepened through a quickening of the tempo and a singing of verses that implore the arrival of the divine guru in the devotee's home, which is described as *hirdai* (one's inner body or heart).

Over the period of a single *kirtan*, as the intensity of yearning increases, the pinnacle of ecstatic bliss is marked by an explosion of sound, color, light, and texture. This is not an expression of an internal *anahad nād*, as described in *Gurbani*, but an external *anahad nād*, as engineered at Amritvela Trust (see **video ex. 5.5**, starting at 07:39:00). Seven hours into *chaliya*, an extended *simran* of a short phrase (*mantar*), "*Dhan Guru Nanak*," sung in a call-and-response manner, is accompanied by falling confetti. A deepening of the meditative state is marked by an increasing tempo and volume such that the phrase "*Dhan Guru Nanak*" feels automatic and internalized (*ajapa jaap*), as characteristic of *anahad nād*, while the vibrant call of the *ransingha* is heard resounding through *gol maidan* and the surroundings. The *sangat*'s sensory faculties are fully awakened: Above the *mantar* and ecstatic vocal improvisation in the high register, a heterogeneous blend of musical timbres and a dazzling laser light display are accompanied by a countdown announced on the large screens. At the designated moment, haptic phenomena such as bubbles, gold confetti, multicolored streamers, smoke from smoke machines, fireworks, and, finally, hundreds of balloons signal the pinnacle of the final proceedings, which are aligned with *darshan* (a sensing of divine presence) of the guru.

It is almost as if this devotional spectacle has been crafted keeping in mind the descriptions of *anahad nād* in *Gurbani*, many of which emphasize an internalized *simran*: dazzling, multicolored light and the striking sound of the *sinyi* (animal horn) and *toorae* (brass horn), while the rumbling sounds of the fireworks evoke the thunderous *bheri* (drum). I have not witnessed this event in person, but I can imagine the sensory overload that devotees felt, not to mention the sense of elation as this *chaliya* unfolded over a period of ten hours. For this single night, the residents of this district may have had to embrace the (noisy) jubilant calls of the *ransingha* and the fireworks display. In 2023 the celebrations on the final day of *chaliya* were even more ornate in their use of multicolored laser lighting, streamers, fireworks, confetti, and balloons decorated by small tee lights, as seen in this video of the highlights (**video ex. 5.6**).[55] I am reminded that several interviewees mentioned that Amritvela Trust is mindful of not only noise pollution but also environmental pollution and waste. For this reason, products aim to be recyclable and nonpolluting as far as possible.

The synesthetic feel of Amritvela Trust's *kirtan* plays a central role in facilitating a digital experience of *anahad nād*—a feeling of inner bliss that also manifests outwardly. While the expression of this moment may be thoroughly modern, given its heavily mediatized multimedia presentation, the means toward reaching this point have been traditional. This digital rendering of bliss has been achieved through *simran* and *kirtan*, as described in *Gurbani*, while the positive vibration that this experience yields is directed toward *seva* (social responsibility and service) and the well-being of all in the community.

A VIBRATORY FEEDBACK LOOP BETWEEN *KIRTAN* AND *SEVA*

In his reflections on *chaliya* 2022 the treasurer Gurmukh Singh drew out many positive aspects of the preceding forty days, including the *seva* undertaken by hundreds of volunteers around the clock. I was struck by one devotee, who is involved in regular *seva* all year round, not only during *chaliya* (see **fig. 5.6**). She mentioned how she starts chopping vegetables at 1 a.m. so that she can serve *karah prasad* (a sweet, flour-based blessed food, which she emphasized was made in pure ghee) and *langar* (a blessed meal) when *kirtan* ends at 6 a.m. Several interviewees repeatedly mentioned the dedication and stamina of those who prepare the fresh flower decorations for *chaliya*, which also takes up considerable time. Gurmukh Singh commended the exemplary conduct of the devotees, the increasing numbers of attendees at Amritvela Trust centers across the country and the diaspora, and the edifying *kirtan* and *katha/viyakhia* of Bhai Gurpreet Singh and the *kirtaniye*.

Gurmukh Singh also asked a question that stood out to me: "What do

FIGURE 5.6 *Langar seva* at Amritvela Trust.

we want to take away from this experience of *chaliya*?" My interviewees already explained the effects of embodied listening through headphones as a form of positive vibration that improves a sense of well-being while raising one's consciousness. But this experience is not oriented only toward personal growth. Gurmukh Singh's answer reveals the tight relationship between *kirtan* and ethics and points to how this digitally immersive experience impacts a devotee's attitudes toward serving their community in a pursuit of equity.

All forms of *seva* are recognized at Amritvela Trust—*vastra seva* (decorating with fabric), rug placement *seva*, headphone *seva* (removing and inserting batteries; handing out, collecting, and organizing headsets), *langar seva* (preparing food), *jora ghar seva* (organizing and cleaning shoes), transportation *seva*, parking *seva*, pen-drive *seva* (saving recitation and *kirtan* on pen drives to be distributed), taking care of visitor needs, helping people access Amritvela Trust through social media by explaining equipment or data subscription plans, and general maintenance and tidying, especially after *chaliya*. During *chaliya* 2023, I was surprised to learn about "wake-up call" *seva*—those who have difficulty waking up are encouraged to place their names and cities on a list to receive a wake-up call from a volunteer. Gurmukh Singh also asks devotees to go back to their communities and notice how to make things better for all. This applies to devotees consuming Amritvela Trust *chaliya* through online media, too. Even as the multimedia packaging of *chaliya* is oriented toward digital *darshan*—whether in person or online—animated icons are constantly flashing across the screen with information on how to donate, who to contact for various forms of *seva*, and practicalities for obtaining updates via WhatsApp and other social media sites.

Food vulnerability remains a pervasive challenge across India, and one aspect of Amritvela Trust that he draws attention to is Nanak Roti Trust, a volunteer program run through donations, which makes and distributes food in surrounding communities. Hundreds of centers offer Nanak Roti and around five hundred thousand people are fed through this program.[56] An interviewee mentioned that Nanak Roti continued during COVID, when food was prepared and packaged into individual portions that met safety standards. Volunteers would then drive these packages into local areas and slums through car *seva*. Amritvela Trust also used to run stores called 13-13 Mart (a pun on the word *tera*, which means "yours" and, in this case, implies that the mart and its business belong to the divine one), which offered groceries at discounted prices. Also during the devastating surge of the delta variant of the coronavirus, Amritvela Trust participated, along with other *Gurudware* across India, in coordinating and sharing oxygen cylinders and other medical services.

Amritvela Trust's use of headphones in a synesthetic context of worship creates a fascinating counterpart to Hagood's study of "orphic media," where headphones allow users to create safe spaces of isolated freedom. In contrast, Amritvela Trust uses this technology to amplify individual bodily vibrations and create a strong resonance that binds an entire community together. While *chaliya* has been attended by up to fifty thousand people in person, many thousands are also accessing these early morning events globally through their personal headsets at home and via group live streaming events. The goal of bringing the *sangat* together in this way is twofold: First, gently repeating melodies embed the ideas of *Gurbani* deep into the body, where attunement to divinity, as facilitated through a heightened focus, enables the experience of *swarag* and *jannat*; second, the opportunity to contemplate the teachings of *Gurbani* over a long period of time, accompanied by a shifting consciousness, readies the *sangat* for social action and engagement with initiatives that facilitate a betterment of the entire community.

The case of Amritvela Trust shows how digital technology and media work toward facilitating bliss, forging social bonds, and engendering civic kinship. This example continues to broaden prevailing notions of Sikh *kirtan* and highlights the many styles and forms that it can take. Key to my study is an acknowledgment of members of the *sangat* as powerful consumers and tastemakers. Their translation of digital bliss into social responsibility brings to mind the following phrase in *rāg Sri* by Guru Nanak: "The body is softened by *Gurbani*. / One feels contentment undertaking *seva*."[57]

VIBRATING BODIES OF THE TWENTY-FIRST CENTURY

Other than its flexible attitude toward the use of designated *rāg*, Amritvela Trust embodies the ideal of *kirtan* as articulated in *Gurbani* for the twenty-first century: Thousands of devotees sit together in a *sangat* and share their corporeal vibrations with one another through their environment. The amplification of this positive feeling is channeled into social activism, and this cycle of *kirtan* and *seva* continues to repeat in a manner that evokes Guru Amardas's instruction in *rāg Majh*: "Focus your awareness on *seva* and orient your consciousness toward the *shabad*."[58] The digitally immersive experience of hearing multi-hour-long *kirtan* in a mediatized setting along with thousands of devotees, live and remote, during the sacred time of the early morning offers a unique approach for understanding communal devotional worship. As I observed the residents of Ulhasnagar steeped in meditation, I was reminded of

Guru Arjan's verse in *rāg Gauri*: "Only a few attain the fourth state of absorption."⁵⁹

During my exploration of *anahad nād*, I have been struck by the emphasis on *virlai* in *Gurbani*—the idea that only a few can experience the vibrant fullness of an internal, synesthetic bliss. While I understand that not everyone is capable of controlling their consciousness in a manner conducive to deepening the meditative state, the case of Amritvela Trust has prompted me to consider how a multimedia conception of *anahad nād* offers daily worship to overcome the strains of a digitally overstimulated and distracted mind-body connection. This chapter has shown how Amritvela Trust's innovative use of technology engineers an inwardly attuned experience of sound that many in their *sangat* experience as affording access to the divine. At Amritvela Trust, one does not have to be an experienced devotee. Everyone is able to feel the sensation of ecstatic bliss both as an internal phenomenon—facilitated through headphones—and as an external spectacle, produced through the intervention of media and technology. This vibrant output and its gentle manipulation of our senses ask us to consider sound differently: as an outward manifestation that can be actively taken into and absorbed by the body in altering our consciousness.

An engaged experience with *anahad nād* allows divine resonance to be rendered as fully accessible and capable of uniting individuals within their immediate and global communities. Sikh scripture places great emphasis on the potential of *kirtan* to facilitate mindful ethical conduct. Amritvela Trust draws on an array of digital means to reinforce this message while democratizing the feeling of bliss so that it is no longer a privilege of a spiritually accomplished elite but potentially accessible to all who are willing to allow technology to lead the way.

CHAPTER SUMMARY

Sikh perspectives have been missing in current research on digital religion. This chapter takes the activities of Amritvela Trust as a case study. Their innovative adaptation of Bluetooth headphone technology for the purposes of early morning recitation and *kirtan* facilitates an unprecedented experience of *anahad nād*: one that is carefully engineered in the outer realm to facilitate conscious meditation in the inner realm.

Amritvela Trust's distinctive style of *slow kirtan* makes creative use of multiple forms of technology and media. The forty-day *chaliya*, which commemorates the birth anniversary of Guru Nanak every year through a daily gathering of devotees during the early morning hours at an outdoor field in Ulhasnagar, demonstrates how this innovative *kirtan* transports twenty-first-century minds and bodies to the celestial realm through a means of inversion: The sensory magnificence of an inner *anahad nād* is now rendered in the outer material realm. Devotees participate in a cross-modal experience of worship, as the senses are stimulated by a mesmerizing display of light, color, sound, texture, fragrance, and taste. The vibration of these individual elements in parallel with and through one another facilitates an experience of divinity that is rooted in community and whose transformative and lasting impact is seen through Amritvela Trust's dedication to caring for their community through forms of *seva*.

| 6

The Digital Journeys of *Kirtan*

Pursuing Innovation and Gender Equality

In one of his ballads Bhai Gurdas observes, "The Sikhs of the gurus are like pearls. They are threaded into a necklace when they get together in religious assemblies [*sadh sangat*]." *Sri Guru Granth Sahib* (*SGGS*) expands this beautiful imagery by emphasizing how the divine guru resides within these *sadh sangat*. This closing chapter places *kirtan* at the center of research on digital religion by asking, Can a global *sangat* feel connected to one another and to divinity through a digital experience of *kirtan*? Following Bhai Gurdas, I wonder, How does the divine guru become manifest within a virtual *sangat*?

In observing how Sikhs create, consume, worship through, and share digital content about *kirtan*, this chapter focuses on the "intimacy and infrastructure of new digital technologies" while exploring the affordances for worship and meditation offered by these modalities.[1] The springboard for this inquiry is a comment made by an anonymous participant in my survey (see the appendix): "Our gurus were innovators. . . . Somehow I always imagine them smiling when they hear their Sikhs trying out new tunes or praising the divine in whichever medium." These kinds of viewpoints speak to the continued innovation in *kirtan*, which is evident in the wide range of styles that are shared through social media, streaming platforms, apps, radio, TV broadcasting, and commercial recordings. Although many Sikhs experience *kirtan* in the sacred space of a *Gurudwara*, they are also simultaneously consuming *kirtan* through a variety of digital modalities. How does this behavior speak to the topic of corporeal vibration as discussed in earlier chapters? How might devotees participate in digital *darshan* (*darshan* refers to "seeing" the divine, but in the Sikh context, where divinity exists without form, this term points to a sensing of divine presence)?

These questions direct my conversations with five practitioners, all of whom use technology in creative ways to craft original compositions and styles of *kirtan* that have a vibrant digital and live presence. In addition to listening intensively to their *kirtan*, my preparation for these interviews came in the form of several in-depth conversations with the audio engineer, Davwinder (Dindae) Sheena. It is rare for "behind-the-scenes techies" to take center stage in discussions about music, but I begin with this perspective because Dindae's work is integral to the digital experience of sonic auras that are felt as sacred and divine. In *Gurbani* the feeling of a sustained, unbroken connection to divinity is called *liv* (attunement). When enhanced in the digital realm, this experience is carefully calibrated by audio engineers, their masterful manipulation of sound systems, and other software and hardware. As explored in chapter 5, the use of technology to create an experience of bliss (*anand*) in the exterior realm is ultimately directed toward realizing bliss in the interior realm of consciousness.

Several threads that have been woven throughout the book are tied together here. The locations of Dindae (Singapore), Jasleen Kaur (Punjab), Taren Kaur and Veer Manpreet Singh (United Kingdom), Bhai Nirmal Singh Khalsa (Pipli Wale) (Bangkok), and Shivpreet Singh (California) once again bring the topic of journeys and innovation into focus. Their collective interest in promoting collaboration between traditional string instruments of the Sikh *darbar* (courts) and newer instruments such as synthesizers, digital pianos, guitars, and contemporary percussion speaks to the debates about tradition and colonial modernity covered in the first half of this book. Discussions with these *kirtaniye* about how technology enhances vocal and instrumental timbres bring a new perspective to the study of *anahad nād* offered in chapters 3 and 4. As shown in chapter 5, and now from a different vantage point in this final chapter, this blissful state becomes accessible to all through a careful manipulation of recording and audio engineering techniques and the widespread availability of *kirtan* content through digital media.

We see how technicians use technology to craft specific acoustics that convey vocal liveness, naturalness, and intimacy. In the absence of tangible vibration issuing from a live voice or instrument, technological intervention allows a feeling of transcendence and immersion to be cultivated within the digital space. Sustained efforts to improve sound production and acoustics respond to growing demands by the global *sangat* to have their experience of listening be in lockstep with other instances of high-definition video and high-resolution audio. *Kirtan FI* is a recent online platform that meets these expectations through its production of high-resolution audio for the "kirtanphile."[2]

The five interviews that follow show how innovators use their skills in composition, arrangement, performance, recording, and production to create an experience of *kirtan* that allows listeners to forge personal links to *Gurbani*. Each *kirtaniya* crafts a distinctive sound world and timbral profile: Jasleen Kaur mediates between *Gurmat Sangeet* and a semi-classical or contemporary Bollywood style, while Taren Kaur is firmly based in a Western pop aesthetic. A *slow kirtan* approach connects Veer Manpreet Singh and Shivpreet Singh, given their mutual efforts to create a wholly immersive experience of *Gurbani*; they savor the nuanced meaning of each word and line through repetition and contemplation over an extended period (as seen with Bhai Gurpreet Singh of Amritvela Trust in chap. 5). Inspired by the success of Pakistan's collaborative music platform, Coke Studio, Bhai Nirmal Singh Khalsa (Pipli Wale) presents a contemporary take on *kirtan* within an "aesthetics of intimacy," a phenomenon observed by Anaar Desai-Stephens but tweaked toward devotional ends by Khalsa.[3] Together, these *kirtaniye* have a vibrant live and digital presence, although it must be noted that their efforts in the digital realm do not replace the uplifting impact of corporeal vibration felt live. Rather, their digital *kirtan* allows corporeal vibration to be prolonged through constant access to commercial avenues for consumption.

As indicated in the title, this chapter foregrounds digital innovation while addressing the enduring problem of gender inequality. Female *kirtaniye* are to this day excluded from offering *kirtan* at some *Gurudware*, including Harmandir Sahib (Golden Temple). I continue the work begun in my earlier article of highlighting the contributions and innovations of female *kirtaniye*.[4] The intimate nature of the interview format allowed me to get at some thorny issues surrounding the biases and discrimination that female *kirtaniye* continue to face, as highlighted by Taren Kaur. A lack of opportunity to offer in-person *kirtan* at major *Gurudware* or during important festivals and celebrations has led some female *kirtaniye* to see social media platforms as a refuge, where the digital terrain offers endless possibilities for innovation and distribution without attempts at censorship or control.

Several women have been at the forefront of digital innovation:

Jagdeep Kaur (of *Qi-Rattan*, United Kingdom) focuses on the healing properties of a pop- and new age–inspired *kirtan* that is live streamed as a form of sound therapy. Amrita Kaur (New Zealand) offers *Sufi*-pop and *ghazal*-inspired renditions, as well as recordings that fall into the category of *Gurmat Sangeet*. Arvindpal Kaur and Arpana Kaur (Bangkok) draw on technology to create original children's music, a cappella arrangements, and lyrical pop renditions of *shabad*, all accompanied by high-quality video narratives designed to be consumed via social media. Kaurishma (Toronto) uses social media to share an intimate devotional experience whose immediacy is heightened by the informality of a home-recorded, pop-ballad aesthetic using voice and guitar. Gursimran Kaur (New Delhi/New York) shares visually dramatic interpretations in a fusion style spanning Indian classical, folk, pop, and new age styles.[5] There are many more female singers who are active innovators of digital *kirtan*, and I wish I could interview them all here. I bring select contributions to the center to begin redressing gender imbalance, highlighting the rigorous training and creative vision behind female Sikh initiatives in India and across the diaspora.

DAVWINDER (DINDAE) SHEENA: CRAFTING A "SIKH SOUND"

A third-generation Singaporean, Dindae Sheena is in demand as an audio engineer and audio consultant who uses technology to create a "Sikh sound." This intriguing concept lies behind his company motto and served as the focal point of our conversations. Dindae's training in computer science and audio engineering, coupled with his passion for a variety of musical genres, led to his first jobs as a DJ and recording engineer in Perth, Australia, before he returned to Singapore. His partnership in an independent record distribution company and, eventually, his transition into the domain of sound installation led to a position as chief engineer in China's first commercial recording facility in the late 1990s: a fifteen-thousand-square-foot facility that he first had to build from scratch. Although he had learned Malay while growing up in Singapore, Dindae quickly learned Mandarin, Hokkien, and Cantonese so that he could communicate with his colleagues, technicians, and construction workers. After seven years in China, Dindae moved back to Singapore to establish his own consultancy. Soon after that he was approached by Loud Technologies (based in the United States) to manage sales in the Asia-Pacific region, eventually becoming managing director.

Dindae's recent work at Stealth Sonics, and this company's striking logo, caught my attention. In particular, his creation of custom in-ear monitors, worn by professional musicians, video-game players, and sound engineers, provided an intriguing counterpart to my study of Amritvela Trust headphones (see chap. 5). As it turns out, Dindae was involved in advising Amritvela Trust on how to incorporate Bluetooth technology into their *kirtan*. While developing his in-ear monitors at Stealth Sonics, he worked with leading musicians, including the Red Hot Chili Peppers, Pearl Jam, Boyz II Men, and prominent Bollywood singers such as Shreya Goshal, Arijit Singh, and Saleem Suleiman. Dindae also installed sound systems in Bollywood's leading Yash Raj Studios, Empire Studios, and Ramoji Film City. The more we talked, the more I realized that all roads seem to lead to Dindae: He flies across the world at the request of event organizers, *kirtaniye*, and *Gurudware* to design and install sound systems. I was surprised to learn that he has been responsible for the audio needs of many *kirtaniye* mentioned in my book, some of whom travel with specific microphones that Dindae has picked out for their unique sacred acoustics.

Given his extensive background improving the acoustics of sacred spaces, including famous churches and mosques (notably the Clock Towers of Mecca), I was keen to understand what is idiosyncratic about the "Sikh sound" from the perspective of a sound technician. Dindae explained, "The foundation of all *Gurudware*, of all houses of worship, is intelligibility, because there's always going to be a preacher, a pastor, a father, an *imam*, a *granthi*, giving a speech. So that's very important." He also noted, "I think what's been lacking in many houses of worship is that many a times, installers think, 'Oh, we'll just put a speaker up and it'll be fine.' No! They need to understand the workings of that particular house of worship, how each one is different and how each application is different." He explained how each audio system that he designs for a particular space is different from the next: What is suitable for a mosque is not suitable for a church; similarly, what is suitable for a church is not transferable to a *Gurudwara*. The type of speakers and microphones that are used are unique to the acoustic calibration of that space. Dindae noted that sound systems in mosques are a little easier to set up because prayer involves vocal recitation and no musical instruments, so the focus is squarely on the intelligibility of the voice. Churches, he explained, have become very tech savvy, especially megachurches that have congregations ranging from 2,500 to 10,000. In these spaces, the organizers are seeking more of a "concert feel," he explained.

> They have a full-on band; the pastor is like a superstar. But what churches have started doing is they also have a broadcast division, [that is,] studios

set up just to broadcast to other churches on Sundays. Because they have so many worshippers under the same banner, they set up remote churches around the area and worshippers can go there; they will broadcast what's happening in the main church to the smaller churches.

We saw a similar setup at Amritvela Trust. Dindae mentioned the high cost of speakers and equipment that some churches are willing to purchase to optimize the sacred sonic experience. He paraphrased one reverend:

> You don't realize that for us, on a Sunday when our worshippers come down, we really want them to be involved. We want them to be part of the whole, the energy has to be good, and when the band performs well, everything sounds good, and when I speak and everyone can hear what I'm talking about, they have a good time, everybody's really into it. I don't have worshippers walking out halfway. What happens at the end of the session—I will tell them, "Hey, look, we spent a million dollars just on the speakers alone." Then the pockets go deep.

Dindae now gives this example when advising *Gurudwara* committees who want to improve their sound systems or wealthy individuals who want to financially support the installation of a high-quality audio setup at their local *Gurudwara*.

The "Sikh sound," for Dindae, is versatile and fluid. When he first started out, he thought his job was to put up speakers so that everyone could hear. Then he began to realize the complexity of his work:

> We have *paath* [recitation] going on, where someone's doing it in a very musical sense, then you have announcements that happen, then you have *kirtan*—this is further divided into your traditional *kirtan* [harmonium, tabla, and singing] and then you have *kirtan* that's with *tanti sāz* [traditional string instruments] . . . and then you have *dhaadhi jatha* [a folk ensemble of ballad singers], which is again a different dynamic because that's high energy, loud percussive instruments. You have so many different variations [of sound] in a *Gurudwara*.

Dindae's experience has taught him to be mindful of these variations in sound and he now teaches students at the Gurmat Sangeet Academy in Singapore and Malaysia how to manage their sound needs themselves, especially since many of them play *tanti sāz*. These techniques include microphone placement, which differs from *dilruba* to *rabab* to *sarangi* because the microphones need to "pick up the sound of the bow, the sound of the strings, or the sound of the skin." As a *dilruba* player myself, I was fascinated by this conversation and deeply struck by Dindae's confession that he attributes his acoustic training for working with *tanti sāz* to his time in China:

> When I was working in China, I think one of the most valuable lessons I learned was how to mic-up Chinese traditional instruments because they're the sort where after every song musicians have to retune the instrument... the Guzheng, you know, these instruments are so unique, but they somehow share certain similarities [with *tanti sāz*]. I think I gained a lot of that knowledge, which I now really am desperately trying to pass on. It's not something that many people have the privilege of learning.
>
> I learned how to mic up in Australia when I was studying—a Western orchestra is mic'd up differently from a traditional Chinese orchestra, right? I remember we were doing the mic'ing up for *Crouching Tiger Hidden Dragon*. It was recorded in my studios in China. So they said, "Oh look, we have an eighty-piece orchestra coming in—these are the requirements and setup." I remember I spent two nights setting up the microphones, setting all this stuff up. I had about sixteen microphones set up and made sure everything was according to their specifications. The Chinese engineer walks in, he looks at the system, and he goes, "Oh no, you've got to remove all those mics." I'm like, "What do you mean remove all these mics? Don't you want this?" He goes, "No, I'll show you." He literally had specific mics for the soloists and stereo mic'ing for everyone else. So we only ended up using eight microphones from the sixty. Eight microphones and, my god, the sound was huge. So he knew about placement. Placement, separation, and how an orchestra sits. First, you depend on the acoustics of the hall; second, how each section is placed gives you the stereo imaging. The separation is beautiful because your ears are able to identify every single thing.
>
> And it's the same for me. It's the same when I now go into *Gurdwaras*. The "Sikh sound" is really about identifying those instruments, identifying those individual sounds and making sure that the *sangat* [congregation] is first able to hear it in a live scenario and then in the broadcast as well. In the broadcast you're able to hear the *rabab*, you're able to hear the *dilruba* ... and I'm sure you've performed in *Gurudwaras*—half the time the *dilruba* is not heard.

This last point really hit home for me given how often the naturally louder harmonium swamps poorly amplified *tanti sāz* when they are played together.

In cultivating the "Sikh sound" in *Gurudware*, Dindae explained the importance of microphone and instrument placement, the use of microphones that have more echo or less echo, and the incorporation of a digital mixer that responds to the unique acoustic needs of the *darbar* (hall) and that can be adjusted according to whether the setting is for male voices, female voices, children's voices, recitation, or speaking. The mixers that he creates for each *Gurudwara* are programmed according to these needs. Dindae concluded that the "Sikh sound" is like an onion: "Layers and layers and layers of really complex sounds that are then set up such that you still get intelligibility, you get the clarity, you get the distinction of every instrument." He drew my attention to the importance of considering the acoustic properties of natural materials like marble, stone, and limestone and to how, in tandem with certain architectural features, they work toward reflecting and amplifying sound while drawing the attention of the ear to the ideal vocal frequency of the voice, between one and four kilohertz. Dindae also taught me about the importance of creating a type of amplification that sounds natural and sweet, compared with one that is overly amplified — making it sound as though someone is shouting, which is often the criticism of *dhaadhi jatha* whose *buland* (strong, resonant) voices do not require extensive amplification. His solution has been to create a separate set of microphones for these resonant voice types that are equalized and balanced.

My interview with Taren Kaur is discussed below, but in preparation I share what Dindae taught me about how he helped craft her trademark sound. Because she sings *shabad* in a popular style, accompanying herself on an acoustic guitar, he created custom hardware for her guitar, allowing her to convey the effect of harmony generated by a chorus (an effect that is not traditionally associated with *kirtan*). She projects the quality of four or five singers sitting behind her, harmonizing in the same key. This hardware also allows her to play the guitar and have it sound like a synthesizer or to add the effect of additional instruments while playing. Custom hardware and Bluetooth technology that generate *tabla tāl* (metric cycles) allow Taren Kaur to be a composite musician: one who creates her own melodic, harmonic, and metric material through the multilayered textures of a virtual orchestra (with a maximum potential of 256 voices). Veer Manpreet Singh (interviewed below) was the first to innovate with multilayered textures using nontraditional (Western) instruments. Taren Kaur extends and builds on these innovations using her modified acoustic guitar.

In a final comment on Sikh sacred sound, Dindae revealed to me that he is not able to read *Gurmukhi* and relies on *kirtaniye* to tell him about the *shabad* and *rāg*, crafting acoustics according to their narrative. For a composition like Guru Gobind Singh's well-known *shabad* (in the *khyal* style) "*Mittar Pyare Nu*," Dindae described how he manipulates the sound in a way that creates a "hollow ambience" to reflect the guru's emotional state when composing this verse. He directed me to an example featuring Bhai Gagandeep Singh (Sri Ganganagar Wale), for which he had served as lead audio engineer (**video ex. 6.1**).[6]

TAREN KAUR: "INTEGRATE WOMEN INTO *KIRTAN DARBAR*"

When I hear Taren Kaur's *kirtan*, it's hard not to picture her as a songwriting British Sikh Punjabi Taylor Swift. Having grown up in a musical family that actively participates in *kirtan*, Taren Kaur was exposed to a wide range of musical styles and genres from a young age and decided to take up the guitar as a child in the hope of becoming a singer-songwriter, a term that is not often tied to the context of *kirtan* but that is attracting significant momentum among young female guitar-playing singers, like Kaurishma (Canada), Jasleen Royal (India), and Ruhani Dhillon (Australia). Kaurishma's contributions on social media fall under the "aesthetics of intimacy" and "bedroom aesthetics" categories observed by Desai-Stephens (following Kate Galloway).[7] The trailblazer for these young women is the vocalist and guitar player Jagdeep Kaur (United Kingdom). She and her husband, Amritpal Singh (who plays the *tabla*), founded Qi-Rattan in 2012, an ensemble dedicated to exploring the healing properties of *kirtan* through their work as sound psychospiritual therapists. Their albums from 2013, 2014, and 2016 feature originally composed *shabad* in a meditative style for voice, guitar, *tabla*, piano, and other instruments.[8] Taren Kaur's original compositions honor these innovations while broadening the impact of *kirtan* beyond the realm of healing.

Initially self-taught, Taren Kaur played and composed a variety of music on the guitar, from *kirtan shabad* to pop to jazz and blues. Her musical inspirations include John Mayer, Stevie Wonder, Arijit Singh, Kaushiki Chakraborty, Tori Kelly, U2, and Michael Jackson, among others. She recalls how, one day, she thought to herself,

> What if I was to combine the two, the Western side and the Eastern side, because I had that love. . . . I tried it and I was like, wow, this is awesome! I approached it differently than someone might coming from the Western side. It was a different sort of fusion, but it was very creative. I suppose I approached it from a singer-songwriter aspect, a Western musical aspect, being chords and those sorts of things.

A song she wrote to commemorate Guru Nanak's 550th birth anniversary in 2019, "Guru Nanak You're My Hero," showcases the singer-songwriter persona in a pop-inspired composition that is accompanied by an introspective ballad-styled video (**video ex. 6.2**).[9]

Her 2019 album, *Divine*, showcases her diverse styles in *Gurbani*. Some *shabad*, like "*Ho Bal Bal Jao*," have a Taylor Swift aura to them.[10] Others, like "*Mere Madho Ji*," feel more inspired by rock and roll and blues, given the use of electric guitars and her exploration of distortion and crunch effects.[11] "*Hey Gobind Hey Gopal*" is based directly on a blues riff and draws on a slide guitar, as well as seventh chords.[12] "*Koi Bole Raam Raam*" features a ballad style.[13] "*Chali Thakur Peh Haar*" moves away from the guitar and draws on a more intimate scoring for piano and voice.[14] She explained, "I really wanted to evoke the emotion of it because it was just the way that I felt with that *shabad*. I wanted it to be very simple and stripped back, and I wanted *Gurbani* to be, which I always do, at the center."

While Taren Kaur was experimenting with new ways to offer *shabad* and *simran* (participatory sung repetition of a single word or phrase) on the guitar, she was also studying *kirtan* with her father and with Bhai Gagandeep Singh (Sri Ganganagar Wale). Her decision to become a full-time, professional *kirtaniya* is almost unprecedented among women. She explained,

> *Kirtan* is the message, it's what Guruji is teaching us. The music is the medium that we're able to express that love and that devotion through. I think that's just amazing. And that's what it is for me — *kirtan* is my way to express that longing, or that love, or that feeling of separation from God, or feeling connected with God and seeking that divinity through music. It's just so beautiful and special. So yeah, it's just sort of grown and grown to the point where I didn't want to do anything else in my life. I felt like I couldn't, I just wanted to devote my time and effort in exploring *kirtan* and expressing it in this way because there aren't really many people, I mean, there's very few women, who are, let's say, born in England, or born in a Western country outside of India, who are doing *kirtan* with Western instruments, who are able to, or who are pursuing it full time.

It wasn't long before the two of us were in the midst of a conversation about why there are so few female *kirtaniye* and the hurdles and challenges that continue to follow women in *kirtan* (as discussed in the introduction). Taren Kaur offered her perspective:

> You know, it's quite sad, because the number of times I've had women say to me, "I used to do *kirtan* and then I got married. I haven't touched my

vaja [harmonium] in, you know, ten, twenty years, and I really miss it." Or "I just don't have time because of the kids." Or "When I got married, it was kind of like, okay, stop now." I heard that so much and it upset me so much. I told them, "No, you should still do it." And they responded, "I really wish I had carried it on. I really wish at that time I'd understood that I can take this with me. I can still do *kirtan*." And then, you know, there's people who just do it, and they feel, "I didn't think I would ever have the opportunity to do kirtan in the *Gurudwara*."

For me, I also felt, "You know what? I want more girls who are going to come along and women to feel like they can do *kirtan*." There are so many girls who've come to me and said, "Am I allowed to do *kirtan*?" I say, "Yes, yes, go, you should definitely do it. Please do it." So, yeah, it's become a life's purpose, I suppose, which I never expected, ever.

Taren Kaur also highlighted another topic I addressed in the introduction and in chapter 2, which concerns the prohibition of women undertaking *kirtan* at certain sacred sites—a topic that, she notes, "doesn't get talked about and gets brushed under the carpet." She drew my attention to organizers at *Gurudware* who do not extend invitations to her, despite passionate pleas from the *sangat*, on account of her being female. Sometimes, she is not permitted to sit on the same stage that male *ragi jatha* (professional *kirtaniye*) sit on; she is asked instead to sit on the floor. At other times, she will be given a minimal payment for her *kirtan* from the organizers. This is a deep affront to her rare and celebrated status as a professional female *kirtaniya*. She reminded me that she can count the number of female singers on the fingers of her hands, so small is the number in relation to the thousands of male *ragi*.

In light of the growing global interest among the diasporic *sangat* to hear *nirdharit kirtan* (in designated *rāg*), Taren Kaur pointed to the rising number of *samagam* (events or programs) where multiday *kirtan darbar* (festivals) feature prominent *kirtaniye*, most of whom are men. The challenges she described were disheartening to hear and resonated with the reasons behind the formation of the female-centered organization *Gaavani* that I discussed in the introduction:

> I do this professionally because I feel like someone needs to do it; someone needs to try and break and make a bit of a path for women to be able to do *kirtan*. OK, my style is different, but it is still something, in a sense, to try and help people to connect. I don't want girls thinking they can't do it. And yeah, I do get women coming up to me and saying, "We're just so happy to see a woman on the stage—we feel represented."

She explains that another reason for underrepresentation—other than bias and gender discrimination—has to do with the challenges of being a professional *kirtaniya*, given that women are often not paid the same rate as male *ragi* (which is already very low): "If there are people who are trying to do *kirtan* to a professional standard and they don't get paid, people start thinking, 'Well, we can't afford to keep doing it off our own backs, you know—we can't afford to spend time learning and perfecting and composing, producing, and doing all of that.'"

Of the many reasons for Taren Kaur's popularity, one is tied to her use of technology to create a contemporary soundscape that centers her performance on acoustic guitar accompanied by *tabla*. She emphasized that her approach to playing the guitar is Western. Although I had never thought of the instrument in this way, she explained that the guitar can be considered a Western *tanti sāz*: "It's not an Indian instrument, but then it does have a similar essence due to the strings. Many people have often expressed to me, 'Oh, you know, it is like a *sitar*, and it is a bit like a *rabab* and, you know, it is a bit like those *tanti sāz* instruments.'" Taren Kaur relies on the *tabla*, and sometimes *jori*, to provide the primary layer of rhythm. The fusion of Western instruments like the guitar with *tanti sāz* is something that she enjoys and equates to her diasporic upbringing and musical education:

> Because of my background being what it is, I think it's nice to have something different that people can connect to. Because again, what I feel is that, yes, it's music, and yes, it's really nice to listen to, and we have an experience with the frequencies of the music and the way that it affects us, mind, body, and soul. But for me, the essence of *kirtan* always comes back to *Gurbani* and how we connect to that emotionally and inside. How can we express that to others and help others to connect as well?

Taren Kaur's singer-songwriter persona has influenced the way she uses technology to enhance the experience of connecting with *Gurbani*. She composes, records, produces, mixes, and edits her own work. In collaboration with Dindae, Taren Kaur has developed custom hardware to enhance her efforts to create an experience of *kirtan* that is immersive and meditative: She creates layers of live sounds using her voice, the guitar, and other instruments, resulting in an orchestral soundscape that envelops the *sangat*.

When we turned to the topic of *nirdharit rāg*, Taren Kaur acknowledged the importance of undertaking *kirtan* in designated *rāg* and mentioned that many of her compositions are *rāg* based. At the same time, she emphasized her wide musical influences in the world of popular music and the traditional *kirtaniye* who have inspired her, such as Bhai Balwant Singh (Namdhari), whose *kirtan* on traditional instruments is not something that is oriented toward performance, she explains, but toward inner listening—in other words, the duality between *ahat nād* and *anahad nād*. She describes how, upon hearing his *kirtan* live, she was able to "just immerse in it . . . it just transports you beyond the physical." Channeling this same atmosphere and energy, Taren Kaur mentioned how she also immerses herself in *Gurbani* when offering *kirtan* and how she aims to "connect the *sangat* to what's within." Whereas a disciplined approach to *nirdharit rāg* may be behind Bhai Balwant Singh's moving *kirtan*, Taren Kaur achieves this goal using a global musical style mediated by technology:

> Some people don't connect to *rāg*, they don't understand it, and they're like, "I just don't get it, or I just sort of switch off." It's a shame because *rāg kirtan* is beautiful, but I often then consider it like this: Some people like rock music, some people like rap music, some people like pop, some people like classical music . . . everyone has their genre that they're drawn to. We could essentially apply the same principle for *kirtan*: Some people like Indian classical *kirtan* and some people like Western-style *kirtan*, or some people like the mainstream style with *vaja* [harmonium]. But even when people are doing *kirtan* on the *vaja*, there's those who will sing more classical-style *rāg* and others who will sing a more mainstream or commercial style of *kirtan*. Everyone has their personal preference. So we can't, I don't think, box it up, because then that alienates people, and people feel like, "Oh, well, you know, that's somebody else's version of Sikhi, or somebody else's version of *kirtan*, and I don't feel welcome." Or "I don't feel like I can listen to this or I can do this." And then it starts making those divisions. Whereas if we were to champion each other and encourage ways for people to listen to *kirtan*, I think there's room for everything. I don't think that it's "this or nothing." I think it's "keep it all alive, keep it all going, yes, explore and connect and help others," because there are people in Western countries who say, "I don't really go to *Gurudwara* and I don't really listen to the *giani* [knowledge bearers] doing *kirtan* . . . I just sort of drift off." I have had people come to me and say, "With your *kirtan*, or with this style of *kirtan*, I do connect, and I enjoy it, and you know, I find it very meditative, and it's just something that I relate to and resonate with." Maybe it's the upbringing, maybe it's because they haven't really heard *rāg kirtan* as they grew up, and they heard music on the radio that was more like what I'm singing—pop music, or fusion, whatever—and that's why they can connect to it more.

But the only way to introduce people to *rāg*, or to get them maybe exploring that in their own time, is if you actually introduce them to *kirtan* first. If they're not even aware of what *kirtan* is, they're not going to go and search on YouTube, or try to listen to it, or want to go to a *kirtan darbar*. Whereas people might listen to my *kirtan* because they like the guitar, or they like the way it sounds. Or, they might listen to someone else's different Western style, and then slowly they might explore. They might wonder, "What other styles are out there? What are the origins of *Gurmat Sangeet*? What is the classical style?" And then they'll go and start looking at that, but you have to reel them in first and get them listening, otherwise there's just no point. So yeah, there's room for everything. I'm quite open-minded in that sense. I just think that everything's not black-and-white, there's so much more out there. Surprisingly, I find that nowadays, having these conversations with people, fewer and fewer people disagree.

Taren Kaur's experiences point to diasporic generations connecting with a more popular-based rather than *rāg*-based *kirtan*. She further fine-tuned my understanding of *kirtan* in the diaspora on the basis of her experience performing *kirtan* across the world. In Calgary, for instance, she is asked to offer more *waheguru simran* (participatory sung repetition of the *gur-mantra*, *waheguru*) than individual *shabad*, since the *sangat* tended to enjoy *simran* more, specifically of "a slow, meditative kind." At other places, members of the *sangat* will request their favorite *shabad*: "In Asia, particularly Southeast Asia, they really like '*Mil Jagdish Milan Ki Bariya*.' In Thailand, some *sangat* enjoy a more commercial, mainstream style of *kirtan*—something they can easily sing along and join in with, a melodious *kirtan*. In Manchester [United Kingdom], people will be like, 'Oh, please, can you sing "*Mere Laalan Ki Sobha*."'" She noticed that the requests varied within the same city from *Gurudwara* to *Gurudwara*, which also speaks to differentiated musical tastes within a community and how the *sangat* feels comfortable making requests of an aesthetic nature with *Gurbani*: "Everyone has different likes or interests or dislikes and what keeps them connected or captivated or engaged. That's why I say to you, I feel like you just can't box [*kirtan*] in. Every *kirtaniya* has their own style, whether it's on the *vaja* [harmonium] or another instrument; they have their own vocal tone; they have their own way of doing things. And what's so beautiful is that everyone's different but still coming together collectively."

Taren Kaur has a growing appeal among younger diasporic generations, and she is making a focused effort to connect children with *kirtan* through animated content that introduces meditation, chanting, and Sikh spirituality.[15] Despite being a breakthrough *kirtaniya*, she remains concerned about the future of practitioners in general, especially female *kirtaniye*:

> When you asked about the future of *kirtan*, the one issue I do see is that if it doesn't offer backing and financial support for *kirtaniye*, less and less people will do it as a profession — there have often been times I have felt concerned about doing it professionally. It is difficult for a person to sustain themselves. It's sadly not enough to be able to survive. I've heard people, even *giani* and *ragi*, say, "I can't tell my child to be a *kirtaniya* because there's unfortunately no life in it." I do hold hope, however, that things will change and that there will be more support and grounding for *kirtaniye* to continue doing this professionally.

JASLEEN KAUR: "YOU CAN'T STOP THE REVOLUTION"

Jasleen Kaur is a *kirtaniya* taught in the *Gurmat Sangeet* tradition under Pandit Rajinder Singh (Patiala *gharana*). During her initial period of vocal training, she was encouraged to participate in a new, *kirtan*-based reality singing show called *Gavo Sachi Baani*. The show was organized by the Shiromani Gurudwara Prabandhak Committee (SGPC, which oversees the management of *Gurudware* across India) and aired through the PTC Punjabi network in 2016. Jasleen Kaur participated in season 1 and was struck by the high level of the participants: "They were all like diamonds.... I don't know how I got selected." It was during this show that one of the judges, Principal Sukhwant Singh of Jawaddi Taksal (an institution dedicated to teaching *Gurbani* and *Gurmat Sangeet*), heard Jasleen Kaur and invited her to continue her vocal training under his guidance. By directing promising young musicians of Punjab toward the tradition of *Gurmat Sangeet*, *Gavo Sachi Baani* provides a platform for these singers to share their renditions of *Gurbani* in *nirdharit rāg*. Today, given her deep knowledge of *Gurmat Sangeet*, Jasleen Kaur is regularly invited to offer *kirtan* at *Gurudware*, as well as at major festivals that showcase *kirtan*, such as the Khushwant Singh Literary Festival, *Mela Phulkari*, and the Rajasthan International Folk Festival. She spoke of the rise of *Gurbani* concerts, a growing phenomenon over the last decade or so, dedicated to highlighting the tradition of *kirtan* as a distinctive musical practice.

In 2020 Jasleen Kaur participated in one such event commemorating Guru Nanak's birth anniversary (The Invisible Divine: Kirtaniye — Festival of Women's Voices in Gurbani Sangeet) and spoke of these concerts as offering an important platform for women.[16] As with Taren Kaur,

Jasleen Kaur mentioned similar challenges that she has faced in terms of having fewer opportunities to offer *kirtan* in comparison to her male counterparts. Jasleen Kaur explained that she initially felt a constant need to prove her musical skills in "making a space for herself" and that this effort has taken her considerably longer than it took her male peers. At the same time, she felt that she would not have been able to progress without the support of a "father figure" (Ustad Sukhwant Singh); he helped her navigate the patriarchal structures of *kirtan* by promoting her performance, often asking her to sing first at his programs. Even though *Gurudwara* committees do not always encourage female *kirtaniye*, Jasleen Kaur emphasized that the space she is making in *kirtan* is not only for herself but also for future female *kirtaniye* so that "doors will be open for them" and they won't have to deal with the kinds of obstacles she has had to face throughout her journey, first as a woman and second as a Sikh minority in India. With the incoming generation, Jasleen Kaur echoed what Taren Kaur highlighted as a problem: Accomplished female students shouldn't think, "What can we do with our skills in *kirtan*?" The space she is creating as a versatile singer is one that these aspiring Sikh women can enter and make their own. This space is real and virtual: As with Taren Kaur, the digital terrain offers Jasleen Kaur a safe zone where she can freely experiment and innovate.

As reflected in Jasleen Kaur's rising fame, commercial opportunities offered through TV broadcasting have proved pivotal for aspiring Sikh female singers. The concept of the *kirtan* reality TV show builds on the first reality shows that were broadcast in India during the early 1990s.[17] Desai-Stephens notes that many of today's famous playback singers "have a reality music show as a significant part of their career path." In the Sikh context this includes Harshdeep Kaur, who has recorded *kirtan*, *Gurbani* recitation, and Sufi *qawwali*; Rajwinder Kaur, who competed on *Sa re ga ma* before going on to win *Gavo Sachi Baani* in 2017; Jasleen Royal, who was a semifinalist on *India's Got Talent* (2009) and who has had success in Bollywood with her indie-inspired style; and Hargun Kaur, who was a finalist on *India's Got Talent* (2014) and *The Voice* (2019). Remarkably, Desai-Stephens's research shows how contestants are often encouraged by judges to reanimate and reinscribe familiar voices: "The ideal performance on Indian Idol is one that evokes the original song in terms of musical sound and emotional impact."[18] What would be the equivalent in the Sikh devotional space?

Indeed, if we collate a sample of judges' comments taken from 2016 and 2017, it becomes possible to outline the distinctive qualities of Sikh *kirtan*: Judges focus on how the structure of the *shabad* is understood and conveyed according to tradition (*maryada*), pronunciation (*ucharan*), presentation style (*peshkari*), vocal technique (in terms of accuracy of *rāg* and *tāl*), tuning (*sur*), and improvisation (*alaap* and *taan*). They also appreciate a sweet (*surili*), soothing (*sakoon*) timbre, while the delivery of the *shabad* itself should be filled with loving, sincere devotion (*pyar, bhaav, sharda*) and evoke bliss (*anand*) in the listener.[19] I was drawn in particular to the female voices that were being featured and that continue to privilege a timbre and style that are distinctive from the stereotypical Bollywood female voice: Sikh female voices are often lower in register and use a mixture of *buland* (chest voice) and throat voice without being harsh and shrill. While the female voice has been examined in Bollywood, most recently by Pavitra Sundar, Sikh voices have received relatively little attention.[20] Certainly, these voices do not fit into the vocal paradigms that encompass female timbre in Bollywood, even though they might draw on Bollywood and commercial recording playback techniques in their *kirtan* innovation.

My research on female contestants in *Gavo Sachi Baani* led me to Jasleen Kaur. I began listening to her a few years ago in an effort to improve my own understanding of *nirdharit rāg*. While I learned a great deal from those recordings, I was equally compelled by new content Jasleen Kaur was uploading to YouTube that was clearly intended for digital consumption. This included recordings of daily prayers (*Chaupai Sahib*) and *nirdharit shabad* that are recomposed in a "light" commercial style and accompanied by videos that deepen the spiritual dimension of the lyrics by being shot in nature or against a digitally composed natural environment. The intent to situate *Gurbani* in nature channels the aura of Guru Nanak's *udasi* (extensive travels), a visual aesthetic that is developed by several contemporary *kirtaniye* focused on digital devotion, as seen with Veer Manpreet Singh, Jagdeep Kaur, Amrita Kaur, and Hajara Singh. While these videos add an additional interpretive layer to a *shabad*, they also invite the viewer to embody the sensory experience of bliss as mediated through nature and seen in Jasleen Kaur's "*Mu Lalan Seo Preet Banee*," Veer Manpreet Singh's "*Waheguru Simran*," Jagdeep Kaur's "*Mohe Na Bisaaroh*," and Amrita Kaur's "*So Satgur Pyara*."[21] Hajara Singh's emphasis on the urban dimension develops the visual aesthetic in a different direction to explore how Sikh identity is navigated in everyday life; in "*Aisee Preet Karo Munn Mere*," a contemporary Sikh subjectivity incorporates *kirtan*, meditation, prayer, commuting, work, family commitments, and service into one's daily existence.[22]

Against this varied Sikh sonic landscape, Jasleen Kaur cultivates a uniquely contemporary Sikh feminine timbre that incorporates a "whisper voice," examined recently by Jessica Holmes in American pop music.[23] Speaking about female *kirtaniye*, Jasleen Kaur explained, "Like new age artists, we also have our own sound. . . . It comes naturally." She mentioned several singers of *kirtan* who draw on the vocal techniques of popular music and musical accompaniments that use Western instruments and synthesized beats in crafting their digitized vocal soundscapes: Manika Kaur (Australia), Hajara Singh, Nirvair Khalsa Jatha (United Kingdom), Gursimran Kaur, Kaurishma, and Arvindpal Kaur. She explained that these artists are able to reach younger listeners who "are kind of vibing with it [new styles of *kirtan*]." Also inspirational for her are new age artists based outside of India, who she hears as producing meditational music, like Snatam Kaur, Nirinjan Kaur, and Taren Kaur. In her desire to explore a similar style, Jasleen Kaur learned the piano to enhance her knowledge of Western music theory and aesthetics. She emphasized that she sings "more naturally," unlike the singers of earlier generations who cultivated a "high throat voice" to sonically signal youthful femininity — Lata Mangeshkar's "hegemonic voice," described by Pavitra Sundar as "high pitched, sweet, and contained" is synonymous with this kind of stylized female image in Bollywood from the 1950s through the 1990s. In contrast, Jasleen Kaur's *kirtan* emphasizes the use of lower registers, while drawing on her chest voice, as well as softer upper registers in offering a wide and varied timbral palette that caters to a contemporary experience of devotional love (*bhaav*).[24]

"*Is Munn Ko Basant Ki Lagai Na Soe*" showcases what Matthew Rahaim has termed a "sweet voice" type, which, he explains, "can be a powerful vehicle for a poetics of tenderness and vulnerability" (**video ex. 6.3**).[25] This interpretation is especially compelling for the female voice in *kirtan* and not only for the expressive correlation between timbre and poetic feeling: The Sikh gurus and bhagats often adopted a feminine poetic persona, and when these compositions are sung by women, the affective intensity is doubled. As I see the concept of sweetness applied to various types of female voice — ranging from Bollywood to contemporary *kirtan* — I also observe how essential this quality remains to perceptions of South Asian vocal womanhood and girlhood across genres, almost as if sweetness resides at the core of these identities. In this *shabad* a lack of rhythmic pulse (typically provided by a *tabla*) allows the ear to dwell in the fluid contours of Jasleen Kaur's resonant voice, which receives a sparse accompaniment from sustained chords played by a synthesizer. Interestingly, she specifies her use of a "smaller hammer mic, made by Rajwinder Singh of Gogiaudio, going through the Chandler TG2 500 series mic pre." Jasleen Kaur's willingness to give away this trade "secret" reveals her passion for recording and production. Her keen interest in crafting and controlling vocal timbre speaks to her aim to hone her own sound by being involved in all aspects of production and audio mixing, which extends to her deliberation over high-quality microphones and amplifiers. She spoke at length about the kinds of microphones she likes to use in bringing out a specific texture or vocal register, while addressing the topic of "microphone technique" and the creation of a vocal timbre that feels "palpably *intimate*," as examined by Rahaim in relation to the cultivation of a mellow, gentle, *filmi* voice.[26]

Building on the numerous interpretations of a verse from *Jaap Sahib* by Guru Gobind Singh, "*Gobindey Mukandey*," Jasleen Kaur's version showcases a contemporary female *filmi* voice that is inspired by, yet stands apart from, the post-Lata era (**video ex. 6.4**). This is an example of a studio-recorded composition where a microphone placed close to Jasleen Kaur's mouth is used to bring out the breathy intimacy of her voice, creating for the listener a feeling of immersion *in* the words of *Gurbani* and of being enveloped *by* the sounds of *Gurbani*. In keeping with Desai-Stephens's attention to an "aesthetics of intimacy," this deliberate cultivation of a feminine vocal timbre is directed toward digital consumption on YouTube.[27] Keeping the devotional framework in view, Jasleen Kaur added, "It is the vibration that matters when you're recording—your vibration, where the frequency is. Ultimately that will reach the listener, not the quality or texture of the sound that is produced and mixed." She also explained that she learned to "dance with the microphone" in cultivating a range of vocal timbres that evokes an experience of her voice being close at some moments and distant at others. This remark reminded me of how *kirtaniye* who innovate through popular styles often practice with the technological hardware that becomes an indispensable element of their craft (as we see with Bhai Gurpreet Singh and Shivpreet Singh, discussed below).

"*Gobindey Mukandey*" draws on a digital synthesizer and Western instruments—piano, strings, guitar, and other percussion instruments—to create a plush soundscape. Meanwhile, the vocal timbre is distinctly "cinematic," which we also hear in the production and mixing of her *Chaupai Sahib*. Jasleen Kaur explains that her pursuit of a cinematic sound is "Hollywood inspired" (after Hans Zimmer and Michael Dunn). We can infer how this is signaled through the choice of instruments, the use of a sonic backdrop that prioritizes vocal reverberation, and the gradual pacing of expressive intensity, leading to a moment of climax before—in a true moment of Hollywood-inspired suspense—the music drops out of the texture, leaving only a faint reverberation of the dreamlike composition and its whispery vocal delivery.

Chaupai Sahib builds on an emerging practice among *kirtaniye* of presenting verses that are usually delivered through vocal recitation in daily prayer as sung compositions (see recordings of *Japji Sahib* by Harshdeep Kaur and Rajwinder Kaur, for instance).[28] As with *"Gobindey Mukandey,"* a simple piano accompaniment supports Jasleen Kaur's softly lilting reverberant voice, whose close placement near a microphone creates the singer-songwriter intimacy that Taren Kaur had also spoken of. Again, as Desai-Stephens argues, this "aesthetics of intimacy" is oriented toward a mode of consumption on YouTube that has gained considerable traction in recent years. Jasleen Kaur draws on a nuanced feminine timbre — at times *buland*, at other times whispery and gentle — to help listeners forge a personal, private relationship to *Gurbani*.

Jasleen Kaur is keen to impart her knowledge of *nirdharit rāg* to younger generations so that the full effect (*asr*) of *Gurbani* can be felt. At the same time, she innovates using technology to create a new soundscape — in her case, this means cultivating a contemporary Bollywood or Indian popular commercial sound — so that everyone, not only Sikh devotees, can connect with *kirtan*. Ultimately, she seeks to direct these innovations toward healing, reminding me again that her initial foray into the world of Western music was through new age meditational music and her experience of *Gurbani* as a source of healing: "*Gurbani* is the only solution and the only medicine in our time — nothing can heal in the way *Gurbani* can."

VEER MANPREET SINGH: THE INNOVATION OF SLOW KIRTAN AND HEALING WITH *"TUHI TUHI"*

There are a handful of *kirtaniye* who command a "celebrity" presence — a term that I use cautiously in the Sikh devotional context — and Veer Manpreet Singh is one such figure. When he came to my local *Gurudwara* in Boston, I observed young children running excitedly toward the *darbar* (main hall) after their Khalsa school classes had ended, whispering to one another, "Veer Manpreet is here!" As they ran, some of them were already singing and humming his trademark melody for the *shabad* that propelled his career, *"Tuhi Tuhi,"* hoping that he would sing this again. Veer Manpreet Singh encourages the full participation of the *sangat*, and the *darbar* was resonant with corporeal vibration. After *diwan* (the offering of *kirtan*) had ended, members of the *sangat* flocked to speak with Veer Manpreet Singh to ask him questions about Sikh spiritual practice and to pose for selfies. Although I had been following him — and the different versions of *"Tuhi Tuhi"* — for many years online, where he has a following of thousands of listeners, it was striking for me to witness firsthand how Veer Manpreet Singh builds a connection with the entire *sangat*, from the youngest to the oldest, regardless of their musical knowledge or training.

The phrase *tuhi tuhi* (only you, only you) appears at several moments in *SGGS* and in Guru Gobind Singh's composition *Akaal Ustat*, whose section "*Tav Prasad Lagh Niraajchhand*" is sometimes recited in full by Veer Manpreet Singh.[29] There are many different recordings of this *shabad* by several *ragi*. Veer Manpreet Singh typically offers "Tuhi Tuhi" in *rāg Bhairvi* or *rāg Darbari*: We hear a simple, repeating melody whose four phrases repeat the words *tuhi tuhi*. On New Year's Eve at Westborough *Gurudwara* near Boston, this melody is sung by everyone to ring in the new year at midnight. There is even a "Tuhi Tuhi" app available, where listeners can hear various *mantar* and daily prayers (*nitnem*) on repeat, as well as five versions of "Tuhi Tuhi" produced between 2009 and 2013, which showcase Veer Manpreet Singh's inclusive approach to using different acoustic instruments and synthesized sounds.

Veer Manpreet Singh is a classically trained *kirtaniya* who studied at Baru Sahib (Himanchal Pradesh) and completed his musical education at *Jawaddi Kalan* (Ludhiana) under Ustad Jaswant Singh Bhanwra. Currently, Veer Manpreet Singh's name is synonymous with a style of *kirtan* characterized as "light" or semiclassical. He uses a synthesizer (attached to a looping station using MIDI wires) to create live, meditative orchestral soundscapes built around special effects and layered textures that feature his own looped voice in a "chorus." I asked him about the term *light*, which continues to reinforce hierarchies in the larger practice of Hindustani classical music. Veer Manpreet Singh laughed. "To sing light, you have to have light in here," he said, pointing to his chest. This is a comment he made to someone who was critical about his lyrical, tuneful approach, but Veer Manpreet Singh explained to me that it is difficult to sing in a "light" style and that one can only reach this point after extensive classical training. He noted that after thirty or thirty-five years of training, a *murki* (a grace note ornament) starts to become soft. At this point, how a single *murki* is sung can reveal the depth of a *kirtaniya*'s musical knowledge. As a classically trained musician, I had never thought to see a "light" (popular) style as "the cream of classical" training, as Veer Manpreet Singh taught me.

"*Tuhi Tuhi*" continues to build on Veer Manpreet Singh's interest in exploring "divine frequency"—he cited scholarship on solfeggio frequencies to support his observations of the calming, healing, and joyful effects of these frequencies on the body and mind. He often speaks about the healing effects of the "*Tuhi Tuhi*" verse in his *diwan* (gatherings), and his interpretation of this verse as a force of healing became especially powerful during COVID. He explained to me, "*Kirna*, to cultivate; *tann*, the body: *Kirtan* means to cultivate the actions of the mind, body, and consciousness (our thoughts, words, and deeds) with the guidance of divine frequencies [*Gurbani*]. This is *kirtan*. We are healing the mind, body, and consciousness with the vibrations of the divine name in the form of *kirtan*."

The divine frequencies that he refers to are aligned with the nine solfeggio frequencies that vibrate through natural elements—such as air, water, fire, and the biotic realm—in the form of *anahad nād* (unstruck sound). I have explored the different timbres of *anahad nād* at several points of this book, but thinking about *anahad nād* in terms of a hierarchy of frequencies was new to me. He explained, "Due to the external noise of our daily life, humans are cut off from these divine frequencies, which can be accessed through meditation and through being in nature." Thus, one of the draws of using a top-end synthesizer is that it allows him to tune his instrument to these specific frequencies, which he hears as deepening the healing effect of *kirtan*. He plays at 417 Hz or 432 Hz to induce a calm experience that generates inner peace; indeed, members of his *sangat* have told him that even before he begins singing, their bodies adjust to the frequencies of his synthesizer. Veer Manpreet Singh often begins by playing arpeggiation for several minutes to give time for corporeal adjustment. Some devotees report immediately feeling goose bumps upon attuning to these lower frequencies. On a practical note, singing at a lower frequency also helps preserve his vocal cords and minimize strain, especially during long overseas tours (in April 2024 he completed his first official "*Tuhi Tuhi*" tour in India). Thinking about issues of vocal preservation, I emphasize how his approach to *slow kirtan* involves singing for a long period of time by himself—between one and three hours.

I have coined the phrase *slow kirtan* to describe the style of *kirtan* that Veer Manpreet Singh created during the early 2000s. A "slow living" approach has become appealing in the digital age as a way to ground the mind and body in the present moment. The Slow Food movement of the 1980s has been followed in recent decades by a slow approach to using urban space, consuming culture, professional development, and building personal relationships.[30] We saw a slow approach to *kirtan* with Bhai Gurpreet Singh of Amritvela Trust in chapter 5. *Slow kirtan* establishes a relaxed tempo, to which devotees attune before invocatory phrases, or the *gur-mantar*, *waheguru*, are repeated in a call-and-response manner. With Bhai Gurpreet Singh, this portion of his *kirtan* can take up to an hour and feels more like *simran* (remembrance through repetition). Veer Manpreet Singh offers a similar approach to *slow kirtan*. Gradually, a few lines (*tuke*) of verse (typically the refrain [*rahao*]) are introduced through repetition and begin to familiarize the *sangat* with the central topic of reflection. This *kirtan* is musically simple (sometimes set to *rāg*, sometimes not); it uses an unchanging *tāl* (meter) in the *tabla* and progresses in a *dharna* style, where the *sangat* echoes what is sung by the lead *kirtaniya*. There are spontaneous interpolations (exegesis), through which the *kirtaniya* leads reflection around a few lines of the verse. The emphasis is on depth but also on breadth, which is achieved through repeating the *rahao* and developing its meaning by spiraling outward to create links with other lines of text (*tuke*) from verses that explore related topics.

Another aspect of *slow kirtan* as it evolves through social media platforms is its ability to make a global *sangat* feel connected to one another and to divinity by encouraging participation through live chat. Some devotees will repeat the *rahao* or a particular line of verse that they have connected with. Through simple expressions of gratitude and bliss (*waheguru ji* and *tuhi tuhi*), these comments tie members of the virtual *sangat* to one another and deepen the feeling of experiencing digital *kirtan* via these platforms. Practitioners of *slow kirtan* also incorporate live comments from the *sangat* into their reflections to enhance the experience of live worship and feelings of interconnectedness.

Above all, Veer Manpreet Singh uses *slow kirtan* to instill a feeling of calm wellness in the *sangat*. With the goal of healing in mind, he began holding live sessions on YouTube and Facebook Live, "Healing with Tuhi Tuhi," beginning on March 22, 2020, during the COVID lockdown. These live healing sessions went on for 441 days, and thousands of devotees gathered online for hours at a stretch to experience healing as a global *sangat* during a time when few were able to attend *Gurudware*. Veer Manpreet Singh's early morning (*amritvela*) sessions take us to the heart of his signature sound: Set against a meditative, unchanging rhythm and a daily changing background image — as requested by the *sangat* — a synthesized harmonium blends with a harmonized live layering of his own looped voice, motifs, and textures created on the SX 900 Yamaha synthesizer. Special effects that create a "cosmic" aura are used sparingly as time passes to immerse the listener even more deeply into the virtual realm of the *shabad*, interspersed by moments of contemplation or exegesis (*vichar*) on current social issues and topics that relate to the *shabad* sung that day.

In a session from February 21, 2021, a steady rhythm provides the backdrop for repeating layers of synthesized sounds and effects, above which Veer Manpreet Singh improvises on the *gur-mantar*, *waheguru ji*, before introducing a verse as an invocation ("*Rakh Pita Prabh Mere*"), each line punctuated by improvisation (**video ex. 6.5**).³¹ By 09:50, the *gur-mantar* comes into focus again as he establishes a pattern of circular breathing common in yogic *mantra* practice (deliberate inhalation followed by a strong exhalation). By incorporating these breathing techniques into the practice of *kirtan*, his listeners automatically initiate a process of self-healing. This live loop becomes a backdrop for instrumental improvisation and, by 14:15, for interpolations of *tuhi tuhi*, which are similarly used as loops that prepare a return to *waheguru*. While initiating healing through breathing, the session gradually builds textural richness and incorporates the central *shabad*, which forms the basis for contemplation and exegesis (beginning at 01:29:00): "*Thir ghar baisahu har jan pyare.*"

Given the technical complexity of his setup, which involves a variety of hardware that he manages alone, even during long sessions of in-person *kirtan*, Veer Manpreet Singh proudly describes himself as the "first *kirtan* DJ." This is especially evident in his recent meditation session for the spring celebrations of *Vaisakhi*—over a period of two and a half hours, he composed live choruses with his own voice and above which he introduced new melodies.³² His masterful use of the microphone to evoke a range of vocal nuance from intimate proximity to distant echo also speaks to his active use of technology to craft an idiosyncratic timbre and style.

In addition to maintaining a busy international travel schedule, Veer Manpreet Singh has an extensive commercial output, including six albums.³³ Since the first album (*Journey Begins*, 2011), he has been keen to experiment with different musical instruments (including a variety of drums). A rap version of "*Tuhi Tuhi*" was released on *Mere Sahib* (2019).³⁴ That album showcases three collaborations with rap artist Paramdeep Singh, where Veer Manpreet Singh's fusion style blends hip-hop beats with Western harmony and instrumentation as well as Indian instruments and melodies (**video ex. 6.6**). Veer Manpreet Singh notes that he was the first *kirtaniya* to create a rap version of "*Tuhi Tuhi*" in 2014. Although he began his journey steeped in the classical training of *Gurmat Sangeet*—without which he could not have progressed toward a "light," popular style—his music is distinctive for its thoughtful intertwining of classical elements with features that embrace technology and for bringing nontraditional instruments and popular idioms into the orbit of *kirtan*. Veer Manpreet Singh gives much credit for innovation with musical instruments to Dya Singh (Australia)—whose inclusion of the didgeridoo, electric guitar, *dilruba*, violin, and *tabla*, among other instruments, "gave something very new to this world"—and to Snatam Kaur, who is similarly experimental and inclusive in the way that she blends musical instruments and ideas from Indian and Western popular music. I observe another emerging group that makes novel use of musical instruments and *rāg*-based musical arrangements, *The Kirtan Collective* (Auckland, New Zealand), who are among the first to blend *kirtan* with jazz.[35]

Veer Manpreet Singh's musical innovation and careful interweaving of *vichar* (exegesis) heightens the spiritual experience—his *kirtan* speaks to members of a large global *sangat* who seek to connect with their Sikh heritage through gestures of inclusivity that incorporate the latest innovations in technology and that are rooted in an aesthetics of contemporary popular culture. While the fusion style of his *slow kirtan* is not welcome at all *Gurudware*, the studio aesthetics that he cultivates in an album like *Mere Sahiba* (2019) opens up a new space for devotional listening in the digital realm—one where the virtual *sangat* can gather and forge an intimate experience of the divine.

BHAI NIRMAL SINGH KHALSA (PIPLI WALE) AND KIRTAN STUDIO: "KIRTAN IS LIFE"

A contemporary experience of *kirtan* drives the innovations of the YouTube channel Kirtan Studio. This venture was begun by Nirmal Singh Khalsa with some family and friends, all business entrepreneurs, who sought to promote *kirtan* in the digital domain. He emphasized Kirtan Studio's dedication to supporting *kirtaniye* while raising general awareness about the rich tradition of Sikh *kirtan* in the digital sphere: "Kirtan Studio does not have adverts.... We have not monetized our channel. We could do that. In fact, it would help our advertising! But the concept my father taught me is that if you want to record *kirtan*, you're not going to make money from it. If you want to make money, then you should not record it."

Khalsa grew up in Bangkok and, like many Southeast Asian diasporic Sikhs, he was able to maintain a strong connection with India through the proximity of his location, even while merging with the local culture and learning regional languages, including Malay, Thai, and Indonesian. He spoke to me about the role of *kirtan* in his community and how it brought members closer together, even as children, as they grew up in a foreign culture while striving to understand their Sikh identity. Khalsa's passion for music and *kirtan* from a young age led him to research recordings by well-known *ragi*. The question that motivated his inquiry concerned the legacy of *kirtan*: "What can we leave for the next generations?" His curiosity pushed him toward learning more about how *kirtan* first came to be recorded and the broader history of commercial *kirtan*, which he attributes to the efforts of Kesar Singh Narula (father of the famous playback singer Jaspinder Kaur Narula). In the decades following the early gramophone recordings, Kesar Singh Narula's goal to "bring *Gurbani* to the world" took hold through the format of records and cassette tapes, with Bhai Harjinder Singh (Srinagar Wale) being among the first to be recorded. Khalsa explained that Narula was the first to obtain permission from the *Akal Takht* to record *kirtan* in a studio. Although the Gramophone Company had recorded *kirtan* as early as 1903 through their colonial enterprise, they did not seek official permission to do so.

Khalsa explained that there are two sides to being Sikh for a *kirtaniya*: "One is the legacy they leave when they perform live — you're sitting in the *darbar*, this is a totally different feel. . . . Then there is the studio recordings, which is them [the *kirtaniye*] saying, 'This is my art, this is my *kala*, this is my composition. . . . I want to turn this into a painting, I want to turn this into a body of work' — this is their cassette tapes." While Khalsa notes that he loves the "imperfections of live performance," Kirtan Studio was born from an impulse to combine live performance with the technological capabilities of a recording studio. The end product is seen as equivalent to a live studio performance in the absence of an in-person audience — a type of *kirtan* to be consumed through purely digital means. Khalsa was inspired by similar endeavors in contemporary culture. I sense similarities with Coke Studio, an industry-backed music platform that fosters collaboration between Pakistani and Indian musicians.[36] Khalsa's goal in establishing Kirtan Studio was to innovate in a way that "pushes the next generation musically"; his compelling production offers a high-quality audio experience of *kirtan* that encourages listeners to think, "This is soothing to my ears." Khalsa also mentioned his own satisfaction in helping *kirtaniye* create their legacy, given the precarious nature of their social and economic existence. For seasons 1 and 2, Khalsa showcased well-known *kirtaniye* in the hope of attracting a large virtual *sangat*. It was only during lockdown that his viewership increased substantially — whether due to spiritual needs or the lack of in-person access to *Gurudware*. Khalsa is currently recording season 3, featuring Veer Manpreet Singh, among several other *kirtaniye*. It completion was disrupted due to COVID.[37]

Khalsa mentioned the large number of messages he received during lockdown asking him to record classical *kirtaniye* performing in *nirdharit rāg*. He noted, however, that these episodes didn't get as many views as those that focused on popular *reet* (orally transmitted traditional melodies), such as Bhai Anantvir Singh's "*Madho.*" Ultimately, for Khalsa, it is important to "connect the *sangat* with *kirtan*," whether that is through simple *dharna* (melodies) or *reet*. This outlook doesn't preclude innovation—Khalsa spoke about his interest in using synthetic drums (and varied percussion) to enhance and update the sonic experience of *kirtan* and to attract younger generations. He spoke of his efforts to compose and arrange original and preexisting *shabad kirtan*: "If you lose the connection with your youth, it's not coming back. There's going to be a generation of people who will forget all that the great *kirtaniye* have done, all the sacrifices they made, and as *kirtaniye*, we can't let that happen.... If we don't take care of our artists, we're going to lose them." This concern remains the main impetus behind the formation of Kirtan Studio—"Kirtan Studio is all about taking care of the art form itself," which means giving due respect and support to *kirtaniye* and innovating in *kirtan*.

This experimental attitude can be seen in Khalsa's approach to instrumentation: In addition to a contemporary Western percussion section, he includes such instruments as the slide guitar and digital piano while working within the domain of *rāg*. Khalsa oversees the mixing of the track and the videography to make sure that "the vibe of *kirtan* is intact." Cultivating the right sound involves thinking about "where an instrument should be played, how much someone should play, where the singer will come up, which instrument will pick up from the vocalist—this is called the arrangement. Mixing involves balance between instruments.... The mix defines the vibe.... The next and final stage is called the master—the music should sound the same on headphones, in the car, in a *nagar kirtan* [outdoor procession].... It should sound consistent," he maintains. Rahaim speaks about the strangely uncanny experience of singing in a recording studio. At Kirtan Studio, the musicians and lead *kirtaniye* are aware that the aesthetics of the studio setup are geared toward a special kind of digital consumption, one oriented toward—and created in the presence of—the divine.[38] To this end, each recording session begins and ends with *ardas*, a prayer of supplication and gratitude that is recited by Sikhs at the beginning and conclusion of any important event.

The studio itself is based in Khalsa's ancestral home in Kurukshetra, India, which I was surprised to learn, given the projection of (what looks like) a large, professional, and lavish setting (also closely overseen by Khalsa). **Video example 6.7** shows how vibrant, plush interior furnishings are set against soft, modern lighting, creating a contemporary "lounge chic" vibe that is directed toward a younger audience that seeks to connect with digital *kirtan* though a high-quality, sensorially rich experience. Reminiscent of Coke Studio, the informal, cozy backdrop of this setup prioritizes "an aesthetics of intimacy." Where the cultivation of devotional intimacy differs from the YouTube performance of popular Bollywood hits, as discussed by Desai-Stephens, is in the *peshkari*—the way the *shabad* is delivered. In keeping with Desai-Stephens's concept, the studio setting gives the impression that the *shabad* has been recorded in a single take, but the end product goes through considerable editing geared toward projecting "a compelling sense of physical and temporal proximity."[39]

Also, unlike the singers that Desai-Stephens studies, *kirtaniye* do not sing directly to the camera. She observes how this aesthetic establishes "a diegetic relationship between performers' bodies and the sounds they produced to create a sense of liveness, direct address, and co-presence between performer and viewer."[40] In a sacred context, however, an aesthetics of intimacy imbued with *bhaav* deepens the devotional experience while using liveness to engage viewers on the level of digital worship. The lack of a direct engagement with the camera's gaze speaks to the conception of divinity in Sikh epistemology as *nirankar* (pure, abstract form beyond time and space). This approach also points to *darshan* as being tied to a sensory witnessing of an immaterial divine presence.

In **video example 6.7** the renowned Bhai Gurmeet Singh Shant actively performs *kirtan* within a studio setting oriented toward conveying a live and intimate feel for a global *sangat*. Khalsa pays attention to aspects of balance between the instruments, as well as timbral variety, making sure that key instruments are showcased through the musical interludes that precede and follow the sung portions of the *shabad*: *rahao/pada* (*asthayi/antara*). Here, Bhai Gurmeet Singh Shant performs *kirtan* with the same *bhaav* (devotional love) that would accompany his offering at a *Gurudwara*. "Hakaa Kabir Kareem Tu" begins with a traditional invocation (*manglacharan*) set to a slow (*vilambit*) *ektāl* (twelve-beat cycle): "Waheguru—Nimaanio ke maan, nitaanio ke taan, niotia ki ot, niaasrio ke aas re/dhan dhan guru garib nawaz" (Wondrous guru—giver of respect, giver of physical form, giver of hope, protector of the poor). In keeping with the tradition of *Gurmat Sangeet*, Shant recites the title at 02:36, "Raag Tilang, Mehla Pehla, Ghar Pehla" ("rāg Tilang, first guru, first *ghar*") before commencing the *shabad* with the *rahao* (refrain), "Hakaa Kabir Kareem Tu," in *Rupak tāl* (seven-beat cycle).

Even as he accompanies himself on the *swarmandal* (plucked box zither), an array of instruments, traditional and modern, form the lush soundscape of this *shabad*: *tanti sāz* (rabab and dilruba) take their place next to newer instruments of *kirtan* (harmonium and *tabla*), the *santoor* (hammered dulcimer), and Western percussion and acoustic instruments. With each interlude, a different instrument has an opportunity to shine. The *dilruba*, played by the virtuoso Sandeep Singh sets the mood for this *shabad* through a short *alaap* (improvisation) that introduces the unique *bhaav* of *rāg Tilang*. This *tanti sāz* evokes the sonic aura of a bygone era, although its accompaniment by bar chimes grounds this timbre in a contemporary soundscape. In the next phrase the harmonium, another timbre tied to *kirtan*, is accompanied by bells and chimes. These kinds of timbral combinations—old with new, local with global—lie at the heart of musical innovation at Kirtan Studio.

The incorporation of the original *Gurmukhi* in transliteration and English translation orients this video toward global digital consumption, as do the visual aesthetics, with their soft lighting, plush fabrics, and close-up camera work. Specifically, this production cultivates an intimate experience of *kirtan* whose sensory richness is heightened by digital technology. Following the success of Kirtan Studio, several other *kirtaniye* have sought to replicate this model online with Shabad Elahi Studio and Gurbani Studio.[41] Seen against the long history of commercially recorded *kirtan* geared toward radio and TV channels, digital endeavors continue to use mass media to broadcast *kirtan* into devotional spaces that exist beyond the *Gurudwara*. These efforts help the *sangat* use media and technology to stay spiritually connected and socioeconomically active in the promotion and consumption of *kirtan*.

| SHIVPREET SINGH: "LISTENING TO GURU NANAK"

Shivpreet Singh is a singer-poet with degrees in biochemistry and music from the University of California, Berkeley, and an MBA from the University of Chicago. Although Shivpreet Singh and I knew each other as graduate students, I became reacquainted with him through the digital *kirtan* he has been sharing over the last decade or so on YouTube and Facebook, where he has amassed a large following. His dissatisfaction of recording his album *Ardaas* (1997) with the major record label EMI inspired him to start his own record label (Ekonkar Records). Shivpreet Singh has always been passionate about music composition, arrangement, and improvisation, and he blends his training in Hindustani classical music with Western popular music to create lightly harmonized renditions of *shabad* on digital piano. He turned to this instrument after realizing that the harmonium doesn't sufficiently complement his voice, whereas a digital piano allows him to create the entire musical structure of a *shabad* by himself: "With a piano, I can do rhythm and the melody — the *rabab* can also do rhythm and the melody; in this respect, the piano is closest to Guru Nanak's original music." Even though the harmonium and piano are unable to create a *meend* (glissandi), he explains that intervallic spaces between pitches give the voice room to glide between notes while exploring new harmonies and textures. Shivpreet Singh sees Guru Nanak as inventing fusion "because he chose to sing with a non-Indian instrument, the *rabab*. The key to doing fusion well is to only change a few elements so that the music is palatable. I want my music to sound Hindustani while using fusion to create a sense of familiarity with a different culture."

Shivpreet Singh often collaborates with musicians on acoustic Indian and Western instruments. He incorporates sampled sounds through his MIDI keyboard to create a multicultural interpretation of a *shabad* in a soothing fusion style. Sometimes, as we see with *"Rasna Japti Tuhi Tuhi"* (*rāg Sarang*) and *"Satgur Aayo Saran Tuhari"* (*rāg Todi*), he will offer a *nirdharit* version of a *shabad* even while harmonizing the melody (**video ex. 6.8** and **audio ex. 6.1**). When I spoke with him about the contentious topic of *nirdharit* versus *rāg*-flexible interpretations, he explained his position: He first records the *shabad* in the designated *rāg*, after which he might then record the same *shabad* in a *rāg*-flexible interpretation. Shivpreet Singh also offers compositions that are not composed in the stipulated *rāg* of *SGGS* (such as *"Jaise Tarvar Pankhi Basera"* in *rāg Anandkali*).[42]

As I pressed further on the topic of *nirdharit rāg* and *Gurmat Sangeet*, he told me a story about Bhagat Kabir's verse *"Paati Tore Malini,"* which is now set to a famous melody by Bhai Bakshi Singh (a mid-twentieth-century *kirtaniya*): "A lot of people sing the same melody. It is in *rāg Kafi*, but Kabir wrote this in *Aasa*, so I recomposed it in *Aasa*. I was skeptical and angry with *ragi* [practitioners] who knew all the *rāg* but kept singing it in *Kafi*. Now everyone sings it in *Kafi* — why are they misleading the *aam janta* [the general public]?" Shivpreet Singh continued, "I used to have this anger for wrong *rāg shabad*, but one day, walking down the aisles in Safeway with my seven-year-old son Gobind, he suddenly starts singing 'Paati Tore Malini' in the wrong *rāg*! At that point I had a realization: So what if it [the *shabad*] is in the wrong *rāg*?! This *shabad* will be with this child throughout his life. . . . You don't want bad compositions in the right *rāg*." Shivpreet Singh sees his liberal viewpoint as coherent with *Gurbani*: "It is the love that matters over the correct *rāg*. If you have the love, then it doesn't matter." Despite his unique approach to recording *Gurbani*, and his wavering dislike of the *Gurmat Sangeet* label, Shivpreet

Singh explains that the *sangat* is very supportive of him: He has been asked to judge *Gurmat Sangeet* competitions, even prestigious ones like the Hemkunt Kirtan Darbar Competition, largely because *Gurmat Sangeet* experts are aware of the rigorous classical training that informs the "popular" style of his *kirtan*—an observation that links his approach with the innovations of Jasleen Kaur and Veer Manpreet Singh.

Shivpreet Singh attributes his idiosyncratic vocal style to the musical techniques he learned on the *bansuri* (bamboo flute), which he studied as a child under Pandit Raghunath Prasanna. Whereas most singers are taught to mimic the ornamentation of the *sarangi*, he explained that his *murki* and *gamak* (ornamentation) are adapted from what he learned on the *bansuri*. Meanwhile, he attributes his soothing timbre to his sustained practice in the lower vocal register (*mandar saptak*). He noticed that he has stability on low notes and decided to develop his *mandar saptak* through focused *riyaaz* (practice) in this range, as inspired by the *ghazal* singers Mehdi Hassan and Jagjit Singh, whose soothing voices similarly connote qualities of sweetness.[43] He explained that it's easier to sing higher because the singer can hear the middle and higher octaves clearly, but "when you sing in a lower range, you don't have the same feedback. Good singers can listen to themselves and adjust." Shivpreet Singh has a naturally lower voice and has found that although a singer cannot increase their range to reach higher notes, they can make it lower through *mandar saptak riyaaz*. His efforts to correct his intonation through repetition, coupled with close critique of his own recordings, formed the basis of a vocal practice that helps him internalize a *shabad*. He started this practice about ten to twelve years ago, preparing one *shabad* every two to three months—his aim was to be as musically perfect as possible. After a few years of memorizing lines of verses, he found that he had memorized between twenty-five and thirty complete *shabad*. This approach forms the basis of his meditative *slow kirtan* and, for me, points to the difference between "doing *kirtan*" and "flowing through *kirtan*."

Over the years the refinement of his vocal timbre in a lower register has led to curiosity among his listeners. He explained that he is often asked to divulge which microphone he is using—a question at which he usually laughs, explaining, "It's not the mic; it's *mandar saptak riyaaz!*" However, like Jasleen Kaur, Shivpreet Singh does give credit to hardware other than his digital piano and computer, specifically the Rode NT1, a large diaphragm microphone with round pop-up filters. He explained that these microphones are often installed in studios and tend to enhance sibilance so that *p* and *s* enunciations are louder, while the pop-up filter reduces unevenness between consonant sounds. Also, like Jasleen

Kaur, Shivpreet Singh undertakes his *riyaaz* with the microphone and has trained himself to restrain his *p* and other harsh consonants so that they don't pop as much. As we have seen with masters of the microphone—Bhai Gurpreet Singh, Jasleen Kaur, and Veer Manpreet Singh—Shivpreet Singh similarly conveys a feeling of intimacy through his microphone technique: He sings directly into the mouthpiece and knows how and when to hold back. His goal is to have "the *murkis* and *halak* [ornamentation] sound as though they whisper into our ears." In parallel with Jasleen Kaur, his sparing use of a breathy whisper technique enhances the listener's feeling of devotional intimacy. Audible inhalation signals liveness, while his overall approach to *slow kirtan* heightens the sensation of submerging into the soundscapes of *Gurbani*.

Shivpreet Singh's compositions are an intercultural melding of poetry and music, richly orchestrated through acoustic and sampled sounds. While the tide turns toward the revival of *tanti sāz* among some practitioners of *kirtan*, Shivpreet Singh tackles issues of revival from the perspective of instrument innovation, which he sees as being at the heart of contemporary *kirtan*. Although, in the end, he argues, "instruments ... are all icing on the cake—what I really enjoy is drowning in the word and interconnecting with other words in and outside of *Gurbani* ... like connecting [Bhagat] Kabir to Emily Dickinson to Walt Whitman."

The feeling of "drowning" in *shabad* characterizes his *slow kirtan*. Recently, he has begun to develop live meditation sessions where he explores the meaning of a single *shabad* over the course of an hour or so, sometimes in dialogue with poetry from the Western canon. These are chosen by Shivpreet Singh to forge cross-cultural connections between *Gurbani* and other literary expressions, while illuminating the central verse from different cultural and intellectual perspectives.[44] Similar to Veer Manpreet Singh's method, this approach immerses devotees in *Gurbani* as the repetition of simple melodies presents the primary topic for reflection through introduction of the *rahao* (refrain). After several minutes, Shivpreet Singh begins to gradually incorporate the verses as he reflects on the meaning of the *rahao* through melodic development and exegesis. These meditation sessions thrive on a feeling of participatory liveness: As we saw with Veer Manpreet Singh, devotees use the live chat to announce their presence through greetings of gratitude and bliss and to express their appreciation of the *shabad* and its musical rendition. Live chat also offers the opportunity to participate in a dialogue with Shivpreet Singh's, and the virtual *sangat's*, own spiritual reflections.

When Shivpreet Singh started sharing his music online, it was under the inspiration of Guru Nanak's extensive travels. Like Guru Nanak, he wanted to "sing to strangers, [to] figure out Guru Nanak's recipe of magic, and to move people who know nothing about the language and music." He explained, "I wondered how to turn strangers into friends." When he started his pages on YouTube, Facebook, and Twitter (now X), he felt that he could have ramped up his efforts to get a few thousand more hits, but he chose not to. Instead, he began a one-*shabad*-a-month meditation to start understanding Guru Nanak's journey. His collaborative online platforms introduce *kirtan* to regional audiences across South Asia (in the states of Bengal and Tamil Nadu in India and in Sindh in Pakistan); he notes that less than 25 percent of his listeners are Punjabi. Shivpreet Singh also helps musicians start their own YouTube channels and believes that it is the "intimacy of his technology [that] helps to make connections between him and strangers," a comment that ties in to this chapter's exploration of the devotional intimacy afforded by the digital realm.

Like the other *kirtaniye* discussed in this chapter, Shivpreet Singh offers *kirtan* at his local *Gurudwara*, although he tends to prefer a prerecorded experience over a live one. Through his masterful use of audio technology, he establishes an intimate experience of *kirtan* to facilitate *aatam darshan* (experience of the divine for oneself) rather than *pradarshan* (performance). He is often invited to perform at large gatherings involving thousands of people — the most recent being an event sponsored in March 2024 by the Indian government in Hyderabad, "Global Spirituality Mahotsav [Celebration] — The World's First Congregation of Various Spiritual Traditions, Interfaith Leaders, Yoga Gurus, and Holistic Wellness Experts," where he was a representative of the Sikh tradition alongside a host of writers and spiritual luminaries, including Deepak Chopra, Alice Walker, Sadhguru, and Eckhart Tolle, to mention a few. Despite this global visibility, Shivpreet Singh reminds me that he is an introvert who prefers the quiet ambience of the studio and the comforts of technology.

Epilogue

As I write my closing reflections on *Vaisakhi* 2024, a spring festival that commemorates the founding of the Sikh community (*Khalsa panth*) under the leadership of Guru Gobind Singh, I am reminded of the musical and poetic prowess of the tenth guru—his vivid, multilingual, heart-stirring *bani* and writings, as well as the musical instruments that were played in his court: the *taus*, *tanpura*, *jori*, *pakhawaj*, and many more. The same morning, I receive a WhatsApp message from Veer Manpreet Singh telling me that his new track, "Hey Karunanidh," a collaboration with the young Australian singer-guitarist Ruhani Dhillon, featuring the famous *tuhi tuhi* refrain, has just dropped. Hours before, I was in a texting flurry with Shivpreet Singh, whose newly released *shabad* "*Darshan Dekh*" guides the virtual *sangat* in reflection during this joyful festival. He reminds me to join him for his Saturday morning meditation on the theme of spring. As I search for his meditation on YouTube, I stumble across Taren Kaur's contribution to *Vaisakhi*—an animated *kirtan* sing-along for children of a *shabad* that commemorates Guru Gobind Singh, "*Vah Vah Gobind Singh*." My eyes and ears are filled with these offerings of *kirtan*—some that I imagine have come straight from the times of the gurus, as well as others that are new renditions innovated in the digital realm.[1]

Vaisakhi as a time of reflection also leads me to contemplate my own journey in writing this book over a twenty-year span. Truth be told, if I had completed this work in the first decade of the 2000s, as I had always imagined I would, *Sikh Kirtan and Its Journeys* would have had a much narrower scope. When I wrote my first graduate seminar paper in 1998, I said that *kirtan* was one thing—the model that Bhai Avtar Singh and Bhai Gurcharan Singh offered and little else. The growing debate around *nirdharit rāg* with which my book opens might have absorbed my full attention.

As I pour through my notes and hours of recorded audio from interviews for this final chapter, I am grateful that these remarkable individuals welcomed me into their spiritual, musical, and intellectual worlds to show me that *kirtan* today cannot be defined as a singular spiritual practice. My personal experience of *kirtan* is infinitely enriched when *rāg* combines with *shabad* (verse); the feeling I get when I receive *Gurbani* in *nirdharit rāg* is unsurpassable. A corporeal engagement with *rāg* orients my inner reflection toward the message and sentiment of sacred verse. At the same time, I have also experienced alternative devotional expressions that are invested with *bhaav* (devotional love), whether they are conceived in the form of a pop lyrical ballad for a female voice and a guitar or as a lo-fi version of a *shabad* with rap, jazz, or a cappella beats. Undoubtedly, the internet of the 1990s and the emergence of social media in the early 2000s spearheaded these innovations—but that's not to say that *kirtan* would not have continued to evolve in their absence.

Kirtan innovation has come a long way since the first crossover efforts in the popular style of early Indian cinema discussed in the introduction. Today, new *shabad* are not based on preexisting Bollywood melodies but stand proudly as original compositions that might reference a specific style or genre while holding *Gurbani* as their centerpiece. The interviews shared in this chapter illuminate current innovations that define the practice across the corners of the globe: An audio engineer reveals his trade secrets in pursuing a sacred Sikh acoustics and sound, two young female *kirtaniye* share their passions for technological innovation in crafting a uniquely feminine timbre and style, two male *kirtaniye* speak of their desire to immerse the *sangat* in *Gurbani* through their original approach to *slow kirtan*, and an entrepreneur and *kirtaniya* describes the contemporary digital presentation of *kirtan* as a way to promote and support the tradition and its practitioners.

The results of my survey, discussed in the appendix, had already indicated the emergence of several strands of musical devotion, each with a substantial following. Despite emphasis from spiritual authorities on a *nirdharit* delivery, members of the *sangat* revealed their varied, fluid, and evolving musical tastes. Their reiteration of origin stories—whether of Guru Nanak and Bhai Mardana or of Bhai Satta and Bhai Balwand—does not, to my mind, reflect being bound to a colonized subjectivity. These narratives provoke a misreading of Mandair to suggest that, in the practice of *kirtan*, it is precisely a desire for cycles of repetition that provide "the possibility of a genuinely postcolonial move."[2] Every time these narratives come alive in the Sikh imagination, they infuse a new devotional fervor into the pursuit of *nirdharit rāg* and historically informed instruments, or the digital rendering of *kirtan* using new instruments, or a novel combination thereof. As we saw with the entry of the harmonium, those who undertake *kirtan* have the ultimate agency to decide how they make their offering.

Sikh *kirtan* never was and can never be a static practice: Its agents have included hereditary musicians (*mirasi*), trained practitioners (*ragi*), male and female professionals and amateurs, and children. The diasporic reach of the *sangat* renders the practice even more diverse, as members adopt the sonic cultural inflections of their social environments, whether this is reflected in their incorporation of native instruments such as the didgeridoo; new instruments such as synthesizers; new genres such as jazz, rap, pop, and blues; or new approaches such as *slow kirtan*. *Kirtan* has never stood still: Guru Nanak and Bhai Mardana took *kirtan* with them on their journeys. The guru's Sikhs continue to take *kirtan* with them on theirs, as they negotiate hyphenated identities: literal (as they continue to migrate across the globe) and spiritual (as *ahat nād* opens up within their consciousness an attunement to the inner music of *anahad nād*).

This book has sought to introduce Sikh *kirtan* to a range of readers: Some will already be familiar with the practice as listeners and practitioners. For others, this material will be new, and I hope that teachers and students will be encouraged to explore Sikh *kirtan* in their courses, curricula, and research—it is time that the broad umbrella of Hindustani classical music (*shastriya sangeet*) is expanded to include and acknowledge a robust musical practice that it has excluded and ignored for too long. It is my hope that the trope of journeying has given readers a starting point in *Gurbani*, which forms the basis of theories about *rāg* and *nād*. At the same time I have guided readers toward a deeper understanding of the impact of journeying on the instruments of *kirtan*—from *tanti sāz* to the "colonial" harmonium—and the technologies that continue to inform its innovation. If the impact of this book is such that *kirtan* begins to attract an even wider *sangat* beyond diasporic Sikhs, I hope that among them will be allies and activists keen to support female *kirtaniye* striving for equal opportunities.

The basis of *kirtan*, *Sri Guru Granth Sahib* (*SGGS*), reflects the richness of humanity through the multiple languages, dialects, cultures, histories, philosophies, and geographies that it encompasses. My book captures the ambience of *kirtan* in these spaces and as *kirtan* travels among the interstices of sound, metaphor, nature, technology, and the cosmos. *Sikh Kirtan and Its Journeys* is ultimately about how listening informs a person's sense of their body, consciousness, and connection to their surroundings and other human beings. *Nād* has an aesthetic, material, biotic, and cosmic vibration; it is when we attune ourselves to these frequencies that we are able to function as whole beings whose amplified inner resonance can be directed toward self-growth and societal healing. We often talk about the transformative qualities of music. Sikh *kirtan* presents a living tradition that thrives on that promise.

Appendix

Since talking openly about one's tastes and preferences for *kirtan* is a sensitive issue, I turned to the virtual *sangat* to help me navigate my personal conundrum around *nirdharit kirtan* versus *rāg*-flexible *kirtan* — and also out of sheer curiosity to learn what others were thinking. In 2021 I made a short, anonymous survey (on a Google Form), which was launched across the diaspora, garnering close to three hundred responses in Punjabi and English. Participants were asked to identify their location and give their approximate age. The questions I posed were oriented around what kind of *kirtan* they liked to listen to in the *Gurudwara* and through digital media, the role of *kirtan* in their lives, and its impact on their identities as Sikhs (however they defined this). I was not aiming to collect quantifiable data; rather, I wanted to give participants an opportunity to voice their thoughts and opinions as part of a personal narrative. Thus, the survey was not organized as a multiple-choice questionnaire. Some older participants who were not comfortable using technology sent written responses to me separately. While Pierre Bourdieu's study of taste and social class looms large in the background of this endeavor, I deliberately chose not to ask for information about educational background or income, or any other such markers of class and status.[1] Since the time of the gurus, the Sikh *panth* (community) has been founded on a notion of equality that goes beyond caste, gender, and social status. I was not keen to underscore the semblance of hierarchy, given the high value implicitly ascribed to the performance of *nirdharit kirtan* and to listeners who have the skills to appreciate *rāg* in comparison with other styles—semiclassical, folk, popular, or digital—that might be perceived as tangential to Sikh musical heritage. These skills are not necessarily expensive to acquire, although access to this knowledge may be limited depending on one's location.

In stark contrast to Bourdieu's cultural legitimacy theory, my experience of observing who listened to what kind of *kirtan* over the years has shown me that taste, in the Sikh context, doesn't seem to be linked to education or wealth as much as it is shaped by the inherited values of an individual's family and what they grew up hearing at their local *Gurudwara* or through personal habits of material and digital consumption. This is not to say that listeners' preferences are unchanging—they can grow to enjoy more styles, but, as is the case with childhood memories that involve family and community, listeners are sometimes nostalgic for their earliest sonic encounters, no matter how their tastes evolve. For example, listeners who only listen to classical, *nirdharit kirtan* are not necessarily highly educated or wealthy, just as someone who prefers to listen primarily to digital *kirtan* may not lack a musical education or social status. I have seen that even more important than the issue of how verses are conveyed through music is the overarching belief that all music—regardless of genre, style, or expression—is subservient to *bani*, the divine utterance of the gurus and bhagats. A wide range of sonic means draw devotees closer to contemplating *bani*, thus the emphasis here is not on musical expression but on the process and the end result of spiritual connection and elevation.

These observations were borne out when I sifted through the results of my survey. I also realized my naivety in embarking on this task since I was not expecting this level of honesty and I was not ready for it. Indeed, I had no expectation that a few hundred strangers would trust me with deeply personal stories about what *kirtan* meant to them and their families and about how listening to *kirtan* had helped them through difficult times and moments of personal crisis. I also learned about some of their favorite *kirtaniye*, and I enjoyed listening to recordings and watching videos that respondents shared with me—some showed their family members playing *kirtan*, others showed professionals. Despite my initial hesitations about soliciting opinions about *kirtan* in this way, I learned a great deal about how and why the global *sangat* engages with *kirtan*. I was expecting only a handful of responses. The fact that I received nearly three hundred indicates to me not only the generosity of the global *sangat* but also their collective passion for *kirtan*, the centrality of *kirtan* to their identities as Sikhs, and a desire (maybe a need) to share their experiences. I'm deeply grateful to every person who took the time to complete yet another survey from a total stranger during the COVID era.

A detailed analysis of this data would require at least an entire chapter. Given the limitations of space, this appendix provides a quick summary of my observations. I received responses from India, the United States, Canada, the United Kingdom, France, The Netherlands, Malaysia, Singapore, Thailand, the Maldives, New Zealand, and Australia, with the greatest participation from the age groups of 50–60 (24 percent) and 60+ (24 percent). Those under 20 accounted for 4 percent, the 20–30 age group for 18 percent, the 30–40 age group for 11 percent, and the 40–50 age group for 14 percent.

The data showed a clear preference for listening to classical or *rāg*-based *kirtan* at *Gurudware* (36 percent), with a few participants expressing their specific interest in hearing *puratan reet* (orally transmitted traditional melodies), *partāl* (compositions in multiple *tāl*), *dhurpad shailly* (in the Sikh tradition of *dhurpad*), and traditional instruments (the *dilruba, rabab, taus,* and *jori* were mentioned). Around 14 percent preferred traditional *kirtan* (presumably what one would hear on the harmonium and *tabla* at most *Gurudware*), and 19 percent emerged as flexible listeners who felt that any style of *kirtan* is acceptable. One respondent replied, "*Gurbani* is the Guru's teachings which should become imbibed in our mind, soul, [and] each and every cell of our being. . . . Style doesn't matter." Another participant who was open to all styles added, "*Kirtan* is to listen to and [to] understand the Guru's message and apply [it] in your daily life. It's not to be listened to as entertainment." Others who preferred *rāg* mentioned that they were open to other styles if the practitioner did not have a knowledge of a specific *rāg*. Overall, respondents emphasized that *kirtan* should be soothing, calm, soulful, relaxing, inspirational, healing, and transcendent. One wrote that *kirtan* should "make [them] totally oblivious to [their] surroundings and make [them] sing along with the *rāgis*." Another said that it should transport the "mental state to a different realm." *Kirtan* should not be "too pompous and showy about the prowess of the singer," and "the music should not overshadow the *shabad* [words]." One respondent explained that *kirtan* is not "a one-way delivery . . . it has to be the style in which there is an avenue for the congregation to also sing along." Importantly, I noticed a taste for *AKJ kirtan* (5 percent) and what was defined as semiclassical (5 percent). One respondent each noted their enjoyment of Bollywood-, *ghazal*-, and *thumri*-styled *kirtan*, while two individuals mentioned the emerging style of *dodra samagam* as enjoyable.

Many were willing to share details of their favorite *ragi* (including Bhai Kamaljit Singh, Bhai Harcharan Singh, Bhai Harjinder Singh, Veer Manpreet Singh, Snatam Kaur, Amrita Kaur, Mallika Kaur, to mention a few) when telling me what style they liked best. Some mentioned their preferences for simple *kirtan* (which they described as *dhuniya* [melody based]), the *dharna* style (call-and-response) and *nirol kirtan* (which emphasizes the verse rather than musical complexity), while a few others revealed that they don't enjoy *dhaadhi jatha* because they are too loud. On the one hand, this observation fulfills Bhai Vir Singh's prediction that, as *ragi* take over the role of exegesis from *dhaadhi* (folk musicians or ballad singers) to compensate for a lack of knowledge about *rāg* among members of the *sangat*, the *dhaadhi* will become obsolete. On the other hand, what participants tended to dislike about *dhaadhi jatha* concerned a technical issue: These musicians traditionally sing in a full-bodied (*buland*) chest voice. *Dhaadhi jatha* don't need amplification, and thus the use of microphones gives the effect of shouting. Overall, participants expressed a strong desire to sing along with the *ragi*—hence an emphasis on simple melodies—and a need to understand the *shabad* easily. Some participants enjoyed *katha/viyakhia/parchaar*—moments when the singing of a *shabad* is momentarily halted to incorporate relevant commentary and exegesis, while others didn't.

When listening to *kirtan* outside of the *Gurudwara* via digital media, many respondents maintained similar preferences. For some, the issue of style remained irrelevant: "Guru resides in the tongue of *Keertanis* and where *kirtan* is being performed.... It may be *Gurudwara* or anywhere outside." I noticed a few more respondents veered toward AKJ (8 percent) and digital or contemporary *kirtan* (4 percent), while others expressed a preference for "light" classical or popular styles (5 percent) and older recordings (from the 1960s through the 1980s). Many of these listeners spoke of *kirtan* being played in the background while they attended to other activities, such as household chores or long-distance driving. Other respondents were flexible listeners depending on their mood and mental well-being. One wrote, "If I'm sad then [I listen to] relaxing *kirtan* to disconnect with the whole world, and there is a little chance to clean your inner self. Or I prefer energetic *kirtan* that [helps me] get out of that sadness [...] to keep walking through sadness until the sadness ends. During [a] happy time, I like listening to *kirtan* of love." Another spoke about using media to hear *kirtan* 24/7: "It's like my life lives in *kirtan*."

When dealing with the question "Do you feel *kirtan* should only be performed in *rāg*?," 38 percent responded no and 16 percent responded yes, although the range of written responses reflected considerable flexibility with an overall curiosity to learn more about *rāg*. Some responses were very clear:

> Guru Maharaj [has] given us *hukam* for *rāg Keertan* . . . that's why they wrote many times *Raag Gaudi*. . . . [Deciding on whether to play in *rāg* is] not an option!

> Preferably! That is why *Gurbani* is written in [a] *raga* format.

> *Rāg* is a crucial element that the Gurus intentionally incorporated in *Gurbani*. This is the pinnacle of music and engages the mind to the highest level. . . . Those who are not familiar with *rāg* . . . may prefer the simpler versions of *kirtan* . . . "*dharnas*." However[,] an effort needs to be made to impart as much *rāg* knowledge as possible so that we follow in the Guru's path.

Many other viewpoints were flexible:

> Not necessarily. . . . We should be able to connect with *shabad guru* in whichever form.

> Ideally, yes, but that would restrict amateurs with a passion.

> It depends on the audience . . . however, an effort needs to be made to impart as much *rāg* knowledge as possible so that we follow in the Guru's path.

> No . . . *kirtan* is for the soul. Any *Gurbani* sung from the heart is *kirtan*.

> No. *Kirtan* is an expression of vibration.

> *Keertan* is a conversation between me and my Guru. Only *bhaav* [devotional mood] is required.

> No. Our Gurus were innovators. . . . Somehow I always imagine them smiling when they hear their Sikhs trying out new tunes or praising the divine in whichever medium.

My next three questions were tied to the topic of musical instruments. Devotees were divided on the issue of hearing *kirtan* on digital synthesizers (27 percent said yes and 31 percent no). While most respondents enjoy hearing *kirtan* on *tabla* and harmonium, I saw a keen interest in *tanti sāz* (traditional string instruments) and *jori*. In answering my question of whether *kirtan* should be performed only on traditional instruments, one respondent mentioned, "It [*kirtan*] carries more depth that way." Another offered the following viewpoint: "*Kirtan* should be open to being performed ... [on] any instrument, it should not be restricted but we should not forget or leave behind traditional instruments. These instruments were selected for a reason—the notes and the sound waves resonate the perfect sound for it to touch your soul."

Overall, respondents were sensitive to the fact that traditional instruments and expert players are not always available and thus that the harmonium serves an important role: "The introduction of the *vaja* [harmonium] by Western society has allowed people of many ages to grasp the ability to sing *Gurbani* easily." Another respondent noted that the choice of musical instrument is not as important as "our *pyaar* [love] and thirst for our Guru, whether we're performing on a harmonium, [a] guitar, or a *taus*." Still another maintained that traditional instruments should be played in historic *Gurudware* but that it is acceptable to experiment with different instruments outside of those sacred spaces. I note the answer of one respondent, who did not feel that *kirtan* should be performed only on traditional instruments but did acknowledge that "these instruments have a way to tug on your soul." Several respondents emphasized the priority of *shabad* over musical instrument and that the latter should never overshadow the former.

The next question addressed the topic of technology. In general, the response to the use of technology in *Gurudware* was unanimously positive, especially regarding projector screens that display translations and effective audio engineering. I was particularly struck by the following comment: "Microphones/speakers need to [be] set up correctly for the emotion of *rāg/shabad* to have an impact on the *sangat*." A few respondents bemoaned the outdated language of sikhitothemax.com—which is the default website used by many *Gurudware* for English translations—and mentioned using other apps on their mobile phones during *diwan* to access a different translation. Some complained about microphones being too loud (overmodulation), and a few wondered whether instruments like the *jori* really need amplification, given their loud, resonant timbre.

The most revealing answers came from my final question about how engaging with *kirtan* impacts a devotee's identity as a Sikh. Several respondents directly cited a well-known phrase from *Gurbani* that indicates the elevated place of *kirtan* in their lives: "In this era [of *kaljug*, the age of destruction], *kirtan* is the most exalted."[2] I cite several responses below because it is so rare that devotees have an opportunity to open up in this way. Some felt that *kirtan* offers moral guidance: "*Kirtan* provides direction on how I should lead my life in this world" and "[*Kirtan*] makes me realize the value of life and purpose of life and how precious life is." Many answers were concentrated around mental health and personal growth:

> *Kirtan* has the power to transform a person 360 degrees.

> [*Kirtan*] was a big factor in helping me overcome severe mental illness.

> It helps me get through tough times and keeps me calm.

> It is my stress reliever.

> It is my daily source of courage and strength.

> *Kirtan* is healing and raises one's vibration.

> The vibration [of *kirtan*] is absorbed by everything.

One respondent wrote, "I feel this immense grounding listening to *kirtan*. It's obviously very meditative, but it can bring me back to very positive memories in my life full of love, and reconnecting with that energy is very powerful even in my young-adult life." Another added,

> I grew up participating in Hemkunt Kirtan Competitions, which had the goal of teaching young students different *rāgs* and if you played a classical instrument (in my case, *taus*), we got extra points. This really motivated me to learn as a young child/teenager and participating in these competitions gave me a new set of friends who had *kirtan* as a common hobby. As a Sikh, *kirtan* is really important to me and it really grounds me to my faith.

Another young participant responded, "*Keerthan* is literally my life. I listen to it every day: when I walk to campus, during workouts, when I'm studying, or just chilling in my dorm room. I even do it with a friend every week! *Keerthan* is the one aspect of Sikhi I relate to the most and it helps me be a better Sikh."

Other answers were more spiritual:

> *Kirtan* is the food of my soul [*rooh di khuraak*].

> Sometimes when I am driving, I play *kirtan* through YouTube and it just transports me to a whole new dimension, and I tear up, because it just touches some corner of my soul.

> After my Guru, *kirtan* is my second most priceless treasure in this world. *Kirtan* is the food that revives my soul each day, the raft that steers me across the worldly ocean, and the sanctuary that protects me from worldly bondages. Wherever our Guru's *kirtan* is sung, there is *sachkhand* [the divine realm] for me.

> *Kirtan* is for humanity. Food for [the] soul. It is in fact meditative and *kirtan* is the way of my life, dealing with situations, and remembering the One without any reservation. *Kirtan* is a constant meditative state … I call this *kirtan*.

Reading the results of this survey was a humbling, emotional, uplifting, and thought-provoking experience. I had launched this survey with the goal of resolving my personal dilemma surrounding the practice of *nirdharit kirtan*. These results opened up a wide terrain filled with nuance and complexity where the practice of *kirtan* was tied to the vast landscape of human existence, as marked by varying states of emotion, mood, and wellness, while traversing issues of taste, the economy, and technology. At the end of it all, I was even further from resolving my conundrum than I had been at the start—but with the added insight that few Sikhs were agonizing over this question in the way that I had been. Ultimately, I gained the understanding that many Sikhs are united across the diaspora in the ways that they forge their personal links with *Gurbani* through *kirtan*. For some, it's *rāg* that is of primary importance; for others, it's *shabad* (the divine word); and for still others, it's both or constantly changing depending on their situation, environment, and mood—what life has given them that day. The reach of technology is powerful and vast: Regardless of where Sikhs are located in the world, they are able to access many expressions of *kirtan* and are thus open to several options. What they choose to consume is, of course, their decision, but as long as there is a choice, *kirtan* will always have many different nuances and expressive identities. And technology will continue to allow devotees to forge a connection with *kirtan* that is deeply personal and meaningful for them.

Glossary

| TERMS USED IN THE TEXT

ahat nād: struck sound, played on musical instruments or conveyed through the voice using effort
anahad nād: unstruck sound, constantly reverberating without effort
bhaav: a feeling of heightened or ecstatic devotion
bivastha/avastha: a state of heightened or elevated consciousness
chautha pad (the fourth state): the deepest state of meditation
darbar: court (as in the court of the gurus) or a large hall for ceremonial events (such as the main hall of a *Gurudwara*)
darshan: an intimate, multimodal sensing of divine presence that does not involve idol worship
dasam dwar: an opening at the crown of the head that allows the consciousness to merge with divinity
dhaadhi: folk musicians who play the *dhadh* (a small, double-faced, handheld drum) and sing ballads often accompanied by the bowed *sarangi* in a small ensemble
dhun/dhuni: sacred or divine melody
diwan: presentation (of *kirtan*)
gur-mantar: mantra based on *Sri Guru Granth Sahib*
gurmukh: one who is oriented toward the teachings of the divine guru

Gurudwara (pl. *Gurudware*): a sanctified building where Sikhs gather to worship (lit. the door of the guru)

kaljug: the dark age, or time of destruction, one of the four ages referred to in *SGGS* 445-7 through 446-4 (the other three are the golden age of Sat Yuga [*prathmai*], the silver age of Trayta Yuga [*trithiai*], and the brass age of Dwapur Yuga [*duthiaa*])

katha/viyakhia: narrative interpolation or exegesis

kirtan: Sikh devotional music

kirtaniya (pl. *kirtaniye*): practitioner of *kirtan*

manmukh: one who is oriented toward the materiality of the world (and oriented away from the divine guru)

munn and *tunn*: the mind and the body, their dichotomy and interconnectedness

nād: divine sound

nirankar: manifestation of the divine one as formless, abstract, and beyond time and space

panch shabad: a voluminous blend of heterogeneous timbres that signal different musical instruments

rāg: melodic mode

ragi/ragi jatha: professionally trained practitioners of *kirtan* (typically male)

ras: an aesthetic and ecstatic delight of the senses (lit. essence, juice, or flavor)

sangat: a gathering of Sikh devotees

seva: social responsibility and service

shabad: divine word or composition

simran/nām simran: remembering the divine name through techniques of vocal or silent recitation

Sri Guru Granth Sahib: the sacred utterance of the gurus (abbreviated *SGGS* throughout and often referred to as *Gurbani*)

surti: consciousness, focus

tāl: a repeating metric cycle based on a fixed number of beats

udasi: Guru Nanak's and Bhai Mardana's extensive travels or a state of feeling disconnected from the material world and connected to the divine guru

virla (pl. *virlai*): one of the few chosen ones who are immersed in the divine guru

MUSICAL INSTRUMENTS

bayn/bansuri: bamboo flute
bheri: kettle drum
chhainay: steel tongs overlaid with small cymbals, also called *chimta*

dhadh: small, double-faced, handheld drum
dilruba: a large, fretted, bowed chordophone
ghungroo: small bells
jhunkar: the tinkling of small bells (*ghungroo*)
jori and *tabla*: paired, differently tuned drums used to accompany *kirtan* and played with distinctive hand, palm, and finger techniques
kinguri: a type of bowed chordophone used in folk traditions
mridang/pakhawaj: a large, double-faced drum played sitting down
rabab: plucked chordophone
shankh: conch
saranda: a type of bowed chordophone played in the Sikh courts and introduced by the third guru, Guru Amardas
sarangi: a type of bowed chordophone used in folk and (in an altered version) classical traditions
sinyi: animal horn
tanti sāz: a broad category referring to string instruments used in Sikh *kirtan* (*rabab, taus, dilruba, tār-shehnai, saranda*, etc.)
taus: a large, fretted, bowed chordophone in the shape of a peacock

DATES OF THE TEN SIKH GURUS

Guru Nanak: 1469–1539
Guru Angad: 1504–1552
Guru Amardas: 1479–1574
Guru Ramdas: 1534–1581
Guru Arjan: 1563–1606
Guru Hargobind: 1595–1644
Guru Har Rai: 1630–1661
Guru Harkrishan: 1656–1664
Guru Tegh Bahadur: 1621–1675
Guru Gobind Singh: 1666–1708

Notes

PREFACE

1. On Guru Nanak's travels and the corpus of hagiographical literature (referred to as the *Janamsakhi*) that was created in his memory, see Harjeet Singh Grewal, "Encountering Oneness and Exiled Being: Conceptualizing Udāsī in the Janamsākhīs, Vārān Bhāī Gurdās, and Srī Gurū Granth Sāhib," in *The Sikh World*, ed. Pashaura Singh and Arvind-Pal Singh Mandair (Routledge, 2023), 61–72.
2. Scholarship about the Sikh migrant experience is growing. Select titles include Masako Azuma, *Sikh Diaspora in Japan* (Routledge, 2018); Knut A. Jacobsen and Kristina Myrvold, eds., *Sikhs in Europe: Migration, Identities, and Representations* (Ashgate Pub., 2011) and *Sikhs Across Borders: Transnational Practices of European Sikhs* (Bloomsbury, 2012); Ian Talbot and Shinder S. Thandi, *People on the Move: Punjabi Colonial, and Post-Colonial Migration* (Oxford University Press, 2004); Gurharpal Singh and Darshan Singh Tatla, *Sikhs in Britain: The Making of a Community* (Zed Books, 2006); and Pashaura Singh and Arvind-Pal Singh Mandair, *The Sikh World* (Routledge, 2023), 113–95.
3. Parminder Bhachu, *Movers and Makers: Uncertainty, Resilience, and Migrant Creativity in Worlds of Flux* (Routledge, 2021), 1. On the topic of *kirtan* in the diaspora, see Navtej K. Purewal and Harjinder S. Lallie, "Sikh Kirtan in the Diaspora: Identity, Innovation, and Revivalism," in *The*

Sikh Diaspora: Theory, Agency, and Experience, ed. Michael Hawley (Brill, 2013), 381–403; Gurdeep John Singh Khabra, "Music of the Sikh Diaspora: Devotional Sounds, Musical Memory and Cultural Identity," *Sikh Formations: Religion, Culture, Theory* 8, no. 2 (2012): 147–70; and Inderjit Kaur, "Making Pilgrimage, Making Home: Sikh Sacred Soundings in Kenya," in *Sounding the Indian Ocean: Musical Circulations in the Afro-Asiatic Seascape* (University of California Press, 2023), 181–98.

4   As one might expect with oral narrative, there are multiple variations of this story. I adapt the version I am most familiar with, which is covered by Bhai Gurpreet Singh: "Dhan Guru Ramdas Rakhi Gareeb Di Laaj—Amritvela Chaliya 2022 Day 12—11th October, 2022," posted October 10, 2022, by Amritvela Trust, YouTube, https://www.youtube.com/live/Ioj989oWFoc?feature=share (in Hindi, 05:01:25 to 05:37:00). For other versions, see Harjinder Singh Dilgeer, *The Sikh Reference Book* (Singh Brothers, 1997), 285–86. Macauliffe offers a version in English, although he assigns Bhai Satta and Bhai Balwand to the court of Guru Angad, the second guru, and not Guru Arjan (Max Arthur Macauliffe, *The Sikh Religion: Its Gurus, Sacred Writings and Authors* [Clarendon Press, 1909], 21–28).

5   SGGS 966-14 to 968-17.

6   A recent exception is in work by Radha Kapuria, who observes "artificial boundaries" between the classical, folk, devotional, urban, and rural (*Music in Colonial Punjab: Courtesans, Bards, and Connoisseurs, 1800–1947* [Oxford University Press, 2023], 4, 32).

7   To give one example, anyone can offer *kirtan seva* at my local *Gurudwara* (in Westborough, MA) by way of a Google sign-up sheet.

8   Bhai Ghulam Mohammad Chand was among the last living *rababi* to offer *kirtan* at a *Gurudwara*. See "Bhai Ghulam Mohammad Chand—Dhrupad in Raag Patdeepki," posted by Kirtan Sewa, October 9, 2019, YouTube, https://www.youtube.com/watch?v=uBYT7n3e0GY.

9   See Balbir Singh Kanwal, *Punjab de Parsidh Ragi Rababi, 1604-2004* (Singh Brothers, 2010) and Navtej K. Purewal, "Sikh/Muslim Bhai-Bhai? Towards a Social History of the Rabābī Tradition of Shabad Kīrtan," *Sikh Formations: Religion, Culture, Theory* 7, no. 3 (2011): 365–82.

10 Gobind Singh Mansukhani, *Indian Classical Music and Sikh Kirtan* (Oxford University Press and IBH, 1982), foreword.

| INTRODUCTION

1   Pashaura Singh, "Sikhism and Music," in *Sacred Sound: Experiencing Music in World Religions*, ed. Guy Beck (Wilfrid Laurier University Press, 2006), 161; Mansukhani, *Indian Classical Music and Sikh Kirtan*, foreword.

2   See Bhai Charan Singh, *Sri Guru Granth Bani Biaura* (Khalsa Tract Society, 1902), and Prem Singh, *Gurmat Sangeet Ratan Bhandar* (Chief Khalsa Diwan, 1922).

3   Virinder S. Kalra, *Sacred and Secular Musics: A Postcolonial Approach* (Bloomsbury, 2015), 69–70, 76–82.

4   Bob van der Linden, *Music and Empire in Britain and India: Identity, Internationalism, and Cross-Cultural Communication* (Palgrave Macmillan, 2013), 129–55.

5   Bhai Baldeep Singh, "Memory and Pedagogy of Gurbāṇī Saṅgīta: An Autoethnographic Udāsī," *Sikh Formations: Religion, Culture, Theory* 15, nos. 1–2 (2019): 112. See also Bhai Baldeep Singh, "What Is Kīrtan? Observations, Interventions and Personal Reflections," *Sikh Formations: Religion, Culture, Theory* 7, no. 3 (2011): 245–95; and Francesca Cassio, "Singing the Scripture: Sikh Kīrtan in Literature, Practices, and Musicological Studies," in *The Sikh World*, ed. Pashaura Singh and Arvind-Pal Singh Mandair (Routledge, 2023), 313–27, 324–25.

6   For a helpful overview of the different strands, see Gibb Schreffler, "Music," *Brill's Encyclopedia of Sikhism*, vol. 2, ed. Knut A. Jacobsen, Anshu Malhotra, Kristina Myrvold, and Eleanor Nesbitt (Brill, 2025), 175–86.

7   Parminder Bhachu, *Movers and Makers: Uncertainty, Resilience, and Migrant Creativity in Worlds of Flux* (Routledge, 2021), 16; Amarjit Chandan, *Gopal Singh Chandan: A Short Biography and Memoirs* (Punjab Centre for Migration Studies Publication, 2004), 12.

8   Bhachu, *Movers and Makers*, 32.

9   Chandan, *Gopal Singh Chandan*, 25, 22.

10 See Gurminder K. Bhogal, "Listening to Female Voices in Sikh Kirtan," *Sikh Formations: Religion, Culture, Theory* 13, nos. 1–2 (2017): 48–77; and The Sikh Gramophone Collection (2023), https://sikhgram.com.

11 I discuss *filmi shabad* in "Listening to Female Voices in Sikh Kirtan," 61–66.

12 I thank Bhai Nirmal Singh Khalsa (Pipli Wale) for bringing Kesar Singh Narula to my attention. Narula is the father of the famous Bollywood singer Jaspinder Narula. See Gulzar Singh Sokhi, *Sangeet Di Duniya Da Dharung [Dhruv] Tara Kesar Singh Narula* (Sangam Publications, 2010).

13 Kimani Gecau, "Popular Song and Social Change in Kenya," *Media, Culture and Society* 17, no. 4 (1995): 561–62.

14 I am grateful to Amardev Singh of Kirtansewa.net for this information. See also Navtej K. Purewal and Harjinder S. Lallie, "Sikh Kirtan in the Diaspora: Identity, Innovation, and Revivalism," in *The Sikh Diaspora: Theory, Agency, and Experience*, ed. Michael Hawley (Brill, 2013), 385–90.

15 Bhai Raghbir Singh Diwana, personal communications with author, December 2021 and January 2022.

16 Scott L. Marcus, "On Cassette Rather Than Live: Religious Music in India Today," in *Media and the Transformation of Religion in South Asia*, ed.

Lawrence Babb and Susan Wadley (University of Pennsylvania Press, 1995), 179.

17 Bhai Vir Singh, "Ragi, Dhaadhi te Giani," *Khalsa Samachar* (1906; repr., *Amrit Kirtan* [June 1989]), 4–5, 6. Citations refer to the *Amrit Kirtan* edition.

18 Bhai Kultar Singh, personal interview with author, August 2023.

19 On this topic, see Verne Dusenbery, "Millennial Sikhs of the Diaspora Come of Age," *Sikh Formations: Religion, Culture, Theory* 14, nos. 3–4 (2018): 252–59; and Charles Townsend, "Sikh Millennials of the 'Kirtan Generation' in the Making of an 'American Sikhism,'" *Sikh Formations: Religion, Culture, Theory* 14, nos. 3–4 (2018): 424–34.

20 Harman Khurana discusses challenges faced by Sikh women in *kirtan*: "Sikh Women *Kirtaniyas*: Singing for Equality," PARI Education, November 2, 2022, https://pari.education/articles/sikh-women-kirtaniyas-singing-for-equality/.

21 Not all participants are visible in this photo—I base these numbers on my memory of this workshop.

22 See Gaavani.com. Joy Ashford writes about the Dallas *kirtan darbar*: "D-FW Concerts to Feature Sikh Women Singing Religious Scriptures," January 11, 2024, https://www.dallasnews.com/news/faith/2024/01/11/d-fw-concerts-to-feature-sikh-women-singing-religious-scriptures/. See also Vidya Pradhan, "Raag Kirtan—Songs of the Divine," September 25, 2018, https://www.sikhfoundation.org/raag-kirtan-songs-of-the-divine/.

23 Michael Nijhawan, *Dhadi Darbar: Religion, Violence, and the Performance of Sikh History* (Oxford University Press, 2006).

24 "The Invisible Divine 8," Kirtaniye: A Festival of Women's Voices in Gurbani Sangeet, January 17, 2020, posted May 31, 2020, by Asli Music, https://www.youtube.com/watch?v=pifEULBSqlo.

25 Michael Nijhawan, "From Divine Bliss to Ardent Passion: Exploring Sikh Religious Aesthetics Through the Ḍhāḍī Genre," *History of Religions* 42, no. 4 (2003): 360–63.

26 Bhai Vir Singh, "Ragi, Dhaadhi te Giani," 4. His point is that *dhaadhi* traditionally sang *vār* and told stories in the evening after *Rehras Sahib* (evening prayer) had been recited (5). Thus, *ragi*, *giani*, and *dhaadhi* served distinct roles.

27 This comment does not detract from master players of *chimta*, like Arif Lohar.

28 Inderjit Kaur studies different labels for *kirtan*: Inderjit Kaur, "Sikh Shabad Kīrtan and Gurmat Sangīt: What's in the Name?" *Journal of Punjab Studies* 18, nos. 1–2 (2011): 251–78.

29 See, for example, "Jathedar Suba Sandeep Singh," posted by Sri Bhaini Sahib, May 25, 2019, YouTube, https://www.youtube.com/watch?v=YTgO4P3-vrM&t=391s.

30   In **video ex. 1.3**, Bhai Baljit Singh mentions the vocal traditions of *dhurpad, dhammar, swaariya, partāl, chaturang, horian,* and *guldasta.* On *dhurpad*, see Bhai Baldeep Singh, "Memory and Pedagogy of Gurbāṇī Saṅgīta."

31   See Dya Singh, World Music Group, 2020, https://www.dyasingh.com; and Snatam Kaur, 2024, https://www.snatamkaur.com.

32   Linden, *Music and Empire in Britain and India*, 132.

33   Pashaura Singh, *Life and Work of Guru Arjan: History, Memory, and Biography in the Sikh Tradition* (Oxford University Press, 2006), 79–80.

34   *SGGS* 849-5.

35   *SGGS* 83-2, 311-12. See also 1087-6 for *rāg Kedara* evoking love for the divine word.

36   *SGGS* 1283-4, 1285-16, 1423-17/18.

37   Valuable doctoral dissertations about *kirtan* have been completed in recent decades by Janice Faye Protopapas, "Sikh Śabad Kīrtan as a Musical Construction of Memory" (PhD diss., University of Maryland, 2011); Nirinjan Kaur Khalsa, "The Renaissance of Sikh Devotional Music Memory, Identity, Orthopraxy" (PhD diss. University of Michigan, 2014); Wai Chung Li, "The Sikh Gurmat Saṅgīt Revival in Post-Partition India" (PhD diss., University of Texas at Austin, 2015); Charles Michael Townsend, "Music in the Gurus' View: Sikh Religious Music, Memory, and the Performance of Sikhism in America" (PhD diss., University of California, Riverside, 2015); Inderjit Kaur, "When 'Unheard Sound' (Re)Sounds: Affective Listening, Ethical Affects, and Embodied Experience in Sikh Sabad Kīrtan" (PhD diss., University of California, Berkeley, 2016); and Kirit James Singh, "Sikh Patronage of Hindustani and Śabad Kīrtan in Colonial Punjab, 1857–1947" (PhD diss., SOAS University of London, 2023), to name a few.

38   For a recent companion study along these lines, see Joginder Singh Talwara, *Sri Guru Granth Sahib Bodh: Bani Beora*, ed. Bhai Joginder Singh Talwara (Singh Brothers, 2004). This volume combines original insights with information drawn from leading scholarship of the time, including Kahn Singh Nabha's encyclopedia, *Gur Shabad Ratanakar Mahankosh* (Sudarshan Press, 1930).

39   See Bhai Vir Singh, "Ragi, Dhaadhi te Giani," 4.

40   Rishpal Singh mentions Sundar Singh's *Harmonium Kirtan Sikhiya* (1913) as a significant early publication in addition to Bhai Sahib Singh's "Raag Mala Prabodh" (unknown date). See Rishpal Singh, "Historical Development of Gurmat Sangeet Publications," *Research Review International Journal of Multidisciplinary* (2018): 83.

41   Bhai Charan Singh, *Gurmat Sangeet: Par Hun Tak Mili Khoj* (Central Khalsa Yatimkhana, 2008).

42   Rishpal Singh, "Historical Development of Gurmat Sangeet Publications," 83.

43 Rishpal Singh, "Historical Development of Gurmat Sangeet Publications," 84.
44 Ajit Singh Paintal, "Kirtan: Sikh Devotional Music; The Contribution of Ragis and Rababis," *Sikh Review* 45, no. 11 (1997): 34–39; and "Tradition of Gurbani Kirtan," *Studies in Sikhism and Comparative Religion* 20, no. 2 (2001): 102–10.
45 Bhai Avtar Singh's son, Bhai Kultar Singh, and their close relative, Bhai Baldeep Singh, continue to play a vital role in sharing the depth of their contributions to *Gurmat Sangeet* through pedagogy and *kirtan* (Bhai Kultar Singh) and instrument-making, research, and performance (Bhai Baldeep Singh).
46 Arvind-Pal Singh Mandair, *Religion and the Specter of the West: Sikhism, India, Postcoloniality and the Politics of Translation* (Columbia University Press, 2009), 5, 313, 314.
47 Gurinder Singh Mann, *The Making of Sikh Scripture* (Oxford University Press, 2001), 87–88.
48 A conference held at Punjabi University (Patiala) in October 2024 was dedicated to this topic: "Hermeneutics of Divine Soundscapes: Decoding the Musical Signatures of Sri Guru Granth Sahib."

CHAPTER 1

1 Zachary Wallmark's discussion of a covert subvocalization is apt given the similarity between what I describe here and an "interior rehearsal of the voice, a form of motor imagery in which musical sound (pitches, rhythmic patterns, inflections, and timbre) is traced out by the voice." See Zachary Wallmark, *Nothing but Noise: Timbre and Musical Meaning at the Edge* (Oxford University Press, 2022), 39.
2 Raman P. Sinha argues that the tradition of *rāgakāvya* goes back at least to the third century (Sinha, "Poetry in Ragas or Ragas in Poetry? Studies in the Concept of Poetic Communication," in *Text and Tradition in Early Modern North India*, ed. Tyler Williams, Anshu Malhotra, and John Stratton Hawley [Oxford University Press, 2018], 130).
3 Nikky-Guninder Kaur Singh, *The Feminine Principle in the Sikh Vision of the Transcendent* (Cambridge University Press, 1993), 47.
4 For the sake of inclusivity, my study observes sixty-two *rāg*.
5 See Pashaura Singh, *The Guru Granth Sahib: Canon, Meaning and Authority* (Oxford University Press, 2000), 144.
6 *SGGS* 176-14.
7 Bhai Gurdas, *Bhai Gurdas: Life and Compositions*, vol. 1, trans. Ujagar Singh Bawa (Washington Sikh Center, 2002), 392–93.
8 Gobind Singh Mansukhani, "A Survey of the Poetry and Music of Sri Guru Ram Das," *Journal of Sikh Studies* 11, no. 2 (1984): 77.

9   Jack Stratton Hawley argues that music is important to Sur Das's vision of worship because it contributes to the "mnemonic powers of singing," even as these songs aid remembrance of the divine name (*nām simran*) and function to shape "ethical life" (Hawley, "The Music in Faith and Morality," *Journal of the American Academy of Religion* 52, no. 2 [1984]: 247, 251). See also Eben Graves, "The Marketplace of Devotional Song: Cultural Economies of Exchange in Bengali Padāvalī-Kīrtan," *Ethnomusicology* 61, no. 1 (2017): 52–86; Richard Widdess, *Dāphā: Sacred Singing in a South Asian City: Music, Meaning and Performance in Bhaktapur, Nepal* (Ashgate, 2013); and Anna Schultz, *Singing a Hindu Nation: Marathi Devotional Performance and Nationalism* (Oxford University Press, 2013). Michael Nijhawan also observes the "clear boundary between the pleasure from listening to secular poetry (or music) and the religious aesthetics evoked through listening to the hymns of the Adi Granth," (Nijhawan, *Dhadi Darbar: Religion, Violence, and the Performance of Sikh History* [Oxford University Press, 2006], 51).
10 Barbara A. Holdrege, *Bhakti and Embodiment: Fashioning Divine Bodies and Devotional Bodies in Krsna Bhakti* (Routledge, 2015), 86–88.
11 Kathleen Marie Higgins, "An Alchemy of Emotion: Rasa and Aesthetic Breakthroughs," *Journal of Aesthetics and Art Criticism* 65, no. 1 (2007): 43–44, 50.
12 It is beyond the scope of my book to examine the textual evolution of *SGGS*, especially since access to manuscripts remains heavily restricted. For an accessible discussion, see Pashaura Singh, "The Guru Granth Sahib," in *The Oxford Handbook of Sikh Studies*, ed. Pashaura Singh and Louis Fenech (Oxford University Press, 2014), 125–35; Jeevan Deol, "Text and Lineage in Early Sikh History: Issues in the Study of the Adi Granth," *Bulletin of the School of Oriental and African Studies* 64, no. 1 (2001): 34–58; and Gurinder Singh Mann, *The Goindval Pothis: The Earliest Extant Source of the Sikh Canon* (Harvard University Press, 1997) and *The Making of Sikh Scripture* (Oxford University Press, 2001).
13 It is important to note that the Namdhari Sikh community believes in a living succession of gurus from the time of Guru Gobind Singh.
14 Pashaura Singh, "The Guru Granth Sahib," 126.
15 Swāmī Prajnānandā, *A Historical Study of Indian Music* (Calcutta Oriental Press, 1965), 18–19. Linda Hess mentions how the "old Bengali *pads* of the Buddhist Siddhas (ca. eleventh and twelfth centuries) and the *Gorakh-bānī* (ca. eleventh century)" are organized by *rāg* (Hess, "Three Kabir Collections: A Comparative Study," in *The Sants: Studies in a Devotional Tradition of India*, ed. Karine Schomer and W. H. McLeod [Motilal Banarsidass, 1987], 116).
16 Jayadeva, *Gitagovinda: Love Song of the Dark Lord*, trans. Barbara Stoler Miller (Columbia University Press, 1977). An eighteenth-century copy of *Gita Govinda* on palm leaf is held at the National Museum, New Delhi

(object no. 57.46), and can be seen here: "Manuscripts Collection," National Museum, New Delhi, http://www.nationalmuseumindia.gov.in/en/collections/index/11. Another eighteenth-century version can be seen here: "Gita Govinda, Song of the Cowherd Manuscript," Los Angeles County Museum of Art, https://artsandculture.google.com/asset/gita-govinda-song-of-the-cowherd-manuscript-unknown/XAEUxe2Kyuwo5Q?hl=en. Manuscripts held at the Orissa State Museum are listed here: http://magazines.odisha.gov.in/Orissareview/may-2007/engpdf/Page20-23.pdf.

17 The five parts of a *prabandha* are *udgraha*, *melapaka*, *dhruvā*, *sanchāri*, and *abhōga*. *Prabandha* is now regarded as a precursor to the vocal form of *dhurpad*. See also Jayadeva, *Gitagovinda*, 10.

18 See Jayadeva, *Gitagovinda*, 12; and Arvind Mangrulker, "Gīta-Govinda Structure, Technique and Substance," *Annals of the Bhandarkar Oriental Research Institute* 64, nos. 1–4 (1983): 151. Edwin Gerow suggests that *rāg* and *tāl* information may have been added later (Gerow, "Jayadeva's Poetics and the Classical Style," *Journal of the American Oriental Society* 109, no. 4 [1989]: 536).

19 Mangrulker, "Gīta-Govinda Structure, Technique and Substance," 151.

20 Sinha, "Poetry in Ragas or Ragas in Poetry?," 135.

21 Winand M. Callewaert, "Singers' Repertoires in Western India," in *Devotional Literature in South Asia: Current Research, 1985–1988*, ed. R. S. McGregor (Cambridge University Press, 1992), 29.

22 In his study of textual corruption, Imre Bhanga notes that Kabir's poems have *rāg* attributions in the Fatehpur manuscript but that this is not always the case in other collections (Bhanga, "Kabīr Reconstructed," *Acta Orientalia Academiae Scientiarum Hungaricae* 63, no 3 [2010]: 252).

23 I have not seen this source firsthand and am relying on the collector's information as to its provenance. This manuscript is available at http://indianmanuscripts.com/scriptviewer-book.php?show=4178.

24 Gurinder Singh Mann, "Scriptures and the Nature of Authority: The Case of the Guru Granth in Sikh Tradition," in *Theorizing Scriptures: New Critical Orientations to a Cultural Phenomenon*, ed. Vincent L. Wimbush (Rutgers University Press, 2008), 51.

25 See Bhai Gurdas's mention of the singer Pandha and the scribe Bula at the court of Guru Amardas. Vār 11, Pauri 16, p. 8, https://www.searchgurbani.com/bhai-gurdas-vaaran/vaar/11/pauri/16/line/1.

26 Christian Novetzke, "Note to Self: What Marathi Kirtankars' Notebooks Suggest About Literacy, Performance, and the Travelling Performer in Pre-Colonial Maharashtra," in *Tellings and Texts Music, Literature and Performance in North India*, ed. Francesca Orsini and Katherine Butler Schofield (Open Book Publishers, 2015), 170.

27 Callewaert, "Singers' Repertoires in Western India," 30.

28 Guru Arjan's description of *pandits* and wandering *jogi* (renunciants) as

singing *"geet, nād, kirtan"* indicates his awareness of the different types of devotional music of his time (*SGGS* 216-18). For a detailed study of *bhagat bani*, see Pashaura Singh, *The Bhagats of the Guru Granth Sahib: Sikh Self-Definition and the Bhagat Bani* (Oxford University Press, 2023).

29 Parasnath Tiwari, *Kabir Granthavali* (Bansal Press, 1961), 73, 76.
30 Pashaura Singh, *The Guru Granth Sahib*, 33. Singh also reminds readers that *rāg Sri* is placed first because it was highly venerated by Guru Amardas (*SGGS* 83), among other reasons (139). See also Gian Singh Abbotabad, *Gurbani Sangeet*, vol. 1 (Shiromani Gurudwara Prabandhak Committee, 1961), 3.
31 Gurnam Singh, "Sikh Music," in *The Oxford Handbook of Sikh Studies*, ed. Pashaura Singh and Louis Fenech (Oxford University Press, 2014), 401.
32 Mukund Lath, "An Enquiry into Rāga-Time Association," in *Aspects of Indian Music: A Collection of Essays*, ed. Sumati Mutatkar (Sangeet Natak Akademi, 1987), 113-19.
33 The information about *kirtan chaunki* in **figure 1.4** is based on several works by Pashaura Singh. See Pashaura Singh, "Musical Chaunkis at the Darbar Sahib: History, Aesthetics, and Time," in *Sikhism in Global Context*, ed. Singh (Oxford University Press, 2011), 102-29; *Life and Work of Guru Arjan: History, Memory, and Biography in the Sikh Tradition* (Oxford University Press, 2006), 150; and *The Guru Granth Sahib*, 141-45.
34 Katherine Butler Schofield, *Music and Musicians in Late Mughal India: Histories of the Ephemeral, 1748-1858* (Cambridge University Press, 2023), 41.
35 *SGGS* 1087-6, 83-2, 311-12.
36 *SGGS* 1285-13, 450-12.
37 *SGGS* 368-3/4.
38 Mangesh Ramakrishna Telang, *Nârada, Sangîta Makaranda* (Baroda, 1920), 15. This is from the section on music (sec. 3, l. 19).
39 *SGGS* 178-6/7.
40 Sinha, "Poetry in Ragas or Ragas in Poetry?," 137.
41 Joginder Singh Talwara explores the etymology and possible meanings of the term *mahala* (Talwara, *Sri Guru Granth Sahib Bodh: Bani Beora*, ed. Bhai Joginder Singh Talwara [Singh Brothers, 2004], 56-57). Today, *mahala* is unequivocally understood to indicate authorship. *Mahala* 1 refers to Guru Nanak, *mahala* 2 to Guru Angad, and so on. Pashaura Singh speculates on the meaning of this term in *The Guru Granth Sahib* (103). See also "mahalu" in Christopher Shackle, *A Guru Nanak Glossary* (School of Oriental and African Studies, 1995), 230; and Gurinder Singh Mann, *The Making of Sikh Scripture*, 137n5.
42 A useful discussion of the term *rahao* can be found on the website for the Guru Granth Sahib Project: https://app.gurugranthsahib.io/tggsp/english/SignificantTermsDetail/Rahau.
43 Tara Singh, *Partaal Gayiki* (Gurmat Sangeet Prakashan, n.d.), xiv. In recent times, the vocal genre of *thumri* incorporates *partāl* to

characterize a folk style. At a concert in Boston on April 29, 2023, Kaushiki Chakraborty performed a *thumri* that combined *keherva tāl* and *dadra tāl* in a composition taught to her by Shubha Mudgal.

44 Wai Chung Li lists these fifty-five *partāl* in "The Sikh Gurmat Sangīt Revival in Post-Partition India" (PhD diss., University of Texas at Austin, 2015), 219–20.

45 Singh, *Partaal Gayiki*, xiv.

46 Pashaura Singh conceives of *partāl* as a feature of the *prabandha* style of singing, which was further developed in *dhurpad* (*The Guru Granth Sahib*, 136).

47 Singh, *Partaal Gayiki*, xiv.

48 Schofield, *Music and Musicians in Late Mughal India*, 9.

49 Bhai Baldeep Singh, "The Tradition of Kirtan and Its Discipline," in *Perspectives on Sikhism*, ed. Prithipal Singh Kapur and Dharam Singh (Punjabi University Publication Bureau, 2001), 158–59.

50 In this recording Bhai Avtar Singh offers a valuable commentary on this *shabad* in Punjabi: https://play.sikhnet.com/search?q=Mohan%20Neend%20Na.

51 See also Pashaura Singh, *The Guru Granth Sahib*, 144.

52 Talwara explains that Guru Nanak composed the twenty-four stanzas and forty-five of the sixty *salok* and that Guru Angad composed the other fifteen. *Chhant* and *pade* by Guru Ramdas are also incorporated (*Sri Guru Granth Sahib Bodh*, 30).

53 A helpful study of *Aasa ki vār* can be found on the website for the Guru Granth Sahib Project: https://app.gurugranthsahib.io/tggsp/english/Bani/db/AKV. On *Aasa ki vār*, see Janice Protopapas, "Kīrtan Chauṇkī: Affect, Embodiment and Memory," *Sikh Formations: Religion, Culture, Theory* 7, no. 3 (2011): 339–64; and Pashaura Singh, "The Reverberation of the Sacred Gurbani's Vibrations at the Darbar Sahib: The Issue of Its Television Broadcasting," *Religions* 15 (2024): 6–7, https://www.mdpi.com/2077-1444/15/4/395. There are several narratives about how King Asraj was injured in Punjabi culture.

54 On *pehar*, see Pashaura Singh, "The Reverberation of the Sacred Gurbani's Vibrations at the Darbar Sahib," 3–4.

55 For specific information, see "Travel Guide for Golden Temple Amritsar," https://www.goldentempleamritsar.org/famous-temples-in-india/amritsar/golden-temple/daily-routine.

56 "Aasa Ki Vār Listening Guide," https://docs.google.com/document/d/1B7Bks-gu_qcU0XLCJn4v54EvCx7JqEjFxH53fz3KVUI/edit?tab=t.0.

57 A helpful overview of *Aasa ki vār* is available at the Guru Granth Sahib Project website: https://gurugranthsahib.io/bani/introduction/104/Introduction.

58 Gurnam Singh, *Sikh Sacred Music: Gurmat Sangeet* (Gurmat Prakashan, 2008), 13.

59 There is variation in how *ghar* is indicated in titles, and thus the data

60 See "Bhai Lal Ji," posted by Kirtan Sewa, January 4, 2013, YoutTube, https://www.youtube.com/watch?v=Y2R32ANfgQ8&t=17s, at 04:00 (Punjabi).

61 On the topic of *ghar* and meter, see Gobind Singh Mansukhani, *Indian Classical Music and Sikh Kirtan* (Oxford University Press and IBH, 1982), 71.

62 Charan Kamal Singh, *Ghar in Gurbani: Reading and Singing Gurbani— The Guru's Way* (Notion Press, 2019).

63 Bhai Teja Singh, *Shabdarath Siri Guru Granth Sahib Ji*, vol. 1 (Shiromani Gurudwara Prabandhak Committee, 2009), 14; Bhai Vir Singh, *Sri Guru Granth Sahib Kosh* (Singh Brothers, 1995), 234; Kahn Singh Nabha, *Gur Shabad Ratanakar Mahankosh* (Sudarshan Press, 1930); Lewis Rowell, *Music and Musical Thought in Early India* (University of Chicago Press, 1992), 170, 192; Vikram Singh, "Gurbani Vich Ghar Prabandh," in *Gurmat Sangeet: Adhunik Pripekh* (Singh Brothers, 2016), 36–56.

64 On *ghar* as a *rāg* variant, see Kerry Brown, *Sikh Art and Literature* (Routledge, 1999), 200–201; Winand Callewaert, *Sri Guru Granth Sahib with Complete Index, Part II* (Motilal Banarsidass, 1996), 20; and Inderjit Kaur, "Discovering the Meaning of *Ghar* in *Shabad* Headings of Guru Granth Sahib," Sikh Music Heritage Institute, 2008, http://www.sikhmusicheritage.org. On *ghar* as microtonality, see Surinder Singh, "What Is 'Sikh Music' and Raags? Dr. Pashaura Singh and Professor Surinder Singh interview," posted by Raj Academy, March 23, 2021, YouTube, https://www.youtube.com/watch?v=A3ppcAjfHXw, at 31:00. Persian theory is cited in Gurnam Singh, *Sikh Musicology: Sri Guru Granth Sahib and Hymns of the Human Spirit* (Kanishka, 2009), 9; and Bhai Teja Singh, *Shabdarath Siri Guru Granth Sahib Ji*.

65 See also Deol, "Text and Lineage in Early Sikh History," 44; Pashaura Singh, *The Guru Granth Sahib*, 144–45; and Mann, *The Making of Sikh Scripture*, 91.

66 Pashaura Singh, "The Guru Granth Sahib," 127. See the entry for Bhai Gurdas in Harbans Singh and Dharam Singh, eds., *The Concise Encyclopaedia of Sikhism* (Punjabi University, 2013), 247–48.

67 I thank Linda Hess and Winand Callewaert for sharing their expertise on this topic with me.

68 Jayadeva, *Gitagovinda*, 162.

69 On the basis of *Mahan Kosh*, Talwara proposes that this term refers to a similarity of melody (*Sri Guru Granth Sahib Bodh*, 34). See also the relevant entry in Nabha's *Mahan Kosh*.

70 http://www.gurugranthdarpan.net/0203.html.

71 Ajit Singh Paintal, "Sikh Devotional Music: Its Main Traditions," *Quarterly Journal* 11, no. 2 (1982): 20.

72 *SGGS* 159-2.
73 *SGGS* 884-12.
74 *SGGS* 781-1.
75 *SGGS* 107-18, 177-9, 119-7.
76 *SGGS* 1226-17.
77 *SGGS* 1234-4.
78 *SGGS* 1364-11.
79 *SGGS* 1163-11, 1362-18.
80 *SGGS* 674-2, 610-11, 1083-5, 1096-3, 1296-13, 1296-17, 1309-12.
81 *SGGS* 7-7, 1290-10.
82 *SGGS* 2-8.
83 *SGGS* 401-12.
84 Bethany Lowe, "'In the Heard, Only the Heard . . .': Music, Consciousness, and Buddhism," in *Music and Consciousness: Philosophical, Psychological, and Cultural Perspectives*, ed. David Clarke and Eric Clarke (Oxford University Press, 2011), 115. Later in this paragraph Lowe provides a wonderful analogue to the kind of Sikh listening experience that I capture: A "'pure' experience of listening, where the auditory consciousness is far more active than the so-called mental consciousness, can provide a rich and full experience without our having to take leave of our senses, so to speak."
85 Bhai Avtar Singh and Bhai Gurcharan Singh, *Gurbani Sangeet Prachin Reet Ratnavali*, vol. 1 (Punjabi University, 1979), xix.
86 In contrast, Anna Morcom explains that interludes in Bollywood are "substantially motived by narrative needs" (Morcom, *Hindi Film Songs and the Cinema* [Ashgate, 2007], 65n8).
87 *SGGS* 110-1, 125-19, 88-5, 552-6, 1259-15.
88 *SGGS* 135-19.
89 *SGGS* 718-2.
90 *SGGS* 614-11, 644-15.
91 *SGGS* 857-9.
92 *SGGS* 610-9, 613-6.
93 *SGGS* 1255-6.
94 *SGGS* 1028-9.
95 *SGGS* 246-6, 638-16, 286-19, 474-10.
96 *SGGS* 119-13.
97 *SGGS* 506-12.
98 *SGGS* 176-14, 161-15.
99 *SGGS* 387-9.
100 *SGGS* 741-15.
101 *SGGS* 822-17.
102 *SGGS* 22-5, 22-13, 29-14, 52-12, 158-11.
103 *SGGS* 95-1, 179-18, 191-2, 197-4, 201-11, 253-7, 283-8 (*Sukhmani*), 319-12. See also 114-19, 115-19, 129-14, 362-10, 368-13, 379-2, 382-19.

104. *SGGS* 105-13.
105. *SGGS* 642-7.
106. *SGGS* 303-7, 668-17.
107. See, for example, *SGGS* 542-6.
108. *SGGS* 682-10.
109. *SGGS* 807-4.
110. *SGGS* 115-9. Bhai Gurdas, *Vār* 14, Pauri 18, 5. See https://www.searchgurbani.com/bhai-gurdas-vaaran/vaar/14/pauri/13/line/1.
111. *SGGS* 1182-10.
112. *SGGS* 108-1.
113. See, for example, *SGGS* 44-13, 46-9, 48-17, 236-13. For *kirtan* as food, see 496-6.
114. *SGGS* 1219-12.
115. *SGGS* 401-12.
116. *SGGS* 671-11.
117. *SGGS* 236-4.
118. *SGGS* 893-19.
119. *SGGS* 106-19.
120. *SGGS* 178-6.
121. *SGGS* 199-3, 385-10.
122. *SGGS* 400-18, 962-8.
123. *SGGS* 715-10, 671-11.
124. *SGGS* 520-4, 200-8.
125. *SGGS* 958-6.
126. *SGGS* 1285-16.
127. *SGGS* 602-13/14.
128. *SGGS* 373-10. The significance of the lotus in *Gurbani* is discussed in chapter 3.
129. *SGGS* 171-14.
130. *SGGS* 1204-14.
131. *SGGS* 1180-14/15.
132. *SGGS* 416-4.
133. *SGGS* 453-15.
134. *SGGS* 190-5/6.
135. *SGGS* 1300-11, 671-14.
136. *SGGS* 683-2.
137. *SGGS* 382-19, 1075-19.
138. See Gurminder K. Bhogal "Listening to Nature and the Cosmos Through *Gurbani*," forthcoming in the *Routledge Handbook on Punjab Studies*, ed. Pritam Singh and Meena Dhanda (New York: Routledge, 2026).
139. Ana María Ochoa Gautier, "Acoustic Multinaturalism, the Value of Nature, and the Nature of Music in Ecomusicology," *boundary 2* 43, no. 1 (2016): 138.
140. Andrew Hicks, "Mysticism's Musical Modalities: Philosophies of

Audition in Medieval Persian Sufism," in *The Music Road: Coherence and Diversity in Music from the Mediterranean to India*, ed. Reinhard Strohm (Oxford University Press, 2019), 114–15.

141 *SGGS* 2-8.
142 *SGGS* 2-16.
143 I provide an abbreviated summary of these stanzas. For a more exact translation, see Nikky-Guninder Kaur Singh, *Janamsakhi: Paintings of Guru Nanak in Early Sikh Art* (Roli Books, 2023), 6-7.
144 *SGGS* 455-15.
145 See Nikky-Guninder Kaur Singh, *Janamsakhi*, 15–16. In *rāg* Bihagra Guru Ramdas also speaks to wind, water, and fire singing continuous praises of Hari, the divine one (*SGGS* 540-8).
146 *SGGS* 4-15.
147 *SGGS* 2-17, 1367-4.
148 Ana María Ochoa Gautier, *Aurality: Listening and Knowledge in Nineteenth-Century Colombia* (Duke University Press, 2014), 3.
149 Rebecca Dirksen, "Haiti, Singing for the Land, Sea, and Sky: Cultivating Ecological Metaphysics and Environmental Awareness Through Music," in *Sounds, Ecologies, Musics*, ed. Aaron S. Allen and Jeff Todd Titon (Oxford University Press, 2023), 125–26.
150 Nikky-Guninder Kaur Singh, *Janamsakhi*, 7.
151 Holly Watkins, *Musical Vitalities: Ventures in a Biotic Aesthetics of Music* (University of Chicago Press, 2018), 3.
152 *SGGS* 524-7.
153 *SGGS* 60-2.
154 *SGGS* 323-16.
155 *SGGS* 455-4.
156 *SGGS* 693-12.
157 Sukhbir Singh Kapoor and Mohinder Kaur Kapoor, *The Birds and Guru Granth Sahib* (self-published, 2006), 10. He mentions twelve birds but lists only eleven. The topic of the bird has been pivotal in ecomusicology. See Steven Feld, *Sound and Sentiment: Birds, Weeping, Poetics, and Song in Kaluli Expression* (University of Pennsylvania Press, 1982); and Helena Simonett, "Of Human and Non-Human Birds: Indigenous Music Making and Sentient Ecology in Northwestern Mexico," in *Current Directions in Ecomusicology: Music, Culture, Nature*, ed. Aaron S. Allen and Kevin Dawe (Routledge, 2015), 107–16. Aaron S. Allen and Kevin Dawe provide a useful survey of research about birdsong in the adjacent fields of ecomusicology, bioacoustics, biomusic, and ethnomusicology (Allen and Dawe, "Ecomusicologies," in *Current Directions in Ecomusicology*, ed. Allen and Dawes, 18–19).
158 Kapoor notes that the *saaring*, *chaatrik*, *babiha*, and *papiha* all refer to the same type of species (*Accipiter virgatus*, or northern goshawk); see Kapoor and Kapoor, *The Birds and Guru Granth Sahib*, 16. See also

Eleanor Nesbitt, "Sparrows and Lions: Fauna in Sikh Imagery, Symbolism and Ethics," *Religions of South Asia* 7, nos. 1–3 (2013): 88.

159   *SGGS* 1107-6.
160   *SGGS* 1114-1.
161   *SGGS* 1010-14.
162   Balbinder Singh Bhogal, "The Animal Sublime: Rethinking the Sikh Mystical Body," *Journal of the American Academy of Religion* 80, no. 4 (2012): 865, 867. Bhogal's major point is that the comparison of the human state with the animal state in *SGGS* is not derogatory, as it sometimes is within Western philosophy, but a means to elevate human consciousness to a state of the sublime.
163   Jagjit Singh Grewal, *Imagery in the Adi Granth* (Punjab Prakashan, 1986), 46.
164   *SGGS* 452-1, 96-17.
165   *SGGS* 454-6, 455-1, 100-13, 452-1.
166   *SGGS* 96-15.
167   *SGGS* 668-1.
168   *SGGS* 1107-6/8, 1108-17, 1273-8.
169   *SGGS* 1284-14.
170   *SGGS* 1107-6.
171   *SGGS* 1271-18, 455-4.
172   *SGGS* 1113-17.
173   *SGGS* 1209-19.
174   *SGGS* 1285-3.
175   *SGGS* 165-10.
176   *SGGS* 574-5.
177   Linda Hess, ed., *The Bijak of Kabir*, trans. Linda Hess and Sukhdeo Singh (Oxford University Press, 2002), 15, 181.
178   Grewal, *Imagery in the Adi Granth*, 6, 8.
179   Bhogal, "The Animal Sublime," 867.
180   *SGGS* 1283-2.
181   *SGGS* 1283-2/3.
182   Christopher Key Chapple, "India," in *Routledge Handbook of Religion and Ecology*, ed. Willis Jenkins, Mary Evelyn Tucker, and John Grim (Routledge, 2017), 179.

| CHAPTER 2

1   For a history of the harmonium, see Arthur W. J. G. Ord-Hume, *Harmonium: The History of the Reed Organ and Its Makers* (David and Charles, 1986). An earlier version of this chapter was published as "Tracking the Harmonium from Christian Missionary Hymns to Sikh *Kirtan*," *Yale Journal of Music and Religion* 8, no. 2 (2022).

2   See "AIR's Seminar on the Harmonium," *Sangeet Natak* 20 (April–June 1971): 5–57; and Matthew Rahaim, "That Ban(e) of Indian Music: Hearing Politics in the Harmonium," *Journal of Asian Studies* 70, no. 3 (2011): 657–82.

3   The absence of a written archive has made it difficult to trace a history of instruments associated with the Sikh courts. Although Allyn Miner mentions a nineteenth-century Urdu reference to a *rabab* inspired by Guru Nanak (Sadiq Ali Khan, *Sarmāya-i ʿishrat* or *Qānūn-i mūsiqī* [1875]), I have been unable to locate Persian or other sources that offer details about Sikh musical instruments other than fleeting mentions.

4   See "Esraj" and "Dilruba" in *The Oxford Encyclopaedia of the Music of India: Saṅgīt Mahābhāratī* (Oxford University Press, 2011).

5   See Kamaldeep Singh Brar, "Remove Harmonium from Golden Temple? Sikh Music Scholars Strike Differing Notes," *Indian Express*, May 23, 2022, https://indianexpress.com/article/cities/amritsar/remove-harmonium-from-golden-temple-sikh-music-scholars-strike-differing-notes-7930927/; and Rohit Pathania, "Harmonium Ban in Golden Temple Puts SGPC's Priorities into Question," *Swarajya*, May 29, 2022, https://swarajyamag.com/culture/ban-on-harmoniums-in-golden-temple-puts-sgpcs-priorities-into-question.

6   Arthur Henry Fox Strangways, *The Music of Hindostan* (Clarendon Press, 1914), 163, 16.

7   Philipp W. Stockhammer, "From Hybridity to Entanglement, from Essentialism to Practice," *Archaeological Review from Cambridge* 28, no. 1 (2013): 16–17.

8   Stockhammer, "From Hybridity to Entanglement," 17.

9   Cleveland Johnson, "The Origins of the 'Indian' Harmonium: Evidence from the Colonial Press and London Patent Office," *Journal of the American Musical Instrument Society* 44 (2018): 144–78.

10 Ananda K. Coomaraswamy, "Indian Music," *Hindustan Review* 17, no. 103 (1908): 260. He compares the *sruti* and tempered-interval harmonium, as well as the use of the harmonium in general, in his foreword to Ernest Clements, *Introduction to the Study of Indian Music* (Longmans, Green and Co., 1913), v–ix.

11 For a brief history of the reed organ, see Robert F. Gellerman, *The American Reed Organ and the Harmonium* (Vestal, 1996), 3–42. Origins of the free reed are discussed in Edward F. Rimbault, "Alexandre Père et Fils: The Great French Harmonium Makers," *Choir and Musical Record*, August 1, 1863 (the original article was printed in *The Illustrated Times*, June 6, 1863, 28); and Bigamudre Chaitanya Deva, "The Harmonium and Indian Music," *Journal of the Indian Musicological Society* 12, nos. 3–4 (1980): 45–48.

12 Strangways, *The Music of Hindostan*, 163.

13 Ian Woodfield, *English Musicians in the Age of Exploration* (Pendragon, 1995), 182.

14 See Victor Anand Coelho, "Music in New Worlds," in *The Cambridge History of Seventeenth-Century Music*, vol. 1, ed. Tim Carter and John Butt (Cambridge University Press, 2005), 97.
15 See Woodfield, *English Musicians in the Age of Exploration*, 182–83, 199. Emperor Akbar's son, Jahangir, was also an admirer of European keyboard instruments such as the virginal, clavichord, and harpsichord, as described by Woodfield (211–12). Gerry Farrell notes that Jahangir received a virginal in 1616 from King James (Farrell, "The Early Days of the Gramophone Industry in India: Historical, Social and Musical Perspectives," *British Journal of Ethnomusicology* 2 [1993]: 46).
16 Woodfield, *English Musicians in the Age of Exploration*, 241, 217.
17 Woodfield explains that at this time, "The English came to trade, to settle or to enslave but only rarely to convert" (*English Musicians in the Age of Exploration*, 283).
18 "The Punjab Mission was begun in 1851, soon after the annexation of the province to British India. The first station was Amritsar, the sacred city of the Sikhs; Kangra was occupied in 1854; Peshâwar, 1855; Múltan, 1856; Dera Ismail Khan, 1861; Kashmir, 1863; Bannu, 1864; Lahore, 1867; Pind Dadan Khan, 1876; Batála, 1878; Dera Ghazi Khan, 1879; Quetta, 1886. At Lahore, the capital of the province, the Divinity School was founded in 1870 by the late Rev. T. V. French." See "Punjab and Sindh Mission," *Proceedings of the Church Missionary Society for Africa and the East* (1893–94): 115. See also Tony Ballantyne, *Between Colonialism and Diaspora: Sikh Cultural Formations in an Imperial World* (Duke University Press, 2006).
19 Ashok D. Ranade purports that "Portuguese strongholds were located in Kerala, Maharashtra, Goa, Gujarat and to a certain extent, Bengal" (Ranade, *Essays in Indian Ethnomusicology* [Munshiram Manoharlal, 1998], 227–28). Anilkumar Belvadi makes the point that "the use of an organ or harmonium . . . was an adaptation that Hindustani (North Indian) music allowed more readily than the Carnātic, given that it used few fractional tones" (Belvadi, *Missionary Calculus: Americans in the Making of Sunday Schools in Victorian India* [Oxford University Press, 2019], 177). On the topic of European missionaries, see Owen White and J. P. Daughton, *In God's Empire: French Missionaries and the Modern World* (Oxford University Press, 2012), 283.
20 "Umritsur," *Christian Missionary Review* 2 (1866): 26.
21 "Missionary Itineration in the Punjab," *Church Missionary Intelligencer* (June 1865): 169.
22 "Missions to Mohammedans," *Church Missionary Intelligencer* (February 1877): 95.
23 "Music and Missions," *Encyclopedia of Missions: Descriptive, Historical, Biographical, Statistical* (1904): 517.
24 "The Power of Christian Song in Mission Work," *Missionary Review of the World* (July–December 1897): 526.

25. Charles Wentworth Dilke, *Greater Britain: A Record of Travel in English-Speaking Countries During 1866–1867* (Macmillan, 1872), 485.
26. Frank Vincent Jr., *Through and Through the Tropics: 30,000 Miles of Travel in Polynesia, Australasia, and India* (Harper and Brothers, 1882), 263. Bob van der Linden calls attention to an account by Charles Wilkins from 1781 that speaks to the use of drum and cymbals in *kirtan*; and a description by Max Arthur Macauliffe from 1881 that mentions the use of *sitar* and *sarangi* by Muslim musicians at Harmandir Sahib (Linden, *Music and Empire in Britain and India: Identity, Internationalism, and Cross-Cultural Communication* [Palgrave Macmillan, 2013], 129–30).
27. Belvadi, *Missionary Calculus*, 142–99.
28. Deva speaks to some of these innovations ("The Harmonium and Indian Music," 49–50). The production of high-quality instruments is also behind P. V. Subramaniam's defense of the harmonium in 1971 (Subramaniam, "The Harmonium in Light and Semi-Classical Music," *Sangeet Natak* 20 [1971]: 7–10). For a discussion of the development of the organ in China, see David Francis Urrows, *François Ravary SJ and a Sino-European Musical Culture in Nineteenth-Century Shanghai* (Cambridge Scholars Publishing, 2021).
29. Ranade makes a similar point in *Essays in Indian Ethnomusicology* (231). P. Sambamoorthy, "Harmonium and Karnatak Classical Music," in *AIR's Seminar on the Harmonium: Seminar Papers* (Sangeet Natak Akademi, 1971), 6.
30. Although her focus is not on the harmonium, Radha Kapuria's recent study of the relationship between *mirasi* and missionaries provides a counterpart to my discussion (Kapuria, *Music in Colonial Punjab: Courtesans, Bards, and Connoisseurs, 1800–1947* [Oxford University Press, 2023], 117–53).
31. See *The Freemason: A Weekly Journal of Freemasonry, Literature, Science, and Art* 3, no. 50 (February 19, 1870): 84.
32. *Musical Times*, March 1, 1871, 2.
33. See the *London and China Telegraph*, September 15, 1866, 499.
34. Agnes Giberne, *A Lady of England: The Life and Letters of Charlotte Maria Tucker* (Hodder and Stoughton, 1895), 295 (letter dated November 8, 1878).
35. *Church Missionary Gleaner* 10, no. 118 (October 1883): 113.
36. *Indian Female Evangelist* 6 (January 27, 1881): 69.
37. "Music in Missions," *Woman's Missionary Friend* 28, no. 10 (April 1987): 290. On "nautch," see James Kippen, *Gurudev's Drumming Legacy: Music, Theory and Nationalism in the Mrdang aur Tablā Vādanpaddhati of Gurudev Patwardhan* (Routledge, 2016), 10.
38. Rev. R. Hoskins, "Hindustani Music as an Evangelizing Agent," *Woman's Missionary Friend* 28, no. 11 (May 1897): 302.
39. "Music in Missions," *Woman's Missionary Friend* 28, no. 10 (April 1987), 290.

40 See Otto Waack, *Church and Mission in India: The History of the Jeypore Church and the Breklum Mission (1876–1914)* (SPCK, 1997), 385; and Monier Williams, *Modern India and the Indians* (Routledge, 2000), 31.

41 At a "pardah-ladies" party, we read of a public hall being transformed into a drawing room containing both a piano and a harmonium. See *Indian Education: A Monthly Record for India, Burma, and Ceylon* 1 (August 1902–July 1903): 401. See also Dennis G. Waring, *Manufacturing the Muse: Estey Organs and Consumer Culture in Victorian America* (Wesleyan University Press, 2002), 19–76; and Dianne Lawrence, *Genteel Women: Empire and Domestic Material Culture, 1840–1910* (Manchester University Press, 2012), 117–18.

42 An article documenting a visit to Ulwar (Alwar) by members of the British royal family provides insights on the role played by women who officiated at services on the harmonium. See *United Presbyterian Magazine*, March 1885, 128. See also a description of female missionaries in Amritsar in *India's Women: The Magazine of the Church of England Zenana Missionary Society* 14, no. 98 (August 1894): 382. On the Multan Harmonium School, see *Report on Public Instruction in the Punjab and Its Dependencies* (1902), 20.

43 *Monthly Supplement to the Day of Rest* (September 27, 1873): 94.

44 India's Ministry of Culture claims, "In 1875, Dwarkanath Ghose designed his version of the Indian hand-pumped harmonium in Calcutta." See Indian Culture, Government of India, "Harmonium," https://indianculture.gov.in/musical-instruments/sushir-vadya/harmonium.

45 Ranade, *Essays in Indian Ethnomusicology*, 231. "One of their [the girls'] chief amusements is to stand round the harmonium while one plays, and [others] sing these songs and hymns" (*The Indian Female Evangelist* 7, no. 45 [January 1883]: 38). A lap harmonium is shown in Gellerman, *The American Reed Organ and the Harmonium*, 16. A French hand-operated harmonium by Kasriel is seen in the National Museum of American History, "Kasriel Reed Organ [Harmonium]," https://americanhistory.si.edu/collections/search/object/nmah_606043. Another hand-operated harmonium, the *harmoniflûte*, is seen in The Met, "Harmoniflûte," https://www.metmuseum.org/art/collection/search/501771. Birgit Abels attributes the invention of the hand harmonium to the *harmoniflûte* and table organ (Abels, *The Harmonium in North Indian Music* [New Age Books, 2010], 27, 32). Johnson discusses the *harmoniflûte*, particularly as advertised by Harold & Co., as early as 1878 ("The Origins of the 'Indian' Harmonium," 161–77).

46 This has been documented in several places, but I refer the reader to Michael Kinnear, who observes that Dwarkanath Ghose established his piano tuning and instrument repair company in 1875, eventually bringing out a harmonium in 1887 (Kinnear, *The Gramophone Company's First Indian Recordings, 1899–1908* [Popular Prakashan, 1994], 35–36).

47. "A Punjabi City Service," *Indian Female Evangelist* 5, no. 35 (July 1880): 162.
48. "A Christian Hindu on the Prince's Visit," *Church Missionary Intelligencer and Record* (February 1, 1876): 304.
49. Rosemary Seton, *Western Daughters in Eastern Lands: British Missionary Work in Asia* (Praeger, 2013), 123.
50. See an account of Marchioness Ripon's visit to a school in Benaras in 1882 in "School Girls in India," *Indian Female Evangelist* 7, no. 46 (April 1883): 103. See also "The Alexandra Girls' School, Umritsur," *India's Women* 1, no. 3 (May–June 1881): 151; "A Sunday in the Christian Girls' School, Lahore," *Coral Missionary Magazine* (May 2, 1875); and *Coral Missionary Magazine* 19 (June 1877): 88.
51. Robert Needham Cust, *Pictures of Indian Life: Sketched with the Pen from 1852 to 1881* (Trübner and Co., 1881), 6.
52. "Here and There; or, How Shall We in England Best Forward the Work in India," *India's Women: The Magazine of the Church of England Zenana Missionary Society* (1882): 289.
53. *India's Women: The Magazine of the Church of England Zenana Missionary Society* 1, no. 4 (July–August 1881): 187.
54. "On Woman's Work in the Indian Mission Field," *Report of the Second Decennial Missionary Conference Held at Calcutta* (1882–83): 319.
55. See "Punjab and Sindh Mission: Lahore and Clarkabad," *Proceedings of the Church Missionary Society for Africa and the East* (1893–94): 229.
56. "The Power of Christian Song in Mission Work," *Missionary Review of the World* (July 1897): 526.
57. "Missions in India: Lodiana Mission," *Fifty-Eighth Annual Report of the Board of Foreign Missions of the Presbyterian Church in the United States of America* (Mission House, 1895), 84. Abels discusses the flute-harmonium (*The Harmonium in North Indian Music*, 29–35).
58. *Heathen Woman's Friend* 21, no. 11 (May 1890): 282–83. Jeffrey Cox discusses Scott's anthology of Indian melodies in relation to other similar collections (Cox, *Imperial Fault Lines: Christianity and Colonial Power in India, 1818–1940* [Stanford University Press, 2002], 112–15). See also Alan M. Guenther, "*Ghazals, Bhajans* and Hymns: Hindustani Christian Music in Nineteenth-Century North India," *Studies in World Christianity* 25, no. 2 (2019): 145–65.
59. Rev. E. M. Wherry, "The Ludhiana Convention of Indian Christian Workers," *Herald and Presbyter*, June 8, 1910, 12.
60. "Music in Indian Evangelism," *Homiletic Review* 79, no. 1 (January 1920): 81.
61. Frederick Stock and Margaret Stock, *People Movements in the Punjab* (William Carey Library, 1974), 120.
62. See my discussion of *filmi shabad* in "Listening to Female Voices in Sikh Kirtan," *Sikh Formations: Religion, Culture, Theory* 13, nos. 1–2 (2017): 61–66.

63 Suhail Yusuf recently interrogates the term *mirasi* ("Bridge Overtones: Lessons from the Sarangi" [PhD diss., Wesleyan University, 2024]). See also Kapuria, *Music in Colonial Punjab*, 104-88. Kapuria describes *mirasi* as nomadic, which is an attribution that some scholars find problematic (105). While some *mirasi* may have been nomadic, the figure of the "wandering bard" may be more of an orientalist stereotype than a sociocultural reality of nineteenth-century Punjab. Gibb Schreffler offers an especially nuanced discussion of this label (*Dhol: Drummers, Identities, and Modern Punjab* [University of Illinois Press, 2021], 92-127). Michael Nijhawan also explores the significance of this term in relation to the *dhaadhi* (bard or minstrel) (Nijhawan, *Dhadi Darbar: Religion, Violence, and the Performance of Sikh History* [Oxford University Press, 2006], 60, 73). Other scholars of *mirasi* include Daniel Neumann, Lowell Lybarger, and Adrian McNeil.

64 Anne C. Wilson, *A Short Account of the Hindu System of Music* (Gulab Singh and Sons, 1904), 5. See also "India—the Missionary and His Minstrel," *Church of England Magazine* 63 (September 21, 1867): 178.

65 On the basis of Frederick Stock's observations, Yousaf Sadiq mentions that "in order to collect data and listen to the various commonly used tunes, the missionaries spent a considerable amount of time at ordinary shopping and eating places. Rev. Young adds that help was also received from the *mirasis*, a group of nomadic singers" (Sadiq, *The Contextualized Psalms (Punjabi Zabur): A Precious Heritage of the Global Punjabi Christian Community* [Wipf and Stock, 2020], 16).

66 This image is reproduced in B. N. Goswamy, *Piety and Splendour: Sikh Heritage in Art* (National Museum, 2000), 218.

67 On the distinction between *mirasi* and *jogi* communities, see Mukesh Kumar, "The Art of Resistance: The Bards and Minstrels' Response to Anti-Syncretism/Anti-Liminality in North India," *Journal of the Royal Asiatic Society* 29, no. 2 (2019): 225-26.

68 See Kumar, "The Art of Resistance," 220.

69 From Lowell H. Lybarger's essay, we see that postpartition *rababi* separated themselves from a group they identified as *mirasi*. Lybarger also observes that *mirasi* might be seen as an umbrella term "to denote all hereditary musicians," while acknowledging the complex dynamics that separate each group ("Hereditary Musician Groups of Pakistani Punjab," *Journal of Punjab Studies* 18, nos. 1-2 [2011]: 120). See also Kapuria, *Music in Colonial Punjab*, 18.

70 *Christian Missionary Intelligencer and Record* 2 (June 1877): 332.

71 "Several Baptisms of Converts in India," *Gospel in All Lands* (May 1890): 232. See also "Bombay," *Proceedings of the Church Missionary Society for Africa and the East* (1893): 136.

72 "Western India Mission," *Proceedings of the Church Missionary Society for Africa and the East, 1900-1901* (1901): 316. Relatedly, Joyce Burkhalter Flueckiger explains, "First generation converts to Christianity from

professional musician castes in Phuljhar [Orissa], who had previously supported themselves through professional performance, felt like they needed to 'give up their instruments'" (Flueckiger, *Gender and Genre in the Folklore of Middle India* [Cornell University Press, 1996], 129).

73 Jeffrey Cox alludes to this convergence: "Missionary women and Punjabi musicians worked together to collect village tunes, and put them into Western musical notation so that missionaries and Punjabi catechists could teach village Christians how to sing the New Songs, and play them on the classic missionary instrument, the harmonium" (Cox, "Sing Unto the Lord a New Song: Transcending the Western/Indigenous Binary in Punjabi Christian Hymnody," in *Europe as the Other: External Perspectives on European Christianity*, ed. Judith Becker and Brian Stanley [Vandenhoeck and Ruprecht, 2014], 160).

74 Raj Bahadur Sharma, *History of Christian Missions: North India Perspective* (Mittal, 2005), 107. Rev. R. Hoskins explains, "In North India a stringed instrument, called *chikāra*, is used almost exclusively by the depressed classes, and people of high birth dislike to play it lest they lose position in society" ("Hindustani Music as an Evangelizing Agent," *Woman's Missionary Friend* 28, no. 11 [May 1897]: 303). A photo of a "Stringed Instrument Used by the Scheduled Castes for Worship" (resembling a *vina*) is reproduced in Stock and Stock, *People Movements in the Punjab*, 249.

75 See Christopher Harding, *Religious Transformation in South Asia: The Meanings of Conversion in Colonial Punjab* (Oxford University Press, 2008), 151. He shares a Belgian source that documents the important role of musicians in missionary work.

76 *The Encyclopedia of Missions: Descriptive, Historical, Biographical, Statistical* (Funk and Wagnalls, 1904), 324.

77 Harding, *Religious Transformation in South Asia*, 194.

78 Emma Dean Anderson and Mary Jane Campbell, *In the Shadow of the Himalayas: A Historical Narrative of the Missions of the United Presbyterian Church of North America as Conducted in the Punjab, India, 1855–1940* (United Presbyterian Board of Foreign Missions, 1942), 114.

79 Peter Manuel, *East Indian Music in the West Indies: Tān-Singing, Chutney, and the Making of Indo-Caribbean Culture* (Temple University Press, 2000), 38. On the basis of iconographical evidence, Allyn Miner estimates that *tarab* (sympathetic) strings had begun to appear "on the larger *sitārs* by about 1830" (Miner, *Sitar and Sarod in the 18th and 19th Centuries* [Noetzel, 1993], 49).

80 Anderson and Campbell, *In the Shadow of the Himalayas*, 114.

81 "A Mohammedan Minstrel," *Church Missionary Gleaner* (December 1890): 185.

82 "A Mohammedan Minstrel."

83 "Punjab and Sindh Mission," *Proceedings of the Church Missionary Society for Africa and the East, 1893–94* (1894): 131.

84 "Punjab and Sindh Mission," 118–19.
85 "Work in Narowal," *Church Missionary Gleaner* (July 1891): 106.
86 There are many different traditions of *kirtan* and *bhajan* throughout India. Guy L. Beck investigates the terms *kirtan* and *bhajan* in "Kirtan and Bhajan in Bhakti Traditions," in *Brill's Encyclopedia of Hinduism*, vol. 2, ed. Knut A. Jacobsen (Brill Academic Publishers, 2010), 585–98.
87 *Missionary Herald*, January 1, 1883, 10. Missionary accounts suggest that the concertina was used interchangeably with the harmonium, although the latter seems to have become more popular, whether due to its sturdiness or a preference expressed by Indian congregants. See "Work in Calcutta," *Missionary Herald: Containing Intelligence, at Large, of the Proceedings* (June 1, 1884): 230. Another discussion speaks to the concertina's "power, compass, and portability," which "render it very suitable for use in Missionary work." See *Female Missionary Intelligencer* 19 (1877): 15.
88 Some scholars claim that the *taus* is primarily an instrument of Guru Gobind Singh's *darbar*. See Francesca Cassio and Nirinjan Kaur Khalsa-Baker, "Singing Dharam: Transmission of Knowledge in the Sikh Sonic Path," in *Beacons of Dharma: Spiritual Exemplars for the Modern Age*, ed. Christopher Patrick Miller, Michael Reading, and Jeffrey D. Long (Lexington Books, 2020), 278.
89 "Lucknow and Cawnpore," *Report on India and Persia of the Deputation* (Board of Foreign Missions of the Presbyterian Church in the USA, 1922), 79–80.
90 "Punjab and Sindh Mission," *Proceedings of the Church Missionary Society for Africa and the East, 1900–1901* (1901): 288–89.
91 Samuel A. Mutchmore, *The Moghul, Mongol, Mikado and Missionary*, 2 vols. (1891), 1:164, 1:167.
92 Anthony George Shiell, *A Year in India* (Samuel Tinsley and Co., 1880), 217.
93 See Ashley Carus-Wilson, *Irene Petrie: Missionary to Kashmir* (Hodder and Stoughton, 1901), 98; and Sundar Singh [Ramgarhia], *Guide to the Darbar Sahib or Golden Temple of Amritsar* (Lahore, 1903), 28.
94 "Missions in India," *Home Missions: One Hundred and Third Annual Report of the Board of Home Missions of the Presbyterian Church in the United States of America* (May 1905): 156.
95 Missionary literature mentions conversions of Sikhs from the "Mazhabi" community.
96 Ajit Singh Paintal, "The Contribution of Ragis and Rababis to the Sikh Devotional Music," in *The City of Amritsar: A Study of Historical, Cultural, Social and Economic Aspects*, ed. Fauja Singh (Oriental Publishers, 1978), 266.
97 Aldous Huxley, *Jesting Pilate: An Intellectual Holiday* (George H. Doran Company, 1926), 66–67.
98 "Let Us Preach and Practise Guru Nanak's Ideals," *The "Spokesman"*

Weekly 6 (1920): 10. It is worth noting that Bhai Sahib Randhir Singh's *kirtan* was considered exemplary by the author of this article even though it was played on the harmonium.

99 *Christian Intelligencer and Mission Field*, May 31, 1922, 343.

100 Many *ragi* associated with Harmandir Sahib during the late nineteenth and early twentieth centuries are mentioned by Paintal in "The Contribution of Ragis and Rababis to the Sikh Devotional Music," 265–71, 272–81.

101 In addition to Kinnear, *The Gramophone Company's First Indian Recordings*, see Michael Kinnear, *The Gramophone Company's India Recordings, 1908–1910* (Bajakhana, 2000). I am grateful to Jonathan Ward for alerting me to this publication and for sharing his knowledge of early gramophone recordings with me.

102 Bhai Uttam Singh Hakim is heard at http://kirtansewa.net/index.php/bhai-utam-singh-hakim-amritsar/, and Bhai Sain Ditta is heard at http://kirtansewa.net/index.php/bhai-sain-ditta-amritsar/. Select additional recordings are also available at the Sikh Gramophone Collection, www.sikhgram.com.

103 See Farrell, "The Early Days of the Gramophone Industry in India," 47–48.

104 Yousuf Saeed, "Urdu Musicology in 20th Century South Asia: Defining Religious and National Heritage," *Indo-Persian Musical Confluence: Indo-Persian Texts on Music Conference*, Herb Alpert School of Music, UCLA, April 25, 2021, https://schoolofmusic.ucla.edu/event/indo-persian-confluence-indo-persian-texts-on-music/.

105 Kamaldeep Singh Brar, "Remove Harmonium from Golden Temple? Sikh Music Scholars Strike Differing Notes," *Indian Express*, May 23, 2022.

106 We see an interesting parallel in East Africa. Anna Maria Busse Berger documents how German missionaries found it impossible to play East African music on the harmonium because of the completely different tonal system (Busse Berger, *The Search for Medieval Music in Africa and Germany, 1891–1961* [University of Chicago Press, 2020], 165).

107 Bhai Harjinder Singh (Srinagar Wale) can be heard at "Bhai Harjinder Singh ... on Tanti Saaz Issue," posted by Kirtan Academy, May 25, 2022, YouTube, https://www.youtube.com/watch?v=FLIGr-iyE-0 (in Punjabi). I have translated the gist of his lecture in the main text.

108 Amanda Weidman highlights a discussion in a Tamil journal from the 1930s where the violin upholds its status as a successfully assimilated foreign instrument, while the harmonium is cast as a polluting foreign force (Weidman, *Singing the Classical, Voicing the Modern: The Postcolonial Politics of Music in South India* [Duke University Press, 2006], 47).

109 Giani Harpreet Singh speaks about the importance of *tanti sāz* at an event organized by Jawaddi Taksal. See "Giani Harpreet Singh," posted by Jawaddi Taksal, June 6, 2022, YouTube, https://www.youtube.com

/watch?v=6LF04gafS1M. He argues that the difference between *Gurmat Sangeet* and *Shastriya Sangeet* resides in the prioritization of *shabad* in the former vs. that of *rāg* in the latter. In *Gurmat Sangeet*, *rāg* does not take precedence over *shabad* despite its importance: *Rāg* helps to transport the essence of *shabad* into the ears of one's inner being (*hirdai*).

110 Harjinder Singh Lallie, "The Harmonium in Sikh Music," *Sikh Formations: Religion, Culture, Theory* 12, no. 1 (2016): 65.

111 "SGPC: No Plans to Phase Out Harmonium from Gurmat Kirtan as Yet at Golden Temple," *The Tribune*, May 27, 2022, https://www.tribuneindia.com/news/punjab/sgpc-no-plans-to-phase-out-harmonium-for-now-398805.

112 Neeraj Bagga, "Harmonium Manufacturers in a Fix over SGPC's Flip-Flop," *The Tribune*, June 1, 2022, https://www.tribuneindia.com/news/amritsar/harmonium-manufacturers-in-a-fix-over-sgpcs-flip-flop-400268.

113 See *United Provinces Gazette*, October 1, 1910, 1683; and Alma Latifi, *The Industrial Punjab: A Survey of Facts, Conditions and Possibilities* (Longmans, Green and Co., 1911), 222. I have struggled to document early harmonium manufacturing, patenting, and repair in Punjab. Cleveland does not mention Punjab either. This is an important area for future research.

114 In numerous public interviews, Bhai Baldeep Singh speaks to the need for historically informed instruments. See Suanshu Khurana, "Jathedar of Akal Takht Wants Harmonium Replaced from Gurbani Sangeet; but Is It Still a Foreign Instrument?" *Indian Express*, May 27, 2022, https://indianexpress.com/article/express-sunday-eye/jathedar-akal-takht-harmonium-replaced-gurbani-sangeet-foreign-instrument-7940110/. Nijhawan mentions Punjabi *sarangi* craftsmen in appendix 3 while noting that this tradition is at risk of extinction (*Dhadi Darbar*, 232–36).

115 *SGGS* 368-9.

116 Virinder S. Kalra, *Sacred and Secular Musics: A Postcolonial Approach* (Bloomsbury, 2015), 78.

117 See "Golden Temple Controversy: Controversy over Harmonium in Golden Temple, Know Why Akal Takht Demanded to Separate It from Kirtan," *NewsNCR*, May 25, 2022, https://www.newsncr.com/knowledge-utility/golden-temple-controversy-controversy-over-harmonium-in-golden-temple-know-why-akal-takht-demanded-to-separate-it-from-kirtan/.

118 Coomaraswamy, "Indian Music," 260.

119 Brar, "Remove Harmonium from Golden Temple?"

120 See Raj Academy, 2024, https://rajacademy.com.

121 Brar, "Remove Harmonium from Golden Temple?"

122 On linguistic complexity in *SGGS*, see Christopher Shackle, *A Guru Nanak Glossary* (School of Oriental and African Studies, 1995), viii.

123 Pathania, "Harmonium Ban in Golden Temple Puts SGPC's Priorities into Question."
124 Kalra, *Sacred and Secular Musics*, 82.
125 Surinder Singh Bakhshi, *Sikhs in the Diaspora: A Modern Guide to the Practice of Sikh Faith* (Sikh Publishing House, 2008), 163.
126 Notable soloists include Bhaiya Ganpat Rao (d. 1924), Pandit Rambhau Bijapure (1917–2010), Pandit Bhishmadev Vedi (1910–84), Pandit Muneshwar Dayal (no dates available), Pandit Montu Banerjee (1915–80, student of Dayal), Jnan Prakash Ghosh (1909–97), Pandit Tulsidas Borkar (1934–2018), Awarind Thatte (b. 1958), Pandit Appa Jalgaonkar (1922–2009), Shri Purushottam Walavalkar (1923–2014), and Pandit Vasant Kanakapur (no dates available), to name a few. Missing from this list are numerous Pakistani virtuosos who perform *qawwali* and *ghazal*. A video of Bijapure is available at https://aneeshpradhan.com/a-keyboard-crescendo-innovative-harmonium-players-from-karnataka-and-bengal/. On instrument construction, I mention Pandit Manohar Chimote (a student of Vedi), whose innovations include the incorporation of a *swarmandal* above the reed board, which he plays periodically between phrases and whose addition has warranted a name change to *Samvadini* (prominent among his students is Rajendra Vaishampayan). Dr. Vidyadhar Oke has recently created a twenty-two-*shruti* harmonium, following in the footsteps of Krishna Balwant Deval and G. B. Achrekar, who had attempted this feat several decades earlier (on Deval and Achrekar, see Rahaim, "That Ban[e] of Indian Music: Hearing Politics in the Harmonium," 664–66). For Oke's harmonium, see 22shruti, http://www.22shruti.com.
127 Bhai Vir Singh, "Shabad de Bhaav te Raag di Taseer," in *Gurmat Sangeet: Par Hun Tak Mili Khoj* (Central Khalsa Yatimkhana, 2008), 2–9.
128 Strangways, *The Music of Hindostan*, 18.
129 There are hundreds of harmonium tutors for learning *kirtan* (the purchase of a harmonium is sometimes accompanied by a book that offers introductory lessons). See, for example, Sundar Singh, *Harmonium Kirtan Sikhiya* (Chatar Singh Jeevan Singh, 2008), 16.
130 Deva, "The Harmonium and Indian Music," 52.
131 Herbert A. Popley, "The Use of Indian Music in Christian Worship," *Indian Journal of Theology* 6, no. 3 (1957): 86.
132 See Bhai Vir Singh, "Ragi, Dhaadhi te Giani," *Khalsa Samachar*, Amritsar, 1906, 4. As listed by Kinnear, these include *Pahari*, *Jhog*, *Lilath* (Bhai Mehroo), *Zila/Jila*, *Piloo*, and *Kanra Asawari* (Bhai Uttam Singh Hakim) (*The Gramophone Company's First Indian Recordings*).
133 Popley, "The Use of Indian Music in Christian Worship," 84.
134 See Bhogal, "Listening to Female Voices in Sikh Kirtan," 52.
135 The video for this audio example can be viewed at "Bhai Anantvir Singh and Bhai Amolak Singh," posted by Naam Simran, September 20, 2018, YouTube, https://www.youtube.com/watch?v=8uANVMLc0D0.

136 On ornamentation, see Abels, *The Harmonium in North Indian Music*, 99–105.
137 Deva, "The Harmonium and Indian Music," 49. Deva mentions innovations by Bhishmadev Vedi and G. B. Achrekar. Vedi attempted to create the effect of *meend* by adding extra strings to his instrument (known as *svara darpan*), while Achrekar attached a lever to his instrument to create the same effect (51).
138 See "Raag Basant Hindol . . . ," posted by Prabh Baani, March 6, 2019, YouTube, https://www.youtube.com/watch?v=SYNPx8aPKxE (14:10–14:32 and 18:08–18:51).
139 See *The Indian Listener* 1, no. 2 (January 7, 1936).
140 Gagandeep Kaur, *Namdhari Sikh Parampara Duara Protsahit Shastri Sangeet De Kalakaar* (National Press Associates, 2021), 4–5.
141 Joginder Singh, *Religious Pluralism in Punjab: A Contemporary Account of Sikh Sants, Babas, Gurus and Satgurus* (Routledge, 2018), 236; and Kaur, *Namdhari Sikh Parampara Duara Protsahit Shastri Sangeet De Kalakaar*, 8.
142 Ashok Singh, *Thoughts of Bhai Ardaman Singh*, ed. Bhai Ashok Singh (Institute of Sikh Studies, 1999), 136; and Gibb Schreffler, "Music," *Brill's Encyclopedia of Sikhism*, vol. 2, ed. Knut A. Jacobsen, Anshu Malhotra, Kristina Myrvold, and Eleanor Nesbitt (Brill, 2025), 180.
143 Joginder Singh, *Religious Pluralism in Punjab*, 252–53.
144 TNN, "'Nagar Kirtan' with 550 Young 'Rababis,'" *Times of India*, November 2, 2019, https://timesofindia.indiatimes.com/city/amritsar/nagar-kirtan-with-550-young-rababis/articleshow/71863834.cms.
145 "LIVE from Red Fort Delhi," posted by GSPS Gurbani, April 20, 2022, YouTube, https://www.youtube.com/watch?v=0xFO_BsHK3A.
146 See also Kalra, *Sacred and Secular Musics*, 82.
147 Madan Gopal Singh, "Harmonium and Its Exiles," *The Tribune*, May 29, 2022, https://www.tribuneindia.com/news/comment/harmonium-its-exiles-399045.

| CHAPTER 3

1 Nikky-Guninder Kaur Singh, *Guru Nanak: Poems from the Sikh Sacred Tradition* (Harvard University Press, 2022), 33 (translation modified).
2 Andrew Hicks, *Composing the World: Harmony in the Medieval Platonic Cosmos* (Oxford University Press, 2017), 190.
3 The notion of the Sikh body as vibrating sonic matter is well established in *SGGS* in particular and in Indian metaphysics in general, although this phenomenon is regarded as relatively unusual within a Euro–North American context, as seen in Nina Sun Eidsheim, *Sensing Sound: Singing and Listening as Vibrational Practice* (Duke University Press, 2015).

4 Bhagat Singh Thind, *The Radiant Road to Reality: Tested Science of Religion* (Wetzel Publishing, 1947), 52.
5 *SGGS* 97-11. Numerous verses support my summary of *anahad nād*, although many are too lengthy to cite in full. For the sake of comparison, I refer the reader to similar verses, 124-5/17.
6 *SGGS* 1036-7.
7 Bhai Gurdas, *Vār* 15, Pauri 16, p. 2: https://www.searchgurbani.com/bhai-gurdas-vaaran/vaar/15/pauri/16/line/1.
8 *SGGS* 945-13.
9 *SGGS* 121-5, 671-10/11.
10 A rigorous study of commonalities and differences between Vedic and Sikh notions of *nād* falls beyond the scope of this chapter (and book).
11 *SGGS* 446-9.
12 *SGGS* 400-18. In his discussion of Sufi *samāᶜ*, Andrew Hicks observes an analogous mode of "hearing 'sounds' that are irreducible to vibrating strings or human voices" (Hicks, "Mysticism's Musical Modalities: Philosophies of Audition in Medieval Persian Sufism," in *The Music Road: Coherence and Diversity in Music from the Mediterranean to India*, ed. Reinhard Strohm [Oxford University Press, 2019], 110).
13 See Zachary Wallmark, *Nothing but Noise: Timbre and Musical Meaning at the Edge* (Oxford University Press, 2022), 57; and Isabella van Elferen, *Paradox, Materialism, and Vibrational Aesthetics* (Bloomsbury, 2021).
14 A recent exception is Inderjit Kaur, "Theorizing the (Un)Sounded in Sikhī: Anhad, Sabad, and Kīrtan," *Religions* 12, no. 11 (2021): 1007.
15 Cornelia Fales, "The Paradox of Timbre," *Ethnomusicology* 46, no. 1 (2002): 57, 61.
16 See, for example, the range of essays in Emily I. Dolan and Alexander Rehding, eds., *The Oxford Handbook of Timbre* (Oxford University Press, 2021).
17 See Balwant Singh, *Amolak Hira: Jiwan Samachar Bhai Sahib Bhai Hira Singh Ji Ragi* (Gurmat Missionary Publication, 1995). See a summary of his biography in English: "Bhai Sahib Bhai Hira Singh Ji Ragi Memorial," Sikhnet, https://www.sikhnet.com/news/ragi-bhai-hira-singh-ji-ragi-memorial. See also Harjinder Singh Dilgeer, *The Sikh Reference Book* (Singh Brothers, 1997), 430.
18 Nikky-Guninder Kaur Singh, *The Feminine Principle in the Sikh Vision of the Transcendent* (Cambridge University Press, 1993), 178.
19 *SGGS* 1383-15.
20 This story has been narrated by several *granthi* (knowledge bearers). I use a version by Bhai Sahib Singh (Canade Wale): "Miracle of Kirtan—Bhai Hira Singh Ji Ragi," Soundcloud, https://soundcloud.com/bhaisahibsingh/miracle-of-kirtan-bhai-hira-singh-ji-ragi (in Punjabi).
21 *SGGS* 2-8.
22 *SGGS* 770-15.

23 Wallmark, *Nothing but Noise*, 185.
24 Gobind Singh Mansukhani, "The Unstruck Melody: Musical Mysticism in the Scripture," in *Sikh Art and Literature*, ed. Kerry Brown (Routledge, 1999), 123–25.
25 For more on Bhai Vir Singh, see Anshu Malhotra and Anne Murphy, "Bhai Vir Singh (1872–1957): Rethinking Literary Modernity in Colonial Punjab," *Sikh Formations: Religion, Culture, Theory* 16, nos. 1–2 (2020): 1–13.
26 For Bhai Randhir Singh's life (in English), see Bhai Randhir Singh, *Autobiography of Bhai Sahib Randhir Singh: Freedom Fighter, Reformer, Theologian, Saint and Hero of Lahore Conspiracy Case, First Prisoner of Gurudwara Reform Movement*, trans. Trilochan Singh (Bhai Sahib Randhir Singh Trust, 1995). This autobiography is based on his letters from jail (in Punjabi): *Jail Chithiyaan* (Bhai Sahib Randhir Singh Trust, 2010), which was originally published in 1938.
27 Malhotra and Murphy, "Bhai Vir Singh (1872–1957)," 2.
28 Published in Bhai Charan Singh, *Gurmat Sangeet: Par Hun Tak Mili Khoj* (Central Khalsa Yatimkhana, 2008). See also Rishpal Singh, "Historical Development of Gurmat Sangeet Publications," *Research Review International Journal of Multidisciplinary* (2018): 83.
29 Bhai Vir Singh, "Shabad de Bhaav te Raag di Taseer," in *Gurmat Sangeet: Par Hun Tak Mili Khoj* (Central Khalsa Yatimkhana, 2008), 2.
30 Bhai Vir Singh, "Shabad de Bhaav te Raag di Taseer," 6–7, 8.
31 Bhai Vir Singh, "Shabad de Bhaav te Raag di Taseer," 3, 4.
32 See Harjeet Singh Gill, *The Cosmic Vision of Baba Nanak* (LG Publishers, 2003), x.
33 See Kanwarjit Singh, *Keertan Reets of Bhai Sahib Bhai Randhir Singh Ji* (Kanwarjit Singh, 1999), 1. This passage is also printed in a pamphlet, "Har Kirtan," which is discussed by Virinder S. Kalra (Kalra, *Sacred and Secular Musics: A Postcolonial Approach* [Bloomsbury, 2015], 199n99).
34 This passage by Seva Singh (originally in Punjabi) is cited in the preface to Kanwarjit Singh, *Keertan Reets of Bhai Sahib Bhai Randhir Singh Ji*, 5–6.
35 Bhai Randhir Singh, *Anhad Shabad Dasam Duar* (Bhai Sahib Randhir Singh Trust, 2004), 22. This book was written in 1939–40, as documented on p. 18 of the English translation (Bhai Randhir Singh, *Anhad Shabad Dasam Duar: Open Discussion of Unstruck Ethereal Music at Tenth Door of Abode Divine*, trans. Bhai Jaspinder Singh Ji [Akhand Keertanee Jatha, 2002]).
36 Bhai Randhir Singh, *Anhad Shabad Dasam Duar*, 60; Bhai Randhir Singh, *Anhad Shabad Dasam Duar: Open Discussion of Unstruck Ethereal Music*, 58.
37 Bhai Randhir Singh, *Anhad Shabad Dasam Duar*, 8; Bhai Randhir Singh, *Anhad Shabad Dasam Duar: Open Discussion of Unstruck Ethereal Music*,

5. Nikky-Guninder Kaur Singh also draws attention to how the five senses "must be intensified so that they . . . synchronize . . . the deepening of a multi-sensual experience" (Singh, "Sikh Mysticism and Sensuous Reproductions," in *Ineffability: An Exercise in Comparative Philosophy of Religion*, ed. Timothy D. Knepper and Leah Kalmanson [Springer, 2017], 117).

38. Arvind-Pal Singh Mandair, *Religion and the Specter of the West: Sikhism, India, Postcoloniality and the Politics of Translation* (Columbia University Press, 2009), 377.

39. Bhai Randhir Singh, *Anhad Shabad Dasam Duar*, 87; Bhai Randhir Singh, *Anhad Shabad Dasam Duar: Open Discussion of Unstruck Ethereal Music*, 88.

40. SGGS 109-19 to 110-9. See also Bhai Randhir Singh, *Anhad Shabad Dasam Duar*, 52–53; Bhai Randhir Singh, *Anhad Shabad Dasam Duar: Open Discussion of Unstruck Ethereal Music*, 51.

41. Śārṅgadeva describes these nine openings ("srota-s") as serving to eliminate bodily impurities (*Sangīta-Ratnākara of Śārṅgadeva*, vol. 1, trans. Ravindra Kumar Shringy and Prem Lata Sharma [Motilal Banarsidass, 1978], 71).

42. Bhai Randhir Singh, *Anhad Shabad Dasam Duar*, 18; Bhai Randhir Singh, *Anhad Shabad Dasam Duar: Open Discussion of Unstruck Ethereal Music*, 40–41. SGGS 452-18 and 1162-7.

43. Bhai Gurdas, *Kabit Savaiye*, 59, https://www.searchgurbani.com/kabit-savaiye/kabit-by-kabit. A different translation is available at https://www.sikhitothemax.org/shabad?id=41088&q=joiq%20mY&type=2&source=B&highlight=208004. For the Punjabi, see Bhai Sewa Singh, *Kabitt Savaiyye Bhai Gurdas Ji Satik* (Singh Brothers, 2001). For a recent translation of selected *vār* by Bhai Gurdas, see Rahuldeep Singh Gill, *Drinking from Love's Cup: Surrender and Sacrifice in the Vārs of Bhai Gurdas Bhalla* (Oxford University Press, 2017).

44. SGGS 943-13/15.

45. Bhai Randhir Singh, *Anhad Shabad Dasam Duar*, 87, 23; Bhai Randhir Singh, *Anhad Shabad Dasam Duar: Open Discussion of Unstruck Ethereal Music*, 88, 45; SGGS 415-16.

46. Bhai Randhir Singh, *Anhad Shabad Dasam Duar*, 88; Bhai Randhir Singh, *Anhad Shabad Dasam Duar: Open Discussion of Unstruck Ethereal Music*, 89. Giani Nahar Singh, who wrote the foreword to the second Punjabi edition in 1952, clarifies that the five timbres associated with *dasam duar* in the practices of the yogis are *bansuri* (flute), *chhainay* (steel tongs), thundering clouds, *shankh* (conch), and *ghanti* (bell). See Bhai Randhir Singh, *Anhad Shabad Dasam Duar*, 136; Bhai Randhir Singh, *Anhad Shabad Dasam Duar: Open Discussion of Unstruck Ethereal Music*, 165.

47. In this passage, Bhai Randhir Singh speaks about an encounter with

a close friend who describes his excitement at hearing what he calls *anahad shabad*. On the basis of the quality of timbres that he hears, however, and in the absence of other senses being activated, Randhir Singh maintains that his friend is not hearing *Gurmat anahad shabad*. After some experimentation himself, Bhai Randhir Singh confirms that he can indeed hear *panch shabad*, the five timbres, described by his friend, but he maintains that these are incomparable to those heard at the opening of *dasam duar*. See Bhai Randhir Singh, *Anhad Shabad Dasam Duar*, 89–90; Bhai Randhir Singh, *Anhad Shabad Dasam Duar: Open Discussion of Unstruck Ethereal Music*, 89–90.

48 Bhai Randhir Singh, *Anhad Shabad Dasam Duar*, 90; Bhai Randhir Singh, *Anhad Shabad Dasam Duar: Open Discussion of Unstruck Ethereal Music*, 90.

49 Bhai Randhir Singh, *Anhad Shabad Dasam Duar*, 110; Bhai Randhir Singh, *Anhad Shabad Dasam Duar: Open Discussion of Unstruck Ethereal Music*, 111. Kamala Elizabeth Nayar and Jaswinder Singh Sandhu are among the few to note the sonic richness of *sunn* in contrast to its Sanskrit cognate, *shunya*: "Emptiness (*sunn*) refers to that which is to be filled with the resonance. It is only in this state of *sunn* that one can experience the cosmic resonance of *Ek Oankar*." See Nayar and Sandhu, *The Sikh View on Happiness: Guru Arjan's Sukhmani* (Bloomsbury Academic, 2020), 118.

50 Bhai Randhir Singh, *Anhad Shabad Dasam Duar*, 117–18; Bhai Randhir Singh, *Anhad Shabad Dasam Duar: Open Discussion of Unstruck Ethereal Music*, 119. This observation is likely linked to Bhagat Kabir's verse in *rāg Bilawal*: "The divine melody comes from bronze and returns to it."

51 Bhai Randhir Singh, *Anhad Shabad Dasam Duar*, 53–54; Bhai Randhir Singh, *Anhad Shabad Dasam Duar: Open Discussion of Unstruck Ethereal Music*, 52–53. I am reminded of Linda Hess's observations on vibration and *ajapa jaap* and of how the latter is considered more powerful because vibration is caused by "the movement of inner energy through our own heartstrings," which renders it "most intimate and potent" (*The Bijak of Kabir*, trans. Linda Hess and Sukhdeo Singh [Oxford University Press, 2002], 28).

52 Bhai Randhir Singh, *Anhad Shabad Dasam Duar*, 73; Bhai Randhir Singh, *Anhad Shabad Dasam Duar: Open Discussion of Unstruck Ethereal Music*, 73.

53 Randhir Singh, *Jail Chithiyaan*, 51, letter no. 2, March 20, 1922. See Bhai Randhir Singh, *Anhad Shabad Dasam Duar: Open Discussion of Unstruck Ethereal Music*, 35, for an English translation. This account evokes Elferen's description of how "vibrating sound waves transport sound energy. . . . Once the sound energy is transported to the cochlea, the thousands of little hairs in the organ of Corti translate it into the electrical energy that governs the human nervous system" (Isabella

van Elferen, "Timbrality: The Vibrant Aesthetics of Tone Color," in *The Oxford Handbook of Timbre*, ed. Emily Dolan and Alex Rehding [Oxford University Press, 2021], 82).
54   Wallmark, *Nothing but Noise*, 184–85.
55   *SGGS* 401-12.
56   *SGGS* 888-16/19.
57   *Puratan Janam Sakhi*, "Vaen Parvesh" (Arorbans Press, 1948), 17.
58   Another term that alludes to the state of bodily bliss is "bismaad de ghar." See *Puratan Janam Sakhi*, 94, 122.
59   For example, "Baba [Nanak] Spoke the Sabad in Raag Asa," in *Puratan Janam Sakhi*, 77.
60   For more about Dattatreya, see Alain Daniélou, *The Myths and Gods of India: The Classic Work on Hindu Polytheism* (Motilal Banarsidass, 2017), 183.
61   A translation of this episode as it accompanies the image from the B-40 manuscript can be seen in W. H. McLeod, *The B40 Janam-Sakhi* (Guru Nanak Dev University, 1980), 198–200.
62   Dattatreya's vow of silence is documented in the Puranas and Upanishads, as explored by Antonio Rigopoulos, *Dattātreya: The Immortal Guru, Yogin, and Avatāra; A Study of the Transformative and Inclusive Character of a Multi-Faceted Hindu Deity* (State University of New York Press, 1998), 46, 74.
63   See Bhai Gurpreet Singh, "Jehva Jap Gur Nao," posted by Amritvela Trust Live, October 25, 2021, YouTube, https://www.youtube.com/watch?v=2R8WqyrhraQ&t=12874s, at 03:19:00 (in Hindi).
64   For example, see *Baba Nanak and Mardana with Dattatreya and His Sannyasis* (British Library, MS Panj. B 40); an early nineteenth-century watercolor, *Guru Nanak's Discourse with Datatre on Mount Byar*; and *Guru Nanak Comes Upon the Sanyasi Dattetreya* (1775/1800). These paintings are discussed in chapter 4.
65   *SGGS* 941-5/6.
66   On this topic, see *SGGS* 973-10/16. In his criticism of yogic behaviors, Bhagat Namdev frowned on the act of making pilgrimages to bathe in holy water, and other types of rituals and austerities, as ways to experience *nirbaan* (nirvana). His contributions to the Sikh notion of divine oneness place the concept of *nirbaan* at a distance from Buddhist notions of nirvana, as explained by Nikky-Guninder Kaur Singh in *Guru Nanak*, xxiii. There are various narratives about the birth of Gorakhnath and his spiritual education as a disciple of Matsyendranath. For a summary, see Prabodh Chandra Bagchi, *Kaulajnananirnaya*, trans. Michael Magee (Prachya Prakashan, 1986), 17–19; and Guy L. Beck, *Sonic Theology: Hinduism and Sacred Sound* (University of South Carolina Press, 1993), 97–102.
67   *SGGS* 1126-13.

68 *SGGS* 153-9.
69 *SGGS* 108-16,
70 *SGGS* 126-11.
71 *SGGS* 1250-18.
72 Significantly, Guru Nanak draws on the concept of yogic *chakras* in his discourse with the yogis (*siddhas*), particularly that of the first lotus (known as *muladhara* in tantric yoga), which is located below the navel (*nabh kamal* in *Gurbani*) and is considered the starting point of breath and sound (*SGGS* 945-15). See also Jodh Singh, *The Religious Philosophy of Guru Nanak: A Comparative Study with Special Reference to Siddha Gosti* (Motilal Banarsidass, 1983), 50–52. For a discussion of how *nād* originates from *muladhar*, see Bagchi, *Kaulajnana-Nirnaya*, 53–54. On the basis of Sarngadeva, *Sangīta-Ratnākara* (vol. 1, 90–96), P. H. Pott explains that the *anahata-padma*, a twelve-petaled lotus, lies over the heart, whereas the *sahasrara-padma*, a thousand-petaled lotus, occupies "a position upside-down at the crown of the head" (Pott, *Yoga and Yantra: Their Interrelation and Their Significance for Indian Archaeology*, trans. Rodney Needham [Springer, 1966], 7–8).
73 *SGGS* 974-17.
74 *SGGS* 161-18, 602-14.
75 *SGGS* 236-11/13.
76 *SGGS* 148-18, 1148-4.
77 For detailed studies of the Nath tradition in relation to *SGGS* and Punjabi history and culture, I refer the reader to Nayar and Sandhu, *The Sikh View on Happiness*. The seventy-three stanzas that comprise Guru Nanak's conversations with the yogis in *SGGS* are composed in *rāg Ramkali* (beginning at 938-5 and ending at 946-19).
78 George Weston Briggs, *Gorakhnāth and the Kānphata Yogīs* (Motilal Banarsidass, 1938), 250; Patton E. Burchett, *A Genealogy of Devotion: Bhakti, Tantra, Yoga, and Sufism in North India* (Columbia University Press, 2019), 170.
79 Burchett, *A Genealogy of Devotion*, 170. For more on Gorakh and his followers, see Briggs, *Gorakhnāth and the Kānphata Yogīs*; and David Gordon White, *The Alchemical Body: Siddha Traditions in Medieval India* (University of Chicago Press, 1996). For a study of Sanskrit texts that document Hatha yoga teachings, see James Mallinson, "The Original Gorakṣaśataka," in *Yoga in Practice*, ed. David Gordon White (Princeton University Press, 2011), 257–72. Jodh Singh discusses the significance of the term *Gorakh* in relation to *SGGS* (*The Religious Philosophy of Guru Nanak*, 78–81).
80 *SGGS* 730-10/18.
81 *SGGS* 886-12/17.
82 Nayar and Sandhu, *The Sikh View on Happiness*, 28–29.
83 Nayar and Sandhu, *The Sikh View on Happiness*, 36.

84 See *SGGS* 327-7: "Turn your breath away from the left channel and away from the right channel, and unite them in the central channel of *sushmanaa*. / At their confluence within your mind, take your bath there without water." See also Hess's description of yogic breathing techniques in *The Bijak of Kabir*, 141–42. The network of *nadi* is also discussed by Śārṅgadeva (*Saṅgīta-Ratnākara of Śārṅgadeva*, 99–103).
85 Thind, *The Radiant Road to Reality*, 194–95.
86 Nayar and Sandhu, *The Sikh View on Happiness*, 36–37; William Pinch, "Nāth Yogīs, Akbar, and the 'Bālnāth Ṭillā,'" in *Yoga in Practice*, ed. David Gordon White (Princeton University Press, 2011), 275.
87 On the topic of *raj yoga*, see Jodh Singh, *The Religious Philosophy of Guru Nanak*, 45–50.
88 *SGGS* 903-18.
89 Nikky-Guninder Kaur Singh, *Guru Nanak*, xix. Jodh Singh reminds us about the ancient origins and broad cultural lineage of the "gosti" or dialogue format when seen against the Ramayana, Mahabharata, Vedas, and the *Dialogues of Plato* (*The Religious Philosophy of Guru Nanak*, 16–17).
90 *SGGS* 944-18.
91 *SGGS* 662-18 to 663-1.
92 *SGGS* 877-9/10.
93 *SGGS* 974-5/19.
94 *SGGS* 973-1/5.
95 See, for example, *SGGS* 904-5/8.
96 *SGGS* 1033-8 to 1034-8.
97 *SGGS* 124-5/17.
98 See, for example, *SGGS* 409-7/11, 908-10 to 909-6.
99 *SGGS* 922-11. *Anand Sahib* begins at 917-1 and ends at 922-19.
100 *SGGS* 1061-18/19. Guru Ramdas also explains in *rāg Bilawal*, "Oh Nanak, we are the instruments upon which the divine one plays" (834-11). See also *SGGS* 313-18/19.
101 *SGGS* 908-16/17.
102 *SGGS* 174-17.
103 *SGGS* 1144-11.
104 *SGGS* 907-15/17.
105 Hess draws our attention to the research of Hazariprasad Dvivedi, who maintains that Kabir's ancestors were yogis recently converted to Islam in the generation before his birth (*The Bijak of Kabir*, 142–43).
106 *SGGS* 334-16 to 335-2.
107 *SGGS* 334-10/15.
108 *SGGS* 478-12.
109 *SGGS* 970-16/17.
110 *SGGS* 971-7/8.
111 *SGGS* 971-19 to 972-3.

112 *SGGS* 972-4.
113 *SGGS* 333-3.
114 *SGGS* 730-17.
115 *SGGS* 1158-19.
116 *SGGS* 356-15.
117 *SGGS* 360-2.
118 *SGGS* 909-6.
119 *SGGS* 886-8/10.
120 *SGGS* 972-18 to 973-2.
121 *SGGS* 970-17.
122 Thind describes a similar timbral trajectory. He explains that in the fourth state (what he calls the "Sunna Region") one "hears the Kingri and Sarangi" (*The Radiant Road to Reality*, 126–34).
123 The Vedic context also suggests varying timbral profiles, as seen in slight timbral differences between the ten internalized sounds mentioned in *Hamsa Upanishad* (from the *Shukla Yajurveda*): *chini* (the primal sound of the word), *chini-chini*, bell, conch, string instrument, cymbals, flute, *bheri*, *mridanga*, and thunder. Later, in Matsyendranath's eleventh-century text, *Kaulajnana-Nirnaya*, the flute signals "the highest state of all," which is not the case in *SGGS*. This passage is translated in Beck, *Sonic Theology*, 99. Popular literature on yoga also points to variety in timbre and succession of sounds. See, for example, Eric A. Gustafson, *The Ringing Sound: An Introduction to the Sound Current: The Key to Enlightenment Singing in Your Soul* (Conscious Living Press, 2000), 29.
124 *SGGS* 883-15, 657-2.
125 *SGGS* 345-12/16.
126 The four states of consciousness are outlined in *Mandukya Upanishad*, I. 2–7. See also Nayar and Sandhu, *The Sikh View on Happiness*, 236.
127 Nayar and Sandhu, *The Sikh View on Happiness*, 104.
128 This translation of the three *gunas* is based on Nayar and Sandhu, *The Sikh View on Happiness*, 151n67; and Nikky-Guninder Kaur Singh, *The Feminine Principle in the Sikh Vision of the Transcendent*, 267n53.
129 *SGGS* 1123-4.
130 *SGGS* 7-14 to 8-7. For a discussion of these five realms, see Nikky-Guninder Kaur Singh, *Sikhism: An Introduction* (I. B. Tauris, 2011), 68–70.
131 Nikky-Guninder Kaur Singh, "Sikh Mysticism and Sensuous Reproductions," 113.
132 Nikky-Guninder Kaur Singh, "Sikh Mysticism and Sensuous Reproductions," 113–34. See also Sukhbir Singh Kapoor, *Guru Granth Sahib: An Advance Study*, vol. 1 (Hemkunt Press, 2002), 267. He differentiates between instruments whose sound issues from bodily contact with string, leather, metal, tapping, and breath. Gobind Singh Mansukhani

discusses *panch shabad* as corresponding to five instruments without listing them, although he does categorize his instruments based on the divisions presented in *Natyashashtra* (*Indian Classical Music and Sikh Kirtan* [Oxford University Press and IBH, 1982], 37). Pashaura Singh cites Guy Beck's discussion of *Kaulajñāña-Nirnaya* (Pashaura Singh, *Life and Work of Guru Arjan: History, Memory, and Biography in the Sikh Tradition* [Oxford University Press, 2006], 148); and Beck, *Sonic Theology*, 99. See also Christopher Shackle and Arvind-Pal Singh Mandair, eds., *Teachings of the Sikh Gurus: Selections from the Sikh Scriptures* (Routledge, 2005), 149; Kirpal Singh Singh, *Naam or Word* (Ruhani Satsang, 1960), 186; and Margaret Kartomi, *On Concepts and Classifications of Musical Instruments* (University of Chicago Press, 1990), 55–74.

133 *SGGS* 6-4/15.
134 *SGGS* 1291-1/3.
135 *SGGS* 381-11.
136 Rabinder Singh Bhamra, *Sikhism and Spirituality* (Xlibris, 2015), 44–45.
137 Pashaura Singh, "Musical Chaunkis at the Darbar Sahib: History, Aesthetics, and Time," in *Sikhism in Global Context*, ed. Singh (Oxford University Press, 2011), 109.
138 *SGGS* 888-16/18.
139 *SGGS* 1315-18.
140 The description of five kinds of music in *Ramayana*, as differentiated by timbre and playing techniques, gives a sense of what *panch shabad* might be comprised of in the Sikh context: *tantri*, which refers to chordophones (such as the *rabab* or *kingri* in *SGGS*); *tāl*, which refers to playing instruments (such as the *pakhawaj* or *mridang* in *SGGS*); idiophones, such as *jhanjh* (*ghungroo* in *SGGS*); *nagara* (*bheri* in *SGGS*); and *turahi* (referring to *tūr* and *sinyi* in *SGGS*). See Frederic Salmon Growse, trans., *The Ramayana of Tulsidasa* (North-Western Provinces and Oudh Government Press, 1883).
141 *SGGS* 764-8 to 765-14.
142 *SGGS* 985-4, 1201-3.
143 *SGGS* 464-7. Of the gurus, Guru Arjan mentions the *shankh* once in a verse that pays tribute to Vishnu (*SGGS* 1082-17) and again where he calls on the Vedas in arguing against a fixed (Vaishnavite) form for divinity (*SGGS* 1359-6). In contrast, the conch is central to Bhagat Namdev's sonic markers of divinity (*SGGS* 1105-10). Thind describes the hearing of *panch shabad* in the *Maha-Sunna* (great void) region as comprising "four Sound-currents issuing forth from unseen, invisible sources." He focuses on a constantly fluctuating timbral intensity (*The Radiant Road to Reality*, 134).
144 Isabella van Elferen, "Drastic Allure: Timbre Between the Sublime and the Grain," *Contemporary Music Review* 36, no. 6 (2017): 626.
145 Wallmark, *Nothing but Noise*, 17.

CHAPTER 4

1. There is a lack of primary documentation about musical instruments in Punjab. One oft-cited nineteenth-century source is Sadiq Ali Khan's *Sarmāya-i 'ishrat* (also known as *Qānūn-i-mūsīqī*) (1875/1884). More recently, Yousuf Saeed's research on Urdu scholarship about music around the time of the partition presents a potential treasure trove that should be mined for information about instruments, practices, style, and theory in and around Punjab. His documentary, *Khayal Darpan: A Mirror of Imagination*, is also a useful resource for learning more about the migration of knowledge during the partition.
2. Nikky-Guninder Kaur Singh, "Corporeal Metaphysics: Guru Nanak in Early Sikh Art," *History of Religions* 53, no. 1 (2013): 32–33.
3. Surjit Hans, B-40 *Janamsakhi Guru Baba Nanak Paintings* (Guru Nanak Dev University, 1987), 11. The name of the B-40 manuscript reflects its cataloging by accession number.
4. Hans, B-40 *Janamsakhi Guru Baba Nanak Paintings*, 5. See Nikky-Guninder Kaur Singh, "Corporeal Metaphysics"; Nikky-Guninder Kaur Singh, "Tasting the Sweet: Guru Nanak and Sufi Delicacies," in *Cultural Fusion of Sufi Islam: Alternative Paths to Mystical Faith*, ed. Sarwar Alam (Routledge, 2020); Atsushi Ikeda, "Early Sikh Imagery in Janam-Sakhi Painting: A Comparison of the B-40, the Guler and the Unbound Set," *Sikh Formations: Religion, Culture, Theory* 16, no. 3 (2020): 244–68; Gurdeep Kour, "An Analytical Narration of Sikh Influence in Miniature Paintings of Kangra-Guler Style from 18th–19th Century in Punjab" (PhD diss., Lovely Professional University, 2019); and Gurdeep Kour, *Sikh Miniature Paintings: Patronage, Extension, Stylistic Borrowings and Influences* (Lahore Books, 2022).
5. Following Bharat's *Natyashastra*, Mansukhani further organizes these instruments into two categories: those that provide melody (*svara vad*) and those that provide rhythm (*tāl vad*) (Gobind Singh Mansukhani, *Indian Classical Music and Sikh Kirtan* [Oxford University Press and IBH, 1982], 37-38).
6. Prakash Singh, "Ranjīt Nagārā," in the *Concise Encyclopaedia of Sikhism* (Punjabi University, 2013), 543. He mentions that the *nagara* was installed by Guru Gobind Singh at Anandpur Sahib in 1684. Earlier sources such as Śārngadeva's *Sangītaratnākara* describe the *bheri* as a double-headed drum.
7. See Jagtar Singh Grewal, *Guru Gobind Singh (1666–1708): Master of the White Hawk* (Oxford University Press, 2019), 68. As mentioned by Grewal, the thunderous timbre of the *bheri* was also associated with battle, which is a long-standing association also mentioned in the Ramayana (Sally Sutherland Goldman, Robert P. Goldman, and Barend A. van Nooten, *The Rāmāyaṇa of Vālmīki: An Epic of Ancient India*, vol. 6

[Princeton University Press, 2008], 695). See also "Bherī" and "Bher" in *The Grove Dictionary of Musical Instruments*, 2nd ed., ed. Laurence Libin, https://www.oxfordmusiconline.com/page/grove-dictionary-of-musical-instruments.

8   *SGGS* 1382-2. Bhagat Kabir also refers to the beating of drums as a *naubat* in *SGGS* 1368-14.

9   See "Nagara" in Manorama Sharma, *Tribal Melodies of Himachal Pradesh: Gaddi Folk Music* (APH Publishing, 1998), 36. See also Alka Pande, *Folk Music and Musical Instruments of Punjab: From Mustard Fields to Disco Lights* (Grantha, 1999), 86.

10   *SGGS* 1271-18.

11   *SGGS* 356-15, 381-11.

12   *SGGS* 368-7/12.

13   *SGGS* 237-3/4, 263-14.

14   *SGGS* 1072-6.

15   *SGGS* 1033-19.

16   *SGGS* 1040-4.

17   *SGGS* 436-13 (see also 436-15), 1236-11 (see also 778-9, 783-12/13, 545-3).

18   *SGGS* 1162-9.

19   *SGGS* 483-2.

20   *SGGS* 884-12. See also Bigamudre Chaitanya Deva, *Musical Instruments of India: Their History and Development* (Firma, 1978), 59.

21   *SGGS* 381-11.

22   See entries for "Ran-Singha" and "Turi" in Sharma, *Tribal Melodies of Himachal Pradesh*, 35–36.

23   Deva mentions that this instrument could also be made of silver and that it can also be straight, semicircular, or curved (*Musical Instruments of India*, 111–12). See also entries for "Taturi (turahi)" and "Tūra" in Walter Kaufmann, *Selected Musical Terms of Non-Western Cultures: A Notebook-Glossary* (Harmonie, 1990), 708, 737.

24   Deva, *Musical Instruments of India*, 112–13.

25   *SGGS* 258-1, 393-16, 577-6, 618-9, 626-13/14, 781-6/7, 806-12, 408-11.

26   *SGGS* 943-19, 228-5, 834-19, 344-4, 971-7, 1252-16.

27   *SGGS* 877-9.

28   See "Shing" in *The Oxford Encyclopaedia of the Music of India: Saṅgīt Mahābhāratī*, ed. Nikhil Ghosh (Oxford University Press, 2011). See also Bonnie Wade, *Imaging Sound: An Ethnomusicological Study of Music, Art, and Culture in Mughal India* (University of Chicago Press, 1998), for additional names and background (121–22).

29   See "Siṅggā," "Garo Musical Instruments," and "śṛṅgā" in *The Oxford Encyclopaedia of the Music of India*; Ganesh H. Tarlekar and Nalini Tarlekar, *Musical Instruments in Indian Sculpture* (Pune Vidyarthi Griha Prakashan, 1972), 57.

30   Abu'l Fazl Allami, *Ain-i-Akbari*, vol. 1, trans. H. Blochmann (Baptist

Mission Press, 1873), 51. The description of this instrument remains unclear in this translation.
31 *SGGS* 360-2.
32 *SGGS* 907-15, 908-13.
33 *SGGS* 605-12.
34 *SGGS* 208-5.
35 *SGGS* 334-18.
36 *SGGS* 790-4, 1084-6. My translation of *burgoo* is based on Robert Ermers, *Arabic Grammars of Turkic: The Arabic Linguistic Model Applied to Foreign Languages and Translation of 'Abū Ḥayyān Al-'Andalusī's Kitāb Al-'Idrāk Li-Lisān Al-'Atrāk* (Brill, 1999), 132. My thanks to Persian scholar Harpreet Singh for sharing his expertise.
37 *SGGS* 1082-6.
38 *SGGS* 606-16.
39 *SGGS* 1035-9/17.
40 *SGGS* 1236-3.
41 *SGGS* 907-16, 1039-5/6, 1082-16. For a discussion of how the *bayn* is used in folk traditions, see Kamal Prashad Sharma, *Folk Dances of Chambā* (Indus Publishing, 2004), 121. Sharma explains that this instrument is called *bansuri* when made of bamboo and *murli* when made of wood.
42 *SGGS* 988-10.
43 *SGGS* 972-18 to 973-1.
44 *SGGS* 344-11.
45 *SGGS* 884-12/19.
46 *SGGS* 62-14.
47 See Shashishekhar Gopal Deogaonkar and Shailaja Shashishekhar Deogaonkar, *Tribal Dance and Songs* (Concept Publishing, 2003).
48 Joep Bor, *The Voice of the Sarangi: An Illustrated History of Bowing in India* (National Centre for the Performing Arts, 1986), 52–53, 62.
49 *SGGS* 92-15.
50 Cited in Bonnie Wade, "Performing the Drone in Hindustani Classical Music: What Mughal Paintings Show Us to Hear," *World of Music* 38, no. 2 (1996): 46.
51 *SGGS* 907-11.
52 *SGGS* 908-12, 886-5, 886-9/10.
53 Gurdeep Kour, "Bhai Mardana Ji and Rabab in Sikh Miniature Paintings," paper presented at the Rababi Bhai Mardana Ji Conference, Sultanpur Lodi, December 18, 2021.
54 W. H. McLeod, *Popular Sikh Art* (Oxford University Press, 1991).
55 Kour, "An Analytical Narration of Sikh Influence in Miniature Paintings," 211.
56 McLeod, *Popular Sikh Art*, 4; Karamjit K. Malhotra, "In Search of Early Sikh Art," *Proceedings of the Indian History Congress* 71 (2010): 397–408.
57 See Nikky-Guninder Kaur Singh, "Corporeal Metaphysics," 32. The

broad range of *Janamsakhi* illustrations can be gleaned from W. G. Archer, *Paintings of the Sikhs* (Her Majesty's Stationery Office, 1966); B. N. Goswamy, *Painters at the Sikh Court: A Study Based on Twenty Documents* (F. Steiner, 1975) and *Piety and Splendour: Sikh Heritage in Art* (National Museum, 2000); F. S. Aijazuddin, *Pahari Paintings and Sikh Portraits in the Lahore Museum* (Sotheby Parke Bernet, 1977); Kerry Brown, *Sikh Art and Literature* (Routledge, 1999); Susan Stronge, *The Arts of the Sikh Kingdoms* (V&A Collections, 1999); Paul Michael Taylor and Sonia Dhami, eds., *Sikh Art from the Kapany Collection* (Sikh Foundation and Smithsonian Institution, 2017); and Davinder Toor, *In Pursuit of Empire: Treasures from the Toor Collection of Sikh Art* (Kashi House, 2018).

58   See Gurdeep Kaur and Rohita Sharma, "Sikh Identity and Dogra Alteration: A Study of Sikh Influences on Jammu Paintings of Eighteenth-Nineteenth Centuries," *Sikh Formations: Religion, Culture, Theory* 14, no. 2 (2018): 221–37.

59   This painting and sketch are held at the Government Museum and Art Gallery, Chandigarh (acc. no. 4072 [4] and acc. no. 2354, respectively). Both images are reproduced in Goswamy, *Piety and Splendour*, 18. A version of this image can be seen at "Sikh Painting 18th Century Replica Rare Antique Finish Guru Nanak Sikhism Art," ArtnIndia, https://artandindia.ecrater.com/p/22105538/sikh-painting-18th-century-replica.

60   This image is reproduced in Stronge, *The Arts of the Sikh Kingdoms*, 111. It can be seen at "Guru Nanak Roff," SearchKashmir, https://searchkashmir.org/2012/10/guru-nanak-roff.html.

61   Aitken makes a similar point with respect to Rajasthani court paintings (Molly Aitken, *The Intelligence of Tradition in Rajput Court Painting* [Yale University Press, 2010], 10–55). An emphasis on *bhaav* can also be seen in Govardhan's *A Rustic Concert* (1625), where the support of the *rabab* sends the singer into a state of ecstasy suggested by his closed eyes; this is likely a performance, as signaled by the companions who sit and listen intently. This image is part of the *Royal Album* (Chester Beatty Library, Dublin, MS 7a, No.11).

62   Kour, "An Analytical Narration of Sikh Influence in Miniature Paintings," 233.

63   This painting is reproduced in Goswamy, *Piety and Splendour*, 57. Perhaps the only exception is an early nineteenth-century painting in the Kangra style held at the British Museum (museum no. 1922,1214,0.2), which claims to show Guru Nanak and Bhai Mardana playing a *saranda*, although it is questionable as to whether this painting is correctly attributed: https://www.britishmuseum.org/collection/object/A_1922-1214-0-2.

64   Daljeet Kaur, *The Sikh Heritage: A Search for Totality* (Prakash, 2004), 34.

65   See Hans, B-40 *Janamsakhi Guru Baba Nanak Paintings*, 53–54.

66 Nikky-Guninder Kaur Singh, "Corporeal Metaphysics." My thanks to Suhail Khan for helping me decipher this *asana*.
67 Goswamy, *Piety and Splendour*, 18.
68 The origins and characteristics of *ravanahasta* are discussed by Bor, *The Voice of the Sarangi*, 43–47.
69 Deva, *Musical Instruments of India*, 34.
70 Margaret Kartomi, *On Concepts and Classifications of Musical Instruments* (University of Chicago Press, 1990), 59.
71 These images are reproduced in *Roopa Lekha* 39, no. 1 (1970): 14.
72 Goswamy, *Piety and Splendour*, 33.
73 See Andrew Greig, "*Tārīkh-i Sangīta*: The Foundations of North Indian Music in the Sixteenth Century" (PhD diss., University of California Los Angeles, 1987), 469–70. Greig explains that the origins of the *rabab* "are probably to be found in the Middle East," while he links this instrument to "the contiguous musical cultures of the Eurasian continent" and to a "variety of instruments named Rabāb."
74 K. Krishna Murthy, *Archaeology of Indian Musical Instruments* (Sundeep Prakashan, 1985), 12.
75 The foundational text for the study of ancient Indian musical instruments is Claudie Marcel-Dubois, *Les instruments de musique de l'Inde ancienne* (Presses Universitaires de France, 1941).
76 Subrahmanyam Krishnaswami, *Musical Instruments of India* (Publications Division, Ministry of Information and Broadcasting, Government of India, 1971), 48.
77 Kailash Nath Dikshit, *Prehistoric Civilization of the Indus Valley* (University of Madras, 1967), 28.
78 See the website of the Gujri Mahal Museum Gwalior (Door Lintel [Sirdal]) and at Monika Ohson (blog), January 3, 2017, https://travelerinmeblog.wordpress.com/2017/01/03/gujarimahal/ (see bottom left for the *kacchapi veena*). Kasliwal claims that "the instrument is so clearly shown that one can even count the number of strings—seven.... Prof. Lal Mani Mishra and B. C. Deva identify this instrument as chitra veena, perhaps, because chitra is described as having seven strings by Bharat" (Suneera Kasliwal, *Classical Musical Instruments* [Rupa, 2001], 156). See Deva, *Musical Instruments of India*, 161.
79 Gabriela Currie, "Sonic Entanglements, Visual Records and the Gandhāran Nexus," in *The Music Road: Coherence and Diversity in Music from the Mediterranean to India*, ed. Reinhard Strohm (Oxford University Press, 2019), 41–70.
80 James A. Millward, "The Silk Road and the Sitar: Finding Centuries of Sociocultural Exchange in the History of an Instrument," *Journal of Social History* 52, no. 2 (2018): 210.
81 Currie, "Sonic Entanglements, Visual Records and the Gandhāran Nexus," 67–68.

82   Currie, "Sonic Entanglements, Visual Records and the Gandhāran Nexus," 67; Allyn Miner, *Sitar and Sarod in the 18th and 19th Centuries* (Noetzel, 1993), 61; Misra as cited in Kasliwal, *Classical Musical Instruments*, 159.

83   On a related concern, see Katherine Butler Brown, "Evidence of Indo-Persian Musical Synthesis? The Tanbur and Rudra Vina in Seventeenth-Century Indo-Persian Treatises," *Journal of the Indian Musicological Society* 36–37 (2006): 89–103.

84   As stated in *The Oxford Encyclopaedia of the Music of India*, early modern references to the *rabab* are found in *Ain-i-Akbari* by Abu'l Fazl and *Rāg Darpaṇ* (1666) by the Mughal music theorist Faqirullah. The following *rabab* players are mentioned in *Ain-i-Akbari*: Bayajid, Rabbani Saleh, Rabani Dhadi, Sikharsen (or Sugharsen), and Hayati. Faqirullah mentions Sheikh Bahauddin Burnawa as a well-known exponent of the *rabab* in *Rāg Darpaṇ*.

85   Greig, "*Tārīkh-i Sangīta*," 469–70.

86   Greig, "*Tārīkh-i Sangīta*," 470–74. He explains that the "Persian Rabāb is similar to, but not the same as, Rabābs shown in Indian miniatures [paintings]" (470).

87   Tansen's daughter's lineage cultivated the *been* or *rudra veena*, whereas his son's side of the family cultivated the *rabab* (Kasliwal, *Classical Musical Instruments*, 109, 157 [on Tansen's expertise]). Adrian McNeil traces this *beenkar* lineage in *Inventing the Sarod: A Cultural History* (Seagull Books, 2004), 53–54.

88   These names are mentioned in Kasliwal, *Classical Musical Instruments*, 153–54.

89   Misra as cited in Kasliwal, *Classical Musical Instruments*, 158.

90   McNeil offers a detailed description of the *Afghani* (or *Pathan*) *rabab* in *Inventing the Sarod*, 24–27. Regarding the organological link between the *sarod* and *rabab*, several scholars observe that the *Afghani rabab* was referred to as "surud or sarod long before the invention of the instrument" (28). See also Max Katz, *Lineage of Loss: Counternarratives of North Indian Music* (Wesleyan University Press, 2017), 89.

91   Aygul Malkeyeva observes three different types of *rabab* in the memoirs of Babur (*Bāburnāma*), as well as the portrayal of two different *rabab* within a single image (Malkeyeva, "Musical Instruments in the Text and Miniatures of the 'Bāburnāma,'" *IdIM/RCMI Newsletter* 22, no. 1 [1997]: 12–22).

92   Scholars regard Henry George Farmer's research on this topic as an important starting point ("The Origin of the Arabian Lute and Rebec," *Journal of the Royal Asiatic Society of Great Britain and Ireland* [1930]: 767–83). Recent research can be seen in conference abstracts for Das mittelalterliche Rabab—ein Streichinstrument mit arabisch-islamischer Vergangenheit und Gegenwart (The Medieval Rabab—a Bowed String Instrument with an Arabic-Islamic Past and Present), Switzerland,

November 2021, organized by Marina Haiduk. For additional research on the *rabab* in the Arab world, see Josef Kuckertz, "Origin and Development of the Rabab," *Sangeet Natak Akademi* (1970): 16–30; and Kartomi, *On Concepts and Classifications of Musical Instruments*, 125–27.

93 Murthy, *Archaeology of Indian Musical Instruments*, 29.
94 Krishnaswami, *Musical Instruments of India*, 15.
95 Bhai Baldeep Singh also observes this resemblance in *Yaar Anad Virtual Baithak Series* (season 1, episode 150, "Presentation on Musical Instruments"), beginning at 01:38:00, https://youtu.be/Db1tnzT6OQU.
96 A beautifully painted (in a Rajasthani style) nineteenth-century *rabab*, with a close-up photo of a wooden plectrum, is in storage at the Horniman museum in the United Kingdom (museum no. 3924) (https://www.horniman.ac.uk/object/3924/).
97 Greig, "*Tārīkh-i Sangīta*," 471.
98 Guru Nanak's *udasi* (travels) are broadly understood to have been taken in the direction of the West, South, North, and East and, finally, within Punjab. Sometimes he is said to have undertaken four *udasi*. See Harbans Singh, *Encyclopedia of Sikhism* (Hemkunt Publishers, 2000), 198. Gurinderpal Singh Josan in *Rababi Bhai Mardana te Puratan Kirtaniye* (Shahid-e-Azam, 2020) ascribes the following dates to these *udasi*: 1500–1506, 1506–13, 1514–18, 1519–21, and 1523–24 (27).
99 Miner, *Sitar and Sarod in the 18th and 19th Centuries*, 61. An example of a Persian *rabab* with a characteristic bent neck can be seen in a miniature held at the British Museum (museum no. 1974,0617,0.15.23): https://www.britishmuseum.org/collection/object/W_1974-0617-0-15-23. Another fine depiction of the Persian *rabab* can be seen in "Portrait of a Prince" (inscribed to Aqa Riza, 1590–1600). This image is published in Ashok Kumar Srivastava, *Mughal Painting: An Interplay of Indigenous and Foreign Traditions* (Munshiram Manoharlal, 2000), plate 32, and housed at the Museum of Fine Arts Boston (no. 14. 609).
100 A Persian style *rabab* can also be seen at https://commons.wikimedia.org/wiki/File:Guru_Nanak_With_Bhai_Bala_and_Bhai_Mardana.jpg.
101 Goswamy, *Piety and Splendour*, 18, 19, 23, 25. See also a slightly later painting from Guler (1815–20) shown in Aijazuddin, *Pahari Paintings and Sikh Portraits in the Lahore Museum*, plate 47 (i). A similar image with the angled peg box can be seen in this watercolor painting: *Guru Nanak and His Companions Mardana and Bhai Bala*, object no. 1998.93, Kapany Collection, Asian Art Museum.
102 See Goswamy, *Piety and Splendour*, 20.
103 See *Guru Nanak and His Companions Mardana and Bhai Bala*; *Guru Nanak with Mardana and Bala*, accession no. IM.2:125–1917, Victoria and Albert Museum; *Guru Nanak Seated on a Terrace in Discourse with Raja Shivanabh in Sri Lanka, Mardana in Attendance* (Bonhams); and *Guru Nanak the First Sikh Guru*, Royal Collection Trust (RCIN 925202).
104 Miner, *Sitar and Sarod in the 18th and 19th Centuries*, 62.

105 See *Guru Nanak and Bhai Mardana in a Landscape* (1750–99) (Artnet).
106 https://indianculture.gov.in/museum-paintings/leaf-series-janam-sakhi-0 (accession no. 63.1321).
107 See *Guru Nanak's Meeting with Dhru Bhagat on Mount Kailasha*, object no. 1998.58.27, and *Guru Nanak's Meeting with Praladh*, object no. 1998.58.26, Kapany Collection, Asian Art Museum.
108 On the topic of the drone in Indian painting, see Wade, "Performing the Drone in Hindustani Classical Music," 41–67.
109 See *Guru Nanak Meets Nath Siddhas at the Village of Achal Batala*, object no. 1998.58.31, and *Guru Nanak's Visit to Bhai Lalo the Carpenter*, object no. 1998.58.14, Kapany Collection, Asian Art Museum.
110 Khusrau as cited by Wade, "Performing the Drone in Hindustani Classical Music," 46.
111 Wade, "Performing the Drone in Hindustani Classical Music," 53.
112 See Toor, *In Pursuit of Empire*, 5. This image is also published in Amandeep Singh Madra and Parmjit Singh, *Warrior Saints: Four Centuries of Sikh Military History*, vol. 1 (Kashi House, 2013), 5.
113 See *Guru Nanak and the Cannibal Kauda*, object no. 1998.58.16, Kapany Collection, Asian Art Museum. Here the painter has failed to distinguish between the *rabab*'s skin membrane and its wooden frame (discussed below).
114 See Taylor and Dhami, eds., *Sikh Art from the Kapany Collection*, 84.
115 Govardhan, *Prince and Ascetics* (1630) from the *Late Shah Jahan Album*, accession no. 1971.79, Andrew R. and Martha Holden Jennings Fund, Cleveland Museum of Art. See also Govardhan, *A Rustic Concert* (1625) from *Royal Album*, Chester Beatty Library, Dublin (MS 7a, No.11).
116 We see an early seventeenth-century example of the half-kneeling position in a Rajasthani painting by Nasiruddin. See *Malkos Raga: Folio from the Chawand Ragamala Series* (1605).
117 See *Guru Nanak's Meeting with Sajan the Thug*, object no. 1998.58.32, Kapany Collection, Asian Art Museum.
118 See *Guru Nanak Visiting His Sister Bibi Nanaki*, object no. 1998.58.24; and *Guru Nanak's Discourse with Datatre on Mount Byar*, object no. 1998.58.25, Kapany Collection, Asian Art Museum.
119 See *Bhai Mardana Ji Playing Rabab to Accompany Guru Nanak in Song*, object no. M.2006.2.31, Williams College; and *Guru Nanak (1469–1539) The First Guru of the Sikhs*, accession no. 59.314, National Museum New Delhi.
120 See Hunhar, *A Mughal Prince with a Musician*, in the Richard Johnson Collection, Johnson 4, 5, British Library. This image can be viewed on Bridgeman Images: *Mughal Prince with Musician* (BL3268969).
121 McNeil, *Inventing the Sarod*, 127. A traveler's account that documents musicians playing standing up for "dancing girls" (often described in colonial accounts as *nautch/nach* girls) can be seen in Frank Vincent Jr., *Through and Through the Tropics: 30,000 Miles of Travel in Polynesia,*

Australasia, and India (Harper and Brothers, 1882), 172–73. He describes four musicians: two who appear to play the *sarangi* or another similar bowed instrument supported by a waistband, a *tabla* player who also holds his instruments with the support of a belt, and a percussionist playing the cymbals.

122 See *Guru Nanak with Followers*, accession no. IM.2:33-1917, Victoria and Albert Museum. McLeod describes this woodcut as "Guru Nanak hearing *kirtan* in the presence of his two sons, four attendants and Bhai Salo. Amritsar, 1874–75" (*Popular Sikh Art*, 127).

123 See Aijazuddin, *Pahari Paintings and Sikh Portraits in the Lahore Museum*, plate 47 (vi); *Guru Har Kishan* (1815–20), Guler (place of painting).

124 See Wade, "Performing the Drone in Hindustani Classical Music," 60; and Miner, *Sitar and Sarod in the 18th and 19th Centuries*, 28–31.

125 Paintal, "The Contribution of Ragis and Rababis to the Sikh Devotional Music," 258.

126 *Guru Nanak with the Other Nine Gurus* (1882) is attributed to Bhai Puran Singh and reproduced in Goswamy, *Piety and Splendour*, 40–41. The original image is held at the Government Museum and Art Gallery, Chandigarh (accession no. 3787). It can be viewed on alamy.com.

127 This painting is reproduced in Goswamy, *Piety and Splendour*, 34.

128 See *Three Musicians*, accession no. 47.110/1017, National Museum New Delhi.

129 See *Guru Nanak and His Companions Mardana and Bhai Bala*. For a later rendition from Guler (1815–20), see Aijazuddin, *Pahari Paintings and Sikh Portraits in the Lahore Museum*, 47 (i), *Guru Nanak*.

130 Madanjit Kaur, *The Golden Temple Past and Present* (Guru Nanak Dev University Press, 1983), 147.

131 Miner, *Sitar and Sarod in the 18th and 19th Centuries*, 62–64.

132 McNeil, *Inventing the Sarod*, 128.

133 See also Madhumita Dutta, *Music and Musical Instruments of India* (IBS Books, 2008), 22–23.

134 McNeil, *Inventing the Sarod*, 14, 39. McNeil mentions that the *seniya rabab* had a higher status in India by the time the *Afghani rabab* arrived with Afghani soldiers in the sixteenth or seventeenth century. See also Miner, *Sitar and Sarod in the 18th and 19th Centuries*, 66.

135 Miner cites from Karamatullah Khan, *Isrār-i karāmat urf naghmāt-i na'mat and Risāla sitar* (Allahabad: Janaki Press, 1908), 160 (Miner, *Sitar and Sarod in the 18th and 19th Centuries*, 66).

136 McNeil, *Inventing the Sarod*, 128. See Peter Manuel and Brian Bond, "Rāgs of Western India and Sindh," *Analytical Approaches to World Music* 10, no. 2 (2022): 10.

137 Katherine Butler Schofield, *Music and Musicians in Late Mughal India: Histories of the Ephemeral, 1748–1858* (Cambridge University Press, 2023), 243.

138   See Harish Dhillon, *The Sikh Gurus* (Hay House, 2015), 155; and Schofield, *Music and Musicians in Late Mughal India*, 27–35.

139   There is variation between the details of these family trees and those presented in Balbir Singh Kanwal, *Punjab de Parsidh Ragi Rababi: 1604–2004* (Singh Brothers, 2010); Josan, *Rababi Bhai Mardana te Puratan Kirtaniye*, 63, 77, in particular, although lineages for *ragi* are shown throughout this book; and Navtej K. Purewal, "Sikh/Muslim Bhai-Bhai? Towards a Social History of the Rabābī Tradition of Shabad Kīrtan," *Sikh Formations: Religion, Culture, Theory* 7, no. 3 (2011): 365–82. On this topic, see also Kaur, *The Golden Temple Past and Present*, 210–11; Sharan Arora, "Guru Nanak Dev Ji and the Rababi Tradition," *Journal of Sikh Studies* 24, no. 2 (2000): 161–76; and appendixes by Paintal, "The Contribution of Ragis and Rababis to the Sikh Devotional Music," 265–71, 272–81.

140   Kanwal, *Punjab de Parsidh Ragi Rababi*, 28–29. A photo of Sham Singh playing *saranda* can be seen at Kirtan Anmol Ratan, https://www.kirtananmolratan.com/ragis, and in print in Josan, *Rababi Bhai Mardana te Puratan Kirtaniye*, 89. An English account of Sham Singh's life can be found at "Sham Singh, Sant," The Sikh Encyclopedia, https://www.thesikhencyclopedia.com/biographical/sikh-mystics-and-traditional-scholars/sham-singh-sant/.

141   See also Kapuria's recent study of musical culture in the main courts of Punjab (Radha Kapuria, *Music in Colonial Punjab: Courtesans, Bards, and Connoisseurs, 1800–1947* [Oxford University Press, 2023], 277–339).

142   Kanwal, *Punjab de Parsidh Ragi Rababi*, 28–29; on Mahant Gajja Singh, see p. 29. For information in English about Gajja Singh's training and Mir Rahmat Ali of Kapurthala, see "Gajja Singh, Mahant," *Sikh Encyclopedia*, https://www.thesikhencyclopedia.com/arts-and-heritage/musicology-and-musicians/gajja-singh-mahant/.

143   Bor, *The Voice of the Sarangi*, 62.

144   Miner notes that earlier archival mention of the *Sikandar Rabāb* has yet to be discovered (Miner, *Sitar and Sarod in the 18th and 19th Centuries*, 62). Miner's source for her observation regarding the *rabab sikandari* is Sadiq Khan, *Sarmāya-i 'ishrat*, 283. See also the entry for "Rabāb" in *The Oxford Encyclopaedia of the Music of India*.

145   *Guru Nanak Meets Firanda the Rabab Maker*, object no. 1998.58.13, Kapany Collection, Asian Art Museum. The painter of this *rabab* seems to have colored over the skin membrane, which is a vital distinguishing feature of this instrument, as discussed above. Based on a similar appearance of the *rabab*, the same painter probably prepared *Guru Nanak's Meeting with the Jeweler Salas Rai*, object no. 1998.58.35, Kapany Collection, Asian Art Museum. On Bhai Firanda, see Trilochan Singh, *Guru Nanak: Founder of Sikhism, A Biography* (Gurdwara Parbandhak Committee, 1969), 60. There are differing oral accounts of how Bhai Mardana came to receive his *rabab*. One strand of oral history maintains that at the

bidding of her brother, Guru Nanak's sister, Bebe Nanaki, gave Bhai Mardana seven rupees for the purchase of a *rabab* from Bhai Firanda, who freely gave the instrument once he realized it had been requested by Guru Nanak. As captured in Devender Singh's painting, another prominent narrative is that the *rabab* was presented by Bebe Nanaki to Bhai Mardana. See *Bebe Nanaki* (2011) in Taylor and Dhami, eds., *Sikh Art from the Kapany Collection*, 94. On recent debates regarding the discovery of the *Firanda rabab*, see Gurnam Singh's interview and Bhai Baldeep Singh's response in Bharat Khanna, "Punjabi Varsity's Firandia Rabab Helps Revival of String Instrument," *The Times of India*, November 1, 2019, http://timesofindia.indiatimes.com/articleshow/71851191.cms.

146 See *Guru Nanak in Kamarupa, the Land Ruled by Women*, object no. 1998.58.15, Kapany Collection, Asian Art Museum.

147 Wade, "Performing the Drone in Hindustani Classical Music," 60. For a detailed discussion regarding the emergence of the *sursingar* in the early nineteenth century, see McNeil, *Inventing the Sarod*, 85–88.

148 See Miner, *Sitar and Sarod in the 18th and 19th Centuries*, 69–70.

149 *Guru Nanak Meets the Poet Kabir*, object no. 1998.58.28, Kapany Collection, Asian Art Museum; *Guru Nanak's Meeting with Dev Loot and Other Demons*, object no. 1998.58.20, Kapany Collection, Asian Art Museum. For other examples of a notched waist *rabab*, see *Guru Nanak and Raja Sudhar Sain, Jhanda Badhi the Carpenter, and Indar Sain*, object no. 1998.58.19, Kapany Collection, Asian Art Museum; and *Guru Nanak's Meeting with the Demon Kaliyug*, object no. 1998.58.18, Kapany Collection, Asian Art Museum.

150 The entire series can be seen on the Royal Collection Trust website beginning with this portrait: *Guru Nanak (the First Sikh Guru)* (RCIN 925202).

151 See Kour, *Sikh Miniature Paintings*, 203.

152 Although the *saranda* is thought to have been adapted by Guru Arjan for the purposes of *kirtan*, many scholars credit Guru Amardas with having introduced the instrument on the basis of oral narratives and the observations of Sadiq Ali Khan. Kanwal, *Punjab de Parsidh Ragi Rababi*, 25–26; and Prithipal Singh Kapur and Dharam Singh, eds., *Perspectives on Sikhism: Papers Presented at the International Seminar on Sikhism: A Religion for the Third Millenium Punjabi University, Patiala on 27–29 March 2000* (Publication Bureau, 2001), 156–58.

153 Vishal Rambani, "Rare 400-Year-Old Rabab Thrills Visitors to Gurmat Sangeet Function," *Hindustan Times*, October 8, 2012, SikhNet, https://www.sikhnet.com/news/rare-400-year-old-rabab-thrills-visitors-gurmat-sangeet-function. Josan claims a date of 1605 for this instrument and maintains that it had six strings (*Rababi Bhai Mardana te Puratan Kirtaniye*, 5).

154 At present, published material on this instrument is restricted to newspaper articles. A YouTube video displays the *rabab* and claims that it was made in Afghanistan from a single piece of wood: "Darshan karo ji sri Guru Arjan Dev Ji Rabab sahib de," posted by Sikhs USA Canada, September 7, 2017, YouTube, https://www.youtube.com/watch?v=1u60w6lPzMU. To Bhatia's point, no painting is visible except for the ivory inlay at the top of the peg box and the detailed wooden carving.

155 For the *rabab* that is believed to have belonged to Guru Gobind Singh, see the gallery of photos for Gurudwara Sri Padal Sahib in Himanchal Pradesh (Mandi): http://www.discoversikhism.com/sikh_gurdwaras/gurdwara_sri_padal_sahib.html#gallery[gallery1]/14/. Josan shows a photo of this *rabab* and claims that it was given by Guru Gobind Singh to Maharaj Sidh Sain in 1701 as a gift (*Rababi Bhai Mardana te Puratan Kirtaniye*, 4). Francesca Cassio briefly studies this instrument ("Gurbāṇī Saṅgīt: Authenticity and Influences—A Study of the Sikh Musical Tradition in Relation to Medieval and Early Modern Indian Music," *Sikh Formations: Religion, Culture, Theory* 11 [2015]: 47).

156 Josan, *Rababi Bhai Mardana te Puratan Kirtaniye*, 4.

157 Daljeet [Kaur], *The Sikh Heritage*, 115.

158 S. Bandyopadhyaya also mentions *sāla*, teak, and *tūn* as additional sources of wood for the *rabab* (Shripada Bandyopadhyaya, *Musical Instruments of India* [Varanasi, 1980]: 50).

159 As cited by Miner, Tagore also notes the convenience of the *rabab* as a traveling instrument, and Bor notes its association with active Rajputs and Afghanis (Miner, *Sitar and Sarod in the 18th and 19th Centuries*, 66).

160 Josan has a version of this story (*Rababi Bhai Mardana te Puratan Kirtaniye*, 25).

161 Some oral accounts hold that Bhai Mardana belonged to a caste of hereditary musicians (*mirasi*).

162 Shahab Sarmadee Faqīrullāh, *Tarjuma-i-Mānakutūhala and Risāla-i-Rāgadarpaṇa* (Indira Gandhi National Centre for the Arts and Motilal Banarsidass Publishers, 1996), 125.

163 Greig, "*Tārīkh-i Saṅgīta*," 511, 468.

164 Mohinder Singh, "Golden Temple: Spiritual Capital of the Sikhs," in *Sikh Art from the Kapany Collection*, ed. Paul Michael Taylor and Sonia Dhami (Sikh Foundation and Smithsonian Institution, 2017), 117. See also Wade, *Imaging Sound*, 228–29, n. 10.

165 See Pashaura Singh, "Speaking Truth to Power: Exploring Guru Nanak's *Bābar-vāṇī* in Light of the *Baburnama*," *MDPI Religions* 11 (2020): 16.

166 *SGGS* 934-5.

167 Kasliwal, *Classical Musical Instruments*, 237.

168 This story is recounted in numerous forms and places. I refer the reader to Daniel M. Neuman, *The Life of Music in North India: The Organization of an Artistic Tradition* (University of Chicago Press, 1990),

59. This image is held at the National Museum (New Delhi) and can be viewed at "Swami Haridasa with Tansen and Akbar at Vrindavana," Google Arts and Culture, https://artsandculture.google.com/story/swami-haridasa-with-tansen-and-akbar-at-vrindavana-national-museum-delhi/DQWxgRQXAigBMQ?hl=en.

169 A recent retelling of this narrative by *kirtaniya* Navjodh Singh Harike mentions that Swami Haridas learned for a short time with Bhai Mardana and for a longer time with his sons, Rajada and Sajada, in Kartarpur (https://www.youtube.com/watch?v=ohdAKFI8iA4, starting at 25:00; in Punjabi). See also Gajindar Singh, *A God Made to Order* (Manbir G. Singh, 2006), 175.

170 The name of this manuscript reflects its cataloging by accession number at the British Library: MS Panj B40.

171 Nikky-Guninder Kaur Singh, "Tasting the Sweet," 38.

172 Hans, *B-40 Janamsakhi Guru Baba Nanak Paintings*, 6.

173 Images from B-40 are available for online viewing in a digitization of Hans's book: http://www.discoversikhism.com/sikh_library/english/b-40_janamsakhi_guru_baba_nanak_paintings.html.

174 See images 33, 34, 35, 46, 47, 48, and 55, respectively.

175 See "Two Miniatures from a Janamsakhi Manuscript Punjab Hills, Late 18th Century."

176 Bandyopadhyaya, *Musical Instruments of India*, 34. Ebony and metal are other materials used for a plectrum (50).

177 See my detailed study of the halo, "Anahad Naad and Pictorial Resonance: The Halo and Sonic Vibration in Sikh Art," *Sikh Research Journal* 8, no. 1 (2023): 1–22.

178 Som Prakash Verma, "Symbols and Motifs in the Mughal School of Art," in *Art and Culture: Painting and Perspective*, vol. 2, ed. Ahsan Jan Qaisar and Som Prakash Verma (Abhinav Publications, 2002), 51.

179 See, for example, Ralph Losey, "The Impact on the Aura of Music, Sound, and PrimaSounds," in *Capturing the Aura: Integrating Science, Technology and Metaphysics*, ed. C. E. Lindgren (Motilal Banarsidass, 2008), 135–52.

180 Ernest Binfield Havell, *The Ideals of Indian Art* (E. P. Dutton, 1920), 48.

181 See *Guru Nanak and Bhai Mardana in a Landscape*. Verma, "Symbols and Motifs in the Mughal School of Art," 48. Verma also notes the Mughal preference for a European-styled halo "for the visual representation of their patron's expression and the symbolic form of the divine light."

182 See also Kour, *Sikh Miniature Paintings*, 203.

CHAPTER 5

1 My attention to a sensory experience of *kirtan* is informed by research on embodiment in music studies and sensory studies as guided by

modal anthropology, anthropology of the senses, and sensory ethnomusicology (see François Laplantine, *The Life of the Senses: Introduction to Modal Anthropology*, trans. Jamie Furniss [Bloomsbury, 2015]; and Sarah Pink, *Doing Sensory Ethnography* [Sage, 2009]).

2   The first wave of studies include N. G. Barrier, "Trauma and Memory Within the Sikh Diaspora: Internet Dialogue," *Sikh Formations: Religion, Culture, Theory* 2, no. 1 (2006): 33–56; Doris Jakobsh, "Authority in the Virtual Sangat: Sikhism, Ritual and Identity in the Twenty-First Century," *Heidelberg Journal of Religions on the Internet* 2, no. 1 (2006): 24–40; Doris Jakobsh, "'Sikhizing the Sikhs': The Role of 'New Media' in Historical and Contemporary Identity Construction Within Global Sikhism," in *Sikhs Across Borders: Transnational Practices Among European Sikhs*, ed. Knut A. Jacobsen and Kristina Myrvold (Continuum, 2012), 141–63; Satnam Singh, "Attending the Cyber Sangat: The Use of Online Discussion Boards Among European Sikhs," in *Sikhs Across Borders: Transnational Practices Among European Sikhs*, ed. Knut A. Jacobsen and Kristina Myrvold (Continuum, 2012), 119–40; Susan Elizabeth Prill, "Sikhi Through Internet, Films, and Videos," in *The Oxford Handbook of Sikh Studies*, ed. Pashaura Singh (Oxford University Press, 2014), 471–81; and Francesca Cassio, "Female Voices in Gurbāṇī Saṅgīt and the Role of the Media in Promoting Female Kīrtanīe," *Sikh Formations: Religion, Culture, Theory* 10 (2014): 233–69. Recent scholarship on digital technology includes Arvind-Pal Singh Mandair, "Im/materialities: Translation Technologies and the (Dis)Enchantment of Diasporic Life-Worlds," *Religion* 49, no. 3 (2019): 413–38; and "Media," in Pashaura Singh and Arvind-Pal Singh Mandair, part 9 in *The Sikh World* (Routledge, 2023), which includes chapters by Jasjit Singh, Conner Singh VanderBeek, and Nirinjan Kaur Khalsa-Baker. See also Knut Lundby, "Mediatization," in *The Handbook on Religion and Communication*, ed. Yoel Cohen and Paul Soukup (Wiley Blackwell, 2023), 276–77; Dhanya Fee Kirchhoff, "Ravidassia: Neither Sikh nor Hindu? Mediatized Religion in Anti-Caste Contexts," in *Mediatized Religion in Asia: Studies on Digital Media and Religion*, ed. Kerstin Radde-Antweiler and Xenia Zeiler (Routledge, 2019), 121–38; and Thea Tiramani, "Sikh Religious Music in a Migration Context: The Role of Media," *European Journal of Musicology* 20, no. 1 (2021): 269–90.

3   Jasjit Singh, "Sikh-ing Online: The Role of the Internet in the Religious Lives of Young British Sikhs," *Contemporary South Asia* 22, no. 1 (2014): 82–97.

4   Thomas Brandon Evans, "Listening to the Infinite: Sikh Soundscapes, Media, and Audiovisions" (PhD diss., Harvard University, 2022), 127–29.

5   Heidi A. Campbell, *When Religion Meets New Media* (Routledge, 2010), 5. In response to the diversifying digital terrain, her later books are

broader in scope. For different perspectives on digital religion, see Stef Aupers and Dick Houtman, eds., *Religions of Modernity: Relocating the Sacred to the Self and the Digital* (Brill, 2019).

6   Annette Wilke and Oliver Moebus, eds., *Sound and Communication: An Aesthetic Cultural History of Sanskrit Hinduism* (De Gruyter, 2011); and Murali Balaji, *Digital Hinduism: Dharma and Discourse in the Age of New Media* (Lexington Books, 2018).

7   Taha Kazi, *Religious Television and Pious Authority in Pakistan* (Indiana University Press, 2021), viii; Patrick Eisenlohr, *Sounding Islam: Voice, Media, and Sonic Atmospheres in an Indian Ocean World* (University of California Press, 2018), 3.

8   Naveeda Khan, 2011. "The Acoustics of Muslim Striving: Loudspeaker Use in Ritual Practice in Pakistan," *Comparative Studies in Society and History* 53, no. 3 (2011): 571–94.

9   Pradeep Gupta, "10,000 Tune into Headphones at Ulhasnagar Kirtan Gathering," *Times of India*, October 19, 2017; Ketan Vaidya, "Technology Solution to Problems of Faith," *DNA*, December 27, 2018; Isaac Weiner, *Religion Out Loud: Religious Sound, Public Space, and American Pluralism* (New York University Press, 2014); Lily Wong and Orlando Woods, *Religion and Space: Competition, Conflict and Violence in the Contemporary World* (Bloomsbury, 2016).

10 On this topic, see Samhita Sunya, "High-Fidelity Ecologies: India Versus Noise Pollution in the Contemporary Public Sphere," in *Indian Sound Cultures, Indian Sound Citizenship*, ed. Laura Brueck, Jacob Smith, and Neil Verma (University of Michigan Press, 2020), 106–9.

11 "This Navratri, Mumbai Brings in SILENT GARBA," *Indian Express*, September 20, 2017.

12 W. H. McLeod, *The B40 Janam-Sakhi* (Guru Nanak Dev University, 1980), 260–61.

13 Bhai Gurdas, *Vāran*, Pauri 27, "Guru Nanak Suryodhaya," https://www.sikhitothemax.org/ang.

14 Nikky-Guninder Kaur Singh, *Sikhism: An Introduction* (I. B. Tauris, 2011), 35.

15 Madanjit Kaur, *The Golden Temple Past and Present* (Guru Nanak Dev University Press, 1983), 17.

16 Davwinder (Dindae) Sheena, in conversation with the author, May 15, 2024.

17 Archana Matharu, "Harmandar Sahib Goes Hi-Tech," *Hindustan Times*, June 11, 2012. Matharu writes, "Nearly 90 small Bose speakers have been installed at the parikarma which project 80 decibels of sound and ensure top vocal quality."

18 Evans, "Listening to the Infinite," 25.

19 William Mason, "Some Embodied Poetics of EQ and Compression," paper presented at the Society for Music Theory, November 12, 2022.

20 Paul Théberge, "The Sound of Nowhere: Reverb and the Construction of Sonic Space," in *The Relentless Pursuit of Tone: Timbre in Popular Music*, ed. Robert Fink, Melinda Latour, and Zachary Wallmark (Oxford University Press, 2018), 325.

21 Nikky-Guninder Kaur Singh, *Sikhism*, 36.

22 See, for example, Susan Hale, *Sacred Space, Sacred Sound: The Acoustic Mysteries of Holy Places* (Quest Books, 2007), and David Elkington, *The Ancient Language of Sacred Sound: The Acoustic Science of the Divine* (Inner Traditions, 2021).

23 Catherine Gomes, Lily Kong, and Orlando Woods, eds., *Religion, Hypermobility and Digital Media in Global Asia: Faith, Flows and Fellowship* (Amsterdam University Press, 2020).

24 The TV network that broadcasts from Harmandir Sahib has recently changed from PTC to SGPC. Live *kirtan* can now be accessed on YouTube via the Official SGPC LIVE channel. Pashaura Singh documents the politics surrounding TV broadcasting from Harmandir Sahib in "The Reverberation of the Sacred Gurbani's Vibrations at the Darbar Sahib: The Issue of Its Television Broadcasting," *Religions* 15 (2024): 1–3.

25 Jasjit Singh, "Young Sikhs' Religious Engagement Online," in *Digital Methodologies in the Sociology of Religion*, ed. Sariya Cheruvallil-Contractor and Suha Shakkour (Bloomsbury, 2015), 87.

26 Heinz Scheifinger speaks to similar issues in the practice of Hindu *puja* ("Hindu Worship Online and Offline," in *Digital Religion: Understanding Religious Practice in New Media Worlds*, ed. Heidi Campbell [Routledge, 2012], 121–27).

27 Although I use these apps to access *kirtan* primarily, many other features are available to users, such as podcasts, radio, daily prayers (*nitnem*), exegesis, audiobooks, and stories.

28 Ravneet Kaur, "Bangla Sahib Goes Tech-Savvy to Serve More People," cityspidey.com, February 27, 2021; Srishti Chaudhary and Raphael Reichel, "Amritsar: The Indian City Where No One Goes Hungry," *BBC Travel*, June 13, 2023. An automated *roti* machine is seen at https://www.youtube.com/watch?v=d3D1HQCUMUE. Kitchen workers are volunteers. In this video *kirtan* from the inner sanctum is audible in the kitchen area and across all common areas in the Harmandir Sahib complex.

29 Gomes, Kong, and Woods, eds., *Religion, Hypermobility and Digital Media in Global Asia*, 17.

30 Gurinder Singh Mann, *The Making of Sikh Scripture* (Oxford University Press, 2001), 5.

31 The five *takht* are Sri Akal Takht (Harmandir Sahib, Amritsar), Sri Hazur Sahib (Nanded), Sri Damdama Sahib (Talwandi Sabo), Sri Keshgarh Sahib (Anandpur), Sri Patna Sahib (Patna).

32   See Heidi A. Campbell and Gregory P. Grieve, *Playing with Religion in Digital Games* (Indiana University Press, 2014), 2.
33   Littlesikhs.com is a website featuring pedagogical games directed at children on key topics such as the *panj pyare* (five blessed ones), the five *kakkar* (articles of faith institutionalized by Guru Gobind Singh), the religious significance of the spring festival *Vaisakhi*, the succession of the Sikh gurus, learning Gurmukhi script, and awareness of Harmandir Sahib as an important site of worship. Commercial games have been discussed in gaming communities online for their use of Sikh characters. Many of these games draw on representations of Sikhs as warriors; see *Hitman 2: Silent Assassin* (offensive portrayals of Sikhs have been removed), *Assassin's Creed Chronicles: India* and *Assassin's Creed Syndicate*, *Far Cry 2*, *Battlefield 1*, *Valiant Hearts*, *Day of Infamy*, *Civilization V*, and *Victoria 3*. In *Grand Theft Auto 3* and *Liberty City Stories*, the common trope of the Sikh taxi driver is used.
34   Michael Kinnear notes other Indian recording companies that emerged during the 1920s alongside the Gramophone Company (Michael S. Kinnear, *A Discography of Hindustani and Karnatic Music* [Greenwood Press, 1985], xiv). For a discussion of early Sikh recordings, see Bhogal, "Listening to Female Voices in Sikh Kirtan," 48–77; and https://sikhgram.com.
35   Regula Qureshi's discussion of how the "Gramophone Company pursued a clear policy of exploiting separate religious communities as markets" is useful for understanding the cultural dynamics of *kirtan* in the first half of the twentieth century, as is her focus on *qawwali* recordings ("Recorded Sound and Religious Music: The Case of Qawwālī," in *Media and the Transformation of Religion in South Asia*, ed. Lawrence A. Babb and Susan S. Wadley [University of Pennsylvania Press, 1995], 144–51).
36   Peter Manuel sprinkles brief mentions of Sikh *kirtan* in *Cassette Culture: Popular Music and Technology in North India* (University of Chicago Press, 1993). Although Jayson Beaster-Jones undertakes fieldwork across India, this does not include Punjab (see *Music Commodities, Markets, and Values: Music as Merchandise* (Routledge, 2016). Also relevant is Charles Hirschkind, *The Ethical Soundscape: Cassette Sermons and Islamic Counterpublics* (Columbia University Press, 2009).
37   Evans, "Listening to the Infinite," 32.
38   Théberge, "The Sound of Nowhere," 336, 340–41.
39   Evans, "Listening to the Infinite," 32.
40   Mack Hagood, *Hush: Media and Sonic Self-Control* (Duke University Press, 2019), 3–4, 25, 5.
41   In the Sindhi tradition, the *chaliya* festival involves fasting for a period of forty days. See also Michel Boivin and Bhavna Rajpal, "From Udero Lal in Sindh to Ulhasnagar in Maharashtra: Partition and Memories

Across Borders in the Tradition of Jhulelal," in *Partition and the Practice of Memory*, ed. Churnjeet Mahn and Anne Murphy (Palgrave Macmillan, 2018), 60.

42 "Chaliya 2023," posted by Amritvela Trust Live, October 8, 2023, YouTube, https://www.youtube.com/watch?v=LZuOIeQNbMg&list=PLbv8bF_WvnquWgCwwNcE-NdIVfVBiLXjG&index=3 (Hindi).

43 Utpal Sharma and R. Parthasarathy, eds., *Future Is Urban: Livability, Resilience and Resource Conservation*, Proceedings of the International Conference on Future Is Urban (ICFU 2021) (Routledge, 2023), 264. See also T. K. Karunakaran, "Ulhasnagar: A Sociological Study in Urban Development" (master's thesis, Department of Sociology, University of Bombay, 1958). An abstract of this thesis is cited in *Research in Sociology: Abstracts of M.A. and Ph.D. Dissertations Completed in the Department of Sociology*, University of Bombay (India Council of Social Science Research, 1989).

44 Tarini Bedi and Ka-Kin Cheuk, "Deepak Making Mumbai (in China)," in *Bombay Brokers*, ed. Lisa Björkman (Duke University Press, 2021), 191–98, 193.

45 Himadri Banerjee, "Sindhi Sikhs: Their Histories and Memories," in *Regional Perspectives on India's Partition: Shifting the Vantage Points*, ed. Anjali Gera Roy and Nandi Bhatia (Routledge, 2023), 131.

46 Satram Verhani, "Baba Nanak Dev Ji's Teachings, the Sindhi Community and Ulhasnagar," in *Seeking Nanak: Commemorating the 551st Birth Anniversary of Guru Nanak Devji* (Edusikh Publications, 2021).

47 "Important: Summer Chaliya 2024," posted by Amritvela Trust Live, April 23, 2024, YouTube, https://www.youtube.com/watch?v=ZeRq58tqOJ8 (Hindi).

48 These acts of "timbral thievery" (as coined by Robert Moog) become especially confusing when the synthesizer mimics instruments that are present in the ensemble, thereby engaging in a form of "sonic deception." See Jonathan De Souza, "Timbral Thievery: Synthesizers and Sonic Materiality," in *The Oxford Handbook of Timbre*, ed. Emily Dolan and Alexander Rehding (Oxford University Press, 2021), 347.

49 Bhai Gurpreet Singh uses this technique again in day 17 of *chaliya* 2022 to tie the *sangat* to the main refrain, which forms the basis for his exegesis (04:08:50). He specifically asks the musicians to stop playing, although the synthesizer continues to provide harmonization.

50 On day 5 of *chaliya* 2022 during a discussion of *ras* (taste or sweet essence), Bhai Gurpreet Singh speaks to the importance of *nirol kirtan* ("pure kirtan"), where one becomes *nām de rasiya* (an appreciator or lover of the divine name) in the depths of one's being (*hirdai*), as opposed to *nād de rasiya* (an appreciator or lover of sound) where the devotee experiences *dhun ka ras* (the taste of music, not of the divine name, *shabad ka ras*).

NOTES TO PAGES 210–223 | 323

51   Evans, "Listening to the Infinite," 16.
52   Thomas Everrett, "Ears Wide Shut: Headphones and Moral Design" (PhD diss., Carleton University, 2014), ii.
53   Alex Blue V, "'Hear What You Want': Sonic Politics, Blackness, and Racism-Canceling Headphones," *Current Musicology* 99–100 (2017): 90.
54   Jacob Downs, "Headphones, Auditory Violence and the Sonic Flooding of Corporeal Space," *Body and Society* 27, no. 3 (2021): 58.
55   "Prakash Purab Chaliya 2023," posted by Amritvela Trust Live, November 30, 2023, YouTube, https://www.youtube.com/watch?v=_T8u-Z-aIAM.
56   "Langar Sewa Nanak Roti," posted by Amritvela Trust Live, November 3, 2023, YouTube, https://www.youtube.com/watch?v=V1U2vYGGHZU&list=PLbv8bF_WvnquWgCwwNcE-NdIVfVBiLXjG&index=21 (Hindi).
57   *SGGS* 25-19.
58   *SGGS* 110-1.
59   *SGGS* 297-3.

| CHAPTER 6

1   Kate Galloway, K. E. Goldschmitt, and Paula Clare Harper, "Introduction to the Special Issue on Listening In: Musical Digital Communications in Private and Public," *Twentieth-Century Music* 19, no. 3 (2022): 363.
2   https://kirtanfi.com.
3   Anaar Desai-Stephens, "The Infrastructure of Engagement: Musical Aesthetics and the Rise of YouTube in India," *Twentieth-Century Music* 19, no. 3 (2022): 444.
4   Bhogal, "Listening to Female Voices in Sikh Kirtan," 48–77.
5   "Kirtan Therapy, Live *Qi-Rattan*," posted by *Qi-Rattan*, July 12, 2020, YouTube, https://www.youtube.com/watch?v=tpFKQIq_Qeg; "*Nanak Chintaa Mat Karo*, Amrita Kaur," posted by Amrita Kaur and Bhai Yadvinder Singh, November 7, 2022, YouTube, https://www.youtube.com/watch?v=Tg9LfrSzE5M; "*Taati Vaho Na Laggayi*, Acapella, Arvindpal Kaur feat. Bhai Nirmal Singh Khalsa and Biba Arpana Kaur," posted by Arvindpal Kaur, October 7, 2021, YouTube, https://www.youtube.com/watch?v=L553VCfkuXc; "*Gur Ka Shabad Rakhware*," posted by Arvindpal Kaur, May 12, 2023, YouTube, https://www.youtube.com/watch?v=I8-RIvca3OE; "*Saiyaan*, Arpana Kaur," posted by Arpana Kaur, August 16, 2021, YouTube, https://www.youtube.com/watch?v=EXm6r6dXk-Q; "*Ramaiya Hau Barak Tera*," posted by Kaurishma, August 4, 2020, YouTube, https://www.youtube.com/watch?v=_6s2xMmKtOA; "*Aarti, Kaesi Aarti Hoye*, Gursimran Kaur," posted by Gursimran Kaur, November 19, 2022, YouTube, https://www.youtube.com/watch?v=f3ahJIqmhTA.

6 "*Mitr Pyare Nu*, Bhai Gagandeep Singh," posted by SikhInside, September 20, 2019, YouTube https://www.youtube.com/watch?v=vh4WIy6k5gI.
7 Desai-Stephens, "The Infrastructure of Engagement," 455.
8 https://www.qi-rattan.com/about/.
9 "*Guru Nanak You're My Hero*, Taren Kaur," posted by Taren Kaur, November 13, 2019, YouTube, https://www.youtube.com/watch?v=-kN2IM5yljU.
10 "*Ho Bal Bal Jao*," posted by Taren Kaur, September 12, 2019, YouTube, https://www.youtube.com/watch?v=eAsPyXa2kiY.
11 "*Mere Madho Ji*," posted by Taren Kaur, September 12, 2019, YouTube, https://www.youtube.com/watch?v=sbQiFIirLLc.
12 "*Hey Gobind Hey Gopal*," posted by Taren Kaur, September 12, 2019, YouTube, https://www.youtube.com/watch?v=nWoIigpgn10.
13 "*Koi Bole Raam Raam*," posted by Taren Kaur, September 12, 2019, YouTube, https://www.youtube.com/watch?v=MbmD-K9FNVs.
14 "*Chali Thakur Peh Haar*," posted by Taren Kaur, September 12, 2019, YouTube, https://www.youtube.com/watch?v=LEZJ3yENrT4.
15 "*Satnam Waheguru—Animation Song For Kids*," posted by Taren Kaur, October 17, 2022, YouTube, https://www.youtube.com/watch?v=z2-GEvZh_vw.
16 "The Invisible Divine 4, Balahaari, Jasleen Kaur Monga," posted by Asli Music, May 3, 2020, YouTube, https://www.youtube.com/watch?v=PFtbFPAVk20.
17 Pavitra Sundar, *Listening with a Feminist Ear: Soundwork in Bombay Cinema* (University of Michigan Press, 2023), 42–43; Anaar Desai-Stephens, "Tensions of Musical Re-Animation from Bollywood to *Indian Idol*," in *Music in Contemporary Indian Film: Memory, Voice, Identity*, ed. Jayson Beaster-Jones and Natalie Sarrazin (Routledge, 2016), 76–90.
18 Desai-Stephens, "Tensions of Musical Re-Animation from Bollywood to *Indian Idol*," 79, 86.
19 "Studio Round 02, Gavo Sachi Baani, Episode 8, Full Episode, PTC Punjabi Gold," posted by PTC Punjabi Gold, January 2, 2017, YouTube, https://www.youtube.com/watch?v=Je_m_BPPYAA&list=RDQM365pfYVogSY&start_radio=1; "Gavo Sachi Baani, Episode 3, Ludhiana Auditions, Full Episode, PTC Punjabi Gold," posted by PTC Punjabi Gold, December 20, 2016, YouTube, https://www.youtube.com/watch?v=-s1hlADFaug&list=RDQM365pfYVogSY&index=2.
20 The few exceptions are Bhogal, "Listening to Female Voices in Sikh Kirtan"; Francesca Cassio, "Female Voices in Gurbānī Sangīt and the Role of the Media in Promoting Female Kīrtanīe," *Sikh Formations: Religion, Culture, Theory* 10 (2014): 233–69; and Nirinjan Kaur Khalsa-Baker, "Engendering the Female Voice in Sikh Devotional Music," *Sikh Formations: Religion, Culture, Theory* 15, nos. 1–2 (2019): 246–86.

21 "Mu Lalan Seo Preet Banee, Jasleen Kaur Monga," posted by Asli Music, December 14, 2019, YouTube, https://www.youtube.com/watch?v=4kZzXriiKbE; *Tuhi Tuhi with Waheguru Simran*," posted by Veer Manpreet Singh, April 13, 2019, YouTube, https://www.youtube.com/watch?v=aHN-1Uqd9_Q; "Qi-Rattan—Mohe Na Bisaaroh," posted by Qi-Rattan, December 1, 2015, YouTube, https://www.youtube.com/watch?v=mxUoDecrnH4; "So Satgur Pyara, Amrita Kaur," posted by Amrita Kaur and Bhai Yadvinder Singh, November 7, 2019, YouTube, https://www.youtube.com/watch?v=9D9kMh1ECJw.
22 "Aisee Preet, Bhai Hajara Singh," posted by Hajara Singh, November 11, 2019, YouTube, https://www.youtube.com/watch?v=ccXyUzZYL-0.
23 Jessica Holmes, "Billie Eilish and the Feminist Aesthetics of Depression: White Femininity, Generation Z, and Whisper Singing," *Journal of the American Musicological Society* 76, no. 3 (2023): 785.
24 Sundar, *Listening with a Feminist Ear*, 14.
25 Matthew Rahaim equates a sweet *filmi* voice with Lata Mangeshkar (*Ways of Voice: Vocal Striving and Moral Contestation in North India and Beyond* [Wesleyan University Press, 2021], 95). I expand this category to include more "natural," breathy voices, as we hear with Jasleen Kaur.
26 Rahaim, *Ways of Voice*, 89, 159.
27 Desai-Stephens, "The Infrastructure of Engagement," 454–55.
28 "Official Video—Chaupai Sahib—Jasleen Kaur—Jaskirat Singh," posted by Dharam Seva Records, April 22, 2020, YouTube, https://www.youtube.com/watch?v=F76VunwZeYo; "Japji Sahib Full Path, Harshdeep Kaur," posted by Hindi Songs, February 1, 2023, YouTube, https://www.youtube.com/watch?v=wIHll4Umc00; "Japji Sahib Full Path by Rajwinder Kaur Amritsar," posted by iGurbani Australia, December 18, 2020, YouTube, https://www.youtube.com/watch?v=zEFhcnKVcHY.
29 "Tuhi Tuhi Infinity (Production and Rap by Paramdeep Singh)," posted by Veer Manpreet Singh, November 4, 2019, YouTube, https://www.youtube.com/watch?v=7BE37zGgXLA&list=OLAK5uy_kcT5xkZtWwa0spv8SLtbEUHLTL-6L_dHk&index=.
30 See, for example, N. Osbaldiston, ed., *Culture of the Slow: Social Deceleration in an Accelerated World* (Palgrave Macmillan, 2013); and Maggie Berg and Barbara Seeber, *Slow Professor: Challenging the Culture of Speed in the Academy* (University of Toronto Press, 2016).
31 "Healing with Tuhi Tuhi Kirtan Veechar Day 195," posted by Veer Manpreet Singh, February 20, 2021, YouTube, https://www.youtube.com/watch?v=plqT9rbzoVw.
32 "Healing with Tuhi Tuhi Kirtan Veechar Day 447," posted by Veer Manpreet Singh, April 13, 2024, YouTube, https://www.youtube.com/watch?v=5DssS8CtRpk&t=132s.
33 *Mere Sahiba* (2019); *Begum Pura* (2018); *Ek Tuhi* (2016); *Sabh Gobind Hai* (2015); *Mera Mann Loche* (2013); and *The Journey Begins: Kar Kirpa* (2011).

34 "Tuhi Tuhi Prosperity (Production and Rap by Paramdeep Singh)," posted by Veer Manpreet Singh, December 25, 2018, YouTube, https://www.youtube.com/watch?v=cUUAmeWGzkk.

35 "Raag Tilang, Manjit Singh NZ, The Kirtan Collective, Bhai Mardana Music Festival," posted by RhythmStudios NZ, December 22, 2020, YouTube, https://www.youtube.com/watch?v=25uK9PTXXJw; "Kirtan and Jazz I Mandeep Singh I Bhai Mardana Music Festival," posted by RhythmStudios NZ, December 22, 2020, YouTube, https://www.youtube.com/watch?v=gQMQlLY5reE.

36 On *Coke Studio*, see Rakae Rehman Jamil and Khadija Muzaffar, *Coke Studio: Season 14* (Bloomsbury, 2024); Bidisha Mukherjee, "Coke Studio: A Musical Identity," in *Understanding Pakistan: Emerging Voices from India*, ed. Joseph C. Matthew (Routledge, 2016), 187–204; and Rahaim, *Ways of Voice*, 183.

37 See a creative lockdown video by *Kirtan Studio*, "17 Kirtanis Stay Home Collaboration, Aavoh Sikh Satguru Ke Pyareo," posted by Kirtan Studio, June 7, 2020, YouTube, https://www.youtube.com/watch?v=X0PDi7Vyh70.

38 Rahaim, *Ways of Voice*, 141.

39 Desai-Stephens, "The Infrastructure of Engagement," 455.

40 Desai-Stephens, "The Infrastructure of Engagement," 447.

41 "Bhai Anantvir Singh Ji L.A," posted by Hazoori Ragi Shabad Elahi, August 27, 2020, YouTube, https://www.youtube.com/watch?v=MdgSN-KPk4I; "Ramdas Guru Har Sat Kiyo, Bhai Amarjit Singh, Patiala Wale," posted by Gurbani Studio, October 12, 2019, YouTube, https://www.youtube.com/watch?v=LEPh51IMCbw.

42 "Jaise Tarvar Pankhi Basera, Shivpreet Singh in Raag Anandkali," posted by Shivpreet Singh, August 11, 2023, YouTube, https://www.youtube.com/watch?v=fWLwfyGE0uQ.

43 Rahaim, *Ways of Voice*, 38.

44 "Live Meditation with Shivpreet Singh—Heart's Deep Desire," posted by Shivpreet Singh, January 27, 2024, YouTube, https://www.youtube.com/watch?v=_hLehEhRDcw&t=10s.

EPILOGUE

1 "Hey Karunanidh: An Eternal Plea | Veer Manpreet Singh & Ruhani," posted by Veer Manpreet Singh, April 12, 2024, YouTube, https://www.youtube.com/watch?v=hDNHE8boEAc; "Darshan Dekh—Guru Nanak," posted by Shivpreet Singh, April 11, 2024, YouTube, https://www.youtube.com/watch?v=4gkaCJuqZzU; "Vah Vah Gobind Singh—Kirtan Sing-Along with Taren Kaur," posted by Taren Kaur, April 12, 2024, YouTube, https://www.youtube.com/watch?v=SbSdJ9efHrg.

2   Arvind-Pal Singh Mandair, *Religion and the Specter of the West: Sikhism, India, Postcoloniality and the Politics of Translation* (Columbia University Press, 2009), 314.

APPENDIX

1   Pierre Bourdieu, *Distinction: A Social Critique of the Judgement of Taste*, trans. Richard Nice (Routledge, 2010).
2   *SGGS* 1075-19.

Index

Aasa ki vār, 43–45, 95, 105, 115, 208, 213
Abhinavagupta, 30, 35
acoustics, 22, 185, 187, 188, 190, 221, 222, 224, 227, 228, 254
Afghani *rabab*, 106, 159, 160, 162, 170, 173
ahat nād, 18, 37, 38, 43, 51, 53, 54, 57, 60, 67, 112, 114, 117–21, 123, 127, 128, 131, 137, 141, 178, 182, 183, 210, 232, 255
Ain-i-Akbari, 149
ajapa jaap, 124, 126, 136, 214
Akal Takht, 44, 69, 70, 97, 245
Akbar, Emperor, 34, 41, 74, 149, 159, 161, 170, 171, 176, 177
Akhand Kirtani Jatha (AKJ), 13, 15, 53, 102, 118, 259, 260
Ali, Mir Rahmat, 172
amrit, 52, 56, 67, 110, 122, 128, 131, 132

amritvela, 19, 65, 114, 115, 184, 187, 197, 242
anahad instruments, 18, 113, 143–46
anahad nād, 18–20, 37, 38, 43, 51–54, 57, 60, 65, 67, 110–23, 127–29, 132, 136–38, 141, 143, 146, 178, 180–85, 186, 212–15, 218, 219, 221, 232, 241, 255

Bakhsh, Ustad Rahim, 105
bansuri, 4, 51, 151, 205, 213, 250
bayn, 52, 132–34, 137, 143, 144, 151, 183
bhagat, 19, 31–34, 47, 49, 53, 56, 60, 62–67, 95, 110, 112, 122, 123, 127, 129–38, 141, 142, 147, 149, 150–52, 173, 178, 179, 207, 237, 249, 251, 258
Bhai Firanda, 106, 172, 174
Bhai Gurdas, 30–33, 46, 47, 57, 112, 123, 188, 220

Bhai Mardana, 16, 19, 31, 46, 70, 106, 125, 126, 144, 145, 152, 155–57, 160–62, 164, 165, 167–82, 255
bhajan, 16, 81, 82, 85, 86, 88, 89, 175, 205
bhakti, 16, 21, 28, 30–32, 35, 38, 39, 47, 65, 134, 175–77
bheri, 18, 111, 113, 136, 137, 143, 144, 146–48, 151, 183, 214
been, 170
birdsong in *SGGS*, 63–66

chakras, 127, 128, 130, 131, 135
chaliya, 186, 197–203, 205, 208–11, 213–18
chaunki, 35, 36, 43, 44, 213
chautukla, 176
chimta/chhainay, 11, 12, 15, 102, 123
chitra veena, 159

Dakhanī Rabāb, 161
dandaut/manglacharan, 42, 55, 93, 100, 101, 103, 206
darshan, 20, 44, 64–66, 190, 191, 200, 202, 206, 207, 214, 216, 221, 247, 252
dasam dwar, 113, 121–23, 127–32, 134, 135–37, 139, 146, 149, 180–83
Dattatreya, 125–27, 179
dhadh, 10, 18, 24, 70, 156
dhaadhi, 10, 11, 24, 105, 129
dhaadhi jatha, 10, 11, 84, 225, 227, 260
dhaadhi vār, 10, 70
dhadh, 10, 18, 24, 70, 156
dholak, 18, 85, 205
dholki, 3, 4, 11, 12
dhrupad/dhurpad, 14–16, 21, 38, 41, 55, 163, 170, 171, 259
dhrupad rabab, 160, 163, 164, 170
dilruba, 4, 5, 8, 9, 13, 14, 18, 69, 70, 87, 88, 93, 97, 104–6, 170, 172, 191, 205, 225, 226, 243, 247, 248, 259
Ditta, Bhai Sain, 6, 92, 93, 101
dotara/dutara, 70, 71, 85, 90

ektara, 83, 95

Faqirullah, 176
Fazl, Abu'l, 149, 161
Firanda/Firandia/Phiranda rabab, 172–74, 178
fourth state, 113, 122, 123, 127, 128, 133, 135–41, 144, 147, 151, 152, 178, 218

Gavo Sachi Baani, 9, 106–8, 234–36
gender inequality, 6, 9, 20, 73, 194, 220, 222, 223, 231, 258
ghar, 24, 45–51, 58, 136, 247
Ghose, Dwarkanath, 79, 80
ghungroo, 135–37, 140, 143, 144, 147, 148, 183
Golden Temple. *See* Harmandir Sahib
Gorakhnath, 129
Gramophone Company, 5, 72, 92, 194, 245
Guler painting style, 154, 156, 163, 167
Gurmat Sangeet/Gurbani Sangeet, 2, 8, 9, 12, 14, 21–23, 38, 53, 54, 70, 95, 97, 98, 102, 104, 105, 107, 108, 119, 222, 223, 225, 234, 247, 249, 250
Guru Amardas, 17, 31, 35, 38, 41, 43, 49, 51, 52, 55–58, 65, 66, 70, 122, 128, 132, 133, 135, 150, 152, 173, 176, 188, 207, 217
Guru Angad, 31, 33, 43, 47, 52, 129, 173, 178, 179
Guru Arjan, 7, 16, 19, 26, 31–43, 46, 47, 49–58, 61, 63, 65, 67, 70, 98, 111, 122, 124, 128, 130, 132, 133, 135, 136, 140, 145, 147–52, 174–76, 188, 206, 207, 218
Guru Gobind Singh, 17, 31, 35, 70, 90, 145, 151, 170, 171, 174, 193, 228, 238, 240, 253
Guru Hargobind, 70, 145, 173, 174
Guru Harkrishan, 169, 173
Guru Nanak, 11, 15–17, 19, 31, 33, 34, 43, 45, 49, 52, 53, 56, 58–65, 67, 70,

106, 107, 111, 112, 115, 123–33, 135, 138, 139, 141, 145, 147–52, 154–157, 161–70, 172–82, 187, 197, 207, 217, 218, 229, 234, 236, 248, 249, 251, 252, 255
Guru Ramdas, 17, 31, 38, 40, 41, 43, 49–52, 64, 65, 70, 96, 112, 128, 133, 140, 141, 147, 149, 150, 173, 176, 188, 206

halo (Sikh iconography), 146, 180–83, 195
Hamsa Upanishad, 147, 213
Harmandir Sahib, xvii, 7–9, 11, 17, 16, 35, 43, 69, 75–77, 89–91, 96, 97, 108, 170, 171, 185, 188–91, 210, 213, 222
headphones, 19, 186, 187, 195, 196, 198, 199, 201, 202, 209–13, 216–18, 224, 246

Ibn Sīnā, 160
ida nadi, 130, 131
Indian *rabab*, 159, 160, 162, 163, 176

Jaidev, 31, 32, 38, 47, 49
Jallianwalan Bagh massacre, 91
Janamsakhi, 23, 124–26, 145, 153–56, 163, 164, 167–69, 172, 173, 175, 177–80, 187
Japji Sahib, 18, 53, 59, 60, 62, 116, 131, 138, 139, 179, 201, 203, 239
jhanjh, 14
jogi, 83, 84
jori, 8, 18, 70, 71, 75, 103, 170, 188, 231, 253, 259, 262

kacchapi veena, 157, 158
kainsi, 14, 51
Kaliyuga, 154, 156, 178
kamaicha, 160
Kangra painting style, 154, 170
Kapurthala court, 172
kartāl, 145, 148, 183, 213

Kartarpur Pothi, 46
Khan, Sadiq Ali, 172
Khan, Ustad Udho, 105
khayal, 15, 176
Khusrau, Amir, 41, 152, 167
kinguri, 18, 113, 120, 133–37, 141, 143, 144, 151, 152, 167, 175, 183
kinnari vina, 152
Kitāb al-mūsīkī al-kabīr, 160
Kitāb al-sifa, 160
Kitāb-i-Nauras, 160
Kohabar, Qasim, 159

"Ladies Satsang," 11, 12
langar, 12, 176, 187, 193, 201, 215, 216
lip-reed aerophone, 148
liveness, 188, 189, 210, 221, 247, 251
lotus (*kamal*), 58, 65, 123, 128, 129
loudspeakers, 96, 186–88, 190, 192, 193, 207, 209, 224, 225, 262

mabati, 3
mandariya, 147
manjira, 14, 213
meditation. See *samadhi*
microphones, 96, 188, 189, 210, 224–27, 238, 239, 243, 250, 251, 260, 262
mirasi, 73, 78, 83–86, 95, 109, 255
mridang/pakhawaj, 8, 18, 51, 65, 70, 113, 120, 140, 146, 147, 148, 169, 170, 183, 253
Mughal court, 21, 41, 170, 171, 176
Mughal miniatures, 154, 160, 164
Mughal rabab, 159, 162, 163

Nabha, Kahn Singh, 70, 71, 156
Nabha court, 172
Namdhari, 13, 14, 53, 93, 104, 105, 172, 232
Nanakshahi rabab, 106, 177
naqqarah/nagara/naubat, 146
Nath yogi, 129–31, 134, 135, 150, 151
nirdharit rāg, 2, 3, 8, 10, 13–15, 17, 24, 29, 34, 37, 70, 94, 95, 105, 106,

nirdharit rāg (continued)
    230–32, 234, 236, 239, 245, 249,
    254, 255, 257, 258
nirol kirtan, 13, 94, 102, 260

ornamentation, 92, 94, 99, 102, 103,
    250, 251

Pahari painting style, 154, 157, 164,
    167, 169
panch shabad, 18, 113, 131–33, 136–41,
    146, 147, 149, 212
partāl, 15, 28, 32, 39–41, 50, 51, 259
Patiala court, 105, 172
pehar, 35, 36, 40, 43, 45, 57, 114
Persian rabab, 92, 95, 159, 160, 162,
    163, 179
pingala nadi, 130, 131
prabhat pheri, 199
puratan reet, 3, 15, 22, 171, 259

Qānūn-i-mūsīqī, 172
qawwali, 16, 53, 93, 235
Qutb Shahi dynasty, 162

Rag Darpan, 176
rāg-flexible kirtan, 14, 15, 17, 249, 257
raj yoga, 127, 131
Ramgarhia, Sardar Sundar Singh, 90
ransingha, 44, 149, 213, 214
ravan vina/ravanhasta vina, 156, 157
recording industry, Sikh, 5–7, 72, 195

samadhi, 113, 120, 123, 130, 131, 136
santoor, 248
saranda, 18, 69–71, 90, 106, 156, 171,
    172, 174
sarangi, 8–10, 13, 14, 18, 24, 69, 70, 73,
    78, 83, 85, 93, 104, 157, 172, 174, 175,
    205, 225, 250
Sarmāya-i 'ishrat, 172
sarod, 158, 160
sen-e-rabab/seniya rabab, 159, 168,
    170, 171, 173

shankh, 120, 123, 132, 136, 137, 141, 143,
    144, 213
Sheikh Farid, 115, 146
Shiromani Gurudwara Prabandhak
    Committee (SGPC), 2, 95–97, 106,
    234
shringa/sing/shing, 149
sikandari rabab, 172
silent kirtan, 198, 199, 207, 209, 210,
    212
Sindhi Sikhs, 19, 197–200, 204, 205,
    213
Singh, Bhai Hira, 92, 114–16, 125
Singh, Bhai Randhir, 22, 91, 118–27,
    136, 139
Singh, Bhai Vir, 7, 11, 21, 22, 98, 118–
    22, 125, 127, 138, 139, 260
Singh, Mahant Gajja, 105, 172
Singh, Maharaja Ranjit, 181, 188
Singh, Ustad Surjit, 9, 13
sinyi, 18, 113, 130, 131, 133–37, 143, 144,
    149, 150, 151, 183, 214
sitar, 18, 70, 71, 76, 82, 86–88, 90–92,
    158, 168, 170, 205, 231
slow kirtan, 204, 209, 218, 222, 239,
    241, 242, 244, 250, 251, 254, 255
string instruments. See tanti sāz
sursingar, 170, 173
sushmanaa, 130, 131, 134
Swami Haridas, 176, 177
swarmandal, 101, 193, 205, 247
synthesizer, 205–7, 221, 227, 237, 238,
    240–42, 255, 261

tabla, 3–5, 9, 13, 15, 18, 44, 70, 75, 90,
    96, 102–4, 196, 204, 205, 208, 225,
    227, 228, 231, 237, 242, 243, 248,
    259, 261
tambur/tambura, 90, 163, 169, 177
Tansen, 34, 159, 170, 171, 176, 177
tanpura, 4, 5, 14, 18, 70, 71, 101, 103,
    167, 169, 191, 193, 203, 253
tanti sāz, 7, 8, 69–71, 73, 75, 90–93,
    95–97, 101, 104–9, 170, 171, 173,

205, 225, 226, 231, 247, 248, 251, 255, 262
tār-shehnai, 14
taus, 8, 14, 18, 69–71, 89, 90, 104–6, 170, 172, 205, 253, 259, 262, 263
tenth door. See *dasam dwar*
tumba, 134
tura/turi, 18, 51, 113, 134, 137, 143, 144, 148, 149, 151, 183

udasi, 145, 161, 162, 169, 236
unstruck sound. See *anahad nād*

Vaisakhi, 193, 243, 253, 254
vār, 10, 11, 24, 30, 33, 39, 40, 43–45, 50, 70, 95, 105, 115, 119, 208, 213
veena/vina, 70, 97, 152, 156–59, 175

yoga, 112, 122, 127–33, 135

www.ingramcontent.com/pod-product-compliance
Lightning Source LLC
Chambersburg PA
CBHW022028290426
44109CB00014B/795